D0885602

FIVE PLAYS
OF
ALEXANDER
OSTROVSKY

FIVE PLAYS OF ALEXANDER OSTROVSKY

It's a Family Affair—We'll Settle It Ourselves
The Poor Bride
The Storm
The Scoundrel
The Forest

Translated and edited by Eugene K. Bristow

PEGASUS • NEW YORK

Copyright 1969 by Western Publishing Company, Inc.
Library of Congress Catalogue Card 69-27985
All rights reserved.
This book, or parts thereof,
may not be reproduced in any form
without permission of the publishers.
Printed in the United States of America

for
Norma
Pamela, Michael, Carol, Katherine

PREFACE

Of the chief Russian writers in the last century, perhaps none has received less attention in English-speaking countries than Alexander Ostrovsky, Russia's first and most prolific professional playwright.

A century ago the first English article on Ostrovsky appeared in *The Edinburgh Review,* and since then the major publishing ventures have occurred about once in every generation. In 1898, for example, Constance Garnett made the first English translation of *The Storm.* About fifty years ago the first and only American volume (four plays) was printed, and twenty-five years later the first and only British volume (three plays) was issued. In the seventy years since Garnett's *The Storm,* about one-third of Ostrovsky's plays have received translation, and almost all of these were printed in the magazine *Poet Lore.* Only two of his plays, *The Storm* and *The Scoundrel,* have been translated more than once.

Ostrovsky has had somewhat better luck in western European countries. William Ralston's English article, for example, was translated and published in the *Revue Britannique* in 1868, marking the introduction of Ostrovsky in France. In the next thirty years, several of his plays were translated and staged, and even though French response was controversial, the Russian playwright was given recognition. His best translator, perhaps, was Durand-Grenville who published a volume of three plays in 1889: *Don't Sit in Another's Sleigh, The Storm,* and *The Snow Maiden.*

In that same year, *The Storm,* translated by J. Pavlovsky and Oskar Metenier, was staged at the theatre Beaumarchais in Paris, but was poorly received. The noisy audience laughed at the wrong times, shouted remarks at the bewildered actors, and even tossed coins on the stage. In short, the production was a fiasco, and Chekhov in a letter to Suvorin advised shipping "all these Messrs. Translators to Siberia. . . ."

They only staged the play so that the French may once again put on airs and gossip authoritatively about those things, which for them are insufferably boring and incomprehensible.

Chekhov was partly right. As early as 1875, Courrière published his *Histoire de la littérature contemporaine*, treated Ostrovsky's plays, and drew the wrong conclusions. Using French classical tragedy as his yardstick, Courrière suggested that one of the best plays was *Dmitry Samozvanets and Vasily Shuisky*. In his opinion, *The Storm* marked the Russian playwright's apogee, while the remaining plays were too similar in plot and character. The plays might come alive on stage, Courrière concluded, but reading them was something of a bore.

Ostrovsky had his share of defenders in France; among them were Francisque Sarcey and Jules Lemaître. Having read Durand-Grenville's translation of *The Storm* in 1874, Sarcey tried to get it staged and hoped that the great Russian actress Savina would play Katerina. Distressed over the 1889 production, Sarcey attributed its failure to incompetent acting, but observed that the storm scene with Katerina was beautiful. Like Sarcey, Lemaître saw great merit in *The Storm*, especially the first meeting between Boris and Katerina. "I do not think," Lemaître declared, "the fatality of passion is expressed anywhere in situation and in language that are simpler and stronger." Lemaître suggested that the poor audience response was simply the inability to understand the concepts of sin, heaven, and hell in the upper Volga region.

Finally, in 1912 a definitive criticism of Ostrovsky and his plays appeared in France, J. Patouillet's *Ostrovski et son théâtre de moeurs russes*. As former director of the French Institute in Petersburg, Patouillet brought to his work not only an excellent knowledge of the Russian language but also a thorough background of Russian criticism and literary history. Including a biography of the playwright, Patouillet examined the various classes and occupations in Ostrovsky's day as the bases of his plays and discussed the wide range of character types from the merchants and clerks to government officials and provincial actors. Patouillet's works on Ostrovsky, which included a shorter book, *Le Théâtre de moeurs russes des origines à Ostrovski*, remain today among the finest criticism of the playwright outside Russia.

In Germany, as in France and England, knowledge of the Russian's plays was introduced during his own lifetime. As early as 1865, *A Lucrative Post* (1857) was translated by E. Göring and published in Munich. The translation, as N. P. Kashin observed in 1923, was generally accurate, although now and again the translator invented freely. For example, in place of Belogubov's "Trembling, sir," the following line was inserted: "Ich sage, ein Untergebener muss seinen Vorgesetsten gegenüber eine gewisse Ehrfurcht, ja Zittern und Zagen fühlen." The German translation, however, was by no means an original version of the play; as, say, Rodney Ackland's *The Diary of a Scoundrel* (1948) was an English adaptation based on Ostrovsky's *The Scoundrel*. In 1870 a portion of *The Storm* was printed in German, and two complete translations were issued in 1893 and 1911.

Although there were fewer translations of Ostrovsky's plays in Germany than in France, German criticism was fairly extensive. Among the works by critics like Haller and Reinholdt, Alexander Brückner's *Geschichte der russichen Literatur* (1905) may be considered the best. In a shorter work, *Russlands geistige Entwickelung im Spiegel seiner schönen Literatur* (1908), Brückner summed up his impressions of Ostrovsky.

> Ostrovsky—the great realist of the Russian stage: strict fidelity and truthfulness—his distinctive sign; no concessions to public taste; careful avoidance of all cheap effects; long before the appeal to realism sounded on the European stage, he introduced it on the Russian. He very readily yielded to passionate and tragic conflicts and characters, this optimist, this herald of joy in life, through and through a human being; if only the Slavophile tendency had sometimes clouded his lucid nonsense.

Ostrovsky's plays were translated in other countries, and an international criticism of the playwright eventually developed. For example, a French version of *The Storm* was made in Paris in 1885 but was issued in Belgium. In recent years his plays have been produced in China and in Central Europe. Professional production of his plays on the British and American stage has been rare, and criticism in English has been limited primarily to articles. The only full-length English criticism of Ostrovsky, for example, consists of an American dissertation on one aspect of his plays. It was written more than a decade ago. By contrast, Chekhovian criticism in English has had sufficient titles to require two separate bibliographical studies.

The five plays in this present volume contain only a small share of Ostrovsky's works, but each is considered a masterpiece by many Russian and English-speaking critics. As a group the plays are representative of Ostrovsky's first twenty-five years as a writer, having been selected from his first thirty original plays. Arranged chronologically in the volume, the first two plays are his first full-length comedies; the third play *The Storm* is one of the few Russian tragedies ever written; the last two plays may be counted among his most popular comedies. Of the five plays, only *The Storm* and *The Poor Bride* are currently available in print.

The plays are representative in still another way. His first full-length comedy, *It's a Family Affair—We'll Settle It Ourselves*, based on the merchant class, describes a mode of life *(byt)* which Ostrovsky repeated with variety in numerous plays, such as *Poverty Is No Crime* (1854), *Your Drink—My Hangover* (1856), and *Truth's Good, But Happiness Is Better* (1877). *The Storm*, too, is based on the merchant class, but unlike *It's a Family Affair*, which takes place in Moscow, the scene of the tragedy is an imaginary provincial town in the upper Volga region. The most poetic of the five plays, *The Storm* depends largely on mood and atmosphere. His second full-length comedy, *The Poor Bride*, portrays the plight of a poor girl courted by government officials, and the world of the official *(chinovnik)* was treated in subsequent plays such as *A Lucrative Post* (1857), *The Abyss* (1866), and *Rich Brides* (1876). The fourth play, *The Scoundrel*, includes representatives from the civil service and army, but the scene is the lower level of the nobility. An excellently constructed play, *The Scoundrel* portrays the rise and fall of a young scoundrel trying to make his way in society. The same milieu was repeated in such plays as *Wild Money* (1870), *Wolves and Sheep* (1875), and *Talents and Admirers* (1882). The last play, *The Forest*, not only includes members of the landed nobility, but also returns to the same upper Volga region in which *The Storm* takes place. Since two of the major characters are provincial actors, the play is also representative of works like *Talents and Admirers* and *Guilty Without Guilt* (1884).

Throughout the making of the translations, my chief aim has been to provide versions for the stage. Since the plays were originally written for stage productions, and since Ostrovsky usually assisted in the staging of the plays, I have also tried to learn as much as possible about the first productions as well as the subsequent major productions in Russia. I was fortunate enough to have directed my first Ostrovsky translation in a university theatre production, and this experience provided insights into the plays which could scarcely have been made in the study. My approach to the plays has been that of the stage director, and my guidelines were based on a solution to the problem of translation which Stark Young supplied in an excellent essay, "Seeing the Point." Borrowing from Plato, Mr. Young noted that "most men are blind to the fact of their ignorance of the essential character of each individual thing. They do not see . . . what, if the thing were freed from all but its own characteristics, would remain, and would be the point of it, and would define its existence in the midst of a multitude of things like and unlike. What men are least apt to do is to see the point."

My purpose, then, was to see the point of the original, as it is revealed not only in structure and language but also in character and thought. For example, I tried to make the distinction, to take Elder Olson's phrase, between "speech as action *(praxis)* and speech as meaningful *(lexis)*." One example may illustrate the point. In both *It's a Family Affair* and *The Scoundrel,* the word *pomilui(te)* is frequently used by Podkhalyuzin in the first play and by Glumov in the second. As a Russian word it may be used in instances of disagreement, objection or retort, persuasion, or surprise; and the word may be translated variously as *for pity's sake, for goodness' sake, goodness me, you're not serious,* etc.

Both Podkhalyuzin and Glumov are con men surrounded by dupes, and the word is used by both characters as a stereotyped response, usually in moments when each is furiously pulling samples from his bag of tricks. The chief difference between the two, however, is related to character, situation, and intention of the scene. Podkhalyuzin is a rising young merchant out of the *meshchane* class, characterized by coarseness, hardheaded ambition, and brazen cleverness. Once he sees an opening through which he can make his next move, he bristles and his eyes glint momentarily. His *pomilui(te)* or *goodness me,* employed in the same way a handkerchief might be used by a magician to distract attention while he pulls off the trick, ranges according to the intention of the scene from crass to ironic sweetness.

The character Glumov in *The Scoundrel,* on the other hand, is a rising young man out of the impoverished nobility, characterized by polish, a sense of clear direction, and wit. Glumov is aware of most of the openings since he has cleverly arranged them; and as he makes his moves, he stands outside himself, smiles wickedly at his *savoir-faire,* and almost winks at the audience. His *pomilui(te)* or *for pity's sake,* employed with the facility of a pen rapidly scratching out a word to make way for the next, ranges according to the intention of the scene from an irritated to a pleasant retort. Both Podkhalyuzin and Glumov flatter their dupes. Glumov flatters because he is carried away by the game he is playing; Podkhalyuzin, because he is playing the game for keeps.

The exact balance of sound, sense, and feeling that has been achieved in one language may be transferred only rarely to another. Since the impossibility of total translation exists, my aim in choice of words was governed by approximating in English the colloquial, vulgar, slang, or standard expression found in the original. I did not attempt to use

English appropriate to the last century, nor did I try to come up with the latest slang. Since the language in Ostrovsky's plays is colorful and often colloquial, I tried to approximate in modern English the tone and feeling of the speaker as governed by his intention. I did not follow, however, the principle Stark Young employed in his translation of Chekhov's *The Three Sisters:* "Let Chekhov . . . have it his own way—let him, for example, repeat a word when he chooses to repeat it, invert the word-order when he chooses, and so on." Had I followed this principle with Ostrovsky, the points in the original would easily have been lost in the English.

Throughout the plays I have retained certain elements as signs to the reader or to the audience that the scene is indeed Russian, not midwest American. The chief element is the translation of proper names as they appear in the original. To keep the flavor of the original in production, however, the actors should be trained to pronounce the names in phonetically accurate Russian. The Russian language has numerous variants of proper names which reveal the attitude of the speaker toward the person he refers to, and I have indicated in the notes the various nuances associated with the names. Even though such nuances will generally be lost on audiences who do not know Russian, the actors may make up something of the difference by characterizing the attitudes.

I should like to express my appreciation and thanks to Professor Ernest J. Simmons for his advice and encouragement in the preparation of this volume; to Mr. John Mong, editor, and to Anne Shahenshah of the Pegasus staff, and also to Virginia L. Hawkins and Kathleen Kelly for their helpful suggestions and editorial services; to my wife, Mrs. Norma J. Bristow, for her typing of the various drafts and manuscript copy of the plays; to the cast of the Indiana University production of *The Scoundrel (Enough Stupidity in Every Wiseman)*, to my colleagues who aided in the production, and to my friends who read the first drafts, for their generous and helpful comments; to The Graduate School, Indiana University, for two typing grants; and finally, my acknowledgment and thanks to the Indiana University Foundation, for a research grant in Russian theatre and drama (1964–1965).

Eugene K. Bristow

CONTENTS

INTRODUCTION

However extensive, limited, or indifferent the response to Aleksandr Nikolaevich Ostrovsky has been in other countries, his influence in his own native land may be considered important, widespread, and enduring.

There have been numerous editions of his works, from his first play collection in 1859 to the standard sixteen-volume edition issued in the period 1949 to 1953. And less than ten years after the standard edition, a ten-volume collection of selected works was issued. In his own day every major critic responded immediately to his plays, and the body of theatrical and literary criticism grew steadily in his lifetime. On the centenary of his birth, research on his life and works increased, received fresh impetus with the one hundred and twenty-fifth anniversary in 1948, and since then scarcely a year has passed without one or two critical volumes appearing in print.

Until the death of Stalin, the production of his plays paralleled the growing number of publications by critics and literary historians. His plays, widely produced in his lifetime, became increasingly popular in the years following the Revolution, and their most frequent production throughout Russia was reached in the thirties, forties, and early fifties. In 1939 Rudnev and Durylin noted that there were more performances of Ostrovsky's plays at the Maly Theatre in Moscow during one ten-year period after the Revolution, than the total performances of his plays produced at the Maly from 1853 to 1917. The authors also suggested that the number of Ostrovsky performances on the amateur stage every year totaled 150,000.

Following the death of Stalin, however, the number of Ostrovsky performances dropped substantially. For example, in the Moscow drama theatres in 1953, as de Liencourt observed, 26 per cent of the plays produced were drawn from pre-revolutionary works. Ostrovsky with 274 performances of twenty different plays headed the list. Seven years later, however, the number of pre-revolutionary Russian works in the Moscow drama theatres had dropped to 15 per cent, and the number of Ostrovsky performances in that year, only twenty-five, reflected the significant change in the repertory.

Whether the substantial increase of Ostrovsky performances during the Stalinist period, and the consequential decrease after his death, came about through a genuine interest and subsequent disinterest on the part of the public, the theatrical producing groups, or the CPSU policy makers is anybody's guess. It is difficult to split interest in a planned society. Apparently the public bought the whole repertory headed by Ostrovsky until a few years before Stalin died. In the last of the forties and early fifties, however, audience attendance fell off dramatically and did not pick up until changes had been made in the repertory during the late fifties. "Although it produced no clear directive on the theatre," de Liencourt pointed out, "the 20th CPSU congress encouraged greater boldness in the choice of the repertoire." As a result, the number of Ostrovsky performances diminished in the late fifties and early sixties to make way for contemporary light comedies and foreign plays. Bored with the limited theatrical fare headed by Ostrovsky, the public quickly settled for a more varied diet. Although there is less Ostrovsky produced in the Russian theatre today than twenty years ago, several of his works continue in the repertory, always play to full houses, and show every sign of remaining a part of the living Russian theatre.

Ostrovsky's chief legacy to the Russian theatre was an incredible number of plays. For example, in the late forties of the last century, the critic Belinsky named only three important Russian plays in the repertory: Griboedov's *Woe from Wit (Gore ot uma)*, Pushkin's *Boris Godunov*, and Gogol's *Inspector General (Revizor)*. From 1846 until his death forty years later, Ostrovsky composed seventy-six plays. Subtract seven plays written in collaboration with younger playwrights, twenty-two translations or adaptations of Latin, English, Spanish, and Italian works, and there remains a substantial number of original plays—and eight of these are in verse. Add to this number, however, several of his original plays which were used as libretti—Ostrovsky himself reworked most of them—for operas by Serov, Rimsky-Korsakov, Chaikovsky, etc., and his formation of the Russian repertory is readily seen.

In addition to the more than 700 characters he invented for actors, Ostrovsky influenced the nature and development of the Russian theatre. In 1865, together with N. G. Rubinshtein, V. F. Odoevsky, P. M. Sadovsky and others, Ostrovsky organized the Artistic Circle—a group with a training program for beginning actors and for established provincial actors. In the next eighteen years, the Artistic Circle not only turned out a number of important actors trained in the realistic tradition, but also served as a model for subsequent organizations and programs. Here, for the first time, were discussed ideas which led eventually to the formation of private theatres in the two capitals, the Moscow Philharmonic Society, and the Society of Russian Dramatic Writers and Opera Composers. This last group, organized in 1874, succeeded in raising royalty payments for dramatists, setting up the Griboedov Prize for the season's best play, and forming the professional library. Ostrovsky served as president of the Society until his death.

Ostrovsky brought purpose, plan, and dedication to the Russian theatre. To the playwright, the theatre was an important institution in society, capable of education as well as of entertainment. Taking Periclean Athens as his model, Ostrovsky envisioned a popular theatre which reached all the people.

> In Moscow a mighty, but rough peasant force is being humanized. To assist this new public in its humanization, more than anything else, will be the theatre, for which it so craves and which it has inhumanly been refused. A strong influence is exerted on this public by the so-called domestic *(bytovoi)* repertory. The domestic repertory, if made artistic, *i.e.* if it is made truthful,—is a great thing for the new, receptive public: it will reveal what is good, what is kind in the Russian person, what he must cherish and educate in himself, and what is savage and rough in him, against which he must fight . . . This kind of theatre is necessary for the Moscow public . . . Dramatic poetry is closer to the people than are all other branches of literature. All the other works are written for educated people, but dramas and comedies—for the whole people.

Ostrovsky failed in his quest for a low-priced popular theatre, but he was successful in his efforts to break the monopoly Imperial theatres held in Moscow and Petersburg. In 1882 the government decreed that private theatres could be formed in the two capitals. That fifteen years later Nemirovich-Danchenko and Stanislavsky, incorporating several of the playwright's aims into their policy, were permitted to establish the Moscow Art Theatre was only one of the consequences which resulted from Ostrovsky's total commitment to the Russian theatre.

Another and even more important consequence is that the whole structure of the present Russian theatre is based on the argument first expressed so eloquently by Ostrovsky in "A Note on the Condition of Dramatic Art in Russia at the Present Time" (1881). Ostrovsky's position was essentially the Platonic argument that the theatre, governed by axioms greater than the theatre itself, must hence serve some larger good—if it is to be accepted in society. The playwright's particular line of reasoning, that seeing plays influences ideas and molds human nature, is precisely the same rationale CPSU policy makers subscribe to and accounts for both the high rewards which workers in the Russian theatre receive and the control to which they submit.

Perhaps the first modern stage director in the Russian theatre, Ostrovsky educated the actors, particularly the Maly company, in the realistic tradition. Upon finishing a play, he usually read the play aloud to the actors, gave the tone, *i.e.* the feeling and intention, of each character, and indicated the course of expression. Moreover, he carefully examined each part with the actor separately. As the maker of the language, he was especially concerned with expression and believed that once the actor caught the rhythm of the language the right action would necessarily follow. Convinced that scenic art reflected life, he consistently worked to create an illusion of life on the stage; hence, the concept of *ensemble* was an essential part of his theatrical vocabulary. His school was founded upon, in his words, "natural and expressive acting on the stage." Under Ostrovsky's guidance, the Maly company became famous and excelled the Aleksandrinsky company in Petersburg. "In the Maly Theatre," A. A. Pleshcheev recalled, "they did not act, they performed a rite. It was not a production, but a concert."

As a playwright, Ostrovsky made plays for performance in the theatre; and even though he recognized the importance of drama as literature, his chief task as he saw it was to create plays that could be performed before audiences. For example, when composing a work he always read the dialogue aloud in his study. He took every opportunity to read his plays before friends or large gatherings. Consequently, his plays designed for the theatre achieve their fullest realization in the theatre. Most actors, for example, usually see immediately the strength of an Ostrovsky character as it may be played in the theatre, whereas readers who may lack the actor's insight will sometimes fail to see the point of a particular scene and dismiss it as an example of poor writing.

The framework of Ostrovsky's writings was established early in his career. In 1850 he published a critique of Mrs. Tur's short story *The Mistake,* and in the course of the review estimated world literature in general and Russian literature in particular.

> The writer either formulates the originality of some sort of character as the highest expression in contemporary life, or evaluating him in relation to an ideal common to all mankind,

finds the definition of him too narrow, and consequently the character turns out comic. . . . This occurs in all literatures, with the only difference, that in foreign literatures . . . works formulating the originality of the character, that is, a personality, stand first and foremost, while those that chastise a personality— are secondary and often in the shade; but with us in Russia it is the other way around . . . the public expects from art . . . its judgment on life, expects . . . the contemporary faults and shortcomings of the day. . . . This accusatory trend of our litera- ture might be called the moral-social trend.

To Ostrovsky, "the more aesthetic a work, the more national it is, then the more this accusatory element will be found in it." The play- wright maintained this conviction most of his life, and it is this ac- cusatory element in his plays which either annoyed or persuaded many of his critics. Since most of his plays were contemporary and topical, many Russian critics responded in terms of the ideas expressed. For example, Dobrolyubov consistently related the ideas in the plays to the social conditions of the day; and in a sense he used the plays as case studies, as evidence in the argument that the social environment must be changed.

Ostrovsky's themes and ideas were centered in the mode of life (byt) as it was revealed in various official classes and occupations. Treating almost the entire range of the class structure, the playwright individualized each class or occupation by particularizing common characteristics. The only classes exempt in his plays were the clergy, since it was forbidden to represent them in contemporary plays, and the peasantry, whose representatives appear now and again in crowd scenes. His plays included religious characters, such as Feklusha the pilgrim in The Storm, as well as discussion of pilgrims on the stage, as in the third act of The Scoundrel. Such religious agents were usually characterized as hypocritical, cunning, and selfish.

The remaining official classes and occupations, however, were treated fully by Ostrovsky. The agents in the merchant byt were characterized as poorly educated, ambitious, occupied with making money or aping the nobility. Domestic life featured the tyrannical head (samodur), who firmly ruled the family members. Threats of beatings, fear of drunken rage, and discussion of violence occurred on the stage, but reflected the terror and savage life off the stage. One of the most effective scenes, for example, is in It's a Family Affair. Bolshov is expected to arrive momentarily, but Fominishna fears he will come home drunk and beat everyone in the house. When Bolshov arrives, shouts, and pounds on the locked door, Agrafena his wife quickly disappears and Fominishna the housekeeper urges the *samodur* to go to sleep. The threat of violence disappears, however, when Bolshov enters and is discovered angry but sober. Based on the interrelation of cumulative terror and sudden release, the scene effectively employs comic reversal. Other examples of petty tyranny *(samodurstvo)* occur in *The Storm*, but both Marfa and Dikoy as exemplary agents of the *samodur* have been characterized in a serious action.

Closely allied with the merchant class were the *meshchane*, ranking immediately below the merchants officially and often depicted by Ostrovsky as dominated by the merchant *byt*. For example, Podkhalyuzin in *It's a Family Affair* has come out of the *meshchane*, but is portrayed as making his way in the merchant world. Kuligin and Shapkin in *The Storm*, on the other hand, are both of the *meshchane* and are characterized as hard-working and sympathetic agents. In *The Poor Bride*, Khorkova too is of this class, as are several in the crowd scene of the last act. The term *meshchane* and its derivatives had a cultural meaning, *i.e.* commonplace, vulgar in taste, etc., and Ostrovsky vividly characterized that meaning in the behavior of the agents in *It's a Family Affair*.

Turning from the merchant *byt* in *It's a Family Affair*, Ostrovsky employed the environment of the government official *(chinovnik)* in *The Poor Bride*. Each of the agents Milashin, Merich, and Benevolensky is individualized in terms of his position in the Table of Ranks, his personal drive, and his sense of ethics. At the lower level, Milashin is poor, forced to work for a living, unable to advance up the ladder. At a similar level, Merich is rich; and having entered the service to reach first rank, he has the ambition for advancement. At a somewhat higher level, Benevolensky has made money by taking bribes; although he is sharp enough to make his way in the service, he is poorly educated, with vulgar taste, and capable of cruelty. Each agent, though bound to the occupation of *chinovnik*, is governed by individual traits and motivations. In this way, Ostrovsky gave texture and measure to his world of the *chinovnik*.

The highest official class, the nobility, contained several degrees of position and power, and Ostrovsky included the impoverished, the landed, and the lower circles of the aristocracy. Although usually better educated than those in the other classes and occupations, the noblemen in his plays are often governed by the same motivations as the characters in the merchant *byt* or the *chinovnik* world. Like Podkhalyuzin in *It's a Family Affair*, Glumov in *The Scoundrel* is after money and a bride. Members of the landed nobility in *The Forest* are as narrow-minded and selfish in their own circle as are the characters in *It's a Family Affair*. In keeping with his technique of particularizing agents, Ostrovsky included noblemen who expressed high ideals. Although Neschastlivtsev the actor in *The Forest* has had as poor an education as, say, Kuligin in *The Storm*, he shares with Kuligin similar viewpoints about man's behavior.

Throughout his plays, Ostrovsky raised questions and employed themes which were specifically related to each *byt* and at the same time were often universal to all classes and occupations. How should the family complex be governed? What alienates parents and children? What are the rights of women? Does education eliminate prejudice and vulgarity? What is the role of ethics in business, in government, in the aristocracy? In short, how should man widen his personal aims and arrange his life in society?

Since Ostrovsky wanted to present life situations on the stage, he rarely tempered his plays with conventional rewards and punishments. At the end of Gogol's *Revizor*, the Inspector General is announced and promises justice to the system. At the end of Ostrovsky's plays, however, the criminal often goes free, right seldom triumphs over wrong, and life goes merrily on. Thus, at the end of *It's a Family Affair*, Podkhalyuzin tries to persuade the audience to visit his new shop, "Send the little fellow to us—and we won't rook him when we count the onions." In *The Poor Bride*, the heroine Marya is destined for a life of hardship with Benevolensky. In *The Storm*, Katerina goes to her death, oppressed by inhumanity, but little change is seen for those who remain. In *The Scoundrel*, the aristocratic circle promises to bring Glumov back simply because he is necessary. In *The Forest*, the actors leave the narrow backwoods society in very much the same condition as when they entered.

Taking Ostrovsky at his word, the critics of his day often viewed his plays as life situations on the stage. But their praise or blame was measured by the degrees to which the life situations reflected their own critical viewpoints. Prince Mirsky, the noted literary historian, suggested that Ostrovsky was simply an observer who put together what he saw in Russia.

> He is the least subjective of Russian writers. His would be a
> hopeless case for the psychoanalyst. His characters are not in
> any sense emanations of himself. They are genuine reflections of
> "the other." He is no psychologist; his characters are not, as
> Tolstoy's are, inner worlds to which we are introduced by a
> supreme power of intuition; they are just people as seen by other
> people.°

°D. F. Mirsky, *A History of Russian Literature*, edited by Francis J. Whitfield (New York: Knopf, 1964), p. 235.

Since Ostrovsky did not subscribe to the principles of any particular group, his clear vision was not obscured by any predetermined convictions other than his sense of justice, far-reaching humanity, and firm belief in education. His sensitivity to the changing social scene was mirrored in play after play.

In an excellent article published in the journal *Muscovite* in 1855, Grigor'ev discussed his thesis that Ostrovsky had introduced a "new word" in Russian literature. The playwright's new message, wrote Grigor'ev, is an old message—nationality *(narodnost')*. By returning to the national roots of Russia, Ostrovsky had come up with the concept of *byt*, thereby creating original characters, a new language, distinctive play construction and style. Grigor'ev's conclusions, as valid today as when they were written, provide an answer as to why Ostrovsky's significance has been restricted primarily to his own native land. Although the playwright raised universal questions, he explored their answers in a social milieu peculiar to Russia. His language—threaded by native images, color, texture—was intricately related to national roots, and his plays consequently reflected that indigenous quality.

Ostrovsky's aims in constructing his plays were also related to the Russian society. The playwright does not invent what happens, Ostrovsky declared, since this comes about through life, history, or legend.

> His chief objective is to show on the basis of what psychological facts any given event happens and why exactly this way, and not otherwise. . . . The invention of plot *(intriga)* is difficult, because plot is falsehood, whereas the objective of poetry is truth. Fortunate was Shakespeare who used prepared legends: not only did he not invent falsehoods, but also into the falsehood of stories he thrust the truth of life. The objective of the poet is not to come up with an imaginary plot, but to explain even an unbelievable incident by the laws of life.

Ostrovsky by no means subscribed to the claim of later naturalists that life as it is should be placed on the stage, that form should have little to do with the matter of constructing plays. An examination of his plays usually reveals a careful attention to plotting and form.

In *The Scoundrel*, for example, Ostrovsky informed his scene with the marked stratification of Russian society, exemplified in this play as in others by the Table of Ranks. Ten of the sixteen characters represent the nobility, but even within this group exists a strong division of rank, or *chin*. The established circle of nobility is headed by Turusina, and of the agents within that circle, each holds a specific rank but attempts to displace or to pursue the character with the next highest rank. Thus, Mamaev at the fifth step pursues Krutitsky at the fourth; Krutitsky in turn tries to thrust aside Gorodulin at the third step, in order to pursue Turusina at the second step. In keeping with the comic nature of the revolving circle, Turusina pursues Manefa the peasant fortune-teller—a representative of the lowest official class. Viewing life as a game to be played by the talented, intelligent, and clever, the impoverished nobleman Glumov capitalizes on the vanities of each agent and mirrors the image of the revolving circle.

In the structure of this play, Ostrovsky built the settings sequentially from the lowest in the nobility, Glumov's apartment, through the next in hierarchical rank, Mamaev's apartment, to the highest, Turusina's home. At the center of the play as at the center of the aristocratic circle, the third act takes place in Turusina's mansion. In the fourth act, the settings descend in rank, first to Krutitsky's study, then to Glumov's apartment; in these two settings, the unmasking of Glumov begins. In the fifth act, as in the third, the setting is Turusina's home, but now outside in the garden—an appropriate setting, with nature changing from dusk to darkness, for thrusting Glumov out into the open and shattering the mirror of the circle. That Glumov and his reflecting nature are required by the circle to maintain its image is sufficient reason to bring him back into the revolving circle.

Of the remaining three comedies in this volume, Ostrovsky manipulated the concepts of illusion and reality, role-playing in life situations, and the divisiveness of class and rank. In *It's a Family Affair*, the specific concept of life as a game informs the structure of the play. The characters play the game, however, according to the rules of business. Bolshov, for example, starts the affair on the premise that everybody's doing it and there's no reason why he should stand on the sidelines simply to watch. Since he is a sharper player than Bolshov, and since Bolshov takes himself out of the game when he turns over the rulebook to others, Podkhalyuzin wins despite the objections raised by his cronies. Ostrovsky applied the rules of business to the law. In *Unlucky Days* (1863), the lawyer Mudrov states the rules for lawyers: "Our profession is just the same as a game: and there's no pity in it; if it's possible to take off your shirt, then we'll take it off."

In *The Poor Bride*, Ostrovsky used the concepts of illusion and reality as well as role-playing as central to the structure of the play. The heroine Marya seldom indulges in role-playing, but her chief suitors assume roles appropriate to each in their scenes with Marya. In the fifth act, the three characters clearly indicate their various roles. Early in the act, after agreeing to Marya's demands, Benevolensky crosses to Dobrotvorsky and asks, "What do you say, am I handling myself slick enough?" Ostrovsky added a mirror to the room, and both Benevolensky and Milashin check out their images in it. Merich plays the role of disappointed lover, and Ostrovsky provided a soliloquy for Merich in order to reveal the character unmasked. The concept of illusion and reality has been intricately threaded in the play. For the most part, Marya responds sincerely, openly, essentially realistically; but as the action progresses, she creates illusions for herself, *e.g.,* Merich loves her, he will propose marriage, etc. Disillusioned by Merich, Marya by the fifth act dreams she will be able to change Benevolensky. Throughout the fifth act, Marya's illusion of future happiness is contrasted with the actuality of future hardship.

In *The Forest,* Ostrovsky contrasted role-playing by actors with role-playing in life situations and manipulated the two concepts throughout the action, exemplified in characters like Marfa and Neschastlivtsev the actor, playing a role from Schiller's *The Robbers,* castigates the landed nobility for the false roles they play in life situations: "We are the artists, noble artists, and you are the comedians." By the time the actors walk out, their life of illusion has achieved a greater sense of reality than the illusion of life experienced by the landed nobility.

In Ostrovsky's tragedy the image of the storm was treated as the unifying element in the structure of the play. The storm in the heavens, as M. I. Pisarev noted in 1860, parallels the moral storm in the play. In the same way, the poetic image of the storm occurs throughout the action, exemplified in the characters like Marfa and Dikoy and central to the struggle of Katerina. Waging her own personal storm, the Old Lady advances the action by arousing the moral storm within Katerina. With her death, Katerina's personal storm has been stilled, but the storms of superstition and cruelty continue.

Another key to understanding these plays is viewing them according to Ostrovsky's objective: "to explain even an unbelievable incident by the laws of life." In recent years, the "laws of life" have been examined by social scientists in terms of rituals, pastimes, and games. G. H. Mead's *Mind, Self, and Society* was an early study of games, and recently Dr. Eric Berne has published important studies, such as *Transactional Analysis in Psychotherapy* (1961), as well as the popular *Games People Play* (1964). The work of the social scientists has been used recently as a way to examine drama, and Ostrovsky's plays readily lend themselves to this kind of analysis.

His clear vision, his understanding of people, together with his enormous knowledge of literature and the theatre, inform the splendid drama Alexander Ostrovsky gave to his native land. Few playwrights match the magnitude of his labor, exceed the breadth of his humanity, or serve the muse of theatre with greater dedication.

A NOTE ON TRANSLITERATION AND PRONUNCIATION

There is no generally accepted system of transliterating the Russian alphabet. The Library of Congress uses one system; European and most American scholars use another; and individual writers have invented additional ones. The Russian proper names in the plays have been transliterated in accordance with the following table. The pronunciation guide should be viewed as only approximate, since most of the letters are pronounced in more than one way. An accurate pronunciation of a letter is governed by the place of stress or where the letter occurs in the word. Stress is marked by an acute accent over the vowel.

Russian	English	Pronunciation
а	a	fáther; máma
б	b	bank; top
в	v	vet; deaf
г	g	get; break
д	d	dáddy; vet
е	e	met; yeah
ё	e	bórder; yore
ж	zh	vísion; push
з	z	zeal; miss
и	i	cheese; if
й	i	unstressed vowel; transliterated (i) by Library of Congress, (j) by scholars
к	k	kept
л	l	log
м	m	mama
н	n	no

Russian	English	Pronunciation
о	o	órder; alóne; artístic
п	p	page
р	r	rake
с	s	miss
т	t	ten
у	u	spoon
ф	f	form
х	kh	a voiceless velar fricative; the Russian equivalent of the German ach.
ц	ts	a voiceless alveolar affricate; its
ч	ch	chief
ш	sh	shoe
щ	shch	fish chówder
ы	y	one of the hard tonic vowels, placed high as in beat, placed back as in boot, but spread in place of rounded
э	e	vet; yet
ю	yu	you; sue
я	ya	artístic; its; yah; yip
ъ		the hard sign has no sound value, but influences the sound of the preceding consonant
ь		The soft sign has no sound value, but influences the sound of the preceding consonant

In the text of the plays, the combinations ый and ий have been transliterated as (y), e.g., the name Ostrovsky (Ostrovskii).

The soft sign symbol (') is not used in the text of the plays, but is included in the Textual Notes. No attempt has been made in the pronunciation guide to give examples of soft consonant sounds. The first example listed for each vowel generally indicates the stressed sound; the remaining examples, the unstressed sound. Something of the complexity in pronunciation may be seen in the name Lomonósov: the first vowel is sounded as *a* in *a*rtístic; the second, as *a* in máma; the third, as *o* in órder; the fourth, as *a* in máma. The stress of the characters' names is given in the explanatory section for each play. The stress of the place names in the plays is as follows.

PLACE NAMES IN THE PLAYS

Arbátsky
Arkhángelsk
Ástrakhan
Balchúg
Bessarábia
Butírka
Dvína
Ekaterínburg
Gorélaya
Il'ínka (pronounced
  Ilyínka)
Irbít
Irkútsk
Ivérsky
Kalínov
Kamchátka
Karasubazár
Karétny

Kazán
Kishinev (pro-
  nounced Kishinóf)
Kostromá
Kremenchúg
Krión
Kuznétsky
Lebedyán
Lyskóvo
Mýshkino
Névsky
Nízhny
Novocherkássk
Odéssa
Palenaya (pro-
  nounced Palónaya
Pénky
Poltáva

Preobrazhénskoe
Pyatigórsk
Pyláeva
Rogózhskaya
Rýbinsk
Samára
Sarátov
Sokól'niky
Stávropol
Tiflís
Tróitsa
Túla
Tyákhta
Vólogda
Vorónezh
Voskrensénsky
Yaroslávl

IT'S A FAMILY AFFAIR— WE'LL SETTLE IT OURSELVES

IT'S A FAMILY AFFAIR—
WE'LL SETTLE IT
OURSELVES

I. COMPOSITION

Ostrovsky began writing *It's a Family Affair—We'll Settle It Ourselves*
in 1846, published scenes from it the following January in the newspaper *Moscow City Leaflet*, and after several revisions brought the
four-act comedy to its final form in the fall of 1849. Although the
comedy was his first full-length work, it was the second play he completed. Both *It's a Family Affair* and his first play, *A Portrait of
Domestic Happiness*, grew out of an early interest in the theatre, a
natural bent for writing, and years of observing the mode of life *(byt)*
in the Zamoskvorech'e—a merchant district of old Moscow. His own
family lived in the district until he was eighteen, and his work as a
clerk, first at the Conscience Court (1843–1845) and next at the Commercial Court (1845–1851), brought him into daily contact with business
and family life in times of legal crises.

By 1846 Ostrovsky at the age of twenty-three had written, as he
himself noted, "many scenes from the merchant *byt.*" He dated his
own career as a writer, however, from the fourteenth of February
1847. On that day he finished *A Portrait of Domestic Happiness*, later
entitled *A Domestic Portrait*, and read the play aloud to a group of
literature students at the apartment of Professor S. P. Shevyrev. The
response was enthusiastic. "The most memorable day of my life,"
Ostrovsky recalled years later. "From that day I started to consider
myself a Russian writer, and without doubt or vacillation I already
believed in my calling." The play was published the next month,
but as N. A. Dobrolyubov pointed out in his famous article "The Kingdom of Darkness," *A Domestic Portrait* received little or no attention
at the time, nor was a single word of praise or blame printed in the
journals. Dobrolyubov was mistaken. Significant attention was paid

five months later by the Imperial dramatic censors, who banned the play from stage productions. The censor M. Gedeonov sternly reprimanded its author: "Judging by these scenes, Moscow merchants cheat and drink, while their wives go out for a good time behind their backs."

A *Domestic Portrait* attracted chiefly the Imperial dramatic censors, but two years later *It's a Family Affair* became the talk of Moscow and thrust its young dramatist among the foremost authors of the day. N. V. Berg, who was there, recalled, "The fame of Ostrovsky as a dramatic writer was born and grew in one day." Although both publication and stage production of the play had been prohibited in November of 1849, the author and the actor P. M. Sadovsky read the play almost daily in Moscow homes during the next few months. News of the comedy spread so rapidly, and those who wanted to hear it were so numerous, that on several occasions Sadovsky had to follow a rigorous schedule of readings in separate homes on the same day. Ostrovsky sent a manuscript copy to Petersburg, and the reception of the play there was as enthusiastic as in Moscow.

Perhaps the most important event occurred on the third of December, when Ostrovsky read the play at the home of M. P. Pogodin, professor of Russian history and publisher and editor of the journal *Muscovite.* Berg recorded the occasion. "Gogol was invited also but arrived in the middle of the reading; he quietly crossed to the door, [stopped] and . . . remained standing until the end, listening to all appearances, attentively." The established author praised the work of the younger man. Pogodin was enthralled with the play and used his powerful connections to receive permission for publication in his journal the following March. About the same time the play was issued in a separate printing.

The widespread reaction to the play brought immediate recognition to Ostrovsky, launched him on his long career, and typified the kind of treatment he would receive until the final years of his life. For example, Pisemsky praised the play as "a merchants' *Woe from Wit (Gore ot uma),* or more precisely . . . a merchants' *Dead Souls.*" Nekrasov invited the dramatist to contribute to his journal *Contemporary.* Prince V. F. Odoevsky wrote to a friend:

> Have you read Ostrovsky's comedy, or rather tragedy, *It's a Family Affair—We'll Settle It Ourselves*—its real title is *The Bankrupt?* It was time to bring into fresh water the corrupted soul of this class of people. If this is not a momentary sprinkling, not a mushroom, oozing with every kind of rot, coming of its own accord out of the earth—then here is a man of enormous talent. In Russia I believe there are only three tragedies: *The*

Minor, Woe from Wit, The Inspector General. I am betting on
The Bankrupt as number four.

The favorable response by Pisemsky, Nekrasov, and Odoevsky was
typical, but certain members of the nobility and the merchant class
were violently opposed to the play and denounced Ostrovsky to Tsar
Nicholas I. When in the spring of 1850 Ostrovsky once again peti-
tioned for permission to stage his play, the Tsar ordered the play
examined by his special committee for the control of works, received
a negative report, and upheld the decision. The play was not only
banned from stage productions, but also any comment about the play
in the journals was prohibited. In June Ostrovsky was placed under
surveillance by the secret police, and in connection with governmental
suspicion he was forced to resign from his position as clerk a few
months later. The surveillance by the secret police continued until 1856.

A year following the first publication, gossip spread throughout Moscow that *It's a Family Affair* was the work of the provincial actor
D. A. Gorev-Tarasenkov. Ostrovsky wrote to Gorev, asking that he put
an end to the rumor, but Gorev refused. Even though Ostrovsky
eventually wrote a total of forty-seven original plays, translated another
twenty-two plays, and collaborated with several authors on additional
plays, the scandal attached to his first full-length work persisted for
several years. Finally, in 1856 Ostrovsky wrote a detailed article
about the creation of *It's a Family Affair.* He pointed out that by the
fall of 1846 the comedy "in its general features had been invented,"
that several scenes had been outlined, and that many lines had been
written. Then he chanced to tell the plot to Gorev, who suggested that
the two work together on the play. They spent three or four evenings
together, usually with Ostrovsky dictating and Gorev writing down the
lines. Gorev left Moscow, and that ended the collaboration. To clear
up the matter, Ostrovsky published the scenes (about six pages) written
with Gorev in the *Moscow City Leaflet,* under the two sets of initials,
A.O. and D.G. Turning to the play again in the spring of 1847,
Ostrovsky changed the plan, began a completely different treatment,
and eventually finished the play two years later. The false charge of
plagiarism has been a consistent subject of discussion, and as late
as 1963 one of Ostrovsky's biographers, A. Revyakin, published a substantial article on the topic in *Russian Literature.*

Ostrovsky was forced to make deletions in his play for its first publication, but when he applied to the censor for permission to include
It's a Family Affair in his first collection in 1858, serious changes were
demanded. For example, it was suggested that he include a final scene
in which a police officer appeared to take Podkhalyuzin to his chief.

There Podkhalyuzin must account for his crime of receiving property from the bankrupt Bolshov. To Ostrovsky a change of this nature was like "cutting off a hand or a leg." Nevertheless, he made the requisite changes, and the play was included in the 1859 publication. The play was printed in this version until 1885.

II. STAGE PRODUCTIONS

Almost a decade passed before the play was produced in the theatre. Although many provincial theatres tried unsuccessfully to get the necessary permission, the theatre in Irkutsk had the sole distinction of staging the play before 1860. In November of 1857 the governor was out of the district, and the director of the theatre staged the play. When the governor returned and immediately applied for permission, Petersburg sent a firm refusal, the play was removed from the repertoire, and the governor tried to silence the affair.

Finally, on 18 April 1860 the Voronezhsky Cadet Corps, in behalf of the Literary Fund, produced the play in the 1859 version. A few months later, several of Ostrovsky's friends, chiefly F. A. Burdin and I. F. Gorbunov, were successful in receiving permission to stage the 1859 version. On 16 January 1861 the first production was given by the Aleksandrinsky Theatre in Petersburg for the benefit performance of Yu. N. Linskaya; and on 31 January the play was staged at the Maly Theatre in Moscow for the benefit performance of P. M. Sadovsky. Ostrovsky attended rehearsals in the two capitals and actively participated in their preparation for performance. Both productions were considered the very best of their respective 1860–1861 seasons.

Not all the roles in the two productions, however, were successfully rendered. Neither F. A. Burdin in Petersburg nor M. S. Shchepkin in Moscow caught the essentials of the *samodur* Bolshov. Burdin in the last act presented "an almost kingly lyricism," whereas Shchepkin, in the words of V. I. Rodislavsky, created "a good-natured, roguish old man—and that was all." One reviewer maintained that Shchepkin "in beard and Russian long-skirted frockcoat" was no more than "a mummer." In Petersburg E. M. Levkeeva as Lipochka and P. K. Gromova as Fominishna were singled out by reviewers for their excellent acting. In Moscow reviewers were enraptured over the role of Podkhalyuzin created by P. M. Sadovsky. D. Koropchevsky discussed Sadovsky in the first act.

Humbly, carefully he entered . . . bowed low and came to a

stop some distance away, having put his hand behind the lapel
of his frockcoat and having bowed his head in the direction of
Bolshov. With habitual obsequiousness . . . he answered at first
the questions of Bolshov. And on the exit of Rispolozhensky
his remarks were still monotonous and without passion. But at
the moment Bolshov asked if he were fond of him, the eyes of
Podkhalyuzin lit up, as if a certain inspiration had occurred
in him; however, he still restrained his enveloping joy and he
concluded the act, returning to the former usual servile tone.

All the critics agreed that the role of Podkhalyuzin was Sadovsky's
crowning achievement. V. I. Rodislavsky noted that "we did not dis-
cover words sufficient in praise of him" and added that Sadovsky
brought to the role "a certain enórmous observation, a certain deep,
true understanding which was not only in the comedy, but which must
also have been read between the lines." Sadovsky played in the 1859
version but invented a mimed piece of business at the end of the play.
When the police officer arrived to take Podkhalyuzin away, the latter
shoved a bribe into his hand; the officer walked out, and Podkhalyuzin
was completely freed.

In 1881 the playwright's brother, M. N. Ostrovsky, former minister
of government properties, finally succeeded in getting permission for
the staging of the play in its 1850 version. Permission was granted
only for productions in the Imperial theatres; the people's theatres
were not allowed to stage the earlier version. In that same year, at
A. A. Brenko's private theatre in Moscow, the playwright himself
directed a brilliant production of his 1850 version. M. I. Pisarev,
who played the role of Bolshov, described the memorable event, when
almost the entire intelligentsia of Moscow arrived for the production.

> The place was almost mobbed, notwithstanding the fact that
> the prices were raised significantly. . . . Calls for the author
> began from the first act; however, he refused stubbornly to
> accept them until the end of the play.

Although *It's a Family Affair* was by no means the most popular of
Ostrovsky's works, the play was performed 1,487 times in Russia from
1875 to 1917. Moreover, *It's a Family Affair* remained in the repertory
of theatres after the Revolution. For example, in 1939 there were 262
productions in the U.S.S.R. In 1940, 270 productions. Since 1945
productions of the play have greatly diminished in the professional
theatres, although L. Volkov's new production at the Maly in 1959 is
ample testimony to the continuing interest in Ostrovsky's first full-
length comedy.

III. NAMES OF CHARACTERS

In keeping with traditions established in the classical theatre of Greece and Rome, Ostrovsky tended to incorporate chief character traits into the names of his characters. Although he used this technique more frequently in his early plays, and even though he was by no means consistent, he chose names with care. His choices were governed not so much by their immediately perceived sense, as by their sound, rhythm, and symbolism. Now and again critics have overestimated Ostrovsky's technique, read too much into the name, or summed up the character by the meaning of the name. "The name of the character," as Linin pointed out, "does not complete the full nature of the character."

Since Ostrovsky chose the first name and patronymic with the same skill he gave to the last name, the three names together with their variants often describe the attitude or bent of the character. For example, Samson Silych Bolshov (Bol'shov) may be translated as Samson, son of strength, Bigman. His wife's first name Agrafena suggests not only water bottle but also countess, while her patronymic Kondratevna (Kondrat'evna) connotes daughter of horseflogger. Their daughter's name Olimpiada combines Olympus and Olympia with Hades, but the name Lipa means lime-tree and Lipochka denotes bud of a lime-tree with the connotation of kidneys. The name Lazar (Lazar') derives from two expressions, *lazarya pet'* "pretending misfortune, complaining of his fate" and *naobum lazarya* "by guesswork, without schooling." Podkhalyuzin's patronymic derives from the verb to lick, while his last name suggests groveling, fawning, or sneaky. The name Rispolozhensky, on the other hand, suggests unbuttoned or unfrocked. The name Ustinya (Ustin'ya) combines mustache with slime or ooze, while her patronymic Naumovna connotes crafty. Tishka (Hush! Be still!) is a nickname for Tikhon, denoting quiet or calm. Fominishna suggests familiar niche.

The stress is as follows: Samsón Sílych Bolshóv, Agraféna Kondrátevna, Olimpiáda Samsónovna (Lípochka), Lázar Elizárych Podkhalyúzin, Ustínya Naúmovna, Sysóy Psóich Rispolózhensky, Fomínishna, Tíshka.

IT'S A FAMILY AFFAIR—
WE'LL SETTLE IT OURSELVES
Svoi lyudi—sochtemsya!
A Comedy in Four Acts

CHARACTERS

SAMSON SILYCH BOLSHOV, *a merchant.*

AGRAFENA KONDRATEVNA, *his wife.*

OLIMPIADA SAMSONOVNA (LIPOCHKA), *their daughter.*

LAZAR ELIZARYCH PODKHALYUZIN, *a clerk.*

USTINYA NAUMOVNA, *a matchmaker.*

SYSOY PSOICH RISPOLOZHENSKY, *a lawyer.*

FOMINISHNA, *housekeeper* ⎫
TISHKA, *boy* ⎬ in Bolshov's house.

ACT ONE

The drawing room in Bolshov's house.

LIPOCHKA. [*Seated by the window with a book.*] Ah! dancing, dancing. What a delightful way to pass the time! What could be more delicious? You go to a party, or somebody's wedding, you sit down, naturally. Smothered in flowers, all dressed up like a doll or a picture in a magazine. All of a sudden up flies a cavalier and says, "Grant me the good fortune, miss." Well, you take a good look, now. If the fellow is witty, or belongs to the military, then take him. And what's more, close your eyes a little and answer, "If you please, with pleasure." Ah! [*Heatedly.*] How fas-ci-nat-ing! Simply beyond belief. [*Sighs.*] Most of all, I don't like dancing with students or clerks. Give me an army man any day! Ah, charming! Delicious! What mustaches, and epaulets, and uniforms, and some even have spurs with little tingling bells. I could murder them when they don't wear a saber. And why on earth do they take it off? It's strange, really and truly. The officers themselves have no idea how they'd sparkle, ever more fascinating. You know, if they'd only take a look at the spurs, how they jingle, especially if a uhlan or some colonel is putting on airs. Why, it's a miracle! You could give your eyeteeth just to look at them, the sweetest thing on earth to see. Just let an officer stick on a saber, and there's simply nothing lovelier to see or hear, like crackling thunder. Which is better than a lot of music you've heard. How can you even compare an officer with a civilian? An officer. You see it right away—his nimble mind and everything. And what about a civilian? Nothing more than a vegetable. [*Silence.*] I'd like to know why so many ladies sit cross-legged at dances. Why, there's no difficulty in learning how. At first I was a little embarrassed in front of the teacher, but after twenty lessons I understood everything, perfectly. Why is it they don't learn how? Simply a matter of superstition. But mama used to get angry because the teacher was always grabbing for my knees. Simply a matter of no education. What difference does it make? He's a dancing master, not somebody else. [*Deep in thought.*] I can see it now. All of a sudden an officer proposes to me, and right off a grand betrothal. Candles are burning everywhere. Enter the waiters in white gloves. Naturally, I am wearing tulle or a gauze dress, when all of a sudden a waltz starts up. But now I find myself confused, right in front of him. Oh, it's shameful, shameful. What will become of me? What will he think? "Here," he'll say, "is a silly fool with no schooling." Oh, no, how is it possible! Don't you know it's been a year and a half since I've danced? I'll try it now in my spare time. [*Waltzing badly.*]   One, two, three. One, two, three.

AGRAFENA. [*Entering.*]   So here you are, you shameless hussy! I knew it from the bottom of my heart. Here you are before daybreak; before you've eaten a little of God's bread, and you take up dancing right off.

LIPOCHKA. How's that, mama? I've had some tea and eaten up the cheese-cake. Take a look. Do you think it's all right? One, two, three. One, two . . .

AGRAFENA. [*Chasing after her.*]   So you've eaten something. So, what! If you think I'm going to spend my time looking at you. No sense of modesty. It's a sin, that's what it is. Don't swirl around like that, I tell you.

LIPOCHKA. What do you mean, a sin? Everybody does it this way nowadays. One, two . . .

AGRAFENA. Better crack your head against a table than show off your legs. [*Runs after her.*]   What's the matter with you? Where did you get the idea of not minding me!

LIPOCHKA. What do you mean, not minding you? Whoever told you that! Don't bother me now. Let me finish it properly. One, two, three . . .

AGRAFENA. Why on earth should I keep running after you in my old age? Whew! You're wearing me out, you little barbarian, you. Listen to me. Stop, or I'll tell your father on you.

LIPOCHKA. In a minute, mama, in a minute. This is my last turn. I think God created you just so you could tell father on me. Go ahead! A lot you mean to me, anyway. One, two . . .

AGRAFENA. What's this? You go on dancing and what's more— scold me, to boot. Stop it this minute. If you don't, I'll give it to you. I'll grab your skirt and rip off the whole train.

LIPOCHKA. Go ahead. Rip away—to your heart's content. You'll only have to sew it on again. There, that'll do it. [*Sitting.*] Phew, phew. I'm all steamed up, just as if I'd been hauling a cart. Whew! Give me a little hanky, mama, to wipe away the sweat.

AGRAFENA. Wait a bit, I'll wipe it myself. See, you're dead tired. You know, it's like someone were making you do it. Even if you don't respect your mother, then you ought to be ashamed in this house. Your father, my dear, could scarcely get his legs moving this morning, and here you skim along like some kind of whirligig.

LIPOCHKA. Oh, I've had enough of your old advice. What am I supposed to do, in your opinion? Perhaps you'd like me to get sick. That'd be just fine if I were a doctor's wife. Whew! What repulsive ideas you have. Oh, what are you, mama, really and truly? Really, you make me blush sometimes with your nonsense.

AGRAFENA. What a darling child we have. Just look at the way she abuses her mother. Oh, you muddle-headed chatterbox, you! What gives you the right to insult your parents like this? Is it for this I brought you into the world, taught you, and what's more, took care of you like a little flower?

LIPOCHKA. But you didn't teach me. Outsiders did. That'll do, thank you. To tell the truth, you were never educated for anything. Well, so what? So you gave birth, and what was I then? A child. A child without the first idea about life. I didn't understand manners. But I grew up and looked at the ways of the world, and I can see now I'm much better educated than other people. Why on earth should I put up with your nonsense? Yes, why! Because that's the only thing I get from you—nonsense.

AGRAFENA. Cut it out, you shameless hussy, you, cut it out, you'll make me lose patience. I'll go straight to your father, fling myself at his feet, and say, "Samson, sweetie, there's no living with our daughter anymore."

LIPOCHKA.   Yes, there's no living for you. I can see it now. And what kind of life do you give me? Why did you get rid of my young man? There was no better match anywhere. He was a god of love, Eyeros himself.[1] How could you say he was simple?

AGRAFENA.   Oh, that one was simple all right—simple-minded. He came in mincing and putting on airs, twirling here and fidgeting there. Oh, he was something, he was!

LIPOCHKA.   Yes, that's all you know. Everybody knows that he's well-born, a gentleman, so he acts in a delicate manner. In his circle they always act that way. How dare you find fault with people like that? Why, you know nothing about them. At least he isn't one of your kopek-pinching merchants. [*Whispers aside.*] My dearest, my darling!

AGRAFENA.   Oh, he's some darling all right. Tell us all about it, please do. I'm sorry we didn't marry you off to a clown in a circus. How do you like that! Oh, my, are you full of it! Whisper right under your mother's nose, will you, just to spite her.

LIPOCHKA.   There's reason enough, since you don't want me to be happy. You and daddy only want to find fault and domineer.

AGRAFENA.   Well, if you want to think that, go ahead. Let God be your judge. But nobody worries about her child like the mother who gave her birth. Here you are, getting all worked up and fishing up all kinds of foolishness, while your father and I worry night and day about finding you a good man and getting you fixed up in no time.

LIPOCHKA.   Yes, it's easy for you to talk. But if I may ask one question, what's in it for me?

AGRAFENA.   I bet you think I'm not sorry for you. What can I do, really? Be patient a little longer, even though you've waited so many years already. It's just impossible to find a husband all of a sudden. Only cats catch mice that fast.

LIPOCHKA.   What do your cats have to do with me! It's a husband I'm after. What chance do I have? I'm ashamed to meet my friends. We couldn't get a husband in all Moscow. They were all snapped up, one after another. Who wouldn't be cut to the quick? All my girl friends have been married forever, while I stand around like an orphan. We ran down one man, and then threw him away. Listen, find me a husband, and find him without fail. I'll tell you ahead of time. Either you make certain I get a husband, or it'll be the worse for you. I'll take a lover in secret, and on purpose, just to spite you. I'll run off with a hussar, and we'll get married on the sly.

AGRAFENA.   What's this, you harlot, you! Whoever hammered such rot in your head? Merciful heavens, I can't find my breath. You, you little bitch! Well, there's nothing I can do. I see I must call your father.

LIPOCHKA.   That's all you harp on—father, father. You're ready enough to talk when he's here, but just try it alone.

AGRAFENA.   So that's it. I'm a fool in your opinion, is that it? What kind of hussars do you have, you with your impudent nose? Tphew,[2] to you! A devilish, evil suggestion. I suppose you think I can't keep you in line. Tell me, you green-eyed hussy, you, where did you pick up that suspicious manner? Don't tell me you want to put something over on me. Keep it up, and you'll be stewing sweet peas in the kitchen. How do you like that! See here, you, you . . . Ah! Oh, saints in heaven! You'll wear sackcloth. Yes, I'll make it and over your head it'll go, right now. What's more, I'll pen you up with the pigs, instead of your parents.

LIPOCHKA.   You don't say! As if I'd let you order me around. Oh, that's a good one.

AGRAFENA.   Shut up, chatterbox. Shut up and do as your mother says. Oh, what a balky baby! Don't say another word, or I'll sew a bridle on your tongue. Some consolation the Lord has sent me—an impudent kid. You're a brat, a tomcat, without a womanly thought in your whole brain. You're ready, I suppose, to hop on a horse and dash away like a soldier.

LIPOCHKA.   And you, I imagine, are ready to drag in the police. Better keep quiet, since you haven't had the least bit of schooling. Very well, let's say I'm obnoxious. But what about you, when all's said and done? Would you like to ship me off to the next world before my time? Destroy me with your crackpot ideas? [*She weeps.*]   There, do you see, I'm starting to cough, just like some fly—here today and . . .   [*Weeps.*]

AGRAFENA.   [*Stands and looks at her.*]   There now, that'll do, stop.   [LIPOCHKA *weeps louder and then sobs.*]   There now, that's enough! Stop, I tell you! Very well, I'm to blame. Only stop it. It's all my fault.   [LIPOCHKA *weeps.*]   Lipochka! Lipa! There, that's all. Stop it, do you hear. [*Through her own tears.*] Please don't be angry at me. [AGRAFENA *weeps.*] A stupid old woman, ignorant. [*They weep together.*] There now, forgive me. I'll buy you some earrings.

LIPOCHKA. [*Weeping.*] Keep your earrings. My dressing-table is filled with them. Buy me some bracelets with emeralds.

AGRAFENA. I'll buy them, I will. Only stop crying!

LIPOCHKA. [*Through tears.*] I'll stop crying the day I get married. [*Weeps.*]

AGRAFENA. You'll get married, you will, my darling. There now, kiss me. [*They kiss.*] Good, Christ be with you! There, if you like, I'll wipe away your tears. [*She wipes tears.*] Did you know that Ustinya Naumovna wanted to come today? We're going to have a little talk.

LIPOCHKA. [*In a voice not yet controlled.*] Oh, if only she'd hurry and come here soon. [FOMINISHNA *enters.*]

FOMINISHNA. Just guess, dear Agrafena Kondratevna, who's gone and favored us with a visit?

AGRAFENA. I can't say. What do you think I am, Fominishna, some kind of guessing hag?

LIPOCHKA. Why don't you ask me? Do you think I'm more of a dunce than you or mama, maybe?

FOMINISHNA. I don't know how to put it. You're pretty nimble with words, but when it comes to deeds—well, that's not for you. I asked you time and again—and it's not this or that only. Please give me, if you like, a handkerchief. In your room right now, lolling around, are two piles of things—scattered here and there—but nothing comes my way. No, everything goes to one stranger after the next.

AGRAFENA. This is something, Fominishna, I'll never figure out till the day I die.

LIPOCHKA. Just look at her. You can see she took a drop of beer after breakfast, so now she's as giddy as a fishwife.

FOMINISHNA. It goes without saying. What are you laughing about? What's this about your dying, Agrafena Kondratevna? It happens, and the beginning is worse than the ending.

AGRAFENA. I don't follow a single word. You no sooner start talking than we lose all sense of what you're saying. There now, who is it that just arrived, exactly?

LIPOCHKA.   A man or a woman?

FOMINISHNA.   All men strike your fancy, don't they? Now wherever did you see a man wearing a bonnet? A little widowish something, so what do you call her from that?

LIPOCHKA.   Naturally, a woman without a husband, or a widow.

FOMINISHNA.   Don't tell me I was right? So it turns out a woman, no less!

LIPOCHKA.   She's muddle-headed, that's it! Now, Fominishna, tell us who the woman is, exactly.

FOMINISHNA.   What did I tell you? You're pretty smart but you're not much of a guesser. It's nobody else but Ustinya Naumovna.

LIPOCHKA.   Oh, mama, isn't that nice!

AGRAFENA.   Where's she been till now? Bring her in at once, Fominishna.

FOMINISHNA.   She'll be here any minute now. She stopped outside to fight with the yard-keeper. He didn't swing open the gate fast enough.

USTINYA.   [*Entering.*]   Whew, fa, fa! Why do you have steep stairs like that, my dears? You climb and climb and end up scarcely able to crawl.

LIPOCHKA.   Oh, here she is at last! How do you do, Ustinya Naumovna.

USTINYA.   Not so fast! There are people older than you around here. Your mother and I will have a little talk first.   [USTINYA *and* AGRAFENA *kiss.*]   How do you do, Agrafena Kondratevna. Feel pretty good when you got up? Have a good night? Still alive, aren't you, my dear?

AGRAFENA.   Thanks to the Lord! I'm alive and able to chew bread. I've spent the whole morning joking with my daughter.

USTINYA.   Must've been all about dresses, I expect.   [USTINYA *and* LIPOCHKA *kiss.*]   There, your turn's finally come. Why, it looks as if you've packed on a little weight, precious. God bless you! What can be better than the full bloom of beauty!

FOMINISHNA.   Tphew! Go on with you, you old sinner! You'll put a curse on us yet, no doubt.

LIPOCHKA.   Oh, what nonsense! It only looks like that, Ustinya Naumovna. I'm losing weight all the time. First, it was colic; then, my heart beats like a pendulum. Right now I feel faint, or else I'm getting seasick, and I'm simply overcome with melancholia.

USTINYA.　[*To* FOMINISHNA.]　Well, old soul, let's have a kiss right now. Of course, we've already said our greetings outside, my dear, so there's no reason for wearing out our lips again.

FOMINISHNA.　It's up to you. Sure, we're not ladies or matrons. No doubt, we're pretty ignorant small fry. But we've got souls in us, and not just hot air.

AGRAFENA.　[*Sitting.*]　Sit down, Ustinya Naumovna, sit down. Why're you standing like a cannon on wheels? Fominishna, run and tell them to warm up the samovar.

USTINYA.　I've had my tea, my dear, I have. I'll be damned if I haven't had my tea and only dropped by for a minute.

AGRAFENA.　Fominishna, why are you dawdling around? Start running, old girl, and be quick about it.

LIPOCHKA.　Mama, let me go. I can get there faster. Just see how awkward she is.

FOMINISHNA.　Now don't show off when nobody's asked you to. You know, dear Agrafena Kondratevna, here is what I think. Wouldn't it be nicer to serve some vodka and herring?

AGRAFENA.　Very well, vodka it is, but bring the samovar, too. Or do you grudge someone else's good fortune? Go along and have them bring it here when it's ready.

FOMINISHNA.　As you like. Yes, ma'am. [*Exits.*]

AGRAFENA.　Come now, Ustinya Naumovna, don't you have anything brand-new for us? You can see my little girl here has pined away to nothing, almost.

LIPOCHKA.　Actually, Ustinya Naumovna, you are here all the time. But nothing ever comes of it.

USTINYA.　But don't you see, my dears, it's impossible to put things together that fast. Your daddy keeps harping on a wealthy man. He tells me even a porter would be good enough, so long as he's loaded with money and keeps the dowry low. Your mother, Agrafena Kondratevna, also wants to live in clover. Give her a merchant without fail. Only he must have honors, drive the best horses, and cross himself in the old style. And you also have something in mind. How am I going to please everybody? [FOMINISHNA *enters and puts vodka and hors d'oeuvres on the table.*]

LIPOCHKA.   I'll never marry a merchant. No, I won't—not for anything in the world. I suppose you think I was brought up for that. Why, I learned French, I play the piano, and I can dance! No, no! Find him wherever you can, but get me a nobleman.

AGRAFENA.   There now, you talk to her a little bit.

FOMINISHNA.   What gave you the idea about these noblemen? What special bait do you see in them? Naked chins sticking on naked necks—something you never see in Christians, exactly. They never go to the bathhouses, and just try finding them baking pies on holidays. Say, you're married to one of them; you know you'd get tired of sauce and dressing all the time.

LIPOCHKA.   You, Fominishna, were born between peasants, and you'll stay a peasant till you turn up your toes. What's your merchant to me? What possible influence can he have? Where's his ambition? Do you think I need his fuzzy face?

FOMINISHNA.   Not his fuzzy face, dear miss, but the Lord's own beard, that's what, miss.

AGRAFENA.   You know your daddy isn't one of these shaved heads, and his beard hasn't been peeled off. Yet you still kiss him anyhow.

LIPOCHKA.   Kissing daddy is one thing, but kissing my husband is something else. Why are you pestering me, mama? I've told you already that I won't go to a merchant. So I won't! I'd as soon die right now. I'll cry from now till the day I die. If I run out of tears, I'll eat pepper.

FOMINISHNA.   Don't tell me you're ready to cry? Don't you even think about it! Why do you want to tease her, Agrafena Kondratevna?

AGRAFENA.   Who's teasing her? She's just being squeamish.

USTINYA.   If that's your appletite,[3] maybe, then we'll find you a nobleman. What'd you like: pretty chunky, or a little wiry?

LIPOCHKA.   There's nothing wrong if he's on the fat side, but he shouldn't be short. Of course, it's better if he's tall, than some sort of shrimp. And worse of all, Ustinya Naumovna, if he were some snub-nosed fellow. By all means, he should be dark; and quite naturally, he should be dressed like men in magazines. [Looks in mirror.]   Oh, good Lord, my hair looks like a witch's broom today.

USTINYA.   Do you know I have a husband for you right now?

Exactly like the one you ordered, my dear. He's a nobleman, tall, and colored.

LIPOCHKA.   Oh, Ustinya Naumovna! Not colored at all, but dark. A dark-haired man, a brunette.

USTINYA.   Look here, why should I twist my tongue learning your jargon, at my old age! Just let it go the way I said it! He has peasants and an organ round the neck.[4] Now then, run and dress, and your mama and I'll have a little talk about all this.

LIPOCHKA.   Oh, Ustinya Naumovna, you old sweetie, come to my room soon. I must talk to you. Let's go, Fominishna.

FOMINISHNA.   Oh, you're a squirmy kid today! [*They exit.*]

AGRAFENA.   Wouldn't you like some vodka before tea, Ustinya Naumovna?

USTINYA.   Wouldn't mind at all, precious, not at all.

AGRAFENA.   [*Pouring.*]   Please help yourself.

USTINYA.   You should have it first, dearie.   [*Drinks.*]

AGRAFENA.   I'll keep up with you.

USTINYA.   Ugh! Phew! Where'd you get poison like this?

AGRAFENA.   At the wine shop.   [*Drinks.*]

USTINYA.   Get it by the bucket, I suppose?

AGRAFENA.   By the bucket. What'd we do with anything less? There'd never be enough. We have a big outlay, you know.

USTINYA.   Don't talk about it, dear, don't. Well now, have I been making a fuss, Agrafena Kondratevna, making it just for you. I've cut a swath in the road, I tell you. I've gone and dug up a husband. You'll just gasp, precious, that's for sure!

AGRAFENA.   That's the first smart thing you've said today.

USTINYA.   A nobleman by birth and a very important person. You've never met a prince like this, even in your dreams.

AGRAFENA.   I see I'd better ask Samson Silych for a couple of gold pieces for you.

USTINYA.   Don't worry, dearie, I'll take them. This fellow has peasants, an organ round the neck, and is he smart. To put it simply, he's worth his weight in gold to you.

AGRAFENA.   Then you'd better tell him, Ustinya Naumovna, that to get our daughter, we don't have—and you can quote me— piles of gold.

USTINYA.   Well, he has so much of his own, he don't know where to put it.

AGRAFENA. Oh, that's good; that's a bit too good. There's only one thing, Ustinya Naumovna, so think it over yourself. What'll I do with a nobleman as a son-in-law? I won't be able to say one word to him. Why, I'd be lost in the forest.

USTINYA. That's right, dearie, it's weird at first, but then you'll get used to it. You both will get along somehow. But we must have a little talk with Samson Silych. He might even know him, this very person.

RISPOLOZHENSKY. [*Entering.*] I've come to see you, dear Agrafena Kondratevna. I was planning a little talk with Samson Silych, but I saw he's busy. So I said to myself, I'll drop in to see Agrafena Kondratevna. Is that a little vodka I see next to you? I'll just try a drop or two, Agrafena Kondratevna. [*Drinks.*]

AGRAFENA. Please help yourself, my dear fellow. Sit down, you're more than welcome. How're things going?

RISPOLOZHENSKY. Don't talk to me about things going. Well now, I'm just wasting my life away, Agrafena Kondratevna. You know it yourself—big family and slim pickings. But I won't grumble. It's a sin to grumble, Agrafena Kondratevna.

AGRAFENA. That's it, my dear fellow, grumbling's the last thing.

RISPOLOZHENSKY. So whoever grumbles sets his face against the Lord, Agrafena Kondratevna. The story goes that . . .

AGRAFENA. What do they call you, my dear fellow? I forget all the time.

RISPOLOZHENSKY. Sysoy Psoich, dear Agrafena Kondratevna.

USTINYA. How'd that come about—Psovich, I mean, dearie? What kind of jargon is that?

RISPOLOZHENSKY. I can't tell you for certain. My father's name was Psoy. Well, quite naturally, I come out Psoich.

USTINYA. You mean Psovich, just like sonofabitch! [5] Well, that's nothing. There are worse names around, sweetie.

AGRAFENA. What kind of story did you want to tell us, Sysoy Psovich?

RISPOLOZHENSKY. Well, it went something like this, Agrafena Kondratevna. It's not just a parable, or some fairy tale, but a true happening. I'll just try a drop or two, Agrafena Kondratevna. [*Drinks.*]

AGRAFENA. Please help yourself, my dear fellow, help yourself.

RISPOLOZHENSKY. [*Sitting.*] There lived an old man, a venerable old man. . . . You know I've forgotten where, my dear, but it was in some place, uninhabited. He had twelve daughters, my dear lady—each younger than the next. He was too weak to work; his wife also was an old, old woman; his children were still young. Nonetheless, one must eat and drink. What was left of their property they had run through by their old age. There was no one to feed them, or give them something to drink. What would become of their little brood? So he started thinking, both this way and that. No, my dear lady, thinking like this will get you nowhere. "I'll go," he said, "to the cross-roads; and there receive something from benevolent passers-by." He sat the whole day. "God will feed you," they said to him. He sat another day and heard, "God will feed you." Now, my dear, he grew dissatisfied, started to grumble.

AGRAFENA.   Oh, saints in heaven!

RISPOLOZHENSKY.   "Dear God," he said, "I'm no grafter, I'm no extortioner. It would be better," he said, "to kill myself."

AGRAFENA.   Oh, saints in heaven!

RISPOLOZHENSKY.   And behold, my dear lady, at night in a dream . . . [BOLSHOV enters.]

BOLSHOV.   Oh, so you're here, good sir! What's this you're preaching here?

RISPOLOZHENSKY.   [Bowing.] Everything in good health, Samson Silych?

USTINYA.   What's this, my dear, have you grown thinner? Or did something else put you out of kilter?

BOLSHOV.   [Sitting.] I've probably caught a cold, or I've gotten rid of my hemorrhoids, maybe.

AGRAFENA.   Well now, Sysoy Psovich, what happened to him next?

RISPOLOZHENSKY.   Later on, Agrafena Kondratevna, I'll finish it later on. Some free time or other, I'll come by in the evening and tell you the whole story.

BOLSHOV.   What's this you're up to? Taken up piety, have you? Ha, ha, ha! It's time you woke up.

AGRAFENA.   Oh, are you starting again? You won't let us have a little talk, heart-to-heart.

BOLSHOV.   Heart-to-heart! Ha, ha, ha! Then you ask him, what about the case he lost in court? That's a much better story he can tell you.

RISPOLOZHENSKY.   Oh, no, no! It wasn't lost! That's not true, Samson Silych.

BOLSHOV.   Then what's the reason they threw you out?

RISPOLOZHENSKY.   Here's the reason, dear Agrafena Kondratevna. I took a case home from court, and on the way with friends I dropped into—it's a man's weakness, well, you know. I dropped into—I hope you forgive me for this—I dropped into a wine shop. I left it there—probably had a bit too much—and forgot about it. Oh, well, it might happen to anyone. After that, my dear lady, this particular case was missing in court. They looked and looked. I went home two times with the court clerk—nowhere, absolutely nowhere to be found. They wanted to put me on trial. Then and there I remembered that probably, I thought, I'd forgotten it in the wine shop. The court clerk and I went there. Sure enough, there it was.

AGRAFENA.   So, what? It could happen to a sober man as well as to a drunk. What does it matter, really?

BOLSHOV.   How come they didn't ship you off to Kamchatka?

RISPOLOZHENSKY.   What do you mean, Kamchatka? But for what, if you'll permit me to ask, what should they send me to Kamchatka for?

BOLSHOV.   For what? For being a disgrace! Why should they tolerate you, really? You're nothing more than a habitual drunk and half-pickled most of the time.

RISPOLOZHENSKY.   But they excused me for that. Of course, dear Agrafena Kondratevna, they wanted to put me on trial for that very thing. I went at once to our general and threw myself at his feet. "Your Excellency," I said, "don't destroy me." "I have a wife," I said, "and small children." "God help you," he said, "you don't hit a man when he's down." "Give me," he said, "your resignation, so I won't see you here any more." So he excused me. Oh, well! May the Lord keep him in health! He never forgets me now. Sometimes on a holiday I drop by to visit him. "How're things," he says, "Sysoy Psoich?" "I just came," I say, "to wish your Excellency many happy returns of the day." Well, not long ago I went to Troitsa and brought him some communion bread. I'll just try a drop or two, Agrafena Kondratevna. [Drinks.]

AGRAFENA.   Please help yourself, my dear fellow. Ustinya

Naumovna, let's go now. I suppose the samovar is ready, and I'd like to show you something new we have for the trousseau.

USTINYA.   I suppose, my dear, you have heaps and heaps all laid in.

AGRAFENA.   What do you think! The new materials came, but it seems we didn't have money enough to pay for them.

USTINYA.   Don't talk about it, dearie! You have your own store— it's the same as if they grew in your own garden. [*They exit.*]

BOLSHOV.   Well now, Sysoy Psoich. In your day, I suppose, you've spilled a lot of ink with underhand dealings like this?

RISPOLOZHENSKY.   Hee, hee, Samson Silych, you'll find it's not too expensive. I just came by to see about your business affairs.

BOLSHOV.   Just came by! A lot you need to know. So here you are, you filthy blood-sucker, you. As soon as you get wind of something like this, then you move in with your devilish ideas.

RISPOLOZHENSKY.   Whatever kind of ideas could spring from me, Samson Silych? Now really, what kind of teacher could I be, when you yourself are, perhaps, ten times smarter than I? If someone asks a favor of me, I'll do it, of course. Why shouldn't I do it? I'd be a pig not to. Especially since you, I might say, have done so many favors for me and my little brood. I'm much too stupid to give you any advice. After all, you know your own business affairs better than anyone else.

BOLSHOV.   Know my own business affairs! There you are, that's the whole trouble. We merchants are all alike—fools, who understand nothing. Just ready to fall under the thumbs of leeches, like you. So now you're here to pester, and filch, and haunt me.

RISPOLOZHENSKY.   Why shouldn't I haunt you? If I weren't fond of you, I wouldn't come around to haunt you. Do you really think I don't care? What am I, actually? Some kind of animal, maybe, a dumb beast?

BOLSHOV.   I know you're fond of me. You lawyers love every single one of us merchants. But try and get anything in return. Here I am, eating my heart out over this business of mine. Believe me, I'm sick to death of this one thing. If only I could get it off my head and be done with it—once and for all.

RISPOLOZHENSKY.   Why, Samson Silych, you aren't the first, and you won't be the last. It's true, isn't it, that others are doing it, too?

BOLSHOV.   How can you help it, brother, so long as others are doing it? And how they're doing it! Shamelessly. No conscience at all. Riding on springs, living in three-storied houses. Just watch one of them put up a belvedere with columns. A beautiful place, but the fellow's so repulsive he's ashamed to come out on the balcony. Up to his gills in debt, and try to get anything out of him. His carriages ride off. Where? Nobody knows. All his houses are mortgaged. And what's left for his creditors? Nothing but three pairs of old boots. That's that—the end of the whole business. And what's more, who do you think he swindled? Well, only some poor devils, and he'll toss them out to the world in their shirt sleeves. My creditors, on the other hand, are all rich men. So what will it matter to them?

RISPOLOZHENSKY.   Quite naturally. Why, Samson Silych, it's all in our hands.

BOLSHOV.   I know it's in our hands. But will you be able to manage this thing? You lawyers are sure something! I know what you're like. Fast with words, and before you know it, you've gone and lost everything.

RISPOLOZHENSKY.   You're not serious. Goodness me, Samson Silych, do you think it's my first time? As if I didn't know how to do it! Hee, hee, hee. Sure, I've handled matters like this, and what's more, gotten away with it, too. Anyone else trying tricks like this would've been shipped out long ago—so far away that even Makar couldn't drive cattle there.[6]

BOLSHOV.   Oh, is that so? Then what kind of trick will you pull off now?

RISPOLOZHENSKY.   That all depends on the circumstances. I'll just try a drop or two, Samson Silych. [*Drinks.*] Well, the first thing, Samson Silych, the house and shops must be mortgaged, or sold. That's the first thing, of course.

BOLSHOV.   Yes, exactly. But it must be done as soon as possible. Who do you want to dump this burden on? Say, how about my wife?

RISPOLOZHENSKY.   Illegal, Samson Silych! It's illegal! It's printed in the laws that sales like this won't hold up. You see, it's easy enough to do it; but afterward, you don't want to find yourself hooked. If we do it, Samson Silych, let's make sure it's going to last.

BOLSHOV.   That's the idea—no chance of raking up the past later on.

RISPOLOZHENSKY.   If you can fix it on some outsider, then they can't find fault with anything. Let somebody quibble later on, and he'll find himself up against legal and certified papers.

BOLSHOV.   Only there's a problem here. If you fix your house on an outsider, maybe it'll stick there, like a flea in wartime.

RISPOLOZHENSKY.   Then find a man, Samson Silych, who knows the meaning of conscience.

BOLSHOV.   But where can you find him nowadays? Everybody's trying to grab you by the collar nowadays, and you want a man with a conscience.

RISPOLOZHENSKY.   I'd like to suggest something now, Samson Silych. Listen to me if you like, or not. What kind of person is your shop-assistant?

BOLSHOV.   Which one do you mean? Lazar, maybe?

RISPOLOZHENSKY.   Yes, Lazar Elizarych.

BOLSHOV.   Very well, Lazar. Then let him have it. He's a youngster with ideas; and besides, he has a little money.

RISPOLOZHENSKY.   What is it you'd like, Samson Silych, a mortgage or deed of purchase?

BOLSHOV.   I'll take the one with the lowest percentage rate. If you can turn the trick, Sysoy Psoich, and there're no hitches, I'll give you a cut so big it'll take your breath away.

RISPOLOZHENSKY.   Now don't worry, Samson Silych, I know my part of the deal. But have you spoken to Lazar Elizarych about this matter or not? I'll just try a drop or two, Samson Silych. [*Drinks.*]

BOLSHOV.   Not yet. We're having a little talk here today. He's a sensible boy. Merely wink at him, and he understands. And he'll wrap up the thing so well that you can't slip a finger inside. Now then! We'll mortgage the house, and then what?

RISPOLOZHENSKY.   Then we'll write up a document saying that the situation is like this—twenty-five kopeks on each ruble. Then, off you go to each creditor. If anyone starts kicking hard, then it's possible to add a little. But if somebody's really mad, then pay him off to the last kopek. When you pay him, though, clinch the deal by having him write that he received twenty-five kopeks on each ruble. Do it for the sake of appearances, just to show it to the others. "Here," you say, "it's in black and white." And the others, looking at the receipt, will agree to your terms.

BOLSHOV.   That's it, exactly. It doesn't hurt to bargain a little. If they don't take it at twenty-five, they'll take it at half a ruble. But if they don't take it at a half, then they'll snatch at seventy kopeks with both hands. At any rate, it's a profit. Now then, say what you like, I have a daughter ready for marriage. I'd like to ship her off to the next man and get her out of my house. Just between you and me, old boy, it's time to take a good rest. I'd enjoy lying on my side, and let all this trading go to the devil. Oh, here comes Lazar. [PODKHALYUZIN *enters*.] What do you say, Lazar? Just arrived from town, maybe? How're things with you there?

PODKHALYUZIN.   Thanks to God, coming along, sir. Sysoy Psoich! [*Bows*.]

RISPOLOZHENSKY.   How do you do, my dear Lazar Elizarych! [*Bows*.]

BOLSHOV.   If they're coming along, then let them come.   [*After a pause*.]   See here, Lazar, when you do the balance sheets for me in your spare time, you'd better deduct the retail side of the business to the landowners. As for the remainder, do as you like. We may be selling and selling, brother, but there's not even a half-kopek's profit. The clerks are guilty, maybe—dragging off things to their family and lovers. You'd better appeal to their conscience a little. What's the use of wasting your life without profits coming in? Don't they know the tricks of the trade? About time they did, I think.

PODKHALYUZIN.   How's it possible, Samson Silych, they don't know? It seems to me, I'm forever in town, sir, and forever giving them a little talk, sir.

BOLSHOV.   But what do you say, exactly?

PODKHALYUZIN.   The usual thing, sir. I try to put everything in shape and moving along smartly, sir. "You men," I say, "wake up. See if some sort of fish or customer will turn up, maybe, for the hard-to-sell article. Or that colored piece with the figure may appeal to some young lady." "There you've done it," I say, "and you can add a ruble or two on the yard."

BOLSHOV.   I should think, brother, you know how the Germans in our stores fleece gentlemen. Let's assume that we're not

Germans but orthodox Christians, and what's more, we'll even eat stuffed pies. That right? Hm? [RISPOLOZHENSKY *laughs*.]

PODKHALYUZIN. Quite right, sir. "And you should also measure," I say, "a little more naturally. Stretch and pull the material until it's ready—God help us—to split." "You know," I say, "we're not going to wear it later on." "Now, if the customers stand around gaping, no one's to blame," I say, "if you'd simply count one yard as two."

BOLSHOV. Oh, that's good! You know the tailor will steal it. Hm? Isn't that it—he'd steal it?

RISPOLOZHENSKY. He'd steal it, Samson Silych. No doubt about it, the scoundrel would steal it. I know all about these tailors.

BOLSHOV. That's just it. The whole gang of them are scoundrels, but we get the blame.

RISPOLOZHENSKY. Precisely, Samson Silych, I'd say you're telling the truth about it.

BOLSHOV. Ah, Lazar, profits are bad nowadays. Not like the old days. [*After a pause*.] Now then, did you bring the paper?

PODKHALYUZIN. [*Taking it from his pocket and handing it to* BOLSHOV.] Pray, take it, sir.

BOLSHOV. Let me have it. I'll take a look. [*Puts on his glasses and looks through it*.]

RISPOLOZHENSKY. I'll just try a drop or two, Samson Silych. [*Drinks. Then puts on his glasses, sits next to* BOLSHOV, *and looks at the newspaper*.]

BOLSHOV. [*Reads aloud*.] "Fiscal announcements from several societies: one, two, three, four, five, and six from the Foundlings' Hospital." That's not in our line. We're not about to buy peasants. "Seven and eight from Moscow University, from the District Governments, from the Offices of Public Charity." Well, we'll just go right past that, too. "From the City Council of Six Members." Now don't tell me there's something here! [*Reads*.] "The Moscow City Council of Six hereby announces: Is there anyone who would like to undertake the collection of the past taxes[7] listed below." That's no affair for us. It's necessary to submit a money guarantee. "The Bureau of the Widows' Home hereby invites . . ." Let them invite, but we're not about to go. "From the Orphans' Court." I don't have a father or mother either. [*Glances through the newspaper further*.] Oho! They missed something here! Listen to this, Lazar. "Such-and-such year, September twelfth, according to the Commerce Court's decision, the merchant Fedot Seliverstov Pleshkov[8] of the first guild was declared insolvent, a debtor; in consequence of which . . ." Why try to explain? Everybody knows what the consequences are. There's your Fedot Seliverstych! Oh, he was an ace all right, but he's gone up in smoke now. Say there, Lazar, does he owe us something or not?

PODKHALYUZIN. He owes us a trifle, sir. They took sugar for the home—anywhere from a thousand to fifteen hundred pounds.

BOLSHOV. Bad business there, Lazar. Well, he'll pay me back in full, out of friendliness.

PODKHALYUZIN. I have my doubts, sir.

BOLSHOV. We'll settle it ourselves, some way or other. [Reads.] "The Moscow merchant Antip Sysoev Enotov[9] of the first guild was declared insolvent." Anything coming from him?

PODKHALYUZIN. For vegetable oil, sir. They took about three kegs, sir, around the beginning of Lent.

BOLSHOV. There's your vegetarian[10] for you—won't let a single fast go by. Trying to play up to God at the expense of somebody else. My boy, don't trust their long-faced manners! These people will cross themselves with one hand, and crawl into your pocket with the other. Here's a third: "The Moscow merchant Efrem Lukin Poluarshinnikov[11] of the second guild was declared insolvent." Well, and what about this one?

PODKHALYUZIN. We have his promissory note, sir!

BOLSHOV. Is it protested?

PODKHALYUZIN. It's protested, sir. He's hiding out, himself, sir.

BOLSHOV. Well! And the fourth here, Samopalov.[12] Don't tell me they've all hatched up a scheme together, maybe?

PODKHALYUZIN. A double-dealing, sinister gang, sir.

BOLSHOV. [Turning the pages of the newspaper.] You could read till tomorrow and still not finish with them. Take it away.

PODKHALYUZIN. [Takes the newspaper.] They only soil the newspaper. It's a lesson in ethics for the whole merchant class, that's what it is. [Silence.]

RISPOLOZHENSKY. Good-by, Samson Silych, I'll run home now. I have some things to look after.

BOLSHOV. Why don't you stay a bit longer?

RISPOLOZHENSKY.   No, really and truly, Samson Silych, I haven't time. I'll drop by tomorrow as soon as possible.

BOLSHOV.   Well, you know best.

RISPOLOZHENSKY.   Good-by. Good-by, Lazar Elizarych. [*Exits.*]

BOLSHOV.   I suppose, Lazar, you have a fair idea about trading. But think what it is. Like picking up money free of charge— is that it? "What do you mean, money," the customer will say. "Look at it go, like frogs jumping in a pond." "Here you are," he'll say, "take my promissory note." And what do you get out of notes from some people? Here I am overloaded with notes, probably worth a hundred thousand rubles, and with protests, too. The only thing you do is put some more on the pile each year. If you like, I'll give you all of them for fifty silver kopeks. You'll never trap the debtors through their notes—not even with dogs. Some have started to die out, and little by little some have run off. There's not one you could put in prison. Say you do imprison one of them, Lazar, it won't make you happy. The next one will cling so tight, that you couldn't smoke him out with a bonfire. "I'm just fine here," he'll say, "and you can go to hell." That's right, Lazar, isn't it?

PODKHALYUZIN.   That's exactly how it happens.

BOLSHOV.   Always notes and more notes! And what exactly is a note? That's it—a piece of paper, and nothing more. If you trade it on discount, then the percentage will be scaled so low that your belly will start rumbling. What's more, you'll answer for it afterward with your own property. [*After a pause.*] Better not have anything to do with customers from the provinces. Why, always on credit and more credit. If your provincial customer brings any money, isn't it always in small change— blindman's coin and Arabian pieces. You take a look. There's neither tail nor head to the piece, and the value's been wiped off long ago. Do just as you like here. When it comes to a local tradesman, though, you'd better not show off your wares. Why, he'll climb into every warehouse, and the only thing he'll do is sniff, peck a little, peck some more, and then off he'll go. It'd be fine if there weren't any goods, but how can you trade with only a pointed barge-pole? I have one candle shop, one dry-goods shop, the third is a grocery. Nothing doing. Not one brings me luck. There's no use showing up at the markets. They knock down prices worse than the devil knows how. If you wear a collar, you must also dole out extras like gifts and entertainment, and be prepared for all kinds of shortages because of faulty scales. So, that's the way it is. You're aware of it, aren't you?

PODKHALYUZIN.   I think I should be aware of it, sir.

BOLSHOV.   That's what trading is exactly, and that's the way you should trade. [*After a pause.*]   Now then, Lazar, what do you think?

PODKHALYUZIN.   And how should I think, sir? It's always up to you, sir. My business is in your employment.

BOLSHOV.   What's this about employment? Just say what you think. I'm asking your opinion about the business.

PODKHALYUZIN.   Samson Silych, again I can only answer, it's up to you, sir.

BOLSHOV.   Oh, forget this nonsense, "it's up to you, sir." What do you think, exactly?

PODKHALYUZIN.   I'm unable to say it, sir.

BOLSHOV.   [*After a pause.*]   Tell me, Lazar—and I'd like an honest answer—are you fond of me? [*Silence.*]   Well, are you or not? Why don't you answer? [*Silence.*]   I've fed you, given you drink, set you up in the world. Isn't that so?

PODKHALYUZIN.   Ekh, Samson Silych! Don't even talk about it, sir. You shouldn't doubt me. I have only one thing to say. I am what I am, nothing more.

BOLSHOV.   What do you mean exactly by "nothing more"?

PODKHALYUZIN.   If you ever want somebody or something, then you'll be satisfied with me. I'd never spare myself.

BOLSHOV.   Very well, nothing more should be said. The way I see it, Lazar, right now is the very best time. We have plenty of ready cash, and all our notes have come due. So, why wait? Try waiting and see if somebody like yourself, brother, won't start cleaning you out. Then, you'll see, he'll make a deal at ten kopeks on each ruble; and he'll sit tight on his million and won't even spit on you. But you, an honest tradesman, you look at him and blame yourself and look blank. You know what I think, Lazar? I should offer my creditors a deal like this. Will they take from me twenty-five kopeks on each ruble, or won't they? What do you think?

PODKHALYUZIN.   The way I see it, Samson Silych, if you pay at twenty-five kopeks, then it'd be more decent not to pay at all.

BOLSHOV.   What's this? You know, you're right. You won't bully anyone by putting up a bold front. Better polish off the deal behind closed doors. After that, the Lord can judge you at the Second Coming. The only thing is—it's a heap of trouble. My house and shops I'm giving in mortgage to you.

PODKHALYUZIN.   It's impossible without a little trouble, sir. Of course, you'll have to palm off the notes on someone else, sir. Then transfer the goods somewhere as far off as possible. We'll get busy, sir.

BOLSHOV.   That's it. I may be an old man, but I'll get busy. But will you help?

PODKHALYUZIN.   Goodness me, Samson Silych, I'd go through fire and water, sir.

BOLSHOV.   What could be better? Why the devil should I work for kopeks? One quick pass now, and then no more of it. Only God grant us courage. I thank you, Lazar. You've done me a good turn. [*Rises.*]   Now then, get busy. [*Crosses to him and pats him on the shoulder.*]   Do the job right and proper, and we'll divide the profits. I'll reward you the rest of your life. [*Crosses to the door.*]

PODKHALYUZIN.   Other than your own tranquillity, Samson Silych, I don't want a thing, sir. Why, I've lived with you since I was a youngster, and I've seen all your good deeds. You might even say, sir, you took me as a little brat to sweep the shops. Therefore, I must be thankful.

ACT TWO

Office in Bolshov's house. A door upstage center. On the left a stairway rises to the next floor.

TISHKA. [*At the proscenium with a brush.*]   Oh, so you call this living, do you! Go on, sweep the floors before it's light. Around here everything's different than it is with real folks. With any other master, if you're a boy, why you live with the boys. What I mean is, you're there at the shop all the time. But around this place, it's go there, come here, and you spend the whole day scraping from street to street, like a madman. "Oh," they say, "you'll soon learn your trade." Like the devil I will. Nice folks keep a yardman for running about, but the yardman here lies on the stove with the kittens or else he's fooling around with the cook. So, you're the one they pick on. At other places it's free and easy. Say you get into a little trouble or something, every now and again. Why, they chalk it off to the fact you're a kid. But here? Oh, do you get it! If not from this one or that, then from the old boy himself, or even the old lady. Sometimes there's that clerk Lazar, sometimes there's Fominishna, and there's always . . . Well, all sorts of riffraff can order you around. Living here is disgusting. If you want to snatch a little time out of the house, like playing a game of three-cards with friends or playing stick-to-the-wall . . . Well, better not think about it. There's something not right in my head, exactly. [*Climbs on chair on his knees and looks in the mirror.*]   How do you do, Tikhon Savostyanych.[13] How are you? You finding everything up to God's mark? Now, Tishka, do a little trick. [*Makes a grimace.*]   That's it. [*Makes another.*]   Do one like . . . [*Shouts with laughter.*]

PODKHALYUZIN. [*Sneaks in and grabs* TISHKA *by his collar.*]   And what are you doing, you little imp, you?

TISHKA.   What? Why, everybody knows what! I was rubbing out dust.

PODKHALYUZIN.   I suppose you rubbed it out with your tongue. What do you mean, found dust on the mirror? I'll show you dust, all right. Clowning around, are you! Now I'm going to paste you one or two, so that you'll know it.

TISHKA.   Know it! And what's it for this time?

PODKHALYUZIN.   Just for that, that's for what. Say any more, and you'll see for what. Just try to say something!

TISHKA.   See if I don't say something. I'll tell the master, and then you'll get it.

PODKHALYUZIN.   Tell the master! What's your master to me? As far as that goes, I am your master. You're no more than a little brat who must be taught. What did you think you were? If you little imps, you, didn't get beaten, why you'd never turn out any good. Everybody knows it's the only way to get the job done. Brother, I've gone through both fire and water and copper smokestacks, myself.

TISHKA.   I know what you've gone through.

PODKHALYUZIN.   Shush, you little devil!   [*He threatens* TISHKA.]

TISHKA.   Go on, try it. Think I won't tell on you? Why, I'll tell, really and truly.

PODKHALYUZIN.   And what are you going to tell, exactly, you devilish little pepper box?

TISHKA.   What'll I tell? Why, I'll say that you swear at me.

PODKHALYUZIN.   Oh, that's a big deal, isn't it? See here, you're some gentleman, aren't you? Come here, my little sir. Has Sysoy Psoich been here?

TISHKA.   Sure, he's been here.

PODKHALYUZIN.   Look here, you little imp, talk some sense. Did he want to drop by again, maybe?

TISHKA.   Sure, he did.

PODKHALYUZIN.   Well, run off now. You're on your own.

TISHKA.   Some ashberry brandy, maybe.

PODKHALYUZIN.   Yes, that'll do. I must treat Sysoy Psoich.   [*Gives* TISHKA *money.*]   Buy half a bottle, but keep the change yourself for some cakes. Only see that you get a move on, so you won't be missed here.

TISHKA.   Be back before a short-haired slut can braid her curls. This is the way I'll go, flying off like some everloving bird. [*Exits.*]

PODKHALYUZIN.   [*Alone.*] Here's disaster for you! When it comes, oh, does it hit you—from all sides. What's to be done now, exactly? Well, it's a bad deal, that's for sure. Can't escape declaring our bankruptcy now. Well, let's assume that something is left for the old man, but what's in it for me? Where do I go now? Sell dust in some back-alley market? I've worked, yes, worked for about twenty years, and then to be told, "Move over to the side of the road." Now, how am I going to work out this deal? The merchandise, maybe? He certainly told me to sell the notes. [*Takes out notes and counts them.*] I imagine you could make a profit here. [*Walks about the room.*] They say you must know what conscience is. Yes, quite naturally, you must know what conscience is, but in what spirit should you take it? When it comes to a good man, everybody has a conscience. But if the man himself is swindling other people, then what sort of conscience must you have then? Samson Silych is one of the richest merchants on earth. And he's started this business now, you might say, just to fiddle around. But I'm a poor man. If there's a little extra profit in this business for me, then there's certainly no sin in that. After all, he's acting unfairly himself and going against the law, besides. Why on earth should I feel sorry for him? The line's drawn, so don't make a mistake. He's set his own policy, so you carry out your own business. Oh, I could have done it with him, but the idea doesn't suit me. Hm! Talk about fantasy slipping into a man's head. Of course, Alimpiyada[14] Samsonovna is a cultured young lady and, you might say, there's nobody on earth like her. And you know this suitor won't take her now. He'll say, "Give me some money!" But where can they get the money? And she certainly won't go to a nobleman, because there's no money. Sooner or later they must give her away to a merchant. [*Walks about in silence.*] Once I raise the cash, I'll go to Samson Silych, bow to him and declaim: "Samson Silych, at this time of life, I must start thinking about the continuity of posterity." "And Samson Silych," so I'll say, "I've never regretted my sweat and blood for the sake of your tranquillity." "Of course," I'll say, "Alimpiyada

Samsonovna is a cultured young lady, and you see that even I, Samson Silych, am no boorish peasant. See for yourself, if you like. I have money, and I'm able to keep up with the business." Why shouldn't he hand her over to me? Don't tell me there's something I'm not a man in? I've never been marked down for anything. I even honor the old folks. Besides, Samson Silych has mortgaged his house and shops to me, so it's possible to scare him with the mortgage. I know the way Samson Silych acts, what he's really like, so it might happen very easily. It's a habit with people like that. If something pops in their head, you can't knock it out with anything. Just the same as three years ago, when he wanted to shave his beard. However much Agrafena Kondratevna begged him, however much she cried, "No," he said, "I'll let it grow again later on, but now I'll keep it the way I want." So he went and shaved it. That's the way this thing may go. If you please him, or get to him in the right way— then it's under the wedding crown tomorrow for sure. And *basta*, it's all over but the shouting! Why, I'm so happy with the idea I could leap from the tower of Ivan the Great.

TISHKA.   [*Enters with the bottle.*]   Here it is, I just got here!

PODKHALYUZIN.   Listen, Tishka, is Ustinya Naumovna here?

TISHKA.   She's upstairs now. And the inkslinger's on his way here.

PODKHALYUZIN.   Then put some vodka on the table, and get some tidbits, too.   [TISHKA *puts vodka and hors d'oeuvres on the table, then exits.* RISPOLOZHENSKY *enters.*]   Ah, our best to you, sir.

RISPOLOZHENSKY.   The same to you, my dear Lazar Elizarych, the same to you. Right. I am thinking, and I quote, what of it? Maybe it's important. Is that a little vodka next to you? I'll just try a drop or two, Lazar Elizarych. Somehow my hands have started trembling mornings, especially the right one here. To write something, Lazar Elizarych, I've got to hold it with my left. Really and truly! But drink a little vodka, and it turns out all right.   [*Drinks.*]

PODKHALYUZIN.   Why is it your hands tremble?

RISPOLOZHENSKY.   [*Sitting at the table.*]   From worry, Lazar Elizarych, from worry, my dear fellow.

PODKHALYUZIN.   That so, sir? But I think it comes from robbing people a bit too much. No doubt God's punishing you for telling lies.

RISPOLOZHENSKY.   Hee, hee, hee . . . Lazar Elizarych. Where would I get, robbing anyone? My dealings are little things. Why, I'm like a bird from heaven—just pecking up little seeds.

PODKHALYUZIN.   You deal in small things, of course?

RISPOLOZHENSKY.   You'd go in for small things, too, if there's nowhere else to go. Well, it wouldn't matter if I was single, but you know I have a wife and four chicks. They all like to eat, the little darlings. First, one says, "Daddy, give me." Then another, "Daddy, give me." One boy I've put in high school. He needs a uniform, and something or other. And what'll happen to my poor old house, exactly? Why, you wear out a pair of boots just walking to Voskrensensky Gates from Butirka.

PODKHALYUZIN.   That's it, exactly, sir.

RISPOLOZHENSKY.   And why on earth go? To write a petition for one person, or register another as a townsman.[15] Shoot the whole day and don't take home even a half-piece of silver. Really and truly, I'm not lying. What's there to live on? I'll just try a drop or two, Lazar Elizarych. [Drinks.] But I'm thinking, I'll come over—and I quote—to Lazar Elizarych, and maybe he'll give me some cash or other.

PODKHALYUZIN.   But what sort of scheme is it for, sir?

RISPOLOZHENSKY.   What do you mean, scheme? Why, that's evil, Lazar Elizarych. Come now, haven't I done my duty for you? I'm your servant till death. Whatever you want, only say the word. I've gone to some trouble to get the mortgage for you.

PODKHALYUZIN.   You know you've been paid for it. And you've no right to keep singing the same tune.

RISPOLOZHENSKY.   That's it, exactly, Lazar Elizarych, I've been paid. That's it, exactly! Oh, Lazar Elizarych, poverty's gotten the best of me.

PODKHALYUZIN.   Poverty's gotten the best! It can happen, sir. [Crosses and sits at the table.] I've some extra money here, sir, and there's no place to put it. [Places wallet on the table.]

RISPOLOZHENSKY.   What'd you say, Lazar Elizarych? You don't mean, something extra? You must be joking.

PODKHALYUZIN.   Put all joking aside, sir.

RISPOLOZHENSKY.   If you have something extra, then why

shouldn't you help out a poor man? God'll remember you for it.

PODKHALYUZIN.   Are you going to need a lot?

RISPOLOZHENSKY.   Give me three rubles.

PODKHALYUZIN.   Why so little, sir?

RISPOLOZHENSKY.   Very well, give me five.

PODKHALYUZIN.   Oh, you should ask more.

RISPOLOZHENSKY.   Well, if you'll be so kind, give me ten.

PODKHALYUZIN.   Ten, sir. That much, for nothing?

RISPOLOZHENSKY.   What do you mean, for nothing? I'll deserve it, Lazar Elizarych, then we'll be even some day.

PODKHALYUZIN.   That's nonsense, sir. Let the snail go; she'll get there sometime. Now I've something here I want you to start on. Did Samson Silych promise you a lot for all this tricky business?

RISPOLOZHENSKY.   I'm ashamed to say, Lazar Elizarych. A thousand rubles and an old raccoon-skin coat. Nobody'll take less than me, really and truly. Go ahead and check the price.

PODKHALYUZIN.   Now then, here's something, Sysoy Psoich. I'll give you two thousand, sir, for the very same item, sir.

RISPOLOZHENSKY.   You're my benefactor, Lazar Elizarych. My wife and children and I will go into slavery at once.

PODKHALYUZIN.   One hundred in silver, right now, sir, but the rest later on—once this whole affair's been settled.

RISPOLOZHENSKY.   Well then, how can I help praying to God for people like you? Only some ignorant pig could miss feeling this way. I bow down to your feet, Lazar Elizarych.

PODKHALYUZIN.   Why, whatever for, sir? Only, Sysoy Psoich, don't chase after your tail in all directions, but hit for accuracy— right to the point and stick to the line. Understand, sir?

RISPOLOZHENSKY.   How can I help but understand? You're not serious, Lazar Elizarych. Think I'm a youngster, maybe? High time I did understand.

PODKHALYUZIN.   And what do you understand, exactly? Here's the way things stand, sir. Listen to me first. Samson Silych and I go into town and take along this duckument,[16] like we should. Then he went from creditor to creditor. First this one didn't agree, then that one didn't. That's it. Not one of them will go for the piece. That's the way the thing stands now.

RISPOLOZHENSKY.   What're you saying, Lazar Elizarych? Oh, go on with you! That's the gang for you.

PODKHALYUZIN. What're we going to do now, without making fools of ourselves over this business? Do you understand me or not?

RISPOLOZHENSKY. That is, about the bankruptcy, Lazar Elizarych?

PODKHALYUZIN. Let the bankruptcy speak for itself. But what about my own situation?

RISPOLOZHENSKY. Hee, hee, hee. That is, the house, exactly, and the shops . . . even . . . the house, exactly . . . hee, hee, hee . . .

PODKHALYUZIN. Wha-a-t, sir?

RISPOLOZHENSKY. No, sir, that's the way I am, Lazar Elizarych, my own foolishness; simply a little joke.

PODKHALYUZIN. You know what you can do with your little jokes. Don't you dare joke about this, sir! The house means nothing. My head's filled with such fancies now, that I must have a long talk with you about it. Come to my room, sir. Tiskha! [TISH-KA *enters.*] Clean all this up. Well, let's go, Sysoy Psoich. [TISHKA *wants to take away the vodka.*]

RISPOLOZHENSKY. [*To* TISHKA.] Hold it, hold it! Ekh, brother, how stupid can you get? Look here, if somebody wants to drink, then you wait. Yes, you do. You may be a youngster, but let's see a little courtesy and humility. I'll just try a drop or two, Lazar Elizarych.

PODKHALYUZIN. Go on and drink, only let's hurry. I'm afraid the old boy himself will show up.

RISPOLOZHENSKY. At once, my dear Lazar Elizarych, at once. [*Drinks and eats a little.*] Might be better if we took it with us. [*They exit.* TISHKA *cleans up a little.* USTINYA NAUMOVNA *and* FOMINISHNA *enter from upstairs.* TISHKA *exits.*]

FOMINISHNA. Get it settled for her, Ustinya Naumovna! See for yourself, the girl feels done in, and you know it's time enough, dearie. Being young's not a pot without a bottom, as they say, and it empties out after a while. I found that out myself. I was married by the time I was thirteen, but she'll be nineteen a month from now. Why let her wear out for nothing? Other girls her age have hatched kiddies long ago. There you are, my dear, why let her wear out?

USTINYA. Been going over all that myself, dearie, and the hitch really isn't with me. Look, the suitors I've got are as fast as wolfhounds. But see for yourself, the girl and her mother are terribly picky.

FOMINISHNA. Why shouldn't they pick over them, exactly? Well now, the important thing is that the men must have fresh faces, no bald patches, and no bad smell. Then take anybody, just so long as it's a man.

USTINYA. [Sitting.] Squat down, dearie. I've just used myself up today, all day long. Been knocking about since early morning like an empty pot on a hot stove. You see there's nothing I could let pass. Turns out I'm pretty necessary everywhere. The important thing, dearie, every person is a human being. A man needs a bride; a girl—suitors. Give it to them, even if you take them at birth. And now and again, you come up with a real wedding. But who puts them together? I'm always the one. Ustinya Naumovna's the one who puffs around, doing the work for everybody. Why does she do it? Because that's the way it is, anybody can see that. All set up from the beginning of the world, when the wheel was wound up. To tell the truth, exactly, they don't try to sidestep me for my trouble. One hands me material for a dress, another a shawl with fringe, somebody else will cook up a cap. But some places there's a little gold, and some places you can tumble over something even better— certainly what the job costs and seeing how much they've got to give.

FOMINISHNA. Don't even talk about it, my dear, don't.

USTINYA. Sit down, Fominishna, your legs are old and cracked.

FOMINISHNA. Oh, my dear, haven't the time. You know it's just terrible. Sometimes when the old man doesn't come home from town, all of us just shake in our boots. We're so afraid he'll come home drunk. Oh, dear God, that's something for you to see. You don't know what deviltry that old man can cook up.

USTINYA. Of course, you can understand the devil quicker than you can a rich peasant.

FOMINISHNA. We've seen him just horrible. Here's last week, one night, he came home drunk. He blustered around a lot. What a drunk he had on! Terrible, that's for sure. He broke plates and dishes. "Oh, you," he says, "every last one of you, I'm going to kill you right now."

USTINYA. Ignorant!

FOMINISHNA. That's for sure, my dear! Now I'll run upstairs, sweets. Agrafena Kondratevna is up in my room, alone.
When you're on your way home, come see me, and I'll tie
up a little ham for you. [*Crosses to stairway.*]

USTINYA. I'll drop by, dearie, I will. [FOMINISHNA *exits.*
PODKHALYUZIN *enters.*]

PODKHALYUZIN. Ah, Ustinya Naumovna! Been a long time, hasn't
it, ma'am?

USTINYA. How do you do, dear heart! How're things hopping
for you?

PODKHALYUZIN. Doing what they can, ma'am. [*Sits.*]

USTINYA. If you like, I'll trap a mamzelle[17] for you.

PODKHALYUZIN. No, thank you very much. Don't need one
right now.

USTINYA. Maybe you don't want one, dearie, but I'll do a good
turn for anyone you know. No doubt you have, I'd say, as many
friends around town as there are dogs.

PODKHALYUZIN. Yes, I have about that many, ma'am.

USTINYA. Well, now, if you have, then praise the good Lord!
Any suitor you know in the slightest extent—whether he's single,
unmarried, or a widower—then drag him straight to me.

PODKHALYUZIN. Then you'll marry him off?

USTINYA. That I will. Why shouldn't he get married? Before
you can blink your eye, I'll have him married.

PODKHALYUZIN. That's a good thing, ma'am. But I'd like to
ask you now, Ustinya Naumovna, why is it you're in the habit
of coming here so much?

USTINYA. Why, that's no business of yours! Why shouldn't I
come by? You know I'm no thief, nor a sheep without a name.
What do you mean by asking that?

PODKHALYUZIN. That's so, ma'am, but aren't you coming by
for nothing?

USTINYA. What do you mean, for nothing? How'd you think up
that one, dearie? Take a good look at the suitor I've found. A
nobleman, has peasants, and he's a nice young fellow, besides.

PODKHALYUZIN. Why has the business stopped altogether,
ma'am?

USTINYA. But it hasn't stopped at all. Tomorrow I want to

bring him and introduce him around. Then and there we'll wrap it up. Be tied up before you know it.

PODKHALYUZIN.   Wrap it up, go ahead. He'll be off like a shot.

USTINYA.   You're not serious, dearie, are you feeling all right?

PODKHALYUZIN.   Wait and see.

USTINYA.   May I be dead by this evening! You're either drunk, sweetie, or you've gone out of your mind, somehow.

PODKHALYUZIN.   Pray don't worry about that, but start thinking about yourself. I know what I know.

USTINYA.   What is it you know, exactly?

PODKHALYUZIN.   I know all kinds of things, ma'am.

USTINYA.   If you know so much, then tell me. Don't think your tongue will fall off, exactly.

PODKHALYUZIN.   That's just it. It's impossible to tell you.

USTINYA.   Why impossible? Are you ashamed of me, maybe, sweetie? It's nothing. Speak up. No need for your conscience to get in the way.

PODKHALYUZIN.   This hasn't a thing to do with conscience. Tell you something, and no doubt you'd blab it all over the place.

USTINYA.   Damned if I will. Look here, if I say a word, you can cut off my hand.

PODKHALYUZIN.   That's it, exactly, ma'am. A compact is better than money, ma'am.

USTINYA.   Naturally. Come, what do you know, exactly?

PODKHALYUZIN.   Just this, ma'am. Ustinya Naumovna, it's not impossible to get rid of that suitor, is it, ma'am?

USTINYA.   Don't tell me you gnawed round henbane?[18]

PODKHALYUZIN.   Gnawed round nothing, ma'am! If you'd like a heart-to-heart talk, honestly, ma'am; then here's what it's all about. I know a certain Russian merchant, and he's terribly in love with Alimpiyada Samsonovna, ma'am. "I'd give anything," he says, "just to get married." "There's nothing," he says, "I wouldn't give. Nothing."

USTINYA.   Why didn't you say that before, dearie?

PODKHALYUZIN.   There was nothing to say, simply because I just found out, myself, ma'am.

USTINYA.   It's pretty late now, my dear.

PODKHALYUZIN.   He's really some suitor, Ustinya Naumovna! And he'll shower you with gold from head to foot, ma'am. A fur coat will be made out of live sables, just for you.

USTINYA. Oh, sweetie, impossible! I'd dance for joy, but I gave my word already.

PODKHALYUZIN. Well, it's up to you, ma'am! If you get her engaged to this fellow, you'll make a lot of trouble for yourself. And you won't get out of it later on.

USTINYA. Well, judge for yourself. How can I show my mug in front of Samson Silych? I really laid it on thick—the man is so rich, so handsome, so much in love that he can't live. But what'll I say now? You know yourself what kind of stubborn kid Samson Silych is. Before you can bat an eye, he'll jump on my cap and trample it.

PODKHALYUZIN. Jump on your cap nothing, ma'am.

USTINYA. Well, I've got this girl in a tizzy. Couple times a day she sends word to me, "How goes it with my suitor?" and "What's he like?"

PODKHALYUZIN. Now, Ustinya Naumovna, don't you run off from your own good luck, ma'am. Wouldn't you like two thousand rubles and a sable coat, just by setting up this wedding? But the special compact about the matchmaking will be kept between us, ma'am. I tell you, ma'am, you've never in your life seen a suitor like this. There's only one hitch, ma'am. His origin's not from the nobility.

USTINYA. But is she really from the nobility? Aha, that's the trouble, dearie! That's the way those kind of people operate nowadays. Every girl born with bast sandals tries to make it into the nobility. Now, even though Alimpiyada Samsonovna— God give her good health, of course—favors us like a princess, why her origin, I'm afraid, is worse than ours. Her father, Samson Silych, traded in leather mittens without linings on the Balchug. Nice people called him One-shot Sam and slapped him around. And her mother, Agrafena Kondratevna, just barely made it into the striped skirt class. He picked her out of the Preobrazhenskoe. They put together some money and crawled out into the merchant class. So the daughter is after the rank of princess. Money has done all that. Here I am, no worse than her, but I'm the one who's got to look after her tail, no less. Don't think God doesn't know her kind of upbringing. She writes exactly like an elephant crawls on its belly. Either French or piano, it's the same thing—here a little, there a little, and she's got nothing at all. Now when she breaks out dancing, why then I've got to pretend there's dust up my nose.

PODKHALYUZIN. Now you can see, can't you, it'd be more decent to give her to a merchant.

USTINYA. But what'll happen to me with the present suitor, dearie? I've already convinced him that Alimpiyada Samsonovna is a real beauty, worth three times the going price. "And is she educated," I said, "both in French and she knows various manners, too." What'll I say to him now?

PODKHALYUZIN. Why you tell him now, and I quote, she's a beauty and cultured and has all kinds of manners. Only, and I quote, they've shot all the money. Then he'll give her up, himself!

USTINYA. Well, that's for sure, sweetie! Oh, no, hold it! Wouldn't you know I told him that Samson Silych has so much money the chickens can never peck it up.

PODKHALYUZIN. What'd I tell you? You're pretty nimble when you start blabbing. How come you know how much money Samson Silych has? Don't tell me you've counted it?

USTINYA. Just go ahead and ask anybody about it. Everybody knows that Samson Silych is one of the richest merchants around.

PODKHALYUZIN. Yes! A lot you know! What'll you do after you've engaged a man of distinction, and Samson Silych won't give any money, exactly? Later on the man will stand up for himself and say, "I," so he'll declare, "am no merchant, that you can swindle me out of the dowry!" What's more, like a man of distinction, he will make a complaint in court. Since a man of distinction gets what he wants everywhere, ma'am, Samson Silych and I'll be caught. And don't think you'll escape, either. Why, you know it yourself. It's possible to swindle our own gang out of a dowry—and get away with it. But just try swindling a man of distinction. You'll never make it, never.

USTINYA. Stop it! I've had enough of your scary talk. You've got me all mixed up.

PODKHALYUZIN. Here, take these hundred silver rubles for deposit. Yes, and let's shake on it, ma'am.

USTINYA. Then, my dear, do you say it's two thousand rubles and a sable coat?

PODKHALYUZIN. That's it, exactly, ma'am. You can rest easy!

We'll dress you up in that sable coat, Ustinya Naumovna, and you'll start out for a walk. And all along the way, people will start thinking you're some general's wife.

USTINYA.   So that's what you're thinking, is it? Well! When I put on a sable coat, I'll have a high old time, with my hands in the pockets. Then your gang, the big-bearded fellows, will stand around with their mouths hanging open. They'll start breathing so hard, you couldn't put them out with a fire hose. Their wives will envy me so much, their noses will fall off.

PODKHALYUZIN.   That's it, exactly, ma'am.

USTINYA.   Give me the deposit! Here goes!

PODKHALYUZIN.   Remember, Ustinya Naumovna, you're doing this on your own hook, so don't get scared.

USTINYA.   What do you mean, scared? Just take a look. Two thousand rubles and a sable coat.

PODKHALYUZIN.   I tell you, it'll be made out of live sables. No use talking about it.

USTINYA.   Well, good-by, sweetie. I'm off to the suitor now. See you tomorrow, at which time I'll import[19] everything to you.

PODKHALYUZIN.   Hold on a minute! Where are you off to? Come up to my room—we'll have a little vodka, ma'am. Tishka! Tishka! [TISHKA enters.] Keep watch, you, and if the old boy comes, run for me right away. [PODKHALYUZIN and USTINYA exit.]

TISHKA.   [Sits at the table and takes money out of his pocket.] Half a ruble in silver. Lazar gave that to me today. The other day when I fell from the bell tower, Agrafena Kondratevna gave me ten kopeks. I won twenty-five kopeks at pitch-and-toss. Three days ago the old boy himself forgot a ruble on the counter. Oh, brother, now that's what I call money. [Counts to himself.]

FOMINISHNA.   [Offstage.] Tishka! Oh, Tishka! How long do I have to keep calling?

TISHKA.   What's going on now?

FOMINISHNA.   [Offstage.] But what's become of him?

TISHKA.   How should I know! Do you think he gets the word from me? If he did, I'd sure know.

[FOMINISHNA enters down the stairway.]

FOMINISHNA.   Samson Silych has come, you see, and seems like he's a bit drunk.

TISHKA.   Whew! We've had it!

FOMINISHNA.   Tishka, run for Lazar! That's my boy, run fast! [TISHKA *runs.*]

AGRAFENA.   [*Comes into sight on the stairway.*]   What's all this, Fominishna, my dear? Where's he off to?

FOMINISHNA.   Seems like it's this way, my dear! Oh, I'll lock the door, really and truly I will. Let him go upstairs, but you sit down here, darling.   [*A knock at the door and the voice of* SAMSON SILYCH: "Hey, open up! Who's in there?" AGRAFENA *steals away.*]   Go ahead, dearie, just try to go to sleep. Forget about coming in!

BOLSHOV.   [*Behind the doors.*]   What's this, you old witch, have you gone out of your mind, maybe?

FOMINISHNA.   Oh, it's you, darling! Oh, I'm a blind, stupid old woman! You're showing me what a fool I am—thinking you'd come home drunk. Please forgive me. I've gotten dense in my old age.   [SAMSON SILYCH *enters.*]

BOLSHOV.   Barrister been around today?

FOMINISHNA.   Been stirring bear today? Oh, no, my dear, been cooking cabbage soup, corned beef, roast goose, and potatoes.

BOLSHOV.   Don't tell me you been gnawing henbane, you old fool!

FOMINISHNA.   No, my dear! Gave the order to the cook, myself.

BOLSHOV.   Go away!   [*He sits.* FOMINISHNA *crosses to the door.* PODKHALYUZIN *and* TISHKA *enter.*]

FOMINISHNA.   [*Returning.*]   Oh, I'm a fool. Yes, I am! Please forgive my bad memory. The cold suckling pig jumped and slid out of my head, completely.

BOLSHOV.   Beat it! Off to the pigs yourself! [20]   [FOMINISHNA *exits. To* TISHKA.]   Why are you standing there with your mouth hanging open? Don't you have work to do?

PODKHALYUZIN.   [*To* TISHKA.]   You heard what he said, didn't you!   [TISHKA *exits.*]

BOLSHOV.   Barrister been around today?

PODKHALYUZIN.   Yes, sir.

BOLSHOV.   Did you talk to him?

PODKHALYUZIN.   Come now, Samson Silych, don't tell me he

has any sense? It's obvious even his soul's little more than an ink-pot, sir. He sings only one tune—to declare bankruptcy.

BOLSHOV.   If it's bankruptcy, then it's bankruptcy. And that's that.

PODKHALYUZIN.   Oh, Samson Silych, what's this you're saying, really!

BOLSHOV.   So you think I should pay the money, do you? And where did you find that idea? Why, I'd rather burn up everything than give them a single kopek. Get rid of the goods, sell the notes. Let them steal, filch—whoever wants to, let him. But I'm not going to end up paying them.

PODKHALYUZIN.   Goodness me, Samson Silych, we had this thing moving along first-rate, and now you want to confuse everything.

BOLSHOV.   What's it to you? It's not your affair. Just keep working, doing the best you can, and I won't forget you.

PODKHALYUZIN.   I don't need a single thing, especially after all your good deeds. So don't even think about wanting to help me along this line. I'm ready now to give away my whole soul for you, but I wouldn't say I'm ready to do anything false. You're getting on in years. Agrafena Kondratevna is a delicate lady. Alimpiyada Samsonovna is a cultured young woman, at the right age. And you ought to take a little time thinking about her, sir. Now here are the circumstances—all kinds of things may come out of all this.

BOLSHOV.   What could come out, exactly? I alone am responsible.

PODKHALYUZIN.   What's there to talk about you? You, Samson Silych, have had your day. Thanks to God, you've seen life. But Alimpiyada Samsonovna—quite naturally—is a young woman, and there's no one like her in the world. Samson Silych, I'm going to speak to you honestly. That is, exactly the way I feel. Right now I'm making every effort for your sake, and I don't begrudge one ounce of sweat and blood. But I'm doing all this mostly because I'm sorry for your family.

BOLSHOV.   Oh, come on now, really?

PODKHALYUZIN.   Oh, please, sir! Now, let's assume that all this turns out excellently, sir. That's fine, sir. You'll have enough left over to set up Alimpiyada Samsonovna. There's nothing to say on that score, sir. Should there be money, suitors will turn up, sir. But what a sin, the Lord preserve us, if the creditors find fault, and start dragging you through the courts, and this kind of reputation falls on the family. And what's more likely, they'll take away all your property. Then the women would have to suffer hunger and cold without any sort of charity, like defenseless little chicks. Oh, the Lord preserve them from that! What would ever become of them? [*Weeps.*]

BOLSHOV.   And what are you crying about, exactly?

PODKHALYUZIN.   Of course, Samson Silych, I'm only giving you an example. Be silent at the right time; talk at the wrong time; nothing comes about from words. But let an enemy grow in strength, you know, and he'll rock the mountains.

BOLSHOV.   But what can be done, brother? Everybody knows it is the will of God, and you can't go against it.

PODKHALYUZIN.   That's it, exactly, Samson Silych! But for all that, in keeping with my stupid reasoning, you should set up Alimpiyada Samsonovna for the time being with a good man. Something like having her behind a stone wall, at least, sir. Most important, the man should have a soul; then, he'd know how to feel. When it comes to that nobleman who's after Alimpiyada Samsonovna, why he's checked reins and driven off.

BOLSHOV.   What do you mean, driven off? How'd you make that up?

PODKHALYUZIN.   I didn't make it up, Samson Silych. Just ask Ustinya Naumovna. Someone who knows him probably found out something or other.

BOLSHOV.   Oh, never mind him! The way things are going now, we don't need someone like that.

PODKHALYUZIN.   Samson Silych, think it over. I'm an outsider, not one of the family, but I can't rest day or night, worrying about your welfare. In fact, I've known so little peace and quiet that my heart has just shriveled up. Why, they're giving him a young lady who, you might even say, is an indescribable beauty. What's more, they're giving him money, sir. But he minces around and puts on airs. Well, after all that, can he possibly have a soul?

BOLSHOV.   Well, if he doesn't want her, then he doesn't need her, and you can bet we won't cry over it, either.

PODKHALYUZIN.   No, Samson Silych, just think it over. Is it possible for a person like that to have a soul? Here am I—an outsider, pure and simple—but I can't bear watching all this without tears. Don't get me wrong, Samson Silych! Somebody else would never pay enough attention to waste away grieving over an outsider's affair, sir. You see, even if you drive me away now, even if you beat me, I'd never ever leave you. I cannot, that's why. I just don't have that kind of heart.

BOLSHOV.   But why on earth do you want to leave me? The only hope I have now is you. I'm old, and things are getting a bit cramped. Hold on! Maybe we can work out a deal. Something you're not expecting, maybe.

PODKHALYUZIN.   But I can never do it, Samson Silych! Don't get me wrong now, but I'm not that kind of person at all! To somebody else, Samson Silych, of course it wouldn't matter, sir. He's none the worse if the grass fails to grow, but I'm not made like that, sir. Pray look for yourself, whether I'm hustling or not, sir. Right now I'm wasting away, like some poor devil, because of your affair, sir. Why? Because I'm not made like that, sir. I'm doing it because I'm sorry for you, and not so much for you as for your family. Pray understand that Agrafena Kondratevna is a delicate lady, that Alimpiyada Samsonovna is a young woman, and there's no one like her in the world, sir.

BOLSHOV.   Surely you don't mean, in the world? See here, brother, you're not after . . . ?

PODKHALYUZIN.   What, sir? No, sir, there's nothing I . . .

BOLSHOV.   Aha, brother, better speak right out. Are you in love, maybe, with Alimpiyada Samsonovna?

PODKHALYUZIN.   Pray, Samson Silych, no doubt you're joking.

BOLSHOV.   Joking, ha! I'm asking you, and it's no joke.

PODKHALYUZIN.   Goodness me, Samson Silych, dare I even to think it, sir?

BOLSHOV.   Why shouldn't you dare? What do you think she is, some kind of princess, maybe?

PODKHALYUZIN.   Maybe she's no princess. But since you've been my benefactor, and in fact taken the place of my own father . . . Oh, no, Samson Silych! Goodness me, how is it possible, sir? Do you think I don't feel this?

BOLSHOV.   Then it turns out you don't love her?

PODKHALYUZIN.   How can I help loving her, sir? Goodness me, it seems to me I love her more than anything on earth. Oh, no, sir, Samson Silych. How is it possible, sir?

BOLSHOV.   You should've said right off, "I love her." See what I mean? "I love her more than anything on earth."

PODKHALYUZIN.   And how can I help loving her, sir? Pray judge for yourself. Days I think; nights I think . . . That is to say, quite naturally, Alimpiyada Samsonovna is a young woman, and there's no one like her in the world . . . Oh, no, it's impossible, sir. How can we even talk about it, sir?

BOLSHOV.   Now what's impossible, you giddy fool, you?

PODKHALYUZIN.   But how is it possible, Samson Silych? Knowing you as my own father, and knowing Alimpiyada Samsonovna, sir; and again knowing myself as I do, how can I even talk with my ugly mug, sir?

BOLSHOV.   So what, if it's ugly? A mug is a mug. Better to have a few brains in your head. And you don't have to start borrowing brains, exactly, since God's rewarded you pretty well here. That's it, Lazar, match you up with Alimpiyada Samsonovna, hmm?

PODKHALYUZIN.   Goodness me, do I dare? Maybe Alimpiyada Samsonovna won't want to look at me, sir?

BOLSHOV.   Big deal! I'm not about to dance to her tune in my old age. She'll go to the man I tell her to. It's my kid. If I like, I'll eat her with my cereal, or churn her up into butter. Discuss it with me, will you?

PODKHALYUZIN.   Samson Silych, I don't dare talk to you about it, sir. I don't want to look like a scoundrel in front of you.

BOLSHOV.   You're a fool, brother! If I didn't care for you, do you really think I'd talk to you like this? You understand, don't you, that I can make you happy your whole life?

PODKHALYUZIN.   And don't you know I care for you, Samson Silych, more than for my own father? Oh, God should punish me! What a beast I am!

BOLSHOV.   Very well, but do you love my daughter?

PODKHALYUZIN.   I'm all shriveled up, sir. My whole soul turned upside down long ago, sir.

BOLSHOV.   Well, if your soul's turned upside down, then we'll just fix you up. "Bait her, Vanya—mate our Anya." [21]

PODKHALYUZIN. Daddy, why are you so nice to me? I don't deserve it. No, I don't. And I'd never get by on my looks.

BOLSHOV. Never mind about your looks! Here you go, I'm transferring all the property to you. The creditors will be sorry they didn't grab twenty-five kopeks when they could've.

PODKHALYUZIN. You know how sorry they'll be, sir.

BOLSHOV. Well, off you go to town now, but drop by later on the bride. And we'll play a trick on them.

PODKHALYUZIN. Very well, daddy, sir! [*They exit.*]

ACT THREE

Drawing room in Bolshov's house.

BOLSHOV. [*Enters and sits in the armchair. For a little while he looks from corner to corner and yawns.*] There it is—life, I mean. Never a truer word was said: vanity of vanities; every-thing vanity. The devil knows I can't figure out what I want to do. I'd like to eat a little something, but then dinner'd be spoiled. And to sit here doing nothing, I'll probably fall into a stupor. Or I could treat myself to a little tea, maybe. [*Silence.*] Well, that's about all there is: a person lives and lives, then all of a sudden he dies—and everything goes to dust. Oh, Lord, dear Lord! [*Yawns and looks from corner to corner.* AGRAFENA *enters, together with* LIPOCHKA, *who is dressed up.*]

AGRAFENA. On your way now, come, my little one. Watch out for the door. Don't hook yourself. Look, Samson Silych. Just see, my dear sir, how I've dressed up our daughter. Phew, go on with you! Isn't she something? Just like a peony-rose. [*To her.*] Oh, my angel, my tsarevna,[22] you cherub, you. [*To him.*] What do you say, Samson Silych, it's true, isn't it? Only she should ride in a coach, driven by six horses.

BOLSHOV. She'll ride in one driven by two horses. It's no high and mighty lady of the manor we have here.

AGRAFENA. We all know she's no general's daughter.[23] But she's a beauty, that's for sure. Why don't you cuddle the child and stop grumbling like a bear?

BOLSHOV. How should I cuddle her, exactly? Lick her hands, maybe, or bow down to her feet? What's the fuss about, really! I've seen women more dressed up than her.

AGRAFENA. And what've you seen, exactly? Something this way, or that, I suppose. But you know this is your daughter, your own flesh and blood. You hard-nosed old man, you.

BOLSHOV.   So, what if she is my daughter? Thank the Lord she
has boots, clothes, that she gets fed. What more can she want?

AGRAFENA.   What can she want? Oh, Samson Silych, have you
gone clean off your head, maybe? That she gets fed! All sorts of
things get fed. Christian law says we're bound to feed everybody.
And take care of outsiders, not only our own family. You know
it's a sin to think otherwise—let alone to say it in front of people.
No matter what, she is your own child!

BOLSHOV.   I know she's mine, but what else can she want? Why
go on and on and on with these fairy tales? You don't have to
fix her into a picture frame, do you? It's only too clear I'm her
father.

AGRAFENA.   Well, if you're really her father, my dear, then don't
go on like a father-in-law! It's about time, I think, you came to
your senses. You must give her up soon, but you haven't opened
your mouth to say one kind word. For her own sake, you should
give her a little worldly advice. I don't think there's a single
fatherly thing in you.

BOLSHOV.   No, there isn't. Too bad, isn't it? Probably the way
God made me.

AGRAFENA.   The way God made you! What do you think you
are, exactly? I think she is God's creation, too, isn't she? She
isn't some sort of animal. Oh, dear Lord, forgive me! Well, ask
her something.

BOLSHOV.   But what should I ask? A goose is no friend to a pig.
If you want to ask her something, then go ahead.

AGRAFENA.   Very well, we won't ask you when it comes to practical matters. Here's something to stir you up in the meantime.
A person is coming here, an outsider or stranger. Try as much
as you like, but a man is not a woman. He is coming for the
first time, even though we've never seen him.

BOLSHOV.   Stop it, I said!

AGRAFENA.   Oh, you are some father, all right. You go so far as
to call yourself a relative. Oh, my deserted baby, there you
stand like an orphan, hanging your little head. He renounces
you and doesn't even want to know you. Squat down, Lipochka,
do. My sweet, my darling treasure, you. [AGRAFENA *seats*
LIPOCHKA.]

LIPOCHKA.   Oh, let me alone, mama! You've rumpled me up for good.

AGRAFENA.   Well, then I'll look at you from way over here!

LIPOCHKA.   For pity's sake, go ahead and look. Only don't go on and on and on about it. Shame on you, mama. It's impossible to dress up nicely anymore. You immediately go off in all directions.

AGRAFENA.   Yes, that's it, my child! If I take one look at you, then I think how sorry I am to lose you.

LIPOCHKA.   So, what? You knew it'd happen sometime.

AGRAFENA.   I still feel sorry anyhow, you silly fool. We've been bringing you up; yes, we have, and here you are—all grown up. Now without rhyme or reason, we're handing you over to out-siders. Just as if we've gotten sick of you, and you've bored us with your stupid childish behavior, or your gentle ways. There, we'll drive you out of the house, like an enemy out of town. But then we'll wake up and suddenly realize there's no place to turn. Judge for yourselves, good people, what kind of life it'll be in a strange far-off land—choking on a stranger's bread, wip-ing off tears with your fist. Yes, for God's sake, she's going to the wrong man. Some idiot who's not equal to her, or some kind of fool, is pushing his way in on us. Yes, some idiotic boy!   [*Weeps.*]

LIPOCHKA.   There you've done it, started crying. All right, mama, aren't you ashamed? What's all this about an idiot?

AGRAFENA.   [*Weeping.*]   Well, it just came out that way—I had to say it.

BOLSHOV.   What'd you start crying so loud about? Let anyone ask you, and I bet you don't know, yourself.

AGRAFENA.   I don't know, my dear. Oh, I don't know. The mood just struck me, I guess.

BOLSHOV.   That's it, did it out of silliness. Tears are pretty cheap with you.

AGRAFENA.   Oh, cheap, my dear, cheap. I know how cheap they are, myself. But what can I do?

LIPOCHKA.   Shame on you, mama, how you go on so! Stop it! Well, he'll show up all of a sudden—and then we're in for it.

AGRAFENA.   I'll stop, child, I will. I'll stop right away!

USTINYA.   [*Entering.*]   How do you do, my dears. Why are you out of sorts, down in the mouth?   [*Kisses are exchanged.*]

AGRAFENA.   We're just worn out waiting for you.

LIPOCHKA.   What do you say, Ustinya Naumovna, is he coming soon?

USTINYA.   It's my fault, I'll be damned if it isn't! But things, my sweets, aren't going very well.

LIPOCHKA.   How? What's all this mean?

AGRAFENA.   Yes, what've you come up with now?

USTINYA.   Only that, dearie, it looks like our suitor is shilly-shallying.

BOLSHOV.   Ha, ha, ha! You're some matchmaker! Don't tell me you're going to hitch them up?

USTINYA.   He's sensitive like a horse. Try to make him "giddy-up" or "whoa"! I can't get a sensible word out of him.

LIPOCHKA.   Now, what's it about, Ustinya Naumovna? Just what are you up to, honestly?

AGRAFENA.   Oh, saints in heaven! How can all this happen?

LIPOCHKA.   Yes, how long ago did you see him?

USTINYA.   I was there this morning. He came out, dressed as he was, in a morning gown, but he gave me a snack—much as I wanted—jot that down to his credit. And he ordered coffee and rum, and were they loaded with biscuits—heaps and heaps of them. "Help yourself," he said, "Ustinya Naumovna!" I was there about the affair, you know; it's necessary, so I thought, to get his mind made up—one way or another. "You," I said, "wanted to get introduced around today." But he didn't say one sensible word on that score. "Well," he said, "I'll start thinking and getting advice." Then he just pulls up the cords on his morning gown.

LIPOCHKA.   Why does he stand around in a slipshod manner and sentimentalize? Honestly, it makes me sick to see all this go on and on and on.

AGRAFENA.   Actually, what's he mincing around for? Don't tell me he thinks we're worse than he?

USTINYA.   Oh, to hell with him. Why don't we find another one?

BOLSHOV.   No, don't you spot another fellow, or it will turn out the same way again. I'll get another one for you myself.

AGRAFENA.   Oh, sure you will—sitting there like a lump on the stove. As far as I can see, you've even forgotten you have a daughter, exactly.

BOLSHOV.   We'll see about that.

AGRAFENA.   Go ahead and see about it. You can't see anything, you! Don't even talk to me, please. You're getting me all upset.

[AGRAFENA *sits.* BOLSHOV *shouts with laughter.* USTINYA *walks away with* LIPOCHKA *to the other side of the stage.* USTINYA *examines* LIPOCHKA's *dress.*]

USTINYA. Well, look at you, will you? All spruced up. That dress on you does something or other. Surely you didn't make it yourself?

LIPOCHKA. What a horrible idea! As if we'd have to. Do you think we're beggars, maybe? And what are dressmakers for?

USTINYA. For shame—beggars, no less! Whoever said a silly thing like that? Anyone can figure out from the way your house is run, that you never made it yourself. But there's one thing for certain—the dress looks trashy on you.

LIPOCHKA. You're not serious, you can't be! Have you lost your mind? Don't you have eyes in your head? How'd you get so confused, anyway?

USTINYA. Come now, what made you get up on your hind legs?

LIPOCHKA. Oh, isn't that something! I'm not going to put up with this nonsense! I suppose you think I'm an ignorant kid, maybe.

USTINYA. Where'd you get that idea? Why, that's the silliest thing you've said yet. How could you ever think I was knocking your dress? It's a dress, isn't it? Anyone'd say it's a dress. But it doesn't look good on you. It's not really the kind you need to go with your beauty, exactly. Snuff out my soul, if I lie. A gold dress wouldn't really do it for you. Let's see one trimmed in pearls. Aha, now you've started smiling, sweetie! Why, I know what I'm talking about.

TISHKA. [*Enters.*] Sysoy Psovich told me to ask if it's possible, he says, to come in. He's outside there, right next to Lazar Elizarych.

BOLSHOV. Go on, tell him to come in here with Lazar. [TISHKA *exits.*]

AGRAFENA. Come now, these tasty dishes haven't been prepared for nothing. Let's try them. How about you, Ustinya Naumovna? I expect you've wanted a little vodka for some time now.

USTINYA. You said it. It's one o'clock by the admiral's watch.[24] Time to eat.

AGRAFENA.   Samson Silych, how about getting a move on? Why are you sitting like that, exactly?

BOLSHOV.   Hold on, the others haven't come yet. We've still some time.

LIPOCHKA.   Mama, I'm going to change my dress.

AGRAFENA.   Go along, child, do.

BOLSHOV.   Hold on there about changing dresses—a suitor is coming here.

AGRAFENA.   What kind of suitor is that? Stop fooling around!

BOLSHOV.   Wait, Lipa, a suitor is coming here.

LIPOCHKA.   Who is he, daddy? Do I know him or not?

BOLSHOV.   You'll see him soon enough. Then maybe you'll recognize him.

AGRAFENA.   Why listen to him? What kind of fool is coming here? He's just wagging his tongue, that's all.

BOLSHOV.   I said he is coming here. Don't think I don't know what I'm talking about.

AGRAFENA.   If someone is really coming, then you would've said so right off. All you've said is that he is coming here, here. Only God knows who it is. Oh, you're like this all the time.

LIPOCHKA.   Well then, mama, I'm going to stay. [*Crosses to mirror and looks; then to her father.*]   Daddy, dear!

BOLSHOV.   What is it?

LIPOCHKA.   I'm ashamed to say, daddy, dear!

AGRAFENA.   What do you mean, ashamed, you silly fool! Speak up if you need something.

USTINYA.   Being ashamed isn't like smoke—it won't burn out your eyes.

LIPOCHKA.   No, I'm ashamed, really and truly.

BOLSHOV.   Then, go hide yourself if you're ashamed.

AGRAFENA.   Want a new hat, maybe?

LIPOCHKA.   No, you didn't guess it. It's not a hat at all.

BOLSHOV.   Then what is it you want?

LIPOCHKA.   To marry a military man!

BOLSHOV.   So now it's out, is it?

AGRAFENA.   Now you've done it, you harlot, you. God help you!

LIPOCHKA.   What's wrong? You know, other girls get married to them.

BOLSHOV.   Go ahead and let them marry them. For all I care, you can sit on the seashore and wait for the weather to break.

AGRAFENA. [*To* LIPOCHKA.] Don't you even dare hint at the idea, let alone mention it to me. I shan't give you my mother's blessings.

[LAZAR, RISPOLOZHENSKY, *and* FOMINISHNA *enter.* FOMINISHNA *stands in the doorway.*]

RISPOLOZHENSKY. How do you do, my dear Samson Silych. How do you do, my dearest Agrafena Kondratevna. Olimpiada Samsonovna,[25] how do you do.

BOLSHOV. Hello, brother, how do you do. Please sit down. And, Lazar, you sit down.

AGRAFENA. Have something to eat, won't you? I've had a little tidbit prepared.

RISPOLOZHENSKY. Why shouldn't I take a little something, my dear? Right now I'd like a drop or two.

BOLSHOV. We'll all go in shortly, but now there's time for a little talk and a snack.

USTINYA. A little talk! Why not? I just heard, my dears—supposedly printed in the newspaper, whether it's true or not—that another Bonaparte's been born, and supposedly, my dears . . .

BOLSHOV. Bonaparte's Bonaparte, but I'll trust to God's mercy. We won't talk about that now.

USTINYA. Then about what, sweetie?

BOLSHOV. About our approaching old age. Also about our health, which is falling apart minute by minute, and only God alone can see what's up ahead. We've decided, while we're still alive, to give away our only daughter in marriage. When it comes to her dowry, we also hope that she won't exhaust either our money or good name, but behave herself, especially in front of others.

USTINYA. Just see how sweetly he says all that, the old darling.

BOLSHOV. And now, since our daughter is at hand, and moreover, being assured of the honorable behavior and self-sufficiency of our future son-in-law, which for us is a very important matter. When it comes to God's blessing, then we name him right off in front of everyone, face-to-face. Lipa, come here.

LIPOCHKA. What do you want, daddy?

BOLSHOV.   Come to me. Don't be afraid I'll eat you. There. Now you, Lazar, crawl over here.

PODKHALYUZIN.   Ready, sir, for a long time!

BOLSHOV.   Now, Lipa, give me your hand.

LIPOCHKA.   Come, what's all this nonsense? How'd you think this up, anyway?

BOLSHOV.   It'll be worse, if I have to use force.

USTINYA.   There it is, old girl, you've almost had it.[26]

AGRAFENA.   Dear Lord, what is it that's going on?

LIPOCHKA.   I don't want to, I don't! I won't go to anything so repulsive!

FOMINISHNA.   Oh, Lord, grant us the power of the cross!

PODKHALYUZIN.   I can see, daddy, that there's no happiness for me on earth. I can see, sir, that your wishes will never come true.

BOLSHOV.   [Takes LIPOCHKA's hand by force; then takes LAZAR by his hand.] Why can't they come true, if I want them to? I'm your father, and you do what I say. Have I fed her for nothing, maybe?

AGRAFENA.   You're not serious, you can't be. Come to your senses at once!

BOLSHOV.   Look here, cricket, stay on your side of the hearth. This isn't your affair. Well, Lipa! There is your suitor. I tell you to love and be gracious to him. Both of you, sit down next to each other and have a friendly talk. Then there'll be a good feast and plans for the wedding.

LIPOCHKA.   What makes you think I want to sit next to that ignoramous? It's absolutely silly!

BOLSHOV.   If you don't sit down, I'll sit you down myself. I'll stop your persnickety attitude, right now.

LIPOCHKA.   Where did you ever see educated young ladies given away to their fathers' workers?

BOLSHOV.   Better shut up! If I say so, you'll go off to the yard-keeper.   [Silence.]

USTINYA.   Listen to that, will you, Agrafena Kondratevna? I'd call that trouble, for sure.

AGRAFENA.   Do you know that I feel as . . . and mind you, I'm the mother around here . . . why I feel as lost as if I were boxed in the pantry. I don't understand how in the world it's happened.

FOMINISHNA.   Good Lord! I'm more than sixty, and I can't

count the number of weddings I've celebrated. But I've never ever seen one of them so botched up as this.

AGRAFENA.   What are you doing, you murderers? You've disgraced the child, that's what.

BOLSHOV.   Yes, and I've heard enough of your stuck-up babbling. I'm going to give my daughter to the clerk. I stand by what I say, and don't you dare talk about it. I won't even listen to you. Now we'll go take a bite, and let them fool around together. Maybe they'll come to some kind of understanding.

RISPOLOZHENSKY.   Let's go, Samson Silych, and just for company, I'll try a drop or two. That's it, Agrafena Kondratevna, the first duty is that children must listen to their parents. That little rule didn't start with us, and it won't stop with us, either.
[*They rise and all exit, except* LIPOCHKA, PODKHALYUZIN *and* AGRAFENA.]

LIPOCHKA.   And what's it all mean, mama? What does he want from me—become a cook, maybe?   [*Weeps.*]

PODKHALYUZIN.   Mama, ma'am! You won't ever find a son-in-law like me. Why, I'll respect you. And that means, give you peace in your old age, ma'am.

AGRAFENA.   How're you planning that, exactly, my dear?

PODKHALYUZIN.   Mama, ma'am! God has put so much . . . purpose in me; for the very reason, ma'am, that the other man won't listen to you, mama, ma'am. But till the day I die, [*weeps*] I must have feelings, ma'am.

AGRAFENA.   Oh, saints in heaven! What is all this?

BOLSHOV.   [*Through the doorway.*] Wife, come here!

PODKHALYUZIN.   Mama, remember what I said just now. [AGRAFENA *exits. Silence.*] Alimpiyada Samsonovna, ma'am! Alimpiyada Samsonovna! I bet you loathe me? Say at least one word, ma'am. Let me kiss your hand.

LIPOCHKA.   You fool, you. Ignoramus!

PODKHALYUZIN.   Pray, Alimpiyada Samsonovna, why do you insult me, ma'am?

LIPOCHKA.   I'll tell you once and forever. I will never go to you, never.

PODKHALYUZIN.   It's up to you. However you feel, ma'am. You can't force love. Only I'd like to add now, ma'am . . .

LIPOCHKA.   I don't want to listen. Get away from me! You, a genteel cavalier, ha! You see, I wouldn't marry you, not for all the money in the world. So you'd better give up.

PODKHALYUZIN.   There, Alimpiyada Samsonovna, you've just said it—give up. Only what'd happen then, if I did give up, ma'am?

LIPOCHKA.   If that happened, I'd marry a nobleman.

PODKHALYUZIN.   A nobleman, ma'am! A nobleman would never take you without a dowry.

LIPOCHKA.   What do you mean, without a dowry? What are you talking about, exactly! Look here, do you know what kind of dowry I have? Why, it'd hit you right in the nose.

PODKHALYUZIN.   Those glad rags, ma'am? A nobleman will never take glad rags. A nobleman will take his in money, ma'am.

LIPOCHKA.   Go on! Daddy will give him money!

PODKHALYUZIN.   All right, if he does, ma'am. But what if he's nothing to give? You don't know your daddy's business, but I know it very well. Your daddy is a bankrupt, ma'am.

LIPOCHKA.   What do you mean, a bankrupt? But the house and shops?

PODKHALYUZIN.   The house and shops—mine, ma'am.

LIPOCHKA.   Yours? Go on! Why try to make a fool out of me? Look for someone dumber than me.

PODKHALYUZIN.   But here are the legal documents!   [*Takes them out.*]

LIPOCHKA.   Then you bought them from daddy?

PODKHALYUZIN.   I bought them, ma'am.

LIPOCHKA.   Where did you ever get the money?

PODKHALYUZIN.   Money! Thank the Lord, I have more money than any nobleman.

LIPOCHKA.   What on earth have they done to me? They've raised me, brought me up, then go and bankrupt themselves! [*Silence.*]

PODKHALYUZIN.   Now, let's assume, Alimpiyada Samsonovna, that you married a nobleman. But what's the sense in that, ma'am? Only the glory that you're called a lady, but not one bit of the fun that goes with it. Pray, think it over, ma'am. Very often ladies go on foot to the market, themselves, ma'am. But if they ever drive anywhere at all, then it's only for the glory of showing off four horses. And the four horses are worser, ma'am, than one merchant's horse. Really and truly, they're worser, ma'am. Also they don't dress a whit fluffy, ma'am. But if you marry me, exactly, Alimpiyada Samsonovna, ma'am; then my first word is this. You'll even wear silk dresses at home, ma'am, on visiting or to the theatre, ma'am. We won't let you wear anything except velvet. Regarding hats or coats, we won't look at what's proper here and there in the nobility, but we'll put you in something lovelier. We'll get our horses from the best stud around. [Silence.] If you have any doubts about my looks, then it's up to you. However you feel, ma'am. I'll wear a frock coat as well, and prune my beard or even shave it off, according to the style, ma'am. It's all one and the same to me, ma'am.

LIPOCHKA.   Yes, all of. you talk like that before the wedding. Then swindle us afterward.

PODKHALYUZIN.   Kill me on this spot, Alimpiyada Samsonovna. Damn me forever if I lie! Why, ma'am, should I swindle you, Alimpiyada Samsonovna? What makes you think we'd live in this house? We'll buy right next to Karetny, ma'am, and we'll have it painted up. Birds of paradise will be drawn on the ceilings, sireens, all kinds of Eyeroses [27]—the love god, you know. Why, they'll give money to come and see it.

LIPOCHKA.   Nobody paints Eyeroses these days.

PODKHALYUZIN.   Then we'll let them put up cosarges of flowers.[28] [Silence.] If you'd only agree from your side, then there's nothing more I need in life. [Silence.] It's a misfortune in my life that I'm not able to give any compliments.

LIPOCHKA.   Why is it, Lazar Elizarych, you don't speak French?

PODKHALYUZIN.   Because it didn't matter to me. [Silence.] Give me my happiness, Alimpiyada Samsonovna, grant me your favor, ma'am. [Silence.] Order me to kneel before you.

LIPOCHKA.   Kneel! [PODKHALYUZIN kneels.] Oh, you're wearing a terrible waistcoat!

PODKHALYUZIN.   I'll give Tishka this one, ma'am, and I'll order one for myself on the Kuznetsky Bridge. Only don't destroy me! [Silence.] What about it, Alimpiyada Samsonovna, ma'am?

LIPOCHKA.   Let me think about it.

PODKHALYUZIN.   What are you thinking about, ma'am?

LIPOCHKA.   Why shouldn't I think?

PODKHALYUZIN.   But you don't have to think.

LIPOCHKA. Do you know what, Lazar Elizarych?

PODKHALYUZIN. Only say the word, ma'am!

LIPOCHKA. Carry me away on the sly.

PODKHALYUZIN. But why on the sly, ma'am, when your daddy and mama have said the word?

LIPOCHKA. It's the way they do it nowadays. Well, if you don't want to carry me away, then I think we'll go on just as it is.

PODKHALYUZIN. Alimpiyada Samsonovna! Pray, let me kiss your hand! [*Kisses her hand. Then jumps up and runs to the door.*] Daddy, sir!

LIPOCHKA. Lazar Elizarych! Lazar Elizarych! Come here!

PODKHALYUZIN. What'd you like, ma'am?

LIPOCHKA. Oh, if you only knew, Lazar Elizarych, what kind of life I have here. One minute mama tells me to do something, the next minute—something else altogether. When daddy isn't drunk, then he sits around saying nothing at all. But when he is drunk, then he can flatten you at any moment. How's it possible for an educated young lady to go through all this? If I could've married a nobleman, then I would've left home and forgotten about all this. But now everything will go on and on in the same old way.

PODKHALYUZIN. No, ma'am, Alimpiyada Samsonovna. It won't happen! Alimpiyada Samsonovna, just as soon as we celebrate the wedding, we're going to move into our own house, ma'am. And we won't let them tell us what to do. No, the present is over with, ma'am. In their day they pulled their fool tricks. It's our turn now.[29]

LIPOCHKA. Then, look here, Lazar Elizarych, we'll live by ourselves, and they'll live by themselves. We'll keep up in the latest fashion, and they can do what they want.

PODKHALYUZIN. That's the way we'll play it, ma'am.

LIPOCHKA. Good. Now call daddy.

PODKHALYUZIN. Daddy, sir. Daddy, sir. Mama, ma'am. [BOLSHOV *and* AGRAFENA *enter.* PODKHALYUZIN *meets* BOLSHOV *halfway and falls into his arms.*] Alimpiyada Samsonovna has agreed, sir!

AGRAFENA. Coming, my dear, I'm coming as fast as I can.

BOLSHOV. Well, that does it! What did I tell you? I know what I'm doing. You don't have to tell me anything.

PODKHALYUZIN. [*To* AGRAFENA.] Mama, ma'am! Pray, let me kiss your hand.

AGRAFENA.   Go ahead, my dear, they're both clean. [*To*
LIPOCHKA.] Oh, my baby, you. How'd you get things settled so
fast? Huh? Really and truly! Why, are you sure this is it? I
just didn't know how to decide the thing at all. Oh, my darling,
you!

LIPOCHKA.   Mama, I never guessed that Lazar Elizarych is the
genteel cavalier he is. But all of a sudden I see now that he is
ever so much more respectful than the others.

AGRAFENA.   That's it, exactly, you silly fool! You know father'd
never want to harm you. Oh, my dear, you know it's like a
story. Huh? Oh, saints in heaven, are you sure this is it?
Fominishna! Fominishna!

FOMINISHNA.   Coming, my dear, I'm coming as fast as I can.
[*Enters.*]

BOLSHOV.   Hold on, you chatterbox! There, you two sit down
next to each other, and let's look you over. [*To* FOMINISHNA.]
Now run and get us a bottle of sparkle. [PODKHALYUZIN *and*
LIPOCHKA *sit.*]

FOMINISHNA.   At once, my dear, at once! [*Exits.* USTINYA *and*
RISPOLOZHENSKY *enter.*]

AGRAFENA.   Congratulate the engaged couple, Ustinya Naumovna! There, God has led us to our old age. We've lived to
this day of bliss.

USTINYA.   What'll I use to congratulate you, my sweets? A dry
spoon pricks the mouth.

BOLSHOV.   Come now, we'll soak your gullet for you. [FOMI-
NISHNA *and* TISHKA *enter.* TISHKA *has wine on tray.*]

USTINYA.   That's a horse of a different color. Well, may God give
you a long life; and let you look younger, grow fat and stay rich.
[*Drinks.*] That's miserable, my dears! [LIPOCHKA *and* LAZAR
kiss.]

BOLSHOV.   Give it to me. I'll congratulate them. [*Takes glass.*
LIPOCHKA *and* LAZAR *stand.*] Get on as best you can—you've
got the brains for it. So that life won't be boring for you, Lazar,
the house and shops go to you instead of the dowry. And you
can count on some ready cash, too.

PODKHALYUZIN.   Goodness me, daddy, I'm already pleased you've
done so much.

BOLSHOV.   Why pussyfoot around thanking me? These are my

own goods. I got them myself. I'll give them to the person I want to. Fill it up again! [TISHKA *pours out more wine.*] No use to go on and on about it. They don't put you on trial for good deeds. Take everything. Only feed me and the old woman and pay the creditors at ten kopeks.

PODKHALYUZIN.   Daddy, no use talking about it, sir. Don't tell me I have no feeling? It's a family affair—we'll settle it ourselves!

BOLSHOV.   I tell you, take everything. That's all there is to it. Nobody can lay down the law to me! Do only this. Pay the creditors. Will you do it?

PODKHALYUZIN.   Goodness me, daddy, it's the first duty, sir.

BOLSHOV.   Only you watch out. Don't give them a lot. But you're happy enough, I bet, to give them everything—out of foolishness.

PODKHALYUZIN.   Later on, daddy, we'll settle it ourselves, some way or other. Goodness me, it's a family affair.

BOLSHOV.   That's it, exactly! Don't you give them over ten kopeks on each ruble. That's enough for them. Now, kiss each other! [LIPOCHKA *and* LAZAR *kiss.*]

AGRAFENA.   Oh, my darlings, you! How'd you ever do it? There, I've gone crazy for sure.

USTINYA.   *Oh, did you never behold,*
                Oh, did you never hear told
                Of the bullhead a hen soon begat,
                Or the egg little pig spawned and spat?

[*Pours out wine and crosses to* RISPOLOZHENSKY. RISPOLOZHENSKY
                bows and refuses the wine.]

BOLSHOV.   Drink, Sysoy Psoich, to their happiness!

RISPOLOZHENSKY.   I can't, Samson Silych. I get sick to my stomach.

BOLSHOV.   Stop it. Drink to their happiness.

USTINYA.   There he goes again, putting on airs.

RISPOLOZHENSKY.   I get sick to my stomach, Samson Silych. Really and truly, I do. I'll try a drop or two of vodka. But my nature can't take wine. It's my weak constitution.

USTINYA.   Oh, you wire-necked spoilsport, you! Get you, will you? Your nature can't take wine. If he doesn't drink it, so help me I'll pour it down his collar!

RISPOLOZHENSKY.   That's wicked, Ustinya Naumovna! That's wicked for a lady to act that way. Samson Silych! I can't, sir! Do you think I like turning it down? Hee, hee, hee. Do you think I'm a fool to do something so ignorant? I've been in society. I know how to act right. I've never turned down vodka. If you like, I'll just try a drop or two. But I can't stand the other stuff. I get sick to my stomach. Samson Silych, don't you let this nonsense go on. It's easy to insult a fellow, but it's not good.

BOLSHOV.   Let him have it, Ustinya Naumovna, right now! [RISPOLOZHENSKY *runs from her.*]

USTINYA.   [*Places wine on the table.*]   It's a lie, you hard-hearted old shyster. Don't you run away from me, Sysoy Psovich! [*Drives him into the corner and seizes him by the collar.*]

RISPOLOZHENSKY.   Help! Guards! Help!   [*All laugh loudly.*]

ACT FOUR

A richly furnished drawing room in PODKHALYUZIN's *house.* OLIMPIADA SAMSONOVNA *sits by the window, in a luxurious position. She wears a silk blouse and a cap in the latest style.* PODKHALYUZIN, *dressed in a fashionable frock coat, stands before the mirror.* TISHKA *is pulling* PODKHALYUZIN's *clothing into shape and making the final adjustment.*

TISHKA.   How'd you like that? Fits you like you were born in them!

PODKHALYUZIN.   What do you think, Tishka, do I look like a Frenchman? Huh? Well, take a look from over there.

TISHKA.   Like two drips, of water.

PODKHALYUZIN.   That'll do, you silly fool! Now go and look at me! [*Walks around the room.*] There you are, ma'am, Alimpiyada Samsonovna. And you wanted to go to an officer, ma'am. Wouldn't you say I'm up to snuff? I grabbed the latest frock coat and put it on.

OLIMPIADA.   But, Lazar Elizarych, you don't know how to dance.

PODKHALYUZIN.   Come now, don't think I won't learn. Why, I'll learn the latest style. In the winter we'll go to the Merchants' Assemblies. Why, you won't know us, ma'am. I'll take up dancing the polka.

OLIMPIADA.   Really, Lazar Elizarych, buy that barouche we saw at Arbatsky's.

PODKHALYUZIN.   Just as you say, Alimpiyada Samsonovna, ma'am. Going, going, and it's done, ma'am.

OLIMPIADA.   They've brought me a new mantela, so we should go to Sokolniki on Friday.

PODKHALYUZIN.   Just as you say, ma'am, we'll go for certain, ma'am. And on Sunday we'll go to the park. You know, the barouche costs a thousand rubles, and the horses another thousand, the harness laid in silver. Then, let them look. Tishka! My pipe. [TISHKA *exits. Sits next to* OLIMPIADA.]   There you are, ma'am, Alimpiyada Samsonovna! Let them look at us.   [*Silence.*]

OLIMPIADA.   Why is it, Lazar Elizarych, you don't kiss me?

PODKHALYUZIN.   Just as you say. Goodness me, ma'am! It's my pleasure. Your hand, please, ma'am!   [*Kisses it. Silence.*]   Alimpiyada Samsonovna, tell me something in the French dialect, ma'am.

OLIMPIADA.   What do you want me to tell you?

PODKHALYUZIN.   Just say something or other. Oh, the tiniest bit, ma'am. It's all the same to me, ma'am!

OLIMPIADA.   *Kom vu zet zholi.*

PODKHALYUZIN.   What's that mean, exactly, ma'am?

OLIMPIADA.   How sweet you are!

PODKHALYUZIN.   [*Jumps off his chair.*]   Oh, I have something here. What a wife, ma'am! Ai, ai and Alimpiyada Samsonovna! Do me the honor. Your little hand, please.   [TISHKA *enters with the pipe.*]

TISHKA.   Ustinya Naumovna has come.

PODKHALYUZIN.   What the hell is she doing here!   [TISHKA *exits. USTINYA enters.*]

USTINYA.   How you coming along, my dears?

PODKHALYUZIN.   Much obliged for your prayers, Ustinya Naumovna, much obliged.

USTINYA.   [*Kisses* OLIMPIADA.]   Don't tell me you've gotten prettier, started getting pudgier?

OLIMPIADA.   Oh, you're talking nonsense again, Ustinya Naumovna! How'd you ever get that idea?

USTINYA.   What do you mean, nonsense, baby? It comes down to this. Willy-nilly, like it or not, you can't get away from it. So, if you love sliding down hills, then you'd better love pulling your sled up afterward. Why is it, my dears, you've gone and forgotten me for good? Or didn't you have time to look around? I suppose you've spent all your time gushing and impressing each other.

PODKHALYUZIN.   We have that failing, Ustinya Naumovna. Yes, we do!

USTINYA.   Aha! What did I tell you? Just look at the little cream-puff I put together for you!

PODKHALYUZIN.   There's a lot of satisfaction here, Ustinya Naumovna. Yes, there is. A lot.

USTINYA.   Oh, you couldn't help being satisfied, dearie. Go on with you! [*To* OLIMPIADA.] No doubt you're running after smart clothes now. Been fooling around with a lot of styles, exactly?

OLIMPIADA.   Not so much, really. Mostly because the new materials have just arrived.

USTINYA.   That's natural, sweetie, there's nothing to a commissar without pants: [30] let them be thin, as long as they're blue. What'd you cook up the most—woolens or silks?

OLIMPIADA.   All kinds—both woolens and silks. I just had one made in crepe with gold.

USTINYA.   How many have you got, altogether, sweetie?

OLIMPIADA.   Go ahead, you count. The dress I got married in, the blondish one over a satin cover and three velvets—that's four. Two gauze and a crepe, trimmed in gold—that's seven. Three satin and three grosgrain—that's thirteen. Seven gros de Naples and gros d'Afrique—that's twenty. Three marceline, two mousseline de ligne, two Chine royale—how many does that make? Three and four is seven—that's twenty-seven. Crepe Rachel, four of them—that's thirty-one. Well, still there are muslins, bouffe mousseline and cotton things—up to twenty. And there are blouses and house-coats—either nine or ten. And I had one made out of Persian material not long ago.

USTINYA.   Look at you, will you? God bless you, if you haven't piled them up already. Why don't you hop along and pull out a big one of those gros d'Afrique?

OLIMPIADA.   I shan't give you a gros d'Afrique. I've only got three myself. What's more, you couldn't get it around your waist. If you like, please take a crepe Rachel.

USTINYA.   Why, that'd make me look like a babbling Hebe—a crapped Rachel, no less! [31] Well, I see there's nothing I can do with you. Well, all right, then. I'll be happy with the satin.

OLIMPIADA.   So, it's the satin, too, is it? Somehow it's not right for you. It's made for the ballroom, pretty revealing. Know what I mean? But we'll find a house-coat out of crepe Rachel, let out the pleats, and you'll be snug as a bug in a rug.

USTINYA.   Well, let's have the crapped Rachel! It's your move, dearie. Run open the dresser.

OLIMPIADA.   Right away. Wait a bit.

USTINYA.   I'll wait, sweetie. Yes, I will. What's more, I must have a chat with your husband. [OLIMPIADA *exits*.]   What do you say, dearie, don't tell me you forgot all about your promise?

PODKHALYUZIN.   How could I forget, ma'am? I remember! [*Takes out pocketbook and gives her paper money.*]

USTINYA.   What's this, exactly, sweetie?

PODKHALYUZIN.   One hundred rubles, ma'am.

USTINYA.   What's with this one hundred rubles? But you promised me fifteen hundred.

PODKHALYUZIN.   Wha-a-t, ma'am?

USTINYA.   You promised me fifteen hundred!

PODKHALYUZIN.   Isn't that cutting it a bit thick? Not right for you to overeat.

USTINYA.   Come now, you backyard cock, don't tell me you're joshing me—just a little, maybe? Listen here, brother, I can keep the pot boiling with the best of them.

PODKHALYUZIN.   Why must I give you money, exactly? You'd get it for sure, if it were for something in particular.

USTINYA.   Whether for something or for nothing, only give it to me. You promised me yourself.

PODKHALYUZIN.   I promised all kinds of things! I promised to jump from the Tower of Ivan the Great, if I married Alimpiyada Samsonovna. Did you see me jump?

USTINYA.   Don't tell me you think I won't take you to court? Matters a lot, I suppose, that you're a merchant of the second guild, and I'm stuck in the fourteenth class.[32] No matter what, I'm the wife of a government man all the same.

PODKHALYUZIN.   So what if you're a general's wife! It's all the same to me. I don't even want to know you. And that's all I have to say.

USTINYA.   No, it's a lie. And that isn't all. You also promised me a sable coat.

PODKHALYUZIN.   What's this, ma'am?

USTINYA.   A sable coat! Don't tell me you've gone deaf, maybe?

PODKHALYUZIN.   Sable, ma'am? Hee, hee, hee.

USTINYA.   Yes, sable! Go ahead and laugh. You'll sprain your windpipe.

PODKHALYUZIN.   You shouldn't go traipsing around in sable coats, ma'am, not with your snout.   [OLIMPIADA *brings the dress and gives it to* USTINYA.]

USTINYA.   What're you getting at, really? Want to rob me, maybe?

PODKHALYUZIN.   Robbery, what the hell! Well, if that's the way you feel about it, then good-by and good luck. And that's all I have to say.

USTINYA.   So, you're going to drive me out. Well, I was a soft-headed fool to tie up with you. It's clear what you are—you weak-blooded, common tradesman, you! [33] Trying to pass yourself off as a merchant, no less.

PODKHALYUZIN.   So, ma'am! Go on. Speak right out. Please do.

USTINYA.   As far as that goes, I don't even want to look at you. I wouldn't join up with you again—not for all the money in the world. I'll go thirty versts out of my way before I'd walk past you. I'd sooner close my eyes and stumble into a horse, than to stand here looking at your dump. Even if I had to spit, you can be damn sure I'd never come up this street. Saw me up into ten little pieces, if I lie. You can rot in hell before you see me here again.

PODKHALYUZIN.   Take it easy, auntie, or I'll send for the police. [34]

USTINYA.   I'll expose you yet, my dears. Wait and see! I'll shout from every housetop in Moscow. You'll be ashamed to show up in public. Oh, I was a fool. Yes, I was, to tie up with you. Here I am—a lady of rank, of title. Tphew! Tphew! Tphew!   [*Exits.*]

PODKHALYUZIN.   How'd you like that! Our pure-blooded duchess had a hemorrhage. Oh, good Lord, you can tell she's an official's wife. You know the old proverb. "Thunder hits you, not from the storm-clouds, but from the manure pile." Oh, good Lord, just look at her. What a lady she is!

OLIMPIADA.   Some sport you were, Lazar Elizarych, getting tied up with her.

PODKHALYUZIN.   Yes, goodness me. She's a silly old woman, for sure.

OLIMPIADA.   [*Looks through window.*]   It looks like they let daddy out of the clink. Go and see, Lazar Elizarych!

PODKHALYUZIN.   Well, no, ma'am. They won't let daddy out of the clink that fast. No doubt they set up a meeting of the creditors, [35] and then daddy got permission to come home for

a while. [*Calls to* AGRAFENA.] Mama, ma'am! Agrafena Kondratevna! Daddy's on his way, ma'am! [BOLSHOV *enters; then*
AGRAFENA.]

AGRAFENA.   Where is he? Where? My little ones, you. Oh, my
darlings! [*Kisses are exchanged.*]

PODKHALYUZIN.   Daddy, how do you do, our compliments.

AGRAFENA.   Oh, my darling, Samson Silych, my sweets! Here
you've gone and left me an orphan in our old age.

BOLSHOV.   That's enough, wife. Stop it.

OLIMPIADA.   What're you doing, mama? You're crying as if he
just died. Only God knows what's happened.

BOLSHOV.   That's it, exactly, daughter. Only God knows what's
what. But all the same, your father's doing time in the clink.

OLIMPIADA.   Why, daddy, lots of them are doing time, and many
are better than you and me.

BOLSHOV.   They're doing time, that's for sure. But what's it like
to be doing time? What's it like to walk the streets with a soldier
alongside you? Oh, daughter! Everyone in town's known me
forty years, you see, and forty straight years they've bowed
down to their belts when I've gone by. But now, even the little
brats point their fingers.

AGRAFENA.   And you look awful, my darling. You're just like a
ghost!

PODKHALYUZIN.   Ekh, daddy, God has mercy! As they say, "Grind
long enough, and you'll get flour." Now, daddy, what is it the
creditors say?

BOLSHOV.   Just this—they've struck a bargain. "Why," they say,
"drag it out anymore? Either it will work or it won't. So you
give us something solid, and we'll call it quits with you."

PODKHALYUZIN.   Why not give it to them, sir? Then kick in a
little extra, sir. Are they asking a lot, daddy?

BOLSHOV.   They're asking exactly twenty-five kopeks on each
ruble.

PODKHALYUZIN.   That, daddy, is a lot, sir.

BOLSHOV.   Brother, I know it's a lot, myself. But what can I do?
They won't take anything less.

PODKHALYUZIN.   If they'd take ten kopeks, then everything'd be
all right, sir. Seven and a half for satisfaction, and two a half
for the meeting's expenses.

BOLSHOV.   I told them that, exactly, but they won't listen at all.

PODKHALYUZIN.   Gotten pretty cocky, haven't they! But won't they take eight kopeks over a five-year period?

BOLSHOV.   Why, Lazar, we must give twenty-five kopeks. Just what we offered the first time, didn't we?

PODKHALYUZIN.   But how, tell me, daddy, sir? After all, you went and told me at the time, sir, not to give more than ten kopeks, sir. Think it over yourself. Twenty-five kopeks is a lot of money. Daddy, wouldn't you like a little something to eat, sir? Mama! Tell them to bring some vodka and ask them to put on the samovar. Just for company, we'll drink a little, sir. But twenty-five kopeks is a lot, sir!

AGRAFENA.   Right away, my dear, right away! [*Exits.*]

BOLSHOV.   Why tell me about it? I know it's a lot, myself. But what, tell me, can be done? They'll let you rot in the clink a year and a half, and every week send you along the streets with a soldier. And if you're not careful, they'll send you to prison for good. So you'd be glad to give fifty kopeks. You don't know where to hide from shame alone. [AGRAFENA *enters with vodka.* TISHKA *brings in hors de'oeuvres and exits.*]

AGRAFENA.   Oh, my darling. Please help yourself, my dear, do! I expect they're starving you to death there.

PODKHALYUZIN.   Please help yourself, daddy! Forgive us, it's not much, but you're welcome to all we have.

BOLSHOV.   Thank you, Lazar, thank you! [*Drinks.*] Have something to drink yourself.

PODKHALYUZIN.   To your health! [*Drinks.*] Mama, wouldn't you like something, ma'am? Do me the favor!

AGRAFENA.   Oh, saints in heaven, is there nothing I can do now? It's all come about through the will of God. Oh, dear Lord God! Oh, you poor darling, you.

PODKHALYUZIN.   Ekh, mama, God has mercy. We'll get off somehow or other. Not right away, ma'am.

AGRAFENA.   Oh, God, grant us that! But as I see him now, I just crumple up inside.

BOLSHOV.   Well, what's the answer, Lazar?

PODKHALYUZIN.   If you like, I'll give them ten kopeks, sir. As you told me.

BOLSHOV.   But where, tell me, do I get fifteen more? I can't make them out of wrapping paper.

PODKHALYUZIN. Daddy, I can't do more, sir. God knows I can't, sir!

BOLSHOV. You're not serious, Lazar, you can't be! And what did you do with the money, exactly?

PODKHALYUZIN. Pray, think it over. Why, I'm setting up a business, finished a house. But help yourself to a little something, daddy. If you like, there's some Madeira, maybe, sir? Mama, treat daddy to something.

AGRAFENA. Help yourself, my dear Samson Silych, please do. I'll pour you some punch, my dear.

BOLSHOV. [Drinks.] Save me, children, please save me.

PODKHALYUZIN. There, you were pleased to ask me, daddy, what I did with the money? Tell me, how could you ask, sir? Think it over yourself. I'm starting a business. You know very well, sir, it's impossible without capital. There's nothing to start on. There, I've bought the house. We've added all the usual things that go with it; horses, this thing and that. Pray, think it over yourself. You ought to start thinking about the children.

OLIMPIADA. Why, daddy, it's impossible! We'd be left without a stitch to our name. You know we're not common tradesmen.[36] Nothing like that at all.

PODKHALYUZIN. Daddy, think it over, please. Nowadays, without capital, sir, it's impossible. Without capital you can barely make a living.

OLIMPIADA. Daddy, I lived with you till I was almost twenty, and I didn't see a thing of the world. Why, do you want me to give back the money, and then go around in cotton dresses again?

BOLSHOV. You're not serious, you can't be! Think back. You know I'm not asking for charity, only for my own property. You're human, aren't you?

OLIMPIADA. Naturally, daddy, we're human. We're not animals at all.

BOLSHOV. Lazar, just think back! You know I've given away everything to you. Everything till I'm cleaned out completely. Look and see what's left for me! Nothing. When you were a little brat, you know, I took you into my house—you heartless scoundrel. I fed and clothed you, took the place of your own facther, set you up in the world. And look at the thanks I get from you. Don't you see? Think back, Lazar, how many times

I saw how light-fingered you were? What d'you say to that? I didn't drive you out, you know, like some animal. I didn't spread it all over town. I made you my head clerk. I gave away everything to you, my own property. And to you, Lazar, I even gave away my daughter, with my own hands. Without my help, you'd never have gotten away with it. Why, you'd never have dared even to look at her!

PODKHALYUZIN.   Goodness me, daddy. I feel very deeply about it, sir.

BOLSHOV.   You—feel? You ought to give away everything, like I did, down to your last shirt. Just to help out your benefactor. But I'm not going to ask that. I don't have to. Only, you pay off what they're asking now. Do that for me.

PODKHALYUZIN.   Why shouldn't I pay, sir? But the asking price is completely absurd.

BOLSHOV.   Don't think I'm asking! I begged out of every one of your kopeks. I begged, I got down on my knees. But what can I do, when they won't give in at all?

OLIMPIADA.   Daddy, we told you that we can't give more than ten kopeks. There's nothing more to say about it.

BOLSHOV.   Then you say, daughter, "Get along, you old devil, to the clink! Yes, to the clink! Into prison he goes, the old fool. He's got it coming!" Don't run after a pile of money; be happy with what you've got. If you do run after your pile, they'll take away your last kopek, fleece you till you're cleaned out. And then you'd better run to Stone Bridge and throw yourself into Moscow River. But then they'll pull you out by your tongue and put you in prison. [*All are silent.* BOLSHOV *drinks.*]   And you start thinking. What'll it be like to walk to the clink now? What if I can close my eyes, maybe? To me the Ilinka now will appear a hundred miles long. You start thinking, only what'll it be like to walk along the Ilinka. Just like devils—forgive me, dear Lord—pulling my sinful soul through torment. And then past Iversky: how can I even glance at her, on the Holy Mother? You know, Lazar, Judas also sold Christ for money; you see, like we sell our conscience for money. And what happened to him for doing that? There are also bureaus, like the criminal board. I did everything by design, you know; malice afore-thought, they call it. You know, they'll ship me off to Siberia.

Dear Lord! If you won't give the money for me, then give it for Christ's sake. [*Weeps.*]

PODKHALYUZIN.   You're not serious, daddy, you can't be. There now, enough. God has mercy. Why are you going on so? We'll put it right, somehow or other. It's all in our hands.

BOLSHOV.   I must have the money, Lazar. Yes, the money. There's no other way to put it right. Either the money, or to Siberia.

PODKHALYUZIN.   I'll give money, sir. Only if you'll stop nagging. All right, I'll add five kopeks more.

BOLSHOV.   After all these years! Is there nothing Christian in you? I must have twenty-five kopeks, Lazar.

PODKHALYUZIN.   No, daddy, it's a lot, sir. Really and truly, a lot.

BOLSHOV.   You're all a pack of snakes. [*Puts head down on table.*]

AGRAFENA.   [*To* PODKHALYUZIN.]   You barbarian, you! A robber, that's what you are! You'll never get my blessing, never. You'll shrivel up with your money, see. Shrivel up and die before your time. You're a robber, you. Yes, that's what you are—a robber.

PODKHALYUZIN.   Stop it, mama, you'll make God angry. Why do you swear at me, when you haven't figured out a thing? You see, daddy got a little drunk, then you take off—just ready to jump.

OLIMPIADA.   Come, mama, it'd be better for you to shut up. But then you love damning people to hell. And I know you've done it enough to go there yourself. That's probably the reason God never gave you any more children.

AGRAFENA.   Shut up yourself, you harlot, you! God punished me enough when he sent you.

OLIMPIADA.   The way you look at it, everybody's a harlot. You're the only good one. Just take a look at yourself. Sure, you fast three days a week,[37] but scarcely a day goes by that you don't bark at someone.

AGRAFENA.   Listen to that, will you, just listen. Oh, oh, oh! I'll damn you in every cathedral in town!

OLIMPIADA.   Damn as much as you like, please do.

AGRAFENA.   Yes, that's it. You're going to die, but you'll never rot, never!

OLIMPIADA. What do I care!

BOLSHOV. [*Rises.*] Well, good-by, children.

PODKHALYUZIN. You're not serious, daddy, sit down. We've got to finish up this business, somehow or other.

BOLSHOV. What's there to finish up? I can see already that it's all over. Like they say, "The old peasant woman'll beat herself brown, if she don't cut the stalk at the ground." Don't you pay a single kopek for me. Whatever they want, let them do it. Good-by. It's time I was going.

PODKHALYUZIN. Good-by, daddy. God has mercy. Things'll get settled someway or other.

BOLSHOV. Good-by, wife.

AGRAFENA. Good-by, my dear Samson Silych. When will they let us come visit you in the clink?

BOLSHOV. I don't know.

AGRAFENA. I'll find out. Or you'll die there, and we won't have seen you at all.

BOLSHOV. Good-by, daughter. Good-by, Alimpiyada Samsonovna. Well, you'll be rich now and start to live like the nobility. That is, going to parties, going to dances, and—going to hell. But don't you forget, Alimpiyada Samsonovna, there are cages with iron bars. And in those cages there are poor convicts doing time. Don't forget us poor convicts. [*Exits with* AGRAFENA.]

PODKHALYUZIN. Ekh, Alimpiyada Samsonovna, ma'am! A bit awkward, ma'am. I'm sorry for daddy, really and truly I am, ma'am. I really should go and haggle with his creditors. Or maybe I shouldn't, ma'am? I bet he can soften them up better than me. Hmm? Or maybe I should go? I will, ma'am! Tishka!

OLIMPIADA. Do whatever you want. It's your affair.

PODKHALYUZIN. Tishka! [TISHKA *enters.*] Get my old frock coat, the worst you can find. [TISHKA *exits.*] Otherwise, they'll start thinking I'm rich. And if it comes to that, you'll never make a deal with them. [RISPOLOZHENSKY *and* AGRAFENA *enter.*]

RISPOLOZHENSKY. Pray, my dear Agrafena Kondratevna, haven't you pickled your cucumbers yet?

AGRAFENA. No, my dear! Cucumbers—why cucumbers now? How can they concern me! But have you been pickling?

RISPOLOZHENSKY. And how, my dear; I should say we've been pickling. They're very expensive these days. They say the frost killed them. Lazar Elizarych, my dear fellow, how do you do! Is that vodka? I'll just try a drop or two, Lazar Elizarych. [AGRAFENA *exits with* OLIMPIADA.]

PODKHALYUZIN.   And what's the reason you've been gracious enough to pay us a visit? Would you be good enough to tell us?

RISPOLOZHENSKY.   Hee, hee, hee. You're some joker, Lazar Elizarych. You know the reason, for sure.

PODKHALYUZIN.   And what is the reason, exactly? I'd really like to know, sir.

RISPOLOZHENSKY.   For money, Lazar Elizarych, for money. Somebody else might be after anything at all. But, me—I'm always after money.

PODKHALYUZIN.   I'd say you come much too often for money.

RISPOLOZHENSKY.   And why, tell me, shouldn't I come so much, Lazar Elizarych? When you give me only five rubles at a swat? You know I have a family.

PODKHALYUZIN.   Well, you're not going to get a hundred every time.

RISPOLOZHENSKY.   If you'd give me the whole lump at one stroke, then I wouldn't be coming to see you.

PODKHALYUZIN.   You don't have either the ears or the snout for business. But, brother, can you take bribes! Why give you anything?

RISPOLOZHENSKY.   What do you mean, why? Simply because you promised me yourself.

PODKHALYUZIN.   Promised you myself? You know I gave you money. You made a profit. That should be enough. You shouldn't take advantage of my hospitality.

RISPOLOZHENSKY.   What do you mean, hospitality? You must give me fifteen hundred more.

PODKHALYUZIN.   Must! That's a good one, must! Just as if you have a bill. And for what—for your swindling.

RISPOLOZHENSKY.   What do you mean, swindling? For my hard work, not for my swindling.

PODKHALYUZIN.   Your hard work!

RISPOLOZHENSKY.   Well, for whatever you might want to call it, I don't care. Only give me the money, or a bill for it.

PODKHALYUZIN.   What's this, sir? A bill. No, you'd only come again, after you got the bill.

RISPOLOZHENSKY.   So that's it. You want to rob me, I suppose, and my little kids?

PODKHALYUZIN.   Robbery, what the hell! Well, if that's the way you feel about it, take another five rubles, and then good-by and good luck.

RISPOLOZHENSKY.   No, hold on! You're not going to shake me off with that. [TISHKA *enters*.]

PODKHALYUZIN.   And what, tell me, will you do to me?

RISPOLOZHENSKY.   I haven't sold my tongue so far.

PODKHALYUZIN.   So what! Do you want to lick my boots, maybe?

RISPOLOZHENSKY.   No, I'm not going to lick your boots, but I'm going to tell all the decent people in the world.

PODKHALYUZIN.   What are you going to tell them, exactly, you hard-hearted old shyster? And who do you think will ever believe you?

RISPOLOZHENSKY.   Who will believe me?

PODKHALYUZIN.   Yes. Who will believe you? Only take a look at yourself.

RISPOLOZHENSKY.   Who will believe me? Who will believe me? You'll see! Yes, you will! Saints in heaven, what can I do? It'll be the death of me. He's robbing me, the robber. Yes, he is. No, hold on, you. You'll see, to rob is against the law.

PODKHALYUZIN.   And what will I see, exactly?

RISPOLOZHENSKY.   Here's what you'll see. Wait a bit. Yes, wait! You think I won't take you to court? Wait and see!

PODKHALYUZIN.   Wait and see. Oh, that's a good one—wait and see. I've already waited long enough. You're full of it—trying to frighten me like this. But I'm not scared.

RISPOLOZHENSKY.   You think nobody will believe me, do you? Won't believe me, is it? Well, let them say what they want to me. I will . . . Here's what I'll do. [*Turns to audience*.] Oh, most respectable public!

PODKHALYUZIN.   You're not serious, you can't be! Come to your senses.

TISHKA.   Get him, will you! He's so drunk he can't see where he's going.

RISPOLOZHENSKY.   Hold on a bit, will you! Oh, most respectable public! I have a wife, four children. Look at the holes in my boots.

PODKHALYUZIN. He's lying about everything, ladies and gentlemen. A very shallow person, ladies and gentlemen. That's enough, you, stop it. Look out for yourself, or you'll start getting in over your head.

RISPOLOZHENSKY. Let me alone! He stole his father-in-law blind. And he's robbing me . . . I have a wife, four children, and my boots have holes in them.

TISHKA. You can put soles on them.

RISPOLOZHENSKY. What are you going on about? You're a robber, the same as him.

TISHKA. Not at all, sir. You missed the mark. [*Exits.*]

PODKHALYUZIN. Oh, why bring morality into the picture? Really!

RISPOLOZHENSKY. No, you wait and see. I'll get revenge. I'll ship you to Siberia!

PODKHALYUZIN. Don't believe him. He's lying about everything, ladies and gentlemen! That's it, ladies and gentlemen. A very shallow person, ladies and gentlemen. He's not worth listening to. Ekh, brother, you sorehead, you! I never knew you. I wouldn't get tied up with you, not for all the money in the world.

RISPOLOZHENSKY. Oh, he took everything. Yes, he did. Here's something for you, you dog! I hope you choke on my money now. And you can go to the devil! [*Exits.*]

PODKHALYUZIN. Oh, what a hothead he is! [*To the audience.*] Ladies and gentlemen, don't believe him. That is, the one who was doing all the talking, ladies and gentlemen. He was lying about everything. Why, nothing like that ever happened at all. He probably had a nightmare, dreamed it all up. Right now, ladies and gentlemen, we are opening a little shop, soon. You are most welcome to come! Send the little fellow to us—and we won't rook him when we count the onions.

THE POOR BRIDE

THE POOR BRIDE

I. COMPOSITION

Ostrovsky began writing *The Poor Bride* in the summer of 1850, stopped work long enough in the fall to finish two short plays—*A Young Man's Morning* and *An Unexpected Incident*—and, after numerous revisions, completed the play in December 1851. The five-act comedy was published the following year in Pogodin's journal *Muscovite*. The writing had been difficult, and twenty-five years later Ostrovsky recalled his trial-and-error process, his commitment to differentiate each major character, and his personal drive to finish the play satisfactorily. Having spent a year and a half in the making of *The Poor Bride*, he "conceived a loathing for it."

Since *The Poor Bride* was Ostrovsky's second major work, it was inevitably compared with his first. "I read your comedy with furious pleasure," Pisemsky wrote to the author, adding that he found the play not only superior to *It's a Family Affair* but also sufficiently impressive to give him dreams at night. Pisemsky was almost alone in his unqualified response. Panaev believed that the play as a whole "failed artistically," while Chernyshevsky noted that the play lacked "the merit of novelty." Both agreed, however, that several sections were excellently rendered.

Most of the critics stressed deficiencies in theatrical effectiveness and specifically listed repetitious dialogue, too many similar details, and the lack of vitality in certain characters. Turgenev, for example, admired the obvious talent of the author, especially in delineating the essential egotism of Benevolensky, Milashin and Merich, but he felt that Marya was confusing, vague, and lifeless. Turgenev challenged Ostrovsky to eliminate the "false psychological analysis . . . in which every character incessantly repeats the same words." Druzhinin, on the other hand, believed that the author had caught the "fidelity of a large part of nature," but added that the comedy was "inferior to the dramatic work of Gogol." In short, most of the critics concluded that, in comparison with either Gogol's plays or Ostrovsky's first major work, *The Poor Bride* was at best second-rate.

In 1858 when preparing the first edition of his collected plays, Ostrovsky turned once again to *The Poor Bride* and thoroughly reworked the play. He cut a scene with the family of young ladies, added characteristics to Milashin and Merich, struck out passages of dialogue, and individualized character, thought, and language. Again, the critical response was mixed. Typical of the skeptical reviewers was Rodislavsky; he thought the play weaker than other Ostrovsky plays and noted especially its "long-windedness." But critics like Grigor'ev and Dobrolyubov viewed *The Poor Bride* in a wider context. As early as 1855, Grigor'ev had charged that all the critics, in their irritation over situation and character, had missed the essential quality of Ostrovsky's plays—a quality which Grigor'ev identified as a "new word" in literature. Four years later Dobrolyubov described the universe of the plays as "The Kingdom of Darkness" and related the central question of *The Poor Bride*—"what holds her in this whirlpool?"—to the social conditions of the day.

It is clear that she is a *poor bride*, she has nowhere to go, nothing to do, except wait or look for a profitable bridegroom. Marriage—this is her duty, work, career, the purpose of life. As the workman looks for work, the government official—a position, the beggar—charity; thus the unmarried girl must look for a bridegroom . . . why in our country does a woman in the family find herself in that slavish situation and why does petty tyranny *(samodurstvo)* weigh her down with particular power?

II. STAGE PRODUCTIONS

The Poor Bride was the third Ostrovsky play to receive a production, opening at the Maly Theatre 20 August 1853. Both the first play, *Don't Sit in Another's Sleigh*, and the second, *A Young Man's Morning*, had been produced the previous January. The decision to stage *The Poor Bride* had been delayed by the censorship office, and even though the censor Gedershtern finally recommended production, he expunged the roles of Dunya and Pasha in the last act. Not until 1861 were the roles restored for stage productions. Gedershtern's recommendation was apparently based on his interpretation of the play as a love story. Having assisted with the direction of *The Poor Bride* at the Maly, Ostrovsky observed that the production played well and added, "I am almost satisfied with the performance; the audience is completely satisfied."

The Maly production in 1853 received high praise, and critics singled out S. V. Shumsky, S. V. Vasil'ev, P. M. Sadovsky, and E. N. Vasil'eva for special comment. Although Shumsky played Dobrotvorsky in the usual vaudeville manner, he created essentially a warm-hearted person. Vasil'ev as Milashin not only caught the qualities of the young man hopelessly in love with Marya, but his interpretation also came close to the fool eager and ready to take offense. Grigor'ev was delighted with the actor's characterization, calling it "almost genius-like."

Both Sadovsky as Benevolensky and Vasil'eva as Marya enthralled the audience and critics. Koropchevsky recalled that Sadovsky "compelled the audience to see in the play not so much the marriage of Marya as the marriage of Benevolensky." The actor based his interpretation on the government official's pomposity, "out of which were revealed heartlessness, narrow-mindedness, and vulgarity (poshlost')." Stakhovich was particularly pleased with Sadovsky's first entrance into the home of the poor bride.

> It seemed when he entered that it was not Benevolensky,
> short in stature, stoutish in the uniform frockcoat of the govern-
> ment official, but the Emperor himself . . .

Another critic lauded Sadovsky's skillful variations of pomposity, coupled with his free-and-easy attitude, as well as his French manner of speaking the phrase, "I am in love." Vasil'eva was apparently so believable in her role of Marya that the spectators forgot they were watching a theatrical performance. Critics pointed out not only her complete concentration and involvement but also her consistently mimed responses to action and speech. "Vasil'eva's talent is great," Ostrovsky concluded once, "she made out of my Marya Andreevna something which I never dreamed of myself."

Even though the director of the Imperial theatres hesitated to produce The Poor Bride in Petersburg, the actors there eventually persuaded the officials to open the play on the twelfth of October 1853 at the Aleksandrinsky Theatre. The production in Petersburg, however, was considered colorless when compared with the brilliant staging in Moscow. A. M. Chitau as Marya, Yu. N. Linskaya as Khorkova, and A. E. Martynov as Benevolensky played their roles with distinction, but the actors creating Mikhailo, Merich, and Dobrotvorsky were judged unimaginative, even insipid. Moreover, as A. I. Vol'f put it, the spectators in Petersburg were accustomed to "the high-flown effects of French melodrama" and did not respond to "the suffering of the poor unmarried girl."

Subsequent productions of The Poor Bride in Russia were few in number. The play was rarely staged in the Imperial theatres, and since it was banned from production in the people's theatres until 1893, *The Poor Bride* was performed less than two hundred times from 1875 to 1917. Certainly the play in its day was timely, and this may have accounted in some measure for the official attitude of the Imperial theatre administration. Insulted by the "stagnant repertory" in 1864, D. V. Averkiev wryly observed that *The Poor Bride* had been given but twice, "and then no more of it." As late as 1884, P. A. Strepetova complained to Ostrovsky that every time she played Marya well the officials took the play out of the repertory. After the Revolution, *The Poor Bride* was produced more frequently, but it has never equaled the productions of the more popular Ostrovsky plays like *The Storm* or *The Forest.*

III. NAMES OF THE CHARACTERS

Not all the names selected by Ostrovsky came about through his own invention. Among the Moscow merchants in the forties, as A. I. Revyakin recently observed, there were memorable last names such as Bol'shov, Khor'kov, and Kabanov. Ostrovsky's use of names, however, was skillful and at times witty. For example, the family name of Khorkov (Khor'kov) incorporates the Russian equivalent of polecat, and in the play the characters now and again refer to Mikhailo's mother by her last name Khorkova. Yet the characters never refer to the son by his last name, since the playwright did not want to associate the name Khorkov with Mikhailo.

The name Anna denotes beneficial or abundant, while the patronymic is a variant of Petr meaning stone or jewel. Pointing out the inconsistent use of these names for the character Nezabudkina (*don't forget*), E. G. Kholodov stressed that Ostrovsky could scarcely be held accountable since the number of characters in his total plays adds up to hundreds of names. On the other hand, the playwright may have selected these three names for their ironic meaning. Anna's last name also denotes one of her traits. Certainly, other character names in *The Poor Bride* exemplify an ironic treatment by Ostrovsky. Names such as Milashin (*pretty boy*), Platon Dobrotvorsky (*Plato benefactor*), and Maksim Benevolensky (*benevolent maxim*) are contrasted with the appearance or bent of the characters. Then, too, the matchmaker Karpovna (*carp*) is contrasted with the matchmaker Pankratevna (Pankrat'evna) or Pan—a hundredfold. The name Pankratevna also connotes gentleman—a hundredfold. Ostrovsky used the technique of referring to the matchmakers only by their patronymics.

The stress of the names is as follows: Anna Petróvna Nezabúdkina, Márya Andréevna, Vladímir Vasílevich Mérich, Iván Ivánovich Miláshin, Platón Márkovich Dobrotvórsky, Maksím Doroféevich Benevolénsky, Arína Egórovna Khórkova, Mikháilo Ivánovich Khórkov, Kárpovna, Pankrátevna, Dárya, Dúnya, Pásha.

THE POOR BRIDE

Bednaya nevesta

A Comedy in Five Acts

CHARACTERS

ANNA PETROVNA NEZABUDKINA, *widow of a poor government official.*

MARYA ANDREEVNA, *her daughter.*

VLADIMIR VASILEVICH MERICH ⎱ *young men, acquaintances of*
IVAN IVANOVICH MILASHIN ⎰ *Anna Petrovna.*

PLATON MARKOVICH DOBROTVORSKY, *an old lawyer.*

MAKSIM DOROFEEVICH BENEVOLENSKY, *a government official.*

ARINA EGOROVNA KHORKOVA, *widow in the tradesmen class.*[1]

MIKHAILO IVANOVICH KHORKOV, *her son, a former student.*

KARPOVNA, *a matchmaker who works among the merchant class; wears a kerchief.*

PANKRATEVNA, *a matchmaker who works among the nobility; wears a cap.*

DARYA, *housemaid for Anna Petrovna.*

A BOY, *serving Dobrotvorsky.*

DUNYA.

PASHA.

A WAITER and various people who appear in the fifth act to watch the wedding.

ACT ONE

A room is represented on stage. In the back wall are two doors; the first leads to inner rooms, the second leads to the street. On the left side is a window. By the window is an embroidery frame; farther away, a piano. On the right side are a couch and a large round table. MARYA *is sitting at the embroidery frame;* ANNA *is sitting on the couch.*

ANNA. We're living the best we can. You see that, don't you? If only your papa hadn't spent his money like water, then everything'd be different. As it is, he left us almost nothing at all. And now, everything's in a mess, and if that isn't enough, we've got this lawsuit. Wait and see if they don't strip the house right out from under us. And what are we going to do then, I'd like to know? You better start thinking how we'll live then. And what can I do to stop them? Nothing. I'm just a woman, that's all. I don't know anything, and I'm used to people telling me what to do. [*Silence.*] Maybe if you'd get married, Masha,[2] as soon as possible. If you did, why I wouldn't know how to thank God enough. As it is, I don't see how we can get along without a man in the house. We can't and that's all there is to it.

MARYA. You know, mama, you go on and on about the same old thing.

ANNA. And why shouldn't I go on and on, I'd like to know? Listening to me isn't going to kill you, is it? Go on with you. I suppose you'd rather I'd say nothing at all. What's bothering you, anyway?

MARYA. Do you think it's my fault, mama, that nobody appeals to me?

ANNA. Appeals? What do you mean, appeals? I don't know

what you're talking about. It's a silly idea, Masha. That's what it is, silly.

MARYA.   Silly! Oh, mama, really! Who on earth wanted to court me? You think back about it, and remember the kind of men who came around here.

ANNA.   What can we do, Mashenka?[3] What can we do, my dear? Where on earth can we pick up a good-looking man for you? Nowadays, the good suitors are after money all the time. As for a pretty thing like you, why they wouldn't give you a second glance. Where is it I put my snuffbox, I'd like to know? Just look over there on the little table. Wait, here it is, in my pocket. Looks to me as if nobody'll ever fall in love with you. Young men nowadays are as harebrained as you'll find anywhere. But I've got to admit you're as choosy as they come, you know. Better start thinking about one little thing, my dear. And that is, we don't have a pile of gold lying around. So there's nothing, absolutely nothing, for you to be so picky about.

MARYA.   All right, all right.

ANNA.   Now, what's this "all right" business?

MARYA.   I'll start thinking about it.

ANNA.   Yes, but what exactly are you going to think about? You wouldn't mind telling me that, would you? The way you are, you could go on thinking until you're way past the marrying age.

MARYA.   And what's wrong with that?

ANNA.   Oh, you're a silly fool. Yes, you are.   [*She sits and pouts. Silence.*]   Oh, God in heaven, if only Platon Markych[4] would come! I don't know what I'm going to do. I saw a stocking here a minute ago, and now where on earth did it go to?

MARYA.   Here's the stocking, mama.   [*Hands it over.*]

ANNA.   [*Knits the stocking.*]   Platon Markych isn't going to show up, and that's all there is to it. So, go ahead and do what you want.

MARYA.   Why is it, mama, you need Platon Markych?

ANNA.   Why? What do you mean, why? I suppose you think we know everything, just sitting around here. After all, Platon Markych is a man. Why, the watchman brought me some sort of paper, and who do you think will figure it out? A fine thing for women to do, I must say. And you'd be a fool even to try it! The whole morning's gone by, and I still can't get my money counted. And I don't know how I'll ever do it, without a man around. Why, it's like a person's just asking for trouble. Masha, take a little piece of paper and count my money for me. Do me the favor, please.

MARYA.   You tell me what it is, and I'll count it up.

ANNA.   Wait a minute, Masha. You're pushing me too fast; I'll lose my bearings again. Where on earth is the paper I had? God help me think where . . . Oh, there it is. Wait a minute, I've found it. Here, you take it and start counting. I already finished counting it. I even counted it on the counting board. Either we're missing a ruble, or we're two too many. But it's better not to make Darya[5] do it. Oh, dear Lord, I'm all mixed up. I'm worried sick about that lawsuit, and I must talk to Platon Markych about the house. After all, Platon Markych is a man. [DARYA enters.]

DARYA.   Ma'am. Oh, ma'am! There's a boy who's come from Platon Markych.

ANNA.   Send him in here.   [DARYA exits. A BOY enters.]

BOY.   Platon Markych sends his greetings and best wishes. He's sent yesterday's papers and a note, ma'am, and he told me to ask about your health.

ANNA.   Oh, good Lord! What did I do with my spectacles? Look for them, Masha. Do me the favor, please.   [MARYA looks for the glasses.)

MARYA.   Well, if you like, mama, I'll read it for you. I don't think you and Platon Markych have any secrets.

ANNA.   Read it, Masha! What do you mean, secrets? I asked him about the lawsuit. It's exactly what a woman would do. I'm sorry to bother Platon Markych, you know—he's an old man. But I couldn't do anything else.

MARYA.   [Reads.] "Your most honorable, gracious madam Anna Petrovna! I have the honor to notify you that I have carried out all the errands with precision and with pleasure, and in the future I beg you to entrust me with the same. Herewith I send you a report of yesterday's events. Concerning that point, about which you asked me, I was at the bureau pointed out by you. There are no worthy bachelor officials for Marya Andreevna. There is one, but I doubt that the above-mentioned would appeal to you. For he is a very big person, a good deal bigger than the usual man, and pock-marked . . . " [*She looks at* ANNA *imploringly.*] Mama!

ANNA. Go on, read it. Do!

MARYA. [*Continues.*] "But, according to references gathered from my secretary and others from his colleagues, he appears of good morals and no drinker, which, as is well known to me, you greatly desired. If you want me to look around in other bureaus, I will carry it out with the greatest pleasure. Your lawsuit, because of neglect on your part, has taken a bad turn. But, pray, dear lady, don't worry. For I've turned up a highly regarded person, who can handle the above-mentioned lawsuit. About the other things I shall have the honor of explaining to you in a meeting, face-to-face. I remain, always ready for service, Platon Dobrotvorsky." What is it you're doing, mama? You're sending Platon Markych to bureaus, looking for suitors! Only God knows what will come of this. And you haven't said one word to me. Why, it's like a slap in my face. Oh, mama, what are you doing to me? [*Sits at the embroidery frame.*]

ANNA. It's not a slap in the face at all. You, Masha, don't know a thing about it. Besides, it's up to me, anyway. You know I'm not making you do it. If you want somebody, then go ahead and marry him. Just remember, it's my job to turn up a husband for you. [*Silence. To the* BOY.] My greetings and best wishes, dear, to Platon Markych. Say that I told you to thank him. And, thank the good Lord, I can say I am well.

BOY. Yes, ma'am.

ANNA. Come with me, and I'll give you a note for Platon Markych. [ANNA *and the* BOY *exit.*]

MARYA. [*Alone.*] There you have it. Every single day, the same old thing. Why mama never gets sick and tired of it, I'll never know. On and on and on . . . I'm bored stiff, and I don't think I'll ever escape. [*Embroiders on the frame.* DARYA *enters.*]

DARYA. [*To herself.*] Oh, the hell with you!

MARYA. Why are you mad all the time?

DARYA. And how, miss, can I help getting mad? Oh, men, men! You'd never believe it. Just now, I run out of the shop; and right there on the road, some sort of blockhead stops dead in his tracks. And then he looks me right in the eye. "All right," I said, "why goggle so wall-eyed? You can see, can't you, that nothing's written on me." Then he said, "How can I help looking at a beauty like you?" Well, I spit on him and took off. [*She looks for something.*] She keeps losing it all the time, and then I have to go and hunt for it. Oh, the hell with . . .

MARYA.   What is it you're looking for?

DARYA.   Oh, the mistress lost her snuffbox. . . . Found it.

MARYA.   What do you think, Dasha,[6] am I good-looking?

DARYA.   You, good-looking? Listen, you've got the kind of beauty they write home to mama about.

MARYA.   Let's switch roles. Then they won't make fun of you.

DARYA.   Oh, my dear, as if your beauty would help me.

MARYA.   And how does it help me?

DARYA.   Oh, come on, miss. Think what you're saying. Look here, some boy will fall in love with you. It's a real pleasure just looking at you. Why, some sort of colonel will take you. Wait and see.

MARYA.   And where on earth, Dasha, will he ever see me to fall in love? Mama says it's time I got married.

DARYA.   No, go on with you! Why don't you go and get married, then?

MARYA.   So, what's the use of being a beauty?

DARYA.   What's the use? Simply because your husband will love you even better. You know, there's a neighbor lady around here who has two daughters. The older one's thin as a matchstick. The younger one's rosy and sleek, not yet sixteen years old, but she looks as if she'd raised three kids already. Their mother says right out, "I'm afraid," she says, "to marry off the older girl, 'cause her husband would never get around to loving her." "But this one here," she says, "her husband would love her, don't you think he wouldn't." Oh, miss, I got so carried away talking to you that I suppose the old woman will be mad as hops. [*Exits.*]

MARYA.   Oh, it's easy for mama to say, "Go ahead and get married." But whom should I pick? It's terrible to imagine yourself married to a man for whom you'd feel nothing but disgust. [*Deep in thought.*]   Any silly old codger who chances by will think he has the right to court me. Yes, and even count it a favor, "because she," he says, "is a poor bride." A person will simply bargain for me, as if I were some kind of gadget on the counter. "I have money," he says, "while you have nothing; but I'll take your daughter for her beauty." [*Looks out the window, deep in thought.*]   Merich! That's wonderful. He looks so pathetic and deep in thought. I wish I knew what he's thinking about. Surely, not about me. [*Crosses to mirror.*]   Oh, how silly I am. Why on earth did I turn all red? Yes, and my voice is trembling. I'd better simmer down a bit. Otherwise, he'll notice it, for sure. Oh, good Lord, what am I saying? Maybe I even wanted him to notice it—just to see what he'd do. Oh, don't be silly. I'm just lying to myself. Darya! Darya! [DARYA *enters.*] Run and ask Vladimir Vasilevich[7] to go into the garden.

DARYA.   All right, miss. [*Exits.*]

MARYA.   [*Spruces up in front of the mirror.*]   Any minute now the different matchmakers will show up. As if I want to look nice for them! I've gotten used to them showing up, but I imagine they'll seem pretty wild to him. Oh, I'm tickled to death to see him. Seems he almost never comes around here.

DARYA.   [*Enters.*]   Please, miss, he is in the garden. [MARYA *exits.* DARYA *dusts the furniture.*]   What a marvelous young lady I have. It's true. Oh, dear Lord, please give her a good suitor. [*Stops in the center of the room, with dustcloth in her hand.*] Stop and figure out what goes on in the world. If you're rich, why everybody and his brother will praise you for it. If you're poor, then all their snouts turn up. Well, it's pretty obvious. It's not the man they want—it's his money. [*Spreads her arms out wide.*]   Pretty puzzling, what goes on in the world. [*Having glanced out the window.*]   Oh, the hell with you! Just see what's turned up. [*Crosses to the door.* KARPOVNA *enters.*]

KARPOVNA.   Dasha, how're you today?

DARYA.   How're you, Karpovna? You know I thought you'd died.

KARPOVNA.   Listen, sweetie, I've been knocking myself out lately. Nothing new going on with you, I don't suppose?

DARYA.   Nothing new? Oh, that's a good one. And where did you think it'd pop out from?

KARPOVNA.   [*Sitting.*]   Oh, girlie, sure is hot in here.

DARYA.   Look at you, will you! God help you, you've sure packed on the weight.

KARPOVNA.   Well, I'll tell you, baby, I'd guess I am getting fatter. How come you don't put on a little flesh?

DARYA.   So, you're wondering why I don't put on a little flesh? How on earth do you think I can, I'd like to know? Be a different matter altogether, if I had a little peace and quiet around here, but the way things . . . Oh . . .   [*Crosses to* KARPOVNA *and speaks in a low voice.*]   What I mean, Karpovna, is you'd never believe it. Day in and day out, the mistress runs around like a wound-up clock, saying this isn't right, the next thing's not to her liking. On and on she goes, grumbling here and . . . Listen here, I'm pretty much of a hot-head. I'll only take so much, and then I spit back. And before you know it, all hell breaks loose. . . . Swearing and the best ruckus you'd see anywhere. What it comes down to is this. If I weren't used to this house, from having spent seven years in it, why I wouldn't stick around another day.

KARPOVNA.   Well, just listen to you, girlie! Oh, my . . .   [*Shakes her head.*]

DARYA.   I said I was pretty much of a hot-head. I start boiling inside, and I boil until all of a sudden it's like a mist before my eyes. Then I'd be happy to break somebody's neck. Only my temper doesn't last long. It's there one minute, and gone the next, just as if nothing had ever happened. But she goes on grumbling and . . . Like I said, if I weren't used to it, from having spent seven years here . . . Then, again, I keep thinking, well . . .   [*Waves her hand.*]

KARPOVNA.   Look, baby, nobody thinks it sweet, being in service.

DARYA.   The other day, she said, "You old so-and-so, you! Why'd you take so long going shopping?" "I suppose," she said, "you're keeping company with the shopkeepers." So I said, "What do you mean, ma'am? Who caught me at it?" "No," I said, "don't you even dare . . ." "I'm just a girl," I said, "like any other, and nothing like . . ." Oh, seems to me, it's better not to talk about it.   [*A pause.*]   The old woman's almost choked the life out of the young lady. "Go on," she says, "get married." And the young lady says, "But whom should I pick?" Well, you know it's the truth. Who is it she'll marry? What sort of clown will turn up? Be much better, Karpovna, if you'd find her a good man.

KARPOVNA.   Well, I've gone and got one. But I don't know if she'll like him.

DARYA.   I'll tell you what I think. Go find her an officer. Look out the window and see how many good ones ride by. I think somebody's coming. [*Crosses to door.* PANKRATEVNA *enters.*]

PANKRATEVNA. What do you say, sweetheart, is your mistress home?

DARYA. She's home.

PANKRATEVNA. Tell her that Stepanida Pankratevna[8] is here. [DARYA *exits. Having glanced at* KARPOVNA.] Ba, ba, ba! So, the crow has landed in the great mansion. How is it you fell into this place?

KARPOVNA. Why on earth should I care, so long as I made it here? What's the big idea of you popping in with a demand like that?

PANKRATEVNA. Look who's talking! Dragging yourself in everywhere. You'd be far better off hanging on to your merchants.

KARPOVNA. And I suppose you stick with the nobility all the time. What did I tell you? Just see how the tail of your skirt has become shabby, from tramping around their hallways.

PANKRATEVNA. A lot you know, you ignoramus, you! I'm not going to say another word to you.

KARPOVNA. Ha, ha, ha, ha! You, no doubt, have a lot better breeding. Here you are running around with the nobility, but you look as though you've just come from plucking chickens and are trying to spruce up. I'm ashamed to look at you. But I stick to my merchants, live in my own home, no worse than the next fellow's, and I've got money in the bank. You've squeezed into your little cap, and so there you go, just thinking nobody can touch you with a ten-foot pole. Listen, if I wanted to, I could slap you dizzy, pole and all. So fast you wouldn't know what hit you. [*Laughs.*] I'll have a better reputation than you ever will.

PANKRATEVNA. No use talking to an ignoramus. Why, you know next to nothing about how to behave, simply because you're a silly fool, without a bit of upbringing.

KARPOVNA. I may be a fool, but I'm neater than you. Nobody will try stepping on my toes. [*Silence.*]

PANKRATEVNA. Just wait till Martyn Martyanych[9] finds out why you're visiting him. Then he'll slap the wind out of your sails.

KARPOVNA. But why do I visit him? Well, tell me, why?

PANKRATEVNA. Oh, everybody knows why.

KARPOVNA. How come you don't know? You're lying. Yes, lying through your teeth. I've been a widow for thirteen years, and nobody's ever caught me doing wrong. Just because you're a little sick in the head, you want everybody else to be. [ANNA *enters. The matchmakers rise and bow.*]

ANNA.   How do you do? Well, what have you got? Well? Speak up. [*The matchmakers are silent.*]   Why don't you say something?

KARPOVNA.   Let her talk first. After all, she has the nobility.

ANNA.   Well, what do you have to say, Pankratevna?

PANKRATEVNA.   I have two suitors, Anna Petrovna. Cavaliers, both of them. You should be tickled to death.

ANNA.   What are they like, exactly?

PANKRATEVNA.   They're in the service, my dear, and nobles.[10]

ANNA.   Well, do they have money and property?

PANKRATEVNA.   They are in service, my dear, and receive salaries.

ANNA.   And what kind of life do they lead?

PANKRATEVNA.   They behave themselves. One writes poetry. The other one sings all day. And are they polite! Yes, and amorous, too. As one of them says, "If I see a good-looking girl, I'm not going to stop until I marry her."

ANNA.   What kind of rank do they have?

PANKRATEVNA.   Not too high, but I bet you won't find better looking fellows.

KARPOVNA.   And I'll bet they're both as poor as beggars.

ANNA.   Well, what have you got, Karpovna?

KARPOVNA.   Listen, I've got one, or have I got one! An ace of spades he is. No use even comparing him to her two suitors. Why, he's got more laid aside than all of us put together in this room.

ANNA.   Well, that's all right. Run along, Pankratevna! Drop by for a chat one of these days.

PANKRATEVNA.   Good-by, Anna Petrovna.   [*Exits, having glanced ferociously at* KARPOVNA.]

ANNA.   Oh, Karpovna, if only you'll find a suitor for us, I wouldn't know how to thank you enough. You know yourself, I'm just a woman, and I don't know anything. How is it possible to get along without a man around, I'd like to know?

KARPOVNA.   There you are, dearie. We had scarcely a kopek, and now all of a sudden there are three. An ace of spades he is. Why, you can't touch him with a ten-foot pole.

ANNA.   Who is he? Don't torment me, speak up.

KARPOVNA.   Sava Savich Belugin.[11]

ANNA.   You're not serious. You know he's a millionaire.

KARPOVNA.   A millionaire. That's what he is, all right, a millionaire.

ANNA.   How come he even thought of it?

KARPOVNA.   Why, dearie, simply because the children overwhelmed him. You know the kind of children he has. Well, just imagine living with them. And he can't stand living in that big house. You know, the one with the balcony. Well, his sons lock themselves in up there, start drinking, and drop the anchor on anyone who comes by. And what do you suppose they thought up? One or the other of them jumps out on the balcony, bugs out his eyes, raises his arms, and lets out a scream that'd set your teeth on edge. Then, he pops back into the room. After a little while, the other one jumps out with pranks of all sorts. A nice how-d'ye-do, I must say.

ANNA.   [Shaking her head.]   A-ya-yai, a-ya-yai!

KARPOVNA.   Well, judge for yourself. The father watches and watches . . .

ANNA.   [Having glanced out of the window and having seen the approaching KHORKOVA.]   Well, good enough, Karpovna, thank you. You know yourself, I'm just a woman. Drop by one of these days, and we'll have a talk. Right now I haven't time. I see Khorkova coming.

KARPOVNA.   I'll come by, I will.   [Bows and exits. KHORKOVA enters.]

ANNA.   Arina Egorovna! Welcome. Sit down, won't you.

KHORKOVA.   I'm just here for a minute or so, Anna Petrovna, absolutely a minute or so. Imagine, I was in town. "What do you say," I thought, "I'll drop by Anna Petrovna's; she's getting pretty stuck up, never visits us anymore." "Well, so what," I thought, "I'll drop by anyway."

ANNA.   Forgive me, dearie, I've been so busy, really and truly. Never seem to have a minute. Judge for yourself, I'm just a woman: I have to do everything myself. Right now we have the lawsuit over the house. I don't get a wink of sleep anymore. Well, if they strip the house out from under us, then what're we going to do? Besides, I've got a daughter that's ready for marriage.

KHORKOVA.   Well, I thank the good Lord you do, Anna Petrovna. You know my Misha,[12] as humble and respectful as they come. "Mama," he says, "it doesn't matter to me that you're just an ordinary woman, simple and uneducated." "I may be educated," he says, "but I love and respect you." Just imagine, right now he's on the ladder right smack into the nobility.[13] Only the other day the wife of our clerk says to me, "You have quite a son, Arina Egorovna." "The kind of son," she says, "all of us envy." "Why, he's humble, respectful, and," she says, "you never hear of him getting into mischief." "Why on earth," she says, "don't you marry him off, Arina Egorovna?" Well, I thought to myself, "Don't think I don't know what you're driving at, I do." You see, Anna Petrovna, she has three daughters, and she's ready to give money galore, just to get them off her hands. Only, I tell you, her girls don't have a smidgen of education. I may be an uneducated woman, but I know how much an education means, nowadays. Well, I run home and say to my son, "Misha, my dear, don't you want to get married?" "You know," I say, "I'm having trouble beating off all these rich girls." "All of them, my dear," I say, "are falling in love with your gentleness and upbringing." "And," I say, "my dear, I'm not going to force you to do something you don't want—you're smarter and better educated than I am." "But when you come up with something," I say, "then let me know your thoughts, and I'll find you a bride." Then he says, "I may be an educated man, mama, but I always prefer to talk things over with you." So I say, "Any girl would give her eyeteeth to marry you." "I've got," I say, "a girl with money and beauty." Just imagine, Misha hugs me and tells me, "Mama dear, you don't find happiness in money." "Money, after all," he says, "doesn't have real value." "Go over to Anna Petrovna's," he says, "I respect her, and find out what she thinks of me." "More than anything else," he says, "I would like Marya Andrevna."[14]

ANNA.   I thank you with all my heart, Arina Egorovna. As for myself, I like your son a lot. I kept thinking I'd run over and see you, but it slipped my mind. I forget things all the time. Oh, good Lord, how I forget! You know, more than anything else I want to see Mashenka married as soon as possible. I'm using every way I can to find her a good husband. I'd better say right off

I've been spoiled all my life. When I was married, and with my husband—now at rest—I was spoiled. I lived like I was behind a stone wall, and I didn't fuss with anything at all. But now, you can see yourself, I work and work until I ache all over. Just tell me how you can get along without a man in the house? I'm a weak woman, dull and commonplace and forgetting all the time. If I could get her off my hands, I'd feel ever so much better.

KHORKOVA. You just keep on thinking of that, Anna Petrovna. Now you know my Misha's good points. Well, in society he's highly thought of, considering where he comes from. You take me, for instance. I'm a woman of plain and humble station in life, but I don't hold with the same ideas as people in my station. To tell the truth, I stay as far away from people in my circle as I can. I'm very aristocratic when it comes to my feelings.

ANNA. I'm not about to force Mashenka. She can have her own way. You tell Mikhailo Ivanych[15] he ought to try and please Mashenka. I'd be very happy if she decides to take him.

KHORKOVA. That boy of mine is the shyest thing alive, scared to death of his own shadow. Why, I tell him, "It's strange, Misha; here you're an educated man, and you're the shyest thing alive. With your mind and upbringing, my dear, what're you scared to death of? Any girl would be tickled to death to fall in love with you." That's what I tell him. Well, Anna Petrovna, you'll let me raise his hopes, then.

ANNA. Tell him that, for my part, I'm willing to go along with him. And I'll talk it over with Mashenka.

KHORKOVA. Thank you very much. We'll keep on hoping. [Silence.] That's a cute little cap you're wearing. What did you give for the ribbons?

ANNA. Oh, don't ask me. You know my memory is bad. Seems to me it was eighty or maybe seventy kopeks.

KHORKOVA. It's cute, the cutest thing I've seen. Lend me the pattern of your morning coat. I'd like to get one made of black moiré. Just imagine what I dream about at nights? Black moiré, that's what.

ANNA. Where on earth do you suppose I put it? I'll have to ask Darya. Now, if Mashenka gets married, why I'll get one made to order from somebody on Kuznetsky Bridge. Only a little bit dressier.

KHORKOVA. I'd never advise you to do that, Anna Petrovna. No, I wouldn't. I know a dressmaker pretty well. Why, she'd make you one that'd be simple and swanky. I'm a woman of plain and humble station in life, but I love to dress with taste and to make sure everything's swanky. Misha keeps saying to me: "Mama dear," he says, "who could help being surprised at you, when you have taste and common sense like you have?" "I love and respect you," he says. "It doesn't matter to me," he says, "that you've never received an education." Good-by, Anna Petrovna. Be sure to try and find that pattern for me.

ANNA. [*Rises.*] Let's go. It's probably in my room. We can look for it together. [*The two women cross to the door.* MILASHIN *enters.*]

MILASHIN. How do you do, Anna Petrovna?

ANNA. How do you do, Ivan Ivanych? Mashenka is probably walking in the garden. [MILASHIN *crosses to the window.*]

KHORKOVA. [*Looking keenly at* MILASHIN.] Who's that, Anna Petrovna?

ANNA. Milashin, Ivan Ivanych.[16]

KHORKOVA. Well, he wouldn't be much of a suitor for your daughter.

ANNA. Who said he was? I didn't. [*The two women exit.*]

MILASHIN. [*Alone at the window.*] Oh, no! Merich is here again. Just as I thought. I was expecting it. Boy, that irritates me, damn it all. No, I'm not going to put up with it. [*Walks about the room.*] How much time have I wasted, doing everything I could to please her? Why, I've knocked myself out, I have. And all for nothing. And now this fellow comes by and . . . I simply don't see how she can stand him, let alone be kind to him. If only I could get rid of him, somehow. Get married to her? Well, she won't take me because there is nothing to live on. Besides, she doesn't love me. Then why on earth should I keep knocking myself out? Be far simpler to go away, drop it, and forget about it. But, on the other hand, might be better to make her realize what she's giving up. I ought to say to her, "Marya Andreevna, you may have new acquaintances with whom you're happier than with the old, but you are losing a friend who was devoted to you." Of course, she will disagree with me, but I'll tell her, "All right." I'll say, "If it's better for you, then what can I do here? No doubt I bore you to death. Then, good-by." In fact, I'll say, "Good-by, forever." Then she'll say, "But why forever, Ivan Ivanych?" And I'll say, "If it's good-by, then it's good-by forever. At least I have character." Then, I'll grab my hat and walk out . . . But what happens then? Oh, damn it all. I suppose she'd be only too glad to see me walk out. And Merich would like it even more. Oh, no, you don't. I'll stay around, just to infuriate him. I'm going to come over here every day. I'm going to laugh at Merich, right in his face. So help me, I'll get rid of him, somehow.   [*Walks about the room.* MARYA *and* MERICH *enter.*]

MARYA.   How do you do, Ivan Ivanych? What do you say, have the matchmakers gone?

MILASHIN.   Looks like they have. I came across two on the way in.

MARYA.   Oh, I'm bored to death. [*Stands, deep in thought.*] Drop in to see us, Vladimir Vasilich,[17] as often as you can. Promise me.

MERICH.   Dare I disobey when you tell me to? Only I'll say it again, Marya Andrevna, I'm scared of you.

MARYA.   Come now, you're teasing me. I know you are. [MILASHIN *makes faces which are quite noticeable.* MARYA *speaks to* MILASHIN.]   What's the matter with you? Are you out of sorts today?

MILASHIN.   Yes, ma'am. I've a headache, somehow.

MERICH.   Headache? Too bad. Better do something for it. Good-by, Marya Andrevna, please give my best regards to your mama.

MARYA.   When are you coming back?

MERICH.   Tomorrow, if I may.

MARYA.   Of course you may. Be sure you come tomorrow. I'll expect you.

MERICH.   Without fail. [*Exits.* MARYA *crosses to the door.*]

MARYA.   Please don't fail me.

MERICH.   [*Behind the setting.*]   Word of honor!

MILASHIN.   What were you two talking about in the garden, Marya Andrevna?

MARYA.   But what's it to you? Seems to me you're pretty nosy.

MILASHIN.   Forgive me, Marya Andrevna, I didn't think you and Merich had deep, dark secrets. I didn't know. Maybe it's something or other you can't talk about?

MARYA.   Maybe.

MILASHIN.   [*After a brief pause.*]   Marya Andrevna, how come you don't like me?

MARYA.   Oh, go on with you. You're not serious. Why shouldn't I like you?

MILASHIN.   Of course, I'm not so good-looking, like Merich. I don't run around in society, and I don't speak French, either. Those are the things that count nowadays. Oh, do they count! Go on, be a silly ass, if you want to. Only you'd better know how to flirt and chatter on and on . . . That's what they like nowadays. Boy, that irritates the devil out of me.

MARYA.   Come now, you get along with people pretty well.

MILASHIN.   Please forgive me, Marya Andrevna, but I'm telling you the truth. It's not my fault if you don't like me. Just tell me in what way I'm worse than this Merich fellow. If I wanted to, I could be a hundred times better than he. Whippersnapper! Where on earth did he go to school? Only to some boarding school, where he learned to chatter on and on in French, no less. At least, I completed my course at the gymnasium. How dare he make fun of me? Why, he doesn't do anything. He's only in the service to receive first rank. So what if his father is rich? Doesn't matter in the least.

MARYA.   Come, he hasn't hurt you, has he?

MILASHIN.   Oh, for pity's sake, he is shallow. The most superficial person I know. [*Silence.*]

MARYA.   Look here, Ivan Ivanych, have you fallen in love with me? [MILASHIN *is confused and embarrassed.*] Oh, I'm sorry, poor thing . . . I didn't mean to . . . Forgive me.

MILASHIN.   Please don't feel sorry for me. What's to be done? You can't force someone to love you. Go on, make him happy. He is worthier than I.

DARYA.   [*Enters with samovar.*] Dear miss, Platon Markych has arrived.

MILASHIN.   A fine time!

MARYA.   And why not?

MILASHIN.   Simply because I don't like him, somehow.

MARYA.   Seems to me there's no one you do like. [ANNA *and* DOBROTVORSKY *enter.*]

DOBROTVORSKY.   And so, ma'am, that's the way the thing looks now.

ANNA.   I understand, Platon Markych, I understand. [*Sits at the table and pours tea.*]

DOBROTVORSKY.   How do you do, my dear young lady? Why is it you look unhappy today?

MARYA.   And is there anything special for me to be happy about, Platon Markych?

DOBROTVORSKY.   Well, that's true. A poor crop of suitors today, miss. Yes, a poor crop.

ANNA.   Wouldn't you like some tea?

DOBROTVORSKY.   Yes, ma'am. Nothing for brides to be happy about. Well, and just for you, my dear young lady, I'll try to run down a good one. One you'll thank me for. I knew your papa, now at rest, a long time. He was a benefactor to me. Pray, then don't worry about it. I'm going to try. Your hand, please.

MARYA.   No, what for, Platon Markych!

DOBROTVORSKY.   It's nothing, miss. Please. [*Kisses her hand.*]

ANNA.   Move over, Platon Markych, a little closer, here. [ANNA *and* DOBROTVORSKY *sit at one side of the table;* MARYA *and* MILASHIN, *at the other.*]

DOBROTVORSKY.   Yes, ma'am. Young men nowadays, I tell you, ma'am, are about played out. It's difficult to find suitors. In our day when we were young, it used to be that a boy was hardly dry behind the ears before he was in the service. And before you knew it, he was married. At that time, ma'am, Anna Petrovna, bachelors were scarce. In fact, among all of us at the law court, believe it or not, there wasn't a single, solitary bachelor. But nowadays, you can only marvel at the way young people live. Nowadays, everything's out of whack.

ANNA.   Out of whack, you said it! A nice how-d'ye-do, I must say. Oh, my. Oh, my. I think I've forgotten to give you sugar. Masha, did I put sugar in Platon Markych's tea, or not?

MARYA.   Yes, mama, you did.

DOBROTVORSKY.   Pray, ma'am, what were you saying?

ANNA.   I said, a nice how-d'ye-do, I must say. It's all wrong.

DOBROTVORSKY.   Yes, that's quite right. It's all wrong. In our day it wasn't at all like it is now. In fact, brides were far happier. They didn't have to sit around, waiting and waiting. Let's say the prospective bride had some sort of physical defect or other. Say, she was hunchbacked. Well, the boys weren't a bit squeamish about things like that. Why, my own sister-in-law, ma'am, had six fingers on her right hand, and her mother kept gasping because, she said, nobody'd ever take the girl . . .

ANNA.   Go on, tell me all about it.

DOBROTVORSKY.   A pretty good man came along, took her, and nothing ever happened. Like I told you, ma'am, brides were far happier then. They didn't have a thing to worry about.

MARYA.   Well, I certainly don't worry about it.

DOBROTVORSKY.   What do you mean, not worry about it, young lady? You don't talk about it, but how on earth can you stop worrying? Of course, it's the girls' affair. I know they don't talk about it, and they act as if they were guilty of something. But how can they help worrying? They do, every last one of them. I know what I'm talking about, ma'am, don't I?

ANNA.   Oh, you do, Platon Markych. Yes, you do. You can say that again. Would you like another little cup?

DOBROTVORSKY.   Please. There you are, my dear young lady, even your own mama says so. [Whispers to ANNA.]

MILASHIN.   Silly fool.

MARYA.   Why are you calling him names?

MILASHIN.   He doesn't understand you at all. He thinks you're worried about suitors, the same as his sister-in-law who had six fingers.

MARYA.   Oh, let him think what he wants to. He's a very good man.

MILASHIN.   All the same, what are they whispering about over there?

MARYA.   Obviously, something that concerns them.

DOBROTVORSKY.   [In a low voice.] A fine-looking person, ma'am, and he's still a young man. Very young. He is a secretary.

ANNA.   What?

DOBROTVORSKY.   [Louder.] A secretary, I tell you. His rank isn't high, but he has a good place. And plenty of things at home. His own horses, even.

ANNA.   What? I can't hear you.

DOBROTVORSKY.   His own horses, even.

MARYA.   What did he say?

MILASHIN.   Must be something interesting.

ANNA.   Listen here, Mashenka. Platon Markych has done us a

nice favor. He has found a man who'd like to take care of our affairs. He says he is a very good young man.

DOBROTVORSKY.   A fine-looking person, miss. And a smart dealer, to boot. Really knows his way around. Oh, does he!

ANNA.   I think I've forgotten all about you, Ivan Ivanych. [*Pours him tea.*] This person you're speaking of, Platon Markych, he doesn't drink, does he?

DOBROTVORSKY.   What do you mean, doesn't drink? Yes, he probably does drink. A little. If he drank a lot, everybody would hear about it.

ANNA.   There, Mashenka. It'd be nice if he liked you.

MARYA.   There you go again, mama, with the same old thing.

ANNA.   Oh, good Lord, what difference does it make? You know, you haven't seen him yet. Look him over and maybe you'll like him yourself.

DOBROTVORSKY.   I'll bring him over to see you, ma'am.

ANNA.   Oh, Platon Markych, how can I ever thank you? I really don't know how to tell you enough. You can see yourself, we're just women. What can we know? We just endure, that's all.

DOBROTVORSKY.   Oh, ma'am, no need to say anything. I had a lot of obligations to your husband, now at rest. I'll carry them to my grave. He was a benefactor to me. May God grant him the heavenly kingdom, the place of rest. How on earth can I ever pay him back? Well, I'm getting old. My brain can't hang on to everything.

MARYA.   [*Rises.*]   You heard it, Ivan Ivanych, didn't you?

MILASHIN.   [*Rises.*]   Yes, I did. It's terrible.

MARYA.   That's what I hear around here all the time. It goes on and on.

MILASHIN.   I don't know. I can't bring myself to it. The pure and simple thought that someday you'll belong to someone else is killing me. I don't think I can stand it.

MARYA.   The only person you think about is yourself. Why don't you think a little about me?

MILASHIN.   About you? Oh, I like that. Listen here, you. Maybe you'll like him. You'll be happy, then. Well, what about it? As for me, I'm ready right now to sacrifice my life, just so you'll be happy.

MARYA.   What are you going on for? I've heard about enough.

Stop it, please. Let's go into the garden.   [MARYA *and* MILASHIN *exit.*]

DOBROTVORSKY.   I'll bring him over tomorrow, ma'am. We'll talk a little about business, and he can take a look at Marya Andrevna. Maybe, he'll like her. There, we'll do two things at the same time.

ANNA.   That's good, Platon Markych, very good. I can't get the lawsuit out of my head. You know I can't sleep nights. Well, if they strip the house out from under us, what am I going to do then, I'd like to know? It's about time to marry off Mashenka. About time, really and truly.

DOBROTVORSKY.   Why on earth wait, my dear? The time is right now. I thank you a lot, ma'am. [*Turns his cup upside down.*] I'll bid you good-by.

ANNA.   Good-by, Platon Markych. We'll be expecting you, then.

DOBROTVORSKY.   Very good, ma'am.   [*They exit.*]

ACT TWO

SCENE ONE.

A small, shady garden is represented on the stage. To the right of the audience, a bench, behind which is a large bush. MIKHAILO KHORKOV, *his head hanging down, is sitting on the bench.*

MIKHAILO. I walked out, got cold feet. I'm just a coward. Yes, cowardly and miserable. After all's said and done, look what I'm doing to myself. Why is it I'm destroying myself? Three years have gone by already since I finished my course of study. And in those three years I've done nothing for myself. Absolutely nothing. I feel cold all over whenever I think how I spent those three years. In laziness, spending each day like a holiday, going through the motions of a shameful bachelor's life. And no aspirations at all to get out of a life like that, not one single drop of ambition. If I had to depend on myself to make a decision, I'd never make it. I know I wouldn't. I have one saving grace, and that's Marya Andrevna. But I don't dare tell her that I love her. No, it's time I stopped this nonsense. Surely, she will find compassion for me. Won't she? I'll start to work for her sake. Yes, I'll toil for her. She, and she alone, could lead me back to life again. [*Sits.*] Oh, dear God, how I love that girl! How I love her! [KHORKOVA *enters.*]
KHORKOVA. [*Sitting on the bench.*] Aren't you ashamed of yourself, Misha? Why did you go away? I'd just started telling Marya Andrevna how you love her and how you regard her, and right

then and there you ran off. I'm an uneducated woman, and I never get mixed up. But you? Why, you get mixed up over everything.

MIKHAILO.   Oh, mama! Do me a favor and don't talk to Marya Andrevna. I'll talk to her myself. The way it is now, you're forever saying God knows what about me.

KHORKOVA.   Yes, wait for you! It's strange, Misha, here you're an educated man, and . . .

MIKHAILO.   Yes, mama, I'm educated. I've a good heart. Besides that, I know she'd be happy with me, that I alone can appreciate her. I know too that she might be destroyed in that circle, a victim of calculation or ignorance. But I'm afraid she'll turn me down.

KHORKOVA.   Oh, good Lord! Look here, she's not the only girl in the world. We'll find another.

MIKHAILO.   Where will I find another like her? It's a good thing I happened to meet Marya Andrevna, to come to know her, and to fall in love. Believe me when I say I love only Marya Andrevna. I can see no one but her. I didn't think I could fall so much in love. I've worn myself out the past few days. You see, I'm weeping. I can't live without her.

KHORKOVA.   Well, if you love her, then tell her how you feel. That's the way it's always done.

MIKHAILO.   I'll talk to her. I've got to talk to her. It's time I stopped this nonsense, somehow. But what if she refuses me? Now, at least I have hope, I have dreams. But what will I have then?

KHORKOVA.   It's strange, Misha, here you're an educated man. But what you're doing, how can I even look at you? You don't have one solitary friend. You're not doing a single thing. You lie around the house in your dressing gown, with a pipe. Right now you've fallen in love, but you're scared to death to tell her. Just look around you and see how other educated men live. Why, the girls themselves are running after them. There, looks like Marya Andrevna is coming here.

MIKHAILO.   Mama, for God's sake, don't say a word!

KHORKOVA.   Do me a favor and don't start teaching me. I may be an uneducated woman, but I know how to behave myself. [MARYA *enters.* KHORKOVA *rises.*]   You're out to take a little walk.

MARYA. Yes, to get a little fresh air. [*To* MIKHAILO.] What are you doing here?

MIKHAILO. Why, miss, I'm dreaming . . .

KHORKOVA. Oh, you can see he feels miserable.

MARYA. About what?

KHORKOVA. Probably fallen in love. I notice it by the way he talks.

MIKHAILO. Mama!

KHORKOVA. Just see how he's pining away. Really, my heart aches just to look at him.

MIKHAILO. Mama! Oh, good Lord!

MARYA. I can't believe it, really. And whom has Mikhailo Ivanych fallen in love with?

KHORKOVA. Now, that's one you should ask yourself, if you've got a mind to. Misha! [*Makes a sign to him and exits.*]

MARYA. [*Sitting next to* MIKHAILO.] Why are you down in the dumps? Tell me the truth. Are you in love?

MIKHAILO. Yes. I don't know what's happened to me.

MARYA. And I've spent the whole day in tears.

MIKHAILO. What were you crying about?

MARYA. Mama keeps pestering me with suitors. Yesterday it was some old merchant, and today an official[18] is to arrive. What do you think about that?

MIKHAILO. It's terrible.

MARYA. Yes, it is. Besides— Mikhailo Ivanych, I'm going to talk openly to you, because we are good friends. Isn't that so? [*Holds out her hand to him.*]

MIKHAILO. [*Takes her hand.*] Say what you want. I'm listening.

MARYA. I'm a little in love, myself.

MIKHAILO. [*Rises quickly.*] You?

MARYA. What frightened you so much? Don't worry, it's not you.

MIKHAILO. No, miss. It's just that I . . . Forgive me.

MARYA. Oh, my, that frightened you, didn't it? Did you think I'd fallen in love with you? Don't be afraid, don't. I'm not going to disturb your composure. [*Silence.*] Well, that's the kind of situation I'm in, Mikhailo Ivanych. What would you advise me to do?

MIKHAILO. I, miss? I've nothing definite in mind.

MARYA. Right now I can't marry anyone. Maybe a week ago I'd have gotten married if the right man had come by.

MIKHAILO.   Do you mean, there's no one?

MARYA.   Definitely, no one.

MIKHAILO.   And if I were to ask for your hand, myself? [*Forces a laugh.*] I ask you, just for the fun of it.

MARYA.   I wouldn't marry you, either. We are friends, but I can't love you.

MIKHAILO.   [*With growing excitement.*] But what if I loved you? Tried to please you, what then? If I were willing and ready to grant your slightest wish? Receive every caress with my heartfelt thanks?

MARYA.   [*Having glanced at him.*] You're joking, aren't you? But say you were to ask, it wouldn't be difficult for me at all. I could tell you frankly that I don't love you, and you wouldn't be hurt in the least. Anyone else would resent it, but not you.

MIKHAILO.   Yes. Yes, of course. [*Silence.*]

MARYA.   Tell me, what sort of man is Merich?

MIKHAILO.   Merich?

MARYA.   Yes, Vladimir Vasilich?

MIKHAILO.   I don't know what to say, Marya Andrevna. Really, I don't know.

MARYA.   That means you don't want to say. All right, then. Good-by. I'd better go in now. I must go see mama. [*Exits.*]

MIKHAILO.   What a silly fool I am! To dream of happiness. Oh, dear God. Dear God in heaven! [*Sits, covering his face with his hands.* MILASHIN *and* MERICH *enter.*]

MERICH.   What are we celebrating here today? Darya is all dressed up. Dolled up so much she won't look at you. Just runs back and forth in her starched skirts.

MILASHIN.   They're expecting guests.

MERICH.   What kind of guests, exactly?

MILASHIN.   Oh, a certain official is coming to handle Anna Petrovna's business. And I suppose they have every intention of looking him over as a suitor for Marya Andrevna. Boy, that irritates me, damned if it doesn't.

MERICH.   Why don't you marry Marya Andrevna?

MILASHIN.   I, sir? For the simplest possible reason. What do you think we'd live on? Nothing, nothing at all. I don't have property, and she doesn't, either.

MERICH.   What about love? Even a hut is paradise with the man you love. Seems to me she loves you.

MILASHIN.   Sure she does. Yes, sir, you can say that again. Ha! Don't tell me you've noticed something?

MERICH.   No, Ivan Ivanych. I just said it for fun. She doesn't love you.

MILASHIN.   Why do you think so?

MERICH.   I don't think so. I know so. She told me herself.

MILASHIN.   It's strange Marya Andrevna would say something like that. It's even insulting. Of course, it's all the same to me whether she loves me or not. I'm not about to pay attention to that. In fact, I'm not a bit concerned about her. But why discuss it? By saying that she wants to prove I'm running after her. Well, I'm not. Let the other fellows do the running.

MERICH.   Nicely put! And if I were in your place I'd do the same. Still, it's too bad she's getting married. She's a mighty pretty girl. I always think it's too bad when pretty girls get married. What about you? Do you feel the same way?

MILASHIN.   No, I don't.

MERICH.   Not so long ago Sofi Barashkova[19] got married, too. You knew her, didn't you?

MILASHIN.   No, I didn't.

MERICH.   We were pretty much attached to each other. I'm going to tell you a secret, Ivan Ivanych. And, of course, you won't say a word to anyone. Sofi Barashkova was madly in love with me. Say, just look at the sort of letter she wrote me before the wedding. [*Takes out the letter.*]   Like to read it?

MILASHIN.   Why on earth should I read someone else's letter?

MERICH.   All right, it's up to you. [*Hides it again.*]   I hope you won't say a word to anyone. No doubt Marya Andreva is inside. I'll go see her. [*Exits.*]

MIKHAILO.   Ivan Ivanych.

MILASHIN.   Oh, you're here. I didn't even notice you.

MIKHAILO.   Tell me, does that Merich come around here often?

MILASHIN.   It used to be he was around scarcely at all, but lately he's started coming every day.

MIKHAILO.   That's bad?

MILASHIN.   Well, just put yourself in my situation. He comes here every day, the devil knows why.

MIKHAILO.   So, what's it to you?

MILASHIN.   No, say what you like, Mikhailo Ivanych, but it irritates the devil out of me.

MIKHAILO.   But it hasn't a thing to do with you. He might have
a bad effect on Marya Andrevna. Very bad. I've known him a
long time. Listen, when he was still a kid at boarding school,
he used to write letters to himself and then brag to his buddies
that he'd received them from young women. If you have influence on Marya Andrevna, then tell her to be on guard. I'd
be terribly sorry if she believed him. Why, he's shallow.
Superficial.

MILASHIN.   All right, Mikhailo Ivanych. Thanks a lot for opening my eyes to that fellow. I'll tell her, for sure.

MIKHAILO.   She'll believe you, won't she?

MILASHIN.   Believe me? Certainly, she'll believe me. She loves
me very much.

MIKHAILO.   Hardly, Ivan Ivanych. Seems to me she doesn't love
you at all.

MILASHIN.   Why do you think that? Don't tell me I'm worse
than the other fellows? No, excuse me, please! You don't know
me. Listen, women like me a lot.

MIKHAILO.   Well, let's assume you're right. Only you'd better
be pretty clever about it, so Marya Andrevna doesn't think
we're fooling around out of jealousy. Ekh, I don't want anything to do with him, or I'd chase him out of here right now.

MILASHIN.   You'd like me to do it, wouldn't you? Listen, I'm
going to laugh at him, right in his face.

MIKHAILO.   Nothing will come of it, then. Marya Andrevna will
get mad at you, and then you've had it. Oh, what business is it
of ours? Let them do what they want.   [*Silence.*]   That Merich
is some character all right. One time, part of his diary accidentally
fell into my hands, together with several letters he'd written to
our neighbor, a woman. Of course, she'd handed them over to
her husband. Boy, you should read them. What didn't he put
in them!

MILASHIN.   Let me have those letters for a while.

MIKHAILO.   What are they to you? All right, they're yours, if
you like.

MILASHIN.   Thank you, ever so much.   [*Takes him by the hand.*]
You've done me a great favor.

MIKHAILO.   Why thank me for it? I'm concerned about Marya
Andrevna, not about you, because I love her very much and I'm
interested in her welfare.

MILASHIN.   And I love . . .

MIKHAILO.   I believe you. Merich might do a lot of harm to Marya Andrevna. He is a man without principles. Completely without principles.

MILASHIN.   And I'm sick and tired of him. He's trying to smear me in the eyes of Marya Andrevna. He's getting in my way.

MIKHAILO.   Let's go home, Ivan Ivanych. I don't think there's a thing we can do here.

MILASHIN.   No, I can't walk out now. I must stay here. Marya Andrevna will no doubt get mad if I leave.

MIKHAILO.   Don't worry about it. She won't get mad, either. Right now you're the farthest thing from her thoughts. You know Anna Petrovna's expecting some official or other today. She wants to ask him about her lawsuit. What can you possibly do here?

MILASHIN.   All right, let's go. [MIKHAILO *and* MILASHIN *exit.* MERICH *and* MARYA *enter from the other side.*]

MERICH.   Good-by, Marya Andrevna.

MARYA.   Where are you going? I'll be bored to death here alone. Sit down a little longer. [*They sit.*]

MERICH.   I heard from Milashin, Marya Andrevna, they're after some sort of husband for you.

MARYA.   Yes, Vladimir Vasilich, it goes on and on. One minute, it's this fellow; the next minute, that one.

MERICH.   And you'll take one of them?

MARYA.   I don't know. But what can I do? I must get married, it seems.

MERICH.   Well, as far as I'm concerned, I don't see the necessity for it at all. Surely, there's nothing forcing you into this marriage?

MARYA.   There are many reasons. You don't know the difficulties we're in.

MERICH.   But, good Lord, don't tell me they're that pressing?

MARYA.   Mama says they are.

MERICH.   It's terrible. To sacrifice yourself. What are you doing, Marya Andrevna? You were created to love and to be loved. Pretty as you are, you were made so men could admire your beauty. Why, you don't have the right to deprive us of that treat. To go and give yourself to one man for the rest of your life.

MARYA. Oh, you're always joking.

MERICH. No, I'm not joking. Just think, Marya Andrevna, what kind of a life you'll lead. One moment of true love is worth far more than binding yourself to one man the rest of your life. Well, when it comes to matters of the heart, I wouldn't listen to your mama. You want to destroy your own happiness and the happiness of others, just for your mama's sake. Why, keep thinking that way, and you're no more than a child.

MARYA. Yes, if only happiness like that were possible for me. The way it is now, I have nothing to regret, nothing to expect. Nothing at all. No one loves me, and I don't love anyone, either.

MERICH. You love no one?

MARYA. No one.

MERICH. And no one loves you?

MARYA. As far as I know.

MERICH. Well, that's a horse of a different color, isn't it? But, all the same, it's terrible to sacrifice yourself, just to settle someone else's accounts.

MARYA. What can I do? I'll choose some person with property, and hopefully he will satisfy some of the things I want in a man.

MERICH. Where on earth did you find such determination, I'd like to know? Such practical principles, too.

MARYA. Necessity teaches us, that's all.

MERICH. If you've made up your mind, I'm not about to shake your decision. It's pretty admirable of you. But tell me something. What would happen if you fell in love with someone? If you happened to meet a man who loved you with all his heart, with all the fire of youthful passion?

MARYA. I don't know, Vladimir Vasilich, but I doubt if it would ever happen.

MERICH. [In a melancholy tone.] Now, when the whole thing's over, when you've agreed to sacrifice yourself, just for your mama's sake—of course, something like that's very admirable— but when you've agreed to all that, I can tell you that I loved you, Marya Andrevna, loved you passionately. And I still love you in a way nobody else will ever love you.

MARYA. Vladimir Vasilich, you're not leading me on, are you?

MERICH. Oh, no. No . . .

MARYA. You're not deceiving me?

MERICH.   Listen, I swear before . . .

MARYA.   No, don't. You don't need to. Oh, Vladimir Vasilich. Don't deceive me, for God's sake. It's easy for you to lead me on because I . . . I love you . . .

MERICH.   My angel. I can't believe my own happiness. Why are you weeping? Oh, Marya Andrevna . . . Mashenka . . . Meri! [20] [*Kisses her hand.*] Now, look at me. God in heaven, you're pretty. Oh, how pretty you are, right at this moment. I wish everyone in the whole world could see you now. Yes, see you with tears in your eyes.

MARYA.   I was wrong, wasn't I? Wrong to tell you.

MERICH.   Why on earth, wrong? You feel guilty, simply because you have a heart. Why, you're worth far more than those puppet-like girls, those dolls without an ounce of feeling, who go around bragging that they've never been in love. Listen, I can appreciate your love.

MARYA.   I hope so. [*Presses herself against him.*] Oh, don't look at me. I'm a silly fool, really. I thought I had the strength to hide my love.

MERICH.   But why hide it?

MARYA.   Yes. Now, of course, there's no reason to. On the contrary, now I want to open my heart, all at once, so you will know how much I love you.

MERICH.   Why? The way you are now, you are worth more to me than anything in the whole world.

MARYA.   No, Vladimir, no. You don't love me the way I love you. You are everything to me now. Everything, everything. Do you believe what I say?

MERICH.   Do you believe me?

MARYA.   I don't know. I want to believe, but I'm afraid. It would be cruel of you to deceive me.

MERICH.   Why all these gloomy thoughts? Just see how all nature smiles on us. [*They sit for a while, silently.*]

MARYA.   Oh, good Lord, I completely forgot. A certain official is coming to see us today. Mama's running around inside now. She told me to dress up.

MERICH.   He isn't some sort of suitor, is he?

MARYA.   I don't know. Now, there's no reason for you to worry. I'll tell mama I don't like him. I'll do it, somehow.

MERICH.   Think he'll come soon?

MARYA.   Yes, pretty soon.

MERICH.   Then I'd better go. Good-by, dear. [*Rises from the bench.*]

MARYA.   Good-by. When will I see you again? Come tomorrow, in the morning. Mama won't be home.

MERICH.   [*Kisses her.*] I'll be here, I will. Good-by, dear. [*Exits.*]

MARYA.   [*Alone, leaning against a tree.*]   He's gone. Was I right to do it? I'm ashamed, and yet I'm happy. But, what if it's only joking on his part? Oh, dear God, I'm ashamed of myself. Ashamed. [*Silence.*]   But, what if he should really love me? Before, he seemed bored, even melancholy. He told me that up till now he's been constantly deceived in women. Oh, I'd really like to know if he loves me. And I love him so very much. What I wouldn't do for him! Everything, everything, everything! [*Stands, covering her face with a handkerchief.* DARYA *enters.*]

DARYA.   Oh, the hell with you! [21] I've run my legs off the whole day long. Miss! Oh, miss! Are you here?

MARYA.   Oh, what?

DARYA.   I'm looking for you, my dear. Been running around like a cat on fire. Somebody's just arrived, and your mama is asking for you.

MARYA.   He's here. Oh, dear God!

DARYA.   Let's go. I'll fix your hair, and you'd better put on another dress.

MARYA.   Let's go, let's go.   [*They exit.*]

SCENE TWO.

The same room as in the first act. DOBROTVORSKY *and* BENEVO-LENSKY *enter.*

DOBROTVORSKY.   This way, Maksim Dorofeich,[22] please. I must confess we didn't expect you this early. You hurried, dear boy, didn't you? Just to favor us as early as possible. Well, as you know, it has to do with a woman's lawsuit. You don't mind waiting a bit.

BENEVOLENSKY.   You told me there was a young lady here, a pretty young lady. Watch out, you know I'm discriminating.

DOBROTVORSKY.   Come now, no question about it, Maksim Dorofeich, for pity's sake. The young lady's something, so much so a general wouldn't be ashamed to take her. I knew her papa very well. . . .

BENEVOLENSKY.   But has she had a good education?

DOBROTVORSKY.   Oh, the best, the very best.

BENEVOLENSKY.   Aha, that's it. Surely, you know me, Platon Markych. I have property and position. Yes, and colleagues. I must have the kind of bride I wouldn't be ashamed to show off in society. Well, she must be the hostess in my home, you know, and wear the little cap they wear nowadays. She must receive whoever comes to the house. . . . Well, her tone must be fashionable. Understand me?

DOBROTVORSKY.   Why shouldn't I? Of course, no sense of you going to extremes and marrying a bad-looking woman, is there? You're something special yourself, you know. How about it, my boy? You old reprobate, you. [*Pats him on the back and then bows.*]

BENEVOLENSKY.   Aha, that's it, exactly. Tell me, has my shirt gotten out behind?

DOBROTVORSKY.   No, sir, nothing's wrong. Everything's right in order. No doubt you'd like to comb your hair. Here's a comb.

BENEVOLENSKY.   [*Takes it and combs his hair in front of the mirror.*]   Well, that's the way it goes, brother. You say the young lady's good-looking?

DOBROTVORSKY.   Oh, you'll see soon enough, Maksim Dorofeich. Why talk ahead of time? You can see for yourself.

BENEVOLENSKY.   We'll take a look, brother, we will. But will they give her to me, if I like her?

DOBROTVORSKY.   Of course, I don't see why they wouldn't. Well, you know what they always say, "To get it is one thing, to ask for it is another."

BENEVOLENSKY.   All right, brother, all right. [*Sits.*]   Platon Markych! Have you seen my drozhky,[23] or not?

DOBROTVORSKY.   No, I haven't, sir.

BENEVOLENSKY.   But you've seen my black horse, haven't you, the new trace-horse? Here, take a look!   [*Points out the window.*] Tell me, he's a good one, isn't he?

DOBROTVORSKY.   Oh, you old rascal, you. At it again, aren't you, Maksim Dorofeich? I suppose you're going to say you didn't buy it?

BENEVOLENSKY.   Of course not.

DOBROTVORSKY.   Well, then don't look a gift horse in the mouth. [*Silence.*]

BENEVOLENSKY.   Listen, Platon Markych, find me a mouth organ somewhere.

DOBROTVORSKY.   If you like, my boy. What do you need it for?

BENEVOLENSKY.   To teach canaries.

DOBROTVORSKY.   All right, I'll look for one.

BENEVOLENSKY.   Do that.   [*Pulls out his snuffbox and takes a pinch.*]   Like some?

DOBROTVORSKY.   [*Takes a pinch; then takes snuffbox and weighs it, first in one hand, then in the other.*]   A beautiful little thing. Pray, where did you get it?

BENEVOLENSKY.   Well, a good man ran into me unexpectedly. You remember, don't you, we had a case of the merchant Peresemkin with the young heirs of the merchant's niece, Akulina Nezamaikina.[24] It got as far as the government senate and was sent back for information. . . .   [ANNA *enters.*]   I have the honor to present myself, Collegiate Secretary Benevolensky.[25]

ANNA.   I'm very happy to meet you. Won't you please sit down? Pray, are you in the service, sir?

BENEVOLENSKY.   Why, I've been in service, ma'am, since 1838. I can tell you I'm very pleased with my position and with my superiors. I'm a hard-working man in the service, strict with my subordinates.

ANNA.   And do you have relatives here in Moscow?

BENEVOLENSKY.   No, absolutely no one, ma'am.

ANNA.   I'm thinking you . . .   [*To* DOBROTVORSKY.]   What's his name, Platon Markych? I keep forgetting it.

DOBROTVORSKY.   Maksim Dorofeich.

ANNA.   I've no memory, Maksim Dorofeich, none at all. Well, what are you going to do, really? I believe you must be pretty bored, Maksim Dorofeich. See, I judge by myself. I'm just a woman, you know. When my husband was still alive I got along somehow. Well, I was pretty well up on things. But now I simply don't know what to do.

BENEVOLENSKY.   I agree with you, ma'am.

ANNA.   Here's this legal action now. How can I do it without a man around? No doubt I'll lose it.

BENEVOLENSKY.   But pray tell me what your lawsuit consists of.

ANNA.   I don't remember all of it. If I did I'd muddle it up, no doubt. But Platon Markych here can tell you the story.

DOBROTVORSKY.   Go into the matter, dear Maksim Dorofeich, please do.

BENEVOLENSKY.   All right, I'll look into it. If it's possible, ma'am, to do anything at all, we'll do it. If there's nothing we can do, then don't get upset. We have a way of getting things done. Of course, whoever isn't a sinner before God, isn't to blame before the tsar. But I can tell you right off that nowadays they're pretty strict about it.

DOBROTVORSKY.   Precisely, my dear lady, strict. He's telling you the truth. They've gone and tightened everything up. Yes, that's it exactly.

ANNA.   Tell me, please.

BENEVOLENSKY.   Nowadays you've got to be on guard, keep your ears cleaned out. I'll tell you about myself. I'm in constant fear. It's impossible not to slip up here and there. Before you know it, they'll drag you into court, drive you out of the service, and then where do you go? Well, all right, I'm a bachelor, but a married man . . .

ANNA.   But don't you intend to settle down as a married man?

BENEVOLENSKY.   That question, ma'am, is very important in life, especially in mine. I have property, plenty of things at home. I keep my own horses, even. If you could only see what I have in my apartment. Platon Markych here has seen it. You've seen my apartment, Platon Markych, haven't you?

DOBROTVORSKY.   How could I help seeing it, sir? An excellent apartment.

BENEVOLENSKY.   Therefore, what should I look for, I ask you?

ANNA.   A companion for life, Maksim Dorofeich. I think that's it.

BENEVOLENSKY.   I agree with you, ma'am. But, as far as I know, every wife is a companion for life. I must first of all look for a hostess. My business is to make as much as I can, but her business is to run the house. There's no sense of order in my house; I suppose you know they pilfer from a bachelor. Anything at all can happen, anything.

ANNA.   I shouldn't wonder, Maksim Dorofeich.

DOBROTVORSKY.   It's no wonder sinning happens so easily. That's for sure.

BENEVOLENSKY.   The girl I want should be good-looking and well-educated, so I wouldn't be ashamed to show her off in society, or out riding anywhere. Although the circle I run around in isn't high up in society, almost all of them are minor officials; but all the same, don't you know, I'll say right out it's nice to have a pretty and well-educated wife. But most of all, I need a hostess.

ANNA.   Your argument is fair, Maksim Dorofeich. But maybe you want someone with a big dowry?

BENEVOLENSKY.   I? No, ma'am, I'm not looking for that. They're not about to give me a girl with property, simply because my origin's pretty insignificant. And my place in society isn't high, either. Of course, there are available girls in the aristocracy who are educated but poor. And for them—I tell you without pride—a suitor like me would be a godsend.

ANNA.   I agree with you, Maksim Dorofeich.

BENEVOLENSKY.   Goes without saying, nobody can praise me for my good looks. As for my education, I received—as the expression goes around common folks—a copper-money training. But I've been around enough so I don't get muddled up in society. And I can say that with the ladies I'm pretty free and easy. Now I ask you, what are good looks in a man, exactly? It's the last thing you think of.

ANNA.   Silly and foolish to give it a single thought, Maksim Dorofeich. That's all it is, giddy and outlandish.

BENEVOLENSKY.   A smart girl pays no attention to good looks. For her it's enough if the man has brains. . . . Well, then he must know how to dress the right way.

ANNA.   And he doesn't drink . . .

BENEVOLENSKY.   Of course, but don't you know, ma'am, if I may put it bluntly, that in a man even that doesn't mean a thing. Platon Markych, what do you think about it?

DOBROTVORSKY.   Doesn't mean a thing, ma'am, Anna Petrovna. It doesn't bother a man. He could be a good person and still . . .

ANNA.   Well, how do you mean, Platon Markych? Perhaps if now and again, but more than . . .

BENEVOLENSKY.   In a woman it's a crime, I agree with you. But for a man it sometimes constitutes an indispensable need. Especially if he is a man of business. Why, he must have some kind of diversion. Goes without saying, I myself would be the first to denounce those who have a great weakness for it. [*Silence.*]   There it is, ma'am, the kind of opinion I have about marriage. However, there's no reason for me to hurry. I can pick a bride exactly in accordance with my wishes.

DOBROTVORSKY.   Why should you hurry? No need for you to push it!   [MARYA *enters.*]

ANNA.   My daughter, Mashenka. Maksim Dorofeich Benevolensky.

BENEVOLENSKY.   Very pleased to meet you.   [*Crosses to kiss her hand; then sits next to her; very friendly.*]   I hear you like music a lot. That so?

MARYA.   Sometimes if I'm bored, I'll play.

ANNA.   That's not right. No, it isn't. She sits at the piano all the time. You can't drag her away. Now what is it, Masha, you play so much? I keep forgetting.

MARYA.   Really, I don't know. I play a lot of things.

ANNA.   No, there's something. What were you playing today?

MARYA.   From *Robert the Devil*, "Grace."

ANNA.   Yes, yes.   [*In a low voice.*]   Be a little more friendly.

BENEVOLENSKY.   Imagine, I've never seen a single opera. They say the music is very good. One time we got together a group, but the whole thing fell through.

ANNA.   What happened?

BENEVOLENSKY.   Very simple. We went straight from the office to dinner in a tavern, so we could go on from there to the theatre. Well, we were young at the time, and we forgot about the theatre. So we spent the whole evening in the tavern.

MARYA.   [*In a low voice.*]   That's terrible.

BENEVOLENSKY.   I also like music, myself. But, unfortunately, I don't play one single instrument. And for a man of business, who needs it? One time I played the guitar, but later on I gave it up. Had no time for it, absolutely no time.

MARYA. [*To herself.*] Oh, dear God in heaven!

BENEVOLENSKY. [*To* MARYA.] Maybe you've taken up literature? Young ladies usually read novels. In boarding school they even start reading them on the sly, because of the supervisor.

MARYA. Yes, I read a little. And you?

BENEVOLENSKY. I stopped it altogether. There was a time I read. But now, don't you know, I've so much business I read nothing. Nothing at all.

ANNA. You're not serious, Mashenka. When would Maksim Dorofeich find time to read? He has lots to do without it, without all that stuff and nonsense.

BENEVOLENSKY. What is it they're writing these days? Tell me.

ANNA. God knows what they're writing. Whatever it is you can be sure it's never once happened. That's all it is, giddy and outlandish.

DOBROTVORSKY. You said it, ma'am, giddy and outlandish. That's it, daydreams.

BENEVOLENSKY. No doubt they write mostly about love?

ANNA. What do you mean, love? It's all stuff and nonsense, it's never once happened. Wouldn't you like some tea, Maksim Dorofeich?

BENEVOLENSKY. No, ma'am, thank you a lot. You can be sure I'm no lover of that.

DOBROTVORSKY. What's tea good for, ma'am? We're not the kind of guests who drink tea. But if you have something brought in, then Maksim Dorofeich and I might have a drop or two to go with it.

ANNA. At once, my dear, at once. Excuse me, I won't be gone more than a minute. [*Exits.*]

BENEVOLENSKY. That wasn't a bad idea you came up with, Platon Markych. [*Takes out his watch. To* MARYA.] I usually drink vodka about this time. It's something of a habit with me.

DOBROTVORSKY. Hee, hee, hee! What do you mean, tea? You think we're children, little kids, maybe?

BENEVOLENSKY. Your mama argues about love like an old man. I didn't want to contradict her, because I know how to respect old folks. But I have a different opinion altogether about love. I have a tender heart myself, just ready for love. Only I have a lot of business. You'd never believe it, but I've no time to think about love. No time at all. [*Looks at her tenderly.*] What kind of candy do you like?

MARYA. I don't like any at all.

BENEVOLENSKY. It's not possible. You're deceiving me. You'd like me to guess your taste. Permit me to bring you some the next time. Platon Markych, what kind of candy does Marya Andrevna like? She's not about to say.

DOBROTVORSKY. I don't know, sir. Better ask her mama.

BENEVOLENSKY. All right, we'll ask her.

MARYA. Please, don't trouble yourself. I don't want any candy.

BENEVOLENSKY. Well, whatever you like, but I'll bring some all the same. Permit me to ask you to play something or other.

MARYA. I've nothing to play, really.

BENEVOLENSKY. Do me the favor. Otherwise, I'm going to beg you on my knees.

MARYA. Oh, no! Why should you? Very well. [*Sits at the piano, strikes several chords, and starts to play.* ANNA *enters, followed by* DARYA *bringing in hors d'oeuvres.* DARYA *puts them on the table and exits.*]

ANNA. Please help yourself, Maksim Dorofeich. Without ceremony, please.

BENEVOLENSKY. Don't trouble yourself.

DOBROTVORSKY. You go ahead and start. [*Pours vodka.*] Please.

BENEVOLENSKY. [*Drinks, then takes a bite and, before he has stopped chewing, crosses to the piano and starts singing with the music.* MARYA *turns around and glances at him questioningly.*] I didn't get the pitch. Do me the favor to continue.

ANNA. Play, Mashenka.

DOBROTVORSKY. Marya Andrevna plays excellently.

BENEVOLENSKY. Quite nimble-fingered. I had a friend who was a prince regent among singers. And he could play anything, whatever you liked, on the piano. He taught himself and played by ear. Only thing, he had no agility in his fingers. Well, he'd play whatever you liked, but not nimble-fingered.

DOBROTVORSKY. Don't you want to give that old saying, Maksim Dorofeich? How does it go? Repetition . . .

BENEVOLENSKY. *Est mater studiorum.*[26] Yes, that's true. Pour me another.

DOBROTVORSKY. [*Pours vodka.*] Please. It's ready, sir.

BENEVOLENSKY. [*Drinks and takes a bite.*] Excellent sturgeon.

ANNA. That I don't know, Maksim Dorofeich. If the merchant didn't deceive me, then it's good. I have to do and go everywhere myself. I'm just a woman, you know it yourself. Doesn't take much to deceive me. In things like this there's nothing you can do without a man around. How can you ever get along without a man? You just tell me how, yourself.

DOBROTVORSKY. [*Leads* BENEVOLENSKY *to one side and speaks in a low voice.*] Well, dear boy, Maksim Dorofeich, how does our young lady strike you?

BENEVOLENSKY. Listen here, Platon Markych, the only thing I'll say is this. I am in love. I'm a man of business. You know me, I'm not one to fuss around with trifles. But I tell you, I am in love. Seems to me, that's enough. [*Crosses to* MARYA *and again sings with the music.*]

ANNA. [*To* DOBROTVORSKY.] What did he say to you?

DOBROTVORSKY. He says he's in love.

ANNA. What?

DOBROTVORSKY. He is in love, he says.

ANNA. Well, thank the Lord. Keep him entertained, my dear. Really let him have it!

DOBROTVORSKY. All right, ma'am, all right. Maksim Dorofeich, please have a little wine, won't you?

BENEVOLENSKY. Fill it up.

MARYA. [*Stops playing but remains sitting at the piano.*] I am tired.

BENEVOLENSKY. I thank you with all my heart. You play excellently. The important thing is you don't get flustered. Young ladies usually get flustered. [*Looks at his watch.*] Excuse me, Anna Petrovna, it's time I left. I have a lot of things to do. You know I am a man of business. Permit me to drink a glass of wine and bid you good-by. [*Crosses to table and drinks.*] You're coming with me, aren't you, Platon Markych?

DOBROTVORSKY. Yes, I am, Maksim Dorofeich.

BENEVOLENSKY. Well, let's go, I'll take you as far as your home.

ANNA. But, Maksim Dorofeich, wouldn't you like a bite of something?

BENEVOLENSKY. No, ma'am, thank you a lot. I'll drink another glass of wine and do myself the honor of wishing you good-by.

[*Drinks and bows. Crosses to* MARYA *and kisses her hand.*]   Until the pleasure of seeing you again. No doubt, you'll permit me to come visit you once more.

ANNA.   Do us the favor. We'll be very happy.

BENEVOLENSKY.   And I'll bring some candy. Yes, I certainly will. [*Exits with* DOBROTVORSKY.]

ANNA.   Isn't he some man, Mashenka, simply marvelous?

MARYA.   Oh, dear God in heaven. It's killing me. I can't stand it, I can't.   [*Exits, running.*]

ANNA.   Mashenka! Mashenka! Where are you going? Wait a minute. Wouldn't you know it, now I'll have to go and talk it over with her. If that isn't a slap in the face!

ACT THREE

The room is the same as in Act One. ANNA *enters, wearing a cloak, and with a large reticule.* MARYA *enters after her.*

ANNA. [*Sitting at the table, next to the door.*] Hope I don't forget anything. First to town. Did you jot down everything I have to buy?

MARYA. Everything, mama.

ANNA. Now, where is the note, exactly? Wait a minute. Yes, in my reticule. Let's see, first to town. Then, stop by the law court and ask about the suit. Surely, there's something else, isn't there?

MARYA. No, nothing. Better run along, mama, or you'll be late.

ANNA. Good-by, God be with you. [*Exits, then returns.*] Tell Darya not to let anyone in while I'm gone, especially young men. Now that you're ready for marriage the suitors will start chasing after you. Before you can bat an eye, some sort of talk will come of it.

MARYA. All right, mama, all right. Better step along.

ANNA. Well, good-by. I'll be back soon. [*Exits.*]

MARYA. [*Alone.*] Never thought she'd leave. I was scared to death Vladimir would arrive while she was still here. Oh, I wish he'd get here. Do you suppose he knows how anxious I am? [*Sits in an armchair.*] Oh, good Lord, I'm happy. I'm just now realizing how heavenly it is to love and to be loved. Why doesn't he show up? I can't bear this eternal waiting. Do you suppose I did the right thing, telling him to come today? We shall be here, alone. [*Silence.*] If it were only possible to know the future, then I'd like to know how our love will finally turn out. Oh, why should I care how? Right now I feel wonderful. I love him, and he loves me. Well, then—come what may. Someone's on his way here. Suppose it's he? [*Runs to the door.* MILASHIN *enters.*] What are you doing here? Why?

MILASHIN.   What do you mean, why? I'm here to see you.

MARYA.   Mama's not home. She told me to let no one in while she was gone.

MILASHIN.   Oh, stop joking.

MARYA.   I'm not joking, not at all. Really, mama said to allow no one in.

MILASHIN.   Well, I'm not about to listen to your mama. But maybe you don't like the idea that I'm here?

MARYA.   Well, and what if I don't?

MILASHIN.   In that event, I'll walk out.

MARYA.   Well, good-by, then.

MILASHIN.   Good-by. Permit me at least to find out why you're chasing me out?

MARYA.   Oh, dear God in heaven! All right, let's just say it's a passing whim. Well, how about it? Aren't you at least going to do one of the things I've asked?

MILASHIN.   As if you think I wouldn't.

MARYA.   Then run along.

MILASHIN.   I'm on my way. What're you worried about?

MARYA.   Why, you haven't moved one inch.

MILASHIN.   Well, you know it's pretty strange. All of a sudden, without rhyme or reason, you chase me away. And you won't give me a single reason. Boy, you know that irritates me!

MARYA.   All right, stick around. Please do. I'm going to my room, and you can sit here alone. [*Silence.*] So you're not going?

MILASHIN.   I'm on my way, ma'am. Say, you know I came here on business today. [MARYA *sits, turning away toward the window.*] You're not listening to me. And the whole thing concerns you.

MARYA.   All right, what is it?

MILASHIN.   I wanted you to open your eyes about a certain fellow.

MARYA.   So that's it. You've come to spread tales. Then you can do it at some other time, when you have more leisure.

MILASHIN.   No, not to spread tales. I just wanted to put you on your guard.

MARYA.   Some other time, Ivan Ivanych. Please, some other time. Come back again.

MILASHIN.   But you know it's only ten words, Marya Andrevna. I've learned some pretty good things about a certain fellow.

MARYA.   [*Aside.*]   If that isn't the limit!   [*To* MILASHIN.]   About whom, exactly?

MILASHIN.   About Merich . . .

MARYA.   Don't tell me the story, please. I know about it.   [*Aside.*] The scoundrel. He's concocted something or other about him.

MILASHIN.   And it's a darned good thing you know it, then. That's all I wanted. Isn't he something! He sure lays it on thick.

MARYA.   Yes, yes, he's a terrible person.

MILASHIN.   I wouldn't say terrible. Simply ridiculous. He's a kid, that's all. And you end up laughing at all the silly things he does.

MARYA.   Why, yes, ridiculous! Ivan Ivanych, do you love me?

MILASHIN.   I love you, Marya Andrevna, really and truly I love you.

MARYA.   Then do one favor for me.

MILASHIN.   Anything you like. I'm ready to sacrifice my life for your sake.

MARYA.   Only in words, no doubt? I've begged you a whole hour to leave, but you haven't moved one inch.

MILASHIN.   At once, at once.   [*Takes hat.*]   Good-by.   [*Exits, then returns.*]   Marya Andrevna! I implore you. Tell me why you want to stay here alone?

MARYA.   Ivan Ivanych, we are going to quarrel.

MILASHIN.   It's all my fault, my fault.   [*Stands for a short while.*] Permit me to kiss your hand in farewell.

MARYA.   With pleasure!   [MILASHIN *kisses her hand, then exits.* MARYA *is alone.*]   He's gone, at last. Poor Vladimir. That Milashin of all people dares to tell stories about him, even discuss his actions. It's terrible. Vladimir, poor thing, never gets sympathy from anyone. Simply because he is superior to the rest of them, and he feels cramped in this society. Every single one of them is jealous of him. At this moment I love him so very much. So much so I feel I could sacrifice everything for his sake.   [*Deep in thought.*]   Oh, why, why doesn't he show up?   [*Sits by the window and looks out.*]   Oh, I think it's he. I'll throw myself in his arms at once. Oh, I don't care how it will look.   [*Crosses to the center of the room.* MERICH *enters. Shyly, she crosses to him.*]   Oh, dear God, I'm happy. I've waited for you, waited so long, Vladimir.

MERICH.   Are we alone?

MARYA.   Yes, alone.   [MERICH *kisses her.*]   Oh, I've thought about this moment, longed for this moment so much since yesterday. You'd never believe how much. I want to live it all over again, talk about it again and again. I don't want to forget a single thing.

MERICH.   What is it you've longed for?

MARYA.   Maybe you'll laugh at me. I don't care. Laugh if you want to. Let's sit at the window. Then we can see when mama will show up.

MERICH.   How about giving me one more little kiss?

MARYA.   Ten, if you like. Only let's talk about what happened after you left.

MERICH.   All right, let's. What is it you want to tell me?

MARYA.   I have so much to tell you, so very much. Our meeting yesterday was too short, but I've been thinking of you all the time. All last evening, last night, and today all morning. Right now I'm terribly upset. It seems as if I've forgotten everything.

MERICH.   Well, it's a good thing you have forgotten.

MARYA.   Oh, Vladimir, just imagine. Yesterday, all of a sudden, some sort of monster appeared. He talked about music, about literature. He wanted to bring me candy. I was in a terrible state. He was disgusting; I was almost sick to my stomach. But mama's all for running after him. Why, you're not listening to me!

MERICH.   I am looking into your little eyes. Oh, they're beautiful, the prettiest eyes in the world. Makes you want to kiss them. I remember eyes like yours . . . someone else's. . . . She is dead now, poor woman. Oh, there's no use talking about the past. We must make use of the present. Oh, Meri, I've gone through so much in my life . . . I'm afraid I haven't the strength to return your childlike love. If I had only met you, Meri, two long years ago . . .

MARYA.   Oh, listen to me, will you. For God's sake, listen.

MERICH.   All right, all right. I'm listening.

MARYA.   That Benevolensky came yesterday. He is vulgar, uneducated. Simply terrible.

MERICH.   Meri, you know that's pretty boring stuff. Why waste our precious time on a silly thing like that?

MARYA.   But what am I going to do with that Benevolensky? I'm scared to death of him, simply scared to death.

MERICH.   It's not worth thinking about. What does Benevolensky matter to you?

MARYA.   And mama? What am I going to do with mama? Oh, Vladimir, there's a lot you don't know, and you don't want to listen.

MERICH.   What should I know! I know only one thing, that you love me. And if you love me, then you won't go to Benevolensky.

MARYA.   But all the same I'm in a bad situation. Very bad. Advise me. What should I do? [MERICH *kisses her on the shoulder.*] Oh, Vladimir, if you only knew how my heart is breaking, and all you do is make love to me.

MERICH.   Oh, dear God, I love you, Meri. I'm happy, so very happy, I've found you alone. But you spend all your time talking about your mama, about some suitor or other. And what do they matter to me? [*Kisses her again on the shoulder.*]

MARYA.   [*Avoiding him.*] Seems you're not a bit concerned about me. You really don't want to know what I'm going through. If that's the way you feel, I want nothing more to do with you.

MERICH.   You're angry. And you call this love.

MARYA.   And do you call it love when you don't want to listen to me? [*Weeps.*]

MERICH.   Oh, no! Tears, no less. And so early, too. [*Sits on chair.*] Well, I thought as much. It's the usual story, isn't it? Here's your love for you! First, a confession, passion. And then, either papa or mama, or some suitor or other is brought into it. [*Silence.*]

MARYA.   Vladimir, you're angry, aren't you?

MERICH.   No, I'm used to it. But aren't you sorry for me, Meri? I've suffered all my life long. And you won't give me a single moment of pleasure without spoiling it.

MARYA.   Don't be angry, Vladimir. . . . Let's make up. [*Kisses him.*] Will that do?

MERICH.   No, more. [MARYA *kisses him several times.*] Keep it up, Meri, shamelessly. Now I see you're a pretty smart girl. Oh, Meri, I remember one woman. There was love for you!

MARYA.   Why do you say that to me? Do you think I'm happy to hear it?

MERICH.   What's this? Jealousy. Don't tell me you're jealous? Oh, do I love to tease jealous women.

MARYA.   No, it's not jealousy. But it hurts me when you talk of other women while I make love to you. I suppose you'll tell stories about me, even . . .

MERICH.   What do you take me for? No, Meri, I shall love no one but you. Kiss me, Meri.

MARYA.   Enough, Vladimir, enough. We'd better talk about something else.

MERICH.   [*Sits next to her and embraces her.*]   About what, my dear, about what?

MARYA.   [*Quickly glances out the window.*]   Oh, mama!

MERICH.   [*Rising from the chair.*]   Really?

MARYA.   [*Laughs.*]   No, I said it on purpose, just so you'd sit a little farther away. Really, Vladimir, sit farther away and let's talk a little. I'd like to talk to you, very much.

MERICH.   [*Absentmindedly.*]   Next time I'll bring my diary, and we can read it together. But now, what do you say? Let's go into the garden.

MARYA.   How can we? Any moment now, mama will come back.

MERICH.   But is she coming back soon?

MARYA.   Pretty soon, I think.

MERICH.   Then, I'd better say good-by.

MARYA.   You've grown bored already, isn't that so? Are you bored? You're really something, Vladimir! If you only knew how anxious I was for you to come here. How delighted I was to see you. But you won't sit and talk to me for ten minutes.

MERICH.   I'm afraid Anna Petrovna will find me here. And that would be unpleasant for you.

MARYA.   Well, so what? She'll scold me, and that would be it.

MERICH.   You know I'd get it, too. Besides, I've something I must take care of. If you like, I'll stay another ten minutes, but I can't any longer. [*Sits next to her.*]   I'm ready to sit and talk to you the rest of my life, to admire you forever.

MARYA.   You're getting too close to me, don't you know?

MERICH.   Boy, are you girls strange! Leave you, and you only get mad. Get too close to you, and you get upset. Choose one or the other. Either I leave or I sit down next to you.

MARYA.   Stay, but on one condition. Sit and talk to me a little longer.

MERICH.   All right, if you want me to. [*Embraces her. They sit silently for some time.*]   My dear Meri, only wait until I can call you my very own, solemnly and openly. Will you marry me?

MARYA.   Why do you ask?

MERICH.   Or maybe they won't give you to me?

MARYA.   Oh, that's nonsense.

MERICH.   However, I must straighten out some things first. And then, Meri, then you and I shall live together nicely.

MARYA.   But will it ever come true?

MERICH.   It will come true, Meri, it will. Nothing will stop me, nothing. If they won't give you to me, then I'll carry you off.

MARYA.   Mama is coming.

MERICH.   Where on earth can I go now? You know I'll run into her. And I don't want that to happen.

MARYA.   Go through the garden.

MERICH.   Good-by. [*Kisses her.*]

MARYA.   Good-by. When will I see you again?

MERICH.   Soon, soon.

MARYA.   Come back as soon as you can.   [MERICH *exits. Alone,* MARYA *sits down at her work.*]   Dear God in heaven, I'm happy, so very happy. I can't get hold of myself. Right now life doesn't seem so terrifying to me. No matter what happens around me, at least I have hope. [*Sits, deep in thought.* DOBROTVORSKY *and* ANNA *enter.* DARYA *enters, removes* ANNA's *cloak and exits.*]

ANNA.   [*Sitting.*]   What can we do now, Platon Markych?

DOBROTVORSKY.   What's to be done, ma'am? Why, the will of God. Only you mustn't despair.

ANNA.   Where on earth can I go with my daughter? Think, Platon Markych, please think. What do I know? What on earth can I do? Even before this grief I didn't know what to do. But now? Now I'm no more than a complete fool. Advise me, please.

MARYA.   What's happened, mama, what is it?

ANNA.   Right now you and I are no more than beggars, that's what. Our lawsuit has been lost. They'll strip the house right out from under us and fix a heavy fine on top of that.

MARYA.   Oh, that's terrible. The worst possible thing.

ANNA.   What can we do, Platon Markych? Advise me.

DOBROTVORSKY.   What can I possibly tell you, ma'am? There's nothing I can do. Even if you should have me executed on the spot, why I couldn't come up with a thing. I've grown old, and a little foolish. At one time, Anna Petrovna, at one time I was a man of business. But I've gone deaf and dumb; I don't know what's what anymore.

ANNA. Yes, but you're a man, all the same. My mind won't think anymore. I am a weak woman, dull and commonplace. And my memory's gone, absolutely gone.

DOBROTVORSKY. A man, you say. Some man I am. Ekh, ekh! That's the way it happens all the time. You're not waiting for it, you don't expect it. But there it is, all of a sudden, the worst possible luck. Oh, my! Dear Lord God in heaven! [Shakes his head.]

ANNA. Oh, Platon Markych, what grief in my old age! Alone. All alone, without a man. But there's still another burden I've got to bear—I don't know how I can get her off my hands.

DOBROTVORSKY. Precisely, ma'am, precisely. Why talk about it?

ANNA. Yes, why send grief after grief? It won't help a single bit.

DOBROTVORSKY. Not a single bit.

ANNA. We've got to get moving, somehow. They say we must make a complaint to the senate.

DOBROTVORSKY. We must, ma'am, we must, for sure. Why shouldn't we get moving?

ANNA. I have no friends. There's no one I can ask.

DOBROTVORSKY. No one, ma'am, no one at all. Who could ever get it moving? Just to ask, you have to give money.

ANNA. Look around, Platon Markych. Isn't there someone among your friends, someone who could take charge of our business?

DOBROTVORSKY. Well, if you want to know, there's no one to ask except Maksim Dorofeich.

ANNA. That will do it, won't it? Excellent. He was telling you something or other yesterday when he was leaving here, wasn't he?

DOBROTVORSKY. Come to think of it, he was telling me, ma'am. He said, "If they give me Marya Andrevna, then I'll get moving." "It's still possible to fix up that lawsuit," he said, "I like Marya Andrevna a lot." He said, "I sure don't need one better." "Find out her inclination," he said, "and I'm ready at once if you like."

ANNA.   Why haven't you said something about it before now?

DOBROTVORSKY.   Forgive me, ma'am, it slipped my mind completely. Once I got my tongue suited to the words, why I just out and said it.

ANNA.   Hear that, Mashenka?

MARYA.   What was it?

ANNA.   Maksim Dorofeich likes you a lot.

MARYA.   I'm very glad.

ANNA.   Well, thank the Lord, you're glad. He's making a proposal.

MARYA.   Oh, no. Not for anything in the world.

ANNA.   No doubt you've gone out of your mind. How can I even look at you? Can't you see, really, that there's nothing more we can do now? There's nowhere else we can go in the world.

MARYA.   It'd be far better, mama, not to talk of Benevolensky. I don't want to hear another word about him.

ANNA.   You're not serious, you can't be! Now, you just think a minute. You know you don't have ten suitors. You don't have a single one to choose. Why, there aren't a hundred thousand after you just so you can go and brush suitors away. I never in my life expected a match like this.

MARYA.   For God's sake, mama, don't talk to me about Benevolensky.

ANNA.   You are a silly fool, I see. Oh, there's no use talking to her. Her head's full of hot air. She doesn't know what she's talking about, herself. Why on earth listen to her nonsense? Platon Markych, tell Maksim Dorofeich that we're very happy about the formal proposal he has made.

DOBROTVORSKY.   All right, ma'am. I'll tell him today.

MARYA.   [*Quickly rises from her chair.*] What are you doing? Platon Markych, don't go to Benevolensky. I don't like him. He is repulsive to me. I wouldn't marry him for all the money in the world.

ANNA.   Why listen to her? She's babbling again, babbling nonsense all the time. Rubbish, that's all it is. I really don't know who's hammered rubbish into her head. Do as I tell you. Why listen to her? She'll change her mind twenty times before you know it.

MARYA.   I'm not going to say another word. Do what you want to, only I won't marry Benevolensky.

ANNA. You won't marry him?

MARYA. I won't.

ANNA. Seems to me you're just being giddy. Giddy and silly, so you can go against something your mama wants. The only thing I want is to get you settled. And you ought to feel sorry for me in my old age. You see, I can scarcely drag one foot after the other. I am a woman, dull and commonplace, but look at the blow I've received—they're stripping away my last piece of property, right out from under me. Now, they say, I must make a complaint to the senate. But who is going to write it? We are, you suppose, you and I? I don't know A from B. If Maksim Dorofeich doesn't take charge, then you know we'll turn out beggars. You understand that, don't you? Just imagine how happy he's going to be when he takes over our business, and then you go and turn him down flat. If you don't want to think about yourself, then at least start pitying your mother. Where do I go in my old age? I am a weak woman, dull and commonplace, and now I can scarcely drag one foot after the other. I suppose you want me to go? Yes, go out as a cook, no less.

MARYA. Oh, dear God, what can I do!

ANNA. Listen to your mother.

DOBROTVORSKY. You must listen to your mama, my dear young lady.

MARYA. No, whatever you want to do with me, do it. But I can't.

DOBROTVORSKY. Get hold of yourself, somehow.

MARYA. I can't. I can't. I can't.

ANNA. Leave her alone, Platon Markych. Have nothing to do with her! Just how do you think I feel, Platon Markych? A mother, an old woman, no less. [Weeps.] Oh, Lord in heaven. Where's my handkerchief? Just as I thought. I lost it in town, and with my money, too. . . . One thing after another. Ah, let everything burn to dust. There's nothing I want anymore if my own daughter won't think about my grief. [To Marya.] Live the way you want to, but I want nothing more to do with you. [To DOBROTVORSKY.] There, I raised her to my own misfortune.

MARYA. Mama, what are you saying? Why go on hurting me?

ANNA. Then you listen to your mother. You think it's easy for me to talk to you. Sometimes I don't know what to say. I have a heart that's weak, womanly.

MARYA.   Mama, I dislike him very much. I am ready to do anything for you, anything you like. Only don't make me get married. I don't want to marry. I won't marry anyone.

ANNA.   Please tell her, Platon Markych, she is completely mad. [*To* MARYA.] You know you don't know what you're saying. How on earth can you say a thing like, "I won't marry." That's all it is, giddy and outlandish. Oh, it's fun to be an old maid, a lot of fun. And what about me? Off to the poor house, I suppose? In the first place, if you love your mother, then you ought to get married. And in the second place, because you need it. What is an unmarried woman, exactly? Nothing. What does she add up to, anyway? You know it's a bad thing to be a widow, but an old maid is the worst thing possible. A woman is meant to live with a husband, tend to his house, raise children. And just what will you do as an old maid? Knit stockings. You've thought about that, haven't you?

MARYA.   No, mama, I haven't thought about that.

ANNA.   Well, come over here, sit down next to me. Let's have a nice talk. I won't get angry.   [MARYA *sits next to* ANNA.]   Listen to me and keep your head. You see, I know your main subject of conversation. To marry for love. The men who fall in love, Mashenka, are the ones who can't get married. They can't get married because either they're still in boys' jackets and it's too early for them, or there's scarcely a kopek to keep a wife alive. That's always when boys fall in love. Now a decent and proper man isn't going to say he's in love or even look like he's in love. Instead, he'll simply go to the mother and say, "I like your daughter." And sure enough, he'll go straight to you afterward, without any silly fooling around, and say, "Young lady, your mama's agreed; I like you; would you like to make me happy?" And the whole thing is done honorably and nobly. That's the way it happens, Mashenka. Here you haven't said ten words to Benevolensky, and yet you don't want to hear about him. Well, he's going to come here, you're going to get acquainted, and then maybe you'll see he's a good man. You see, those featherbrains of yours are only experts at talking all the time. As for getting anything out of them—the best you'll ever get is a bad reputation.

DOBROTVORSKY.   That's right, young lady.   [*Silence.*]

ANNA.   Mashenka, make me happy in my old age. Listen to your mother.

MARYA.   [*Rises.*]   Mama, right now I can't marry either Benevolensky or anyone else. Please don't force me. I beg only one thing of you. Don't talk to me about marriage. Wait a little while. For God's sake, give me freedom to live a bit.

ANNA.   Gracious me, maidenly life is simply wonderful. You'll be sorry to leave it, I know.

MARYA.   Let Benevolensky come see us. I'll be nice to him, anything you want. Only let him wait . . . Well, a month. Yes, one month. I'll get a good look at him, find out about him. Agreed?

ANNA.   [*Kisses* MARYA.]   Oh, what can I do with you? Well, all right, then. Tell me, feel better now? Oh, my! You silly, silly girl.   [MARYA *exits.*]   What's to be done, Platon Markych! Tell Maksim Dorofeich that I'm very happy, but he must wait a month before making the proposal. Oh, and ask him about the lawsuit.

DOBROTVORSKY.   Very good, ma'am.   [KHORKOVA *enters.*]

KHORKOVA.   Thanks a lot, dear Anna Petrovna, thanks a lot. Yes, I'll have to say it. You've done me a big, big favor.

ANNA.   What is it? What have I done for you?

KHORKOVA.   I may be an uneducated woman, but I'm not going to let somebody laugh at me. Not so long ago you gave me some hope. Goes without saying, I arrive home and say, "Misha, my dear, Anna Petrovna agrees." "Open yourself up," I say, "to Marya Andrevna." And what do you know? She turned him down flat. He comes running home, all shaken up. "Mama," he says, "there's no happiness in my life." "You deceived me," he says. "I, my dear," I say, "I've never been deceitful." "But if they've scorned us," I say, "then there's nothing for you to worry about; you with your education can always find a bride, no worse than Marya Andrevna." And so I thought, "I'm not about to put up with this; let her swear at me, but all the same I'm going to give Anna Petrovna a good dressing down."

ANNA.   What can I do, exactly? It's what she wants, and I can't force her.

KHORKOVA.   That, Anna Petrovna, is sarcasm, pure and simple. And that's the way I'm going to take it, as sarcasm.

ANNA.   But for pity's sake, my dear, how on earth is it sarcasm?

KHORKOVA.   It's sarcasm. That's what it is, it's sarcasm. All you wanted to do was make a silly fool out of me, right in front of my son, too. I may be an uneducated woman, but I understand . . .

ANNA.   What do you understand, I'd like to know? There's nothing here for you to understand, exactly.

KHORKOVA.   Now, don't you start talking. Please. I know a couple of things, don't think I don't. Right now you've got your eye on a certain rich suitor. So you're a little squeamish about the other young fellows. I'll give you a little advice, Anna Petrovna, better hurry it up; otherwise, you might find some talk going around.

ANNA.   What sort of talk? You're not serious. Perhaps you've come to quarrel with me, Arina Egorovna?

KHORKOVA.   There you have it, my dear. Take it whatever way you like. I've been insulted, inside and out. What I don't know, I'm not about to say. But what I do know, I'll publish—point-blank. If people tell an outrageous lie, who am I to never let it die?

ANNA.   A tongue has no bones: it can wag all the time. It's possible to say anything, only there's no use listening.

KHORKOVA.   Listen or not, whatever you like. But if people talk, it means something or other is there.

ANNA.   Anybody can talk, but what does he say? Who can find anything to say about me?

KHORKOVA.   Oh, no, the talk's not about you at all. It's about Marya Andrevna. That girl's got a lot of pride, but this will put her nose out of joint. Well, she turned us down. Wait and see if that rich suitor himself won't turn you down when he hears something or other.

ANNA.   Oh, you're not serious, Arina Egorovna. Lost your mind, no doubt. And who on earth would dare say anything against my Mashenka?

KHORKOVA.   Oh, my dear, you can't stop a person's mouth. Anybody's free to talk. The tongue was made for talking.

ANNA.   What on earth is this, I'd like to know? Listen here, Platon Markych, they've started spreading rumors about Mashenka. Have you ever heard the like?

DOBROTVORSKY.   Well, you can't run around saying, "God bless you," to everyone who sneezes, can you? No need to listen to her.

ANNA. [*To* DOBROTVORSKY.] Now, what can anyone possibly say against my Mashenka? Do me a favor and tell me.

KHORKOVA. Well, here's something for you. Why does Merich come here every day? You know the neighbors see it going on. There's no way to hide it. It goes on when you're here and when you're out of the house. Maybe you yourself don't know a thing about it. I'm an uneducated woman, but you won't catch me letting my daughter get away with that. My son tells me they won't let Merich in a single decent and proper house because of his filthy and vulgar ways. I saw him slinking through your garden just now, saw him with my own eyes. Slinking like a thief, he was.

ANNA. Oh, dear Lord, what's going on? You can see what comes from being without a man in the house. Anybody, just anybody, can tell whatever stories pop into his head. Wouldn't you know it's the kind of thing women can do nothing about? Oh, Arina Egorovna, have pity on me. I'm a weak woman, dull and common-place. Why are you getting me all upset? Don't you know it's sinful!

KHORKOVA. Cut off a man's head, and you won't find him crying for the loss of his hair. You're to blame yourself, for letting her go this far. Just try looking for suitors now, and see if anybody's tempted. Even if you did agree to it, why I'd never allow my Misha to go through with it. No, indeed. Thanks a lot.

ANNA. Well, we don't want Misha or you. Aren't the two of you something! Why, I've never seen the like. The only thing you're good for is spreading gossip, scandal. . . .

KHORKOVA. [*Rises.*] Well, then, dearie, forgive me for not keeping it a secret from other people. I mean, what all I've been hearing.

ANNA. Go on with you keeping it a secret! Why, you'll add plenty of your own. You were as happy as anything that the opportunity came along for you. That's just the thing I'd have expected from you.

KHORKOVA. And the only things I've gotten from you are insults and sarcasm. Only I just couldn't stand not telling you off for Misha's sake. If it hadn't been for that, I'd never step a foot in your house. As for Misha, I'm not going to let him even think about your daughter. With his brains and education, we can come up with a far cleaner girl. That's for sure. [*Exits.*]

ANNA.   What in the world is this? Platon Markych, judge for yourself. You see, I couldn't pull myself together soon enough; otherwise, I'd have given her a song or two. Now you know she may spread it around everywhere, for all I know. She could give me a black eye in no time. That's the way it is without a man, Platon Markych. Run here, run there, doing everything by yourself. And what's more, keep an eye on your daughter. It's impossible even to go out of your own house. And what am I? Just a woman, dull and commonplace. Masha! Masha! Darya! Darya! [DARYA *enters.*] What's wrong with you, gone deaf, maybe? Do I have to scream my head off for you? Call the young lady in.

DARYA.   As if I don't have more than one thing to do. I'm not sitting around with my hands folded, you know. [*Exits.*]

ANNA.   Oh, I've done myself in, today. And now this of all things comes pressing in on me. Both my feet and hands are shaking. What is it Masha's doing to me! I feel I'm a weak mother. Now take my side, Platon Markych. [MARYA *enters.*]

MARYA.   You called me, mama?

ANNA.   What are you doing? Maybe you want to drive me to the grave before my time! What more have you tried?

MARYA.   What do you mean?

ANNA.   Was Merich here while I was away? [*Silence.*] Why don't you say something?

MARYA.   He was, but not for long. I told him you weren't home. He left then.

ANNA.   Don't you try and deceive me. What's going on between you two? Speak up.

MARYA.   What do you mean, going on? Who told you, mama?

ANNA.   Who told me? Everybody's talking. I don't dare poke my face outside anymore. Khorkova came over just now, and even she knows. If that Merich so much as takes one breath in here, I'll have him thrown out. Hear me, young lady?

MARYA.   No, mama, it's impossible.

ANNA.   And why is it? Tell me, do we stand on ceremony with him maybe? He's a man of distinction, I suppose. I'll chase him out, and that's all there is to it. You must get married. But with all this talk making the rounds, you won't find a husband very soon. You've shamed me, shamed me completely. Either you give your word to Maksim Dorofeich at once, or I'll tell Merich tomorrow he can never poke his face in here again.

MARYA.   Don't do that, for God's sake. I beg you, mama, don't. How could you!

ANNA.   Then, take the marriage step.

MARYA.   Mama, give me time to think. I've gone to pieces, my head's going round and round. Give me time to think.

ANNA.   What're you going to think about? We must do something right away, I don't know what, or Maksim Dorofeich will hear the gossip, and very likely he'll turn you down. What would I do with my head then? Oh, what a shame that would be! You must tell Maksim Dorofeich that we are agreed.

MARYA.   No, mama, I don't have the strength.

ANNA.   All right, then live the way you want to. Right now, I want nothing more to do with you. I raised you, educated you, fussed over you, not getting a bit of rest day or night. And you, you want to go against me. For you, mother is cheaper than anyone else, God help you! I won't say another word to you now. Raise as much hell as you like and with whom you like. There, I've said it. You've forgotten mother. Yes, you have. You want nothing more to do for mother. Maybe, oh, maybe, kind people somewhere will show up, somebody who won't abandon the old woman. Let's go to my room, Platon Markych. [*Rises and goes.*]   It's clear I must lead a wretched life in my old age.

MARYA.   [*Following her.*]   Mama!

ANNA.   You, don't you come after me! Right now I never want to see you again. [*Exits.*]

MARYA.   [*Sits on a chair and covers her face with her handkerchief.* DOBROTVORSKY *stands opposite her.*]   It's agonizing, the torment.

DOBROTVORSKY.   What, just because your mama scolded you. Oh, that's nothing. Don't cry, young lady. You two will make up, somehow.

MARYA.   Oh, Platon Markych, it may be mama is right. But she wants something impossible from me.

DOBROTVORSKY.   And why do you say impossible, my dear young lady? It's possible, really and truly. Go along with the old woman, comfort her. You know you won't find a better suitor than Maksim Dorofeich.

MARYA. Listen to me, Platon Markych. You're a good person, and I'm going to speak frankly to you. I love someone else. He's a nice man, smart, educated. Judge for yourself, how can I exchange him for Benevolensky?

DOBROTVORSKY. Then he is a young man, miss?

MARYA. Very young . . .

DOBROTVORSKY. You know they're only whistlers, my dear, not substantial at all. Don't you believe them. Today he's in love, tomorrow he's out of it. A lot of fun for them, but the poor girl ends up weeping.

MARYA. I don't know whether he'll stop loving me or not. I do know I am in love with him.

DOBROTVORSKY. My dear young lady, I knew you when you were about this big. You were a child without a thought in your head when I carried you in my arms. Your papa, now at rest, was a benefactor to me. He made my way in the world. Before he came along I was pretty insignificant. As the poor fellow lay dying, he said, "You, Platon, don't leave my wife and daughter." "I'm listening," I said, "my dear Andrey Petrovich,[27] I will serve them as long as my strength holds out." Young lady, I love you more than my own daughter, if I had one. You don't know how bitter I'd feel if some featherbrain kid would make you the target of his fun. You just spit on them. I know you'll probably say, young lady, that you know better than we do, that we're old folks and have outlived our brains. I don't dare advise you. You'll have to figure it out yourself. Here I am in my old age, and just for your sake, young lady, I worked out your marriage. I turned up a person. And it seems to me he's a nice man, but only God knows for sure. How on earth can I try to make him out? You look him over yourself. It's too much for me, and I don't want a sin like that on my conscience. It comes down to this, my whole advice is . . . better listen to your mama. There'll be fewer sins on your conscience that way.

MARYA. Platon Markych, make up to mama for me. She likes you.

DOBROTVORSKY. Don't worry, my dear. I'll make it up, don't worry about it.

MARYA. Go tell her I'll give her my answer in three days. I must have time to think, to talk about it with him. He promised to marry me!

DOBROTVORSKY. All right, young lady. Want me to see your mama right away?

MARYA. Yes, please, right away. I always feel terrible when she's angry, whether there's reason for it or not.

DOBROTVORSKY. And why shouldn't you feel terrible, my dear? She is your mother after all. All right, miss. [Exits.]

MARYA. What can I do? I don't know, I absolutely don't know. I feel I was wrong to quarrel with mama. But I can't marry Benevolensky, I can't. I love Vladimir. And say I decided to sacrifice myself, why I don't have the right. Why on earth should I deceive poor Vladimir? He loves me so very much.

DARYA. [Enters.] Oh, to hell with you! [28] She loses everything all the time. [Takes ANNA's handkerchief.]

MARYA. Dasha, what is mama doing?

DARYA. Talking with Platon Markych.

MARYA. Is she angry?

DARYA. I don't dare get close to her. [Exits.]

MARYA. I am sorry for mama, really and truly sorry. If I hadn't done that silly, silly thing, I could talk to mama now. Yes, and tell her frankly I don't like Benevolensky. But I can't now. There's only one way out for me. I'll talk it over with Vladimir, then we'll tell mama, and it will be over and done with. Oh, you silly fool, you. What on earth are you crying about? Some fellow says right out that he'll marry me, and I turn around and cry, thinking up all kinds of unhappy thoughts. [She laughs, then deep in thought.] And if he won't? If he won't? What then? Oh, come now. What right have I to think badly of him? I don't even know him yet. Oh, dear God, what is it? What am I saying? I'm all confused, mixed up. Any other girl in my place would jump for joy. But silly, silly stuff and nonsense keeps going through my head. No, no, I won't think about anything. Oh, if I could see Vladimir soon, soon. [DOBROTVORSKY enters.]

DOBROTVORSKY. Go to your mama, young lady, please. I've made a little headway with her. Don't be afraid of anything. She won't scold you now. She wants to talk a little. "Let her see," she said, "that mother's not wishing evil on her." Let's go right now and talk everything over, together. Perhaps, young lady, we'll fix it up somehow. [They exit.]

ACT FOUR

The room is the same as in Act One.

MARYA. [*Alone.*] Here it is the third day, and he hasn't come. What can it mean? Three days of torment, it's agonizing. No doubt he's sick, that's it. Oh, dear God, if he doesn't come today, I think I'll go out of my mind. I feel terrible, absolutely miserable, and I never saw it coming. Why, a week ago I was happy, not a thought in my head. And here I am now, waiting for Benevolensky to arrive and make his proposal. What shall I do? Mama has a lot of confidence in me. She loves me so very much. . . . Right now her peace of mind depends on me. I wonder if I have strength enough to go against her will? [DARYA *enters.*]

DARYA. Oh, to hell . . . Run here, run there, and still find time to . . . How come you're in the dumps, miss?

MARYA. Why on earth should I be happy? Tell my fortune in the cards, Dasha, please.

DARYA. If you like, miss, I'll lay them out right now. [*Distributes the cards.*]

MARYA. Tell me, Dasha, did anything come out yet? I suppose it's a lot of silly nonsense.

DARYA. No, my dear, don't say things like that. Look here, the other day I told my old crony Aksinya's[29] fortune, and the guilty ace kept showing up. "Just look," I tell her, "you're going to come to some kind of grief." What do you know, miss, turns out I was right. Somebody stole her new coat, brand spanking new it was. [*Spreads her hands, making a helpless gesture.*] Just in your anterest[30] we'll try the clubs . . . and stay in that family . . . fulfillment of wishes. Look at that, will you? King of diamonds, sticking right to the clubs, means an admirer enticed.

MARYA.   And who is the king of diamonds?

DARYA.   Oh, that's easy. Vladimir Vasilevich. Who else could it be?   [ANNA *enters.*]

ANNA.   What is it you're doing? Fortune-telling, no doubt. Darya, tell me mine.

DARYA.   If you like, my dear, right away.

ANNA.   Now, what queen do I have for my fortune? You remember, Mashenka, don't you?

DARYA.   I'll lay out hearts for you, my dear. Oh, miss, the postman's coming here.   [*Exits for the letter.*]

MARYA.   Who's it from? Oh, dear God, my heart's beginning to throb.   [DARYA *returns with letter.*]

ANNA.   Dasha, try and find my spectacles.   [*Breaks the seal on the letter.*]

DARYA.   Here they are, my dear.

ANNA.   [*Looks at signature.*]   From Benevolensky.

MARYA.   From Benevolensky? What does he write?

ANNA.   [*Reads.*]   "My dear madam, highly respected Anna Petrovna. Taking into regard your favor and the cheerful reception which you showed me last Thursday, I take upon myself the boldness to offer my hand and heart to your most peerless daughter, Marya Andrevna, with whose virtues and beauty I am charmed. At the same time I have the honor to add that I heard from Platon Markych about your lawsuit, in which, as a learned man, I might be the solicitor. Of course, only in the event that you agree to accept my proposal. I am a man of business, and I've no time to lose in vain on the affairs of others. My property, you know, I strive constantly to increase, using to that end all my own abilities. For as you know only too well, property gives weight in society. Taking into consideration all that and equally the situation in which you find yourself, I don't think you can refuse a relationship with me. I shall expect your answer today, or in the last resort, tomorrow, so I don't remain in ignorance. Please advise Marya Andrevna of my most humble regard for her, and let her know once and for all, that I, as a passionate admirer, await with beating heart her answer. With sincere regard and like devotion, I have the honor to be, Maksim Benevolensky." Well, there you have it, Mashenka. We must write.

MARYA.   [*Excitedly.*]   Wait a bit, mama, please wait.

ANNA.   Wait? Whatever for, Masha? Now you listen to me. You know we can never expect a match like this again. Maksim Dorofeich is a man of delicacy. We must write him something or other, so he'll have no doubts whatsoever.

MARYA.   Wait a bit, mama. For God's sake, wait a bit. Tomorrow, tomorrow.

ANNA.   And why not now, exactly?

MARYA.   I can't do it now. I don't know what to answer. I'm so upset . . . I'm sort of sick, my head aches. I can't, I absolutely can't do it.

ANNA.   All right, do what you want. Tomorrow then. Tomorrow. But right now I'm going to think a little about how to write it as elegantly as possible.   [*Exits.*]

MARYA.   Dasha, you know where Vladimir Vasilich lives?

DARYA.   I know, my dear.

MARYA.   Run to him, Dasha, my darling, run as fast as possible.

DARYA.   You're not serious, my dear. And what happens if your mama finds out?

MARYA.   Oh, hurry. It's nothing. Hurry, please. I'll tell mama, somehow or other. Only, for God's sake, hurry up. Tell him he must come here at once, this minute.

DARYA.   Well, I see I can't do a thing with you.

MARYA.   Oh, quickly, Dasha, quickly.   [DARYA *exits.* MARYA *is alone.*]   No, it can't be, it can't. Vladimir will save me. Oh, what if she doesn't find him in? And, what if . . . No, it can't be. He loves me. Oh, I see now I can't figure out what I think, what I feel. Oh, I feel terrible, absolutely terrible. Oh, if she'd only hurry and come back. Someone is coming. Suppose it's he? No, it's Milashin.   [MILASHIN *enters.*]   Tell me, Ivan Ivanych, have you seen Vladimir Vasilich, or not?

MILASHIN.   What's he got to do with you?

MARYA.   Oh, dear God! If I ask you, it means I want to know. I must know.

MILASHIN.   Who knows anything about him? For pity's sake, how do you expect me to know where people like him hang out?   [MARYA *turns around and weeps.*]   If you think I'm saying it out of jealousy, you're deeply mistaken. I'm sorry for you and nothing more.

MARYA.   Do me a favor and stop being sorry. What gives you the right to feel sorry for me?

MILASHIN.   All right, whatever you like. I say it out of affection for you and your mama. I'll repeat it again. If I were in Anna Petrovna's place, I'd never allow a man like Merich to come near the gates. If Anna Petrovna is pleased to hear him spread it around, even brag that you're in love with him, then let her ask him into the house.

MARYA.   You are lying.

MILASHIN.   I'm lying? No, I never lie, miss. Someone else can tell lies, but I do not.

MARYA.   Why even talk to me about him? You know I'd never believe you. I love him, do you hear? I love him, love him. Don't you dare say anything bad about him while I'm around.

MILASHIN.   You love him? And he loves you, or so you think?

MARYA.   Listen here, I'm beginning to lose patience. Either shut up or clear out! Fast as you can.

MILASHIN.   [Sits on the other side of the room. Silence.]   You've hurt me, Marya Andrevna, hurt me cruelly. I've wished you well. I've known you ever since we were children, but you're driving me away from you. Tell me, please, do I really deserve this? [Silence.]   I only wanted, by virtue of our friendship, to put you on your guard.

MARYA.   On guard against whom? I don't need warnings from you.

MILASHIN.   Right now I see you don't. You believe in him so much you're blind to him, and you won't listen to anyone. I'm not going to disillusion you. But all the same, that doesn't stop me from knowing a few little things about him. Yes, and they're not very good, either.

MARYA.   You can know, and you can say what you want to whomever you please. But all the same, nobody is going to believe you.

MILASHIN.   What am I anyway? I suppose I'm a scoundrel, according to you. So that's what I get for my affection.

MARYA.   All right, what have you found out? Speak up.

MILASHIN.   I found out so much I'd never be able to repeat it all.

MARYA.   And do you have evidence?

MILASHIN.   What do you mean, evidence? His behavior is very clear without evidence.

MARYA. Well, if you don't have evidence then I'll tell you right now, I don't believe you. I don't believe you, I don't.

MILASHIN. Perhaps some time soon I'll prove the truth of what I say with facts. Only it may be too late then.

MARYA. That's no concern of yours. When you have evidence, then speak up. But until you can, don't say another word. [*Silence.*] Why, why so long? [*Looks out the window. Silence.*] Oh, at last!

MILASHIN. Who is it?

MARYA. Vladimir Vasilich. Well, he's certainly going to get it from me. [MERICH *enters.*] Where on earth have you been? Aren't you ashamed!

MERICH. [*Kisses her hand.*] My fault, Marya Andrevna, my fault. But I won't try and put things straight. How do you do, Ivan Ivanych.

MARYA. I must tell you some news. It's pretty unpleasant.

MERICH. Unpleasant? That's bad. You frighten me.

MARYA. Yes, for me it's very unpleasant.

MERICH. If it's unpleasant for you, then you can be sure it is for me, too.

MILASHIN. Why do you say that? Permit me to ask.

MERICH. For a very simple reason, Ivan Ivanych. Anything that concerns Marya Andrevna I take very much to heart. Now do you understand?

MARYA. Yes, Ivan Ivanych, this particular matter concerns both of us.

MILASHIN. In that case, excuse me.

MERICH. Why have you grown thin and pale, Marya Andrevna?

MARYA. I tell you I've put up with a lot of unpleasant things. And isn't it enough that I haven't seen you for three days? What haven't I gone over and over in my mind since then!

MERICH. If I'm the least bit responsible for your grief, then I consider myself guilty. So guilty I won't even try to make excuses. You have a good heart. But I'll try to make up for my guilt. Give me your hand as a sign of truce. [*Kisses* MARYA's *hand.*]

MARYA. It's your fault, of course it is. How could you do it? Not even come by for almost a week. I'd like nothing more to do with you. You know I sent Darya to your place.

MERICH.   Obviously she didn't find me home. We must have missed each other on the way.

MILASHIN.   [*Aside.*]   This is unbearable.

MERICH.   Why on earth did you send Darya for me?

MARYA.   So you'd come here. I want to talk to you. Yes, I must talk to you about a very important matter.

MILASHIN.   Good-by, Marya Andrevna.

MARYA.   Where are you going?

MILASHIN.   After the evidence.

MARYA.   I wish you success. [MILASHIN *exits.*] Vladimir, Vladimir. What are you doing to me? I waited and waited, but you never came.

MERICH.   What is it, what's wrong? Why are you crying?

MARYA.   Vladimir, a terrible thing has happened to us, terrible. We have lost the suit. They'll take everything we have.

MERICH.   Oh, dear God!

MARYA.   What can we do now? Mama says we have nothing to live on. The only thing I can do is sacrifice myself, go to Benevolensky. I can't pull myself together. I must give my answer today.

MERICH.   Oh, that's terrible, terrible.

MARYA.   [*Embraces him.*]   Vladimir, save me.

MERICH.   [*Freeing himself.*]   Wait a minute, wait. Let's talk it over carefully, calmly.

MARYA.   How on earth can I talk about it calmly? Vladimir, what can I do? My life and death depend on that.   [*Embraces him.*]

MERICH.   What are you doing, Meri? Careful, careful. Well, suppose someone saw us, what would they say?

MARYA.   It's all the same to me now. Let them say what they want.

MERICH.   But they'd blame me, wait and see. You know everything will fall on me. They'll say God only knows what about me. You know the reputation I have without adding this to it.

MARYA.   Are you frightened? But you weren't frightened before, if I remember.

MERICH.   Can't you understand that it's different now? A lot different. Your mama wasn't home then.

MARYA.   What can I do? I don't know, really and truly.

MERICH.   Oh, this isn't good, not good at all. And I never really expected it.

MARYA. Vladimir, if I'd never met you, I'd have married anyone mama wanted for me. But I fell in love with you. You said yourself you loved me. How can I ever part with you now?

MERICH. Tell me something, Meri. Do it as a favor and tell me what is it you want from me?

MARYA. Oh, Vladimir, just think what you're saying. Think of the situation you put me in. You make me ashamed of myself. I tell you about this terrible thing. As a friend I tell you, and you turn around and ask, what is it I want? What do you want me to say to you, ask you to marry me? Spare me.

MERICH. Oh, Meri, Meri! You don't know what strange circumstances I'm in now. [*Walks about the room.*] I can't come up with a thing now, absolutely nothing.

MARYA. Nothing?

MERICH. Nothing.

MARYA. Oh, dear God in heaven! [*Covers her face with her hands.*]

MERICH. There, you see. It all comes from inexperience. I had to run away from you. Why, why did I meet you? Oh, fate, fate! It would have been a lot easier for me never to have met you than to stand here and see you in torment. Besides, I didn't think you'd become so attached to me.

MARYA. What did you think?

MERICH. I thought nothing serious would come from our relationship.

MARYA. So you were bored, wanted to amuse yourself, play around a little? Is that it? Why didn't you say it yourself, that you were sick and tired of playing at love?

MERICH. You really don't think I love you, do you? Can't you see the torment I'm in now? Oh, if you could only look into my soul! Well, what can we do? We must accept what we have coming to us. We must be strong, Meri, strong.

MARYA. I was strong until you deceived me. Yes, deceived me cruelly. Aren't you sorry for me? Tell me, for God's sake.

MERICH. I'm very sorry for you, Meri, more than sorry since I can't help you at all. I can't marry you. Why, my father would never allow it. Of course, I'd never listen to him, anyway. But the circumstances, the circumstances pressing in on me my whole life long . . .

MARYA. Oh, dear God! Tell me why you deceived me then? Whatever made you swear, when I asked nothing of you?

MERICH. I love you, Meri. I was carried away, and I never realized. I'm a person with a lot of passion.

MARYA. You loved me? No, you never loved me. I was the only one in love. Well, your behavior is pretty clear to me now. Even though it's late, I found out about you. Oh, dear Lord in heaven! And you even dared to call it love. A nice sort of love that is. Without sacrificing yourself, even without a bit of passion! Well, the whole guilt is mine. And I'll never be forgiven, never. I throw myself in your arms, but you turn around to see if someone is looking. You just remember, and remember it well. It used to be I could scarcely wait for you to come here. I had eyes only for your arrival. But when you came, it meant nothing to you. Nothing at all. I suppose you'd thought it all out at home, just what step you'd take next.

MERICH. You're hurting me. Go on, you can say what you like. You have every right in the world.

MARYA. Don't go on talking, for God's sake. Try to find some conscience now, if you can. You've no reason now to go on lying. Oh, no. Now you can just brag about all your successes.

MERICH. Listen here, what do you take me for?

MARYA. Exactly the kind of person you are.

MERICH. Well, that does it. I'm not going to stand for any more. [*Takes his hat.*]

MARYA. Are you leaving? Good-by.

MERICH. I'm not going to stick around listening to that. All right, it's all my fault, I admit it. But it isn't at all the way you say it is. No matter what you say, I am an honorable man. You see, circumstances mean a lot, Meri. But how will you ever find it out, you women?

MARYA. I believe you. Yes, I do.

MERICH. No, it's the truth. Don't get mad at me. I couldn't have done any differently because of all my love for you. Go on, say what you like. But all the same I maintain I love you. You don't believe it, I know. You're mistaken, and you're hurting me. Can I help it if I'm in love with a beautiful, innocent person like you?

MARYA. Stop it, for God's sake.

MERICH.   Under different circumstances, I'd have given the whole world for the happiness of possessing you.

MARYA.   Stop it, please. Stop it right now.

MERICH.   But I am fated to do otherwise. What can I do? We must part.

MARYA.   Good-by. Good-by. [MERICH *kisses her hand, exits slowly, then returns.*]

MERICH.   No, I can't go, I can't without one more look at you. [*Stands, folding his arms on his chest.*]   You're not mad at me, are you?

MARYA.   I'm not mad.

MERICH.   That's excellent. Good-by, Meri, good-by. I wish you all the happiness in the world.   [*Walks a little farther away.*] Forget about me.   [*Exits.*]

MARYA.   [*Alone.*]   And I believed in that man. How ashamed I am of myself. He's walked out, and it's nothing as far as he's concerned. I think he is even happy that he left me for good. And I, I? Oh, why must I go on and on in torment? What am I guilty of? Oh, dear Lord! Why do we find so little truth in people? Could I help it if he deceived me? How was I going to know? How could I have ever found out, I'd like to know. Why, why did he deceive me?   [*Weeps.* MILASHIN *enters.*]

MILASHIN.   Here is the evidence, Marya Andrevna.

MARYA.   There's no longer any need.

MILASHIN.   So, I spoke the truth. For pity's sake, I know a lot about him.   [*Reads.*]   "Forgive my impudence, but I can no longer hide the passion which is destroying me." Tell me, isn't that tenderness of first rank?

MARYA.   What is it you're reading?

MILASHIN.   Here, see for yourself, please.   [*Hands over some notes.* MARYA *reads to herself.*]   A little while ago you said I was lying. I remember that, Marya Andrevna.

MARYA.   [*Tears the notes and throws them out the window.*] Only one thing was missing. It's terrible.

MILASHIN.   I have some more. Don't you want them?

MARYA.   Oh, dear God. And what do they mean to me? Leave me, for God's sake. You see the state I'm in.   [*Following a brief silence.*]   I saw Vladimir Vasilich just now.

MILASHIN.   What about him?

MARYA. [*Weeps.*] He would have nothing to do with me. Nothing at all. He says we must accept what we have coming to us.

MILASHIN. The scoundrel! Marya Andrevna, stop it, please. Don't cry. I am ready to sacrifice my life for you. Tell me, Marya Andrevna, how can I help you? I am ready for anything.

MARYA. There's nothing you can do for me. Help me calm down a little. My pride was injured, and I'm ashamed of myself. I am not crying because I must sacrifice myself. I'm getting used to that thought. It's just that I was a plaything for a giddy and silly man. How can you help me?

MILASHIN. I can challenge him to a duel, if you want me to. You think I wouldn't? Well, I would, that's for sure.

MARYA. Why did you bring that up? What gives you the right, I'd like to know.

MILASHIN. Yes, I know it's pretty awkward. I only wanted to ask you, but of course it's up to you. My life isn't worth much. I can't stand to see you in torment. Isn't there something I can do, anything to help you? Anything at all?

MARYA. Yes, there's one thing. Leave me in peace.

MILASHIN. You are driving me away. So that's the way you treat me. Well, I'll prove to you I don't deserve it. Marya Andrevna, I am not Merich. I know only too well your situation. Marry Benevolensky? No matter what beast comes along and gets the giddy and outlandish idea to propose to you, you can do nothing but accept him, marry him. No, this is unbearable. It's downright irritating, terrible. Know something, Marya Andrevna? I am a poor man. I can scarcely support myself, let alone a wife. But I would never do what Merich has done. And I certainly wouldn't have given you up as a sacrifice to Benevolensky. Marya Andrevna, I offer you my own hand. I want to prove to you I am a noble person.

MARYA. Oh, Ivan Ivanych, I wouldn't want to hurt you, but there's nothing I can do. I don't need your help, and I don't need your nobility, either. I'd never marry you, not for anything in the world.

MILASHIN. Oh, of course, I am no Benevolensky. He is a suitor to envy, all right.

MARYA. Benevolensky is a person with property. And mama wants me to marry him. That's the reason I prefer Benevolensky.

MILASHIN.   You don't want to? Well, it's up to you. Only one thing hurts me. Why is it you humiliate me, put me lower than a fellow like Merich, of all people? I make you an honest proposal, and you get mad at me. But you didn't chase Merich out when he was running after you.

MARYA.   Listen here, what do you take me for? You don't have a bit of respect for me. No, I must stop this once and for all. Enough of crying. [*Wipes her eyes.*] If Merich made a proposal now, I'd never marry him. I'll marry Benevolensky. That's been decided. Can you see if I've been crying? I want to show mama that I've made my decision without the least bit of effort. Let her be happy, have peace of mind. I'll take all the responsibility. And you can stop sulking, too. Take a look. Can you see any tears at all?

MILASHIN.   Scarcely any at all.

MARYA.   Well, thank God for that. Let's try and laugh, try and talk about something else. Haven't you gone to the theatre the last day or so?

MILASHIN.   I suppose you believe you're deceiving me and yourself to boot. Why are you doing it? You see, I know what's going on inside.

MARYA.   [*Stamps her foot.*]   I'm not deceiving you at all. Really, I'm happy all of a sudden, somehow. Let's play something or other. Oh, here are the cards. Let's play cards.

MILASHIN.   All right, let's play. It's up to you. [*Sits at the table.*]

MARYA.   What do you want to play? Let's play the game of fools.[31]

MILASHIN.   [*Deals the cards.*]   Let's play, let's play. Listen, Marya Andrevna, you are pretending. You don't want me to see your tears. Why try and hide them from me? I'm no stranger to you. Boy, that irritates me, it really does.

MARYA.   Play, keep playing, or else you'll get stranded.

MILASHIN.   You are so proud you don't want me to share your fate. You know it's pretty clear to me that you're pretending.

MARYA.   There you are, you're stranded! [*Laughs.*]

MILASHIN.   Well what do you know? I'm stranded. [*Shuffles the cards and deals.*]   You know it irritates me, irritates the devil out of me. So you call it pride? You humiliate me. You don't think I amount to anything at all.

MARYA. Are you going to take that card? And that one, too? Well, you've done it again, you're stranded. [*Laughs.*]

MILASHIN. You know this is unbearable, simply unbearable.

MARYA. Deal out the cards, deal them. What's wrong with you? [MILASHIN *deals. Deep in thought,* MARYA *covers her eyes with a handkerchief and leans on the table. Then she wipes her eyes and takes the cards.*] Who goes now, me? [ANNA *enters.*]

ANNA. What are you laughing about?

MARYA. Why, Ivan Ivanych gets stranded all the time. You don't know how to play, not at all. Mama, when are we going to write the answer to Maksim Dorofeich? [*Continues to play cards.*] Thank him for his proposal and tell him that I agree.

ANNA. Masha, you agree? Well, thank you, you've given me comfort. And I can see you love me now. You've made me happy. Indeed, so happy I can't say enough. Ivan Ivanych, look at the daughter I have . . . beautiful and smart. Now, where did that paper go? Here, all of a sudden, I don't have the slightest idea what to write now. [*Takes paper and writes.* MARYA *and* MILASHIN *play cards.*]

MARYA. [*To* MILASHIN.] If only it were over soon. I'm losing all my strength. [*Rises.*] Give it to me, and I'll help. What are you writing?

ANNA. Here it is. "My dear sir, Maksim Dorofeich. I thank you for your flattering proposal to us. Mashenka agrees and asks you over for a cup of tea." Think that's good enough? I don't know, really. Hm? Or should I write something else?

MARYA. No, it's excellent, excellent. Now, let it be delivered at once.

ANNA. No, really, is it good enough? Ivan Ivanych, is it all right?

MILASHIN. Very good.

ANNA. Shouldn't I add a little something?

MARYA. No, it's not necessary, nothing more is needed. It's enough. Now, send it at once. Darya! Darya! [DARYA *enters.*] Send someone at once with this letter to Maksim Dorofeich. Go on, Darya, at once. I can't stand it any longer. Ivan Ivanych, I feel faint. [MILASHIN *runs and gives her a chair.* MARYA *sits for several moments, utterly exhausted; then, she dissolves in tears.*]

ANNA. Mashenka! Mashenka! What is it? What's wrong with you?

MILASHIN.   [*Aside.*]   What's going on here?

MARYA.   Nothing, it will pass soon. I feel rather faint. Don't worry.

ANNA.   Kiss me, Mashenka. My sweet, darling . . .

MARYA.   Tell me, mama, is he a good person?

ANNA.   Good? Why, I'd never give you to a bad person.

MARYA.   [*In tears.*]   Is he going to love me? If he'll love me, then I'll love him.

ANNA.   Then what are you crying about, you silly thing, you?

MILASHIN.   Don't tell me you're surprised Marya Andrevna is crying? That's strange.

ANNA.   And what's strange in that, my dear? She said it herself. She wanted to marry Benevolensky, and now she's crying. Don't you think he's a good match?

MILASHIN.   And what's so special about Benevolensky?

ANNA.   Why, aren't you something! You're pretty young to go around telling older people what's what. He is a man of substance, not much over thirty years old. And he has property. He is engaged in business, while the only thing on your mind is silly nonsense. Yes, and downright vulgarity,[32] too.

MILASHIN.   Property! But where did he get that property, I must ask? I have a conscience, and that's the reason I don't have property. Getting property isn't so hard.

ANNA.   All right, go ahead and get some, and then you can talk all you want.

MILASHIN.   I can say right off who is an honorable man and who isn't. Happiness isn't in wealth but in a peaceful soul. To link your fate to a person like that is just asking for trouble. Wait and see if they don't drag him into court. . . .

ANNA.   Oh, as if I have to stand around here listening to reason after reason. I, my dear, am the mother. You think I'm doing it for no purpose. You're a youngster, and you're too young to teach me. Go on, get some kids of your own and then try and marry them off the best you know how. Anybody in the world can teach, but when it comes down to practical matters, they've got nothing going for them. All it comes down to is a lot of giddy and outlandish ideas, silly and stupid. Now then, I've gone and lost my snuffbox. Oh, the hell with you! Darya! Darya!

DARYA.   [*Enters.*]   What do you want?

ANNA. What are you goggling at? Look for my snuffbox. [DARYA *exits*.]

MILASHIN. Scold me as much as you like, but why should you bury Marya Andrevna, I'd like to know?

ANNA. Go on, get out of here. I won't listen to you. Seems to me she must know what kind of a mother I've been to her. Think what it's cost me just to raise her. I should get some kind of comfort or other out of her. Enough of your crying, now.

MARYA. Really, mama, haven't I done my best to please you? Have I ever dissatisfied you, in any way?

ANNA. Why go on jabbering about the past? I don't want to know about it. I suppose you think it's easy for me to remember when you've pleased me, and when you haven't. Oh, I can see your gratitude now. Day or night, there's no peace for your mother in her old age. I'm just a woman, and I'm plain tired out. Well, I found her a husband, the like of which even she isn't worthy of. But she cries and wastes away to nothing just like I was some kind of villain.

MARYA. But, you know, mama, I've agreed to it.

ANNA. Oh, I can see how you've agreed to it.   [DARYA *enters*.] What are you after now?

DARYA. Here's your snuffbox, please.

ANNA. How do you like that! Coming in here at a time like this.

DARYA. [*As she exits*.]   Well, go on, keep on cackling, cackling.

ANNA. Any other girl would be so happy she wouldn't know how to thank her mother for a husband like that, instead of doing her best to get her mother upset. It's a woman's way. I am just a woman, dull and commonplace. But a lot you care. You won't think about your mother or how to make her happy.

MARYA. Mama! For God's sake, what are you saying!   [*Weeps*.] Oh, dear God in heaven, what does it all mean?

ANNA. [*A brief silence; then speaks more calmly*.]   Oh, well, I won't complain about you, of course. You've always listened to me. But what's wrong with you now, Mashenka? Now enough of that. Stop it. You know I'm sorry for you, myself. I've hurt you. But what could I do? Forgive me. You see, I'm a woman. I have a heart that's weak and it gets heated up too fast. It gets to boiling, and I can't stop it. But it's all your fault for driving me to it. Sometimes I go and say something in the heat of the moment. You know it's a sin to get upset with me over that. It's a woman's way.

MARYA. I'm not upset with you . . .

ANNA. What can I do? Good or bad, I am your mother all the same. You'll get married, and then that's the end of me. Well, enough, my dear, enough. I suppose you think I'm happy to see you cry. If you think that way then I want nothing more to do with you. [*All characters are on the left side of the stage.* MIKHAILO *enters and stops in the middle of the stage.*]

MIKHAILO. Marya Andrevna! My mother insulted you. I have come to ask forgiveness for her.

ANNA. Yes, my dear, there's no use talking. That mother of yours is a good woman.

MARYA. [*Softly.*] Mama, it seems he is drunk. Please be quiet.

MILASHIN. [*To* MARYA.] This is the fourth day he's been drinking. As soon as he left you, he started in drinking. All he does is walk around the room crying and drinking.

MARYA. Oh, no! Oh, the poor man.

MIKHAILO. What's this? Tears. What are you crying about? I didn't want to hurt you. I would die for you, Marya Andrevna. That mother of mine . . . She is a simple woman. I didn't know she was at your house, I didn't know. I would never have let her come. She is a simple woman, she doesn't understand anything. How could she understand? What can I do? Mother loves . . . she raised me. Marya Andrevna, forgive me. [*Falls on his knees.*]

MARYA. Oh, don't do it, Mikhailo Ivanych, don't. Get up, please. I'm not angry at you or your mother. On the contrary, I am thankful that you like me.

MIKHAILO. [*Rises.*] What are you crying about? Tell me, what are you crying about? Who hurt you?

ANNA. Oh, young man, young man . . .

MIKHAILO. What's wrong, Anna Petrovna! [*To himself.*] Oh, you don't know. Better keep quiet, then. [*To* MARYA.] Has your mother hurt you, really? Don't be mad at her. . . Never mind about her. She doesn't know . . . Don't be mad at her. You know she loves you . . . raised you . . . taught . . .

ANNA. Let's go, Mashenka, it's time to dress. Maksim Dorofeich will be here soon. [*To* MILASHIN, *softly.*] Show him out, Ivan Ivanych.

MILASHIN.   [*Takes his hat.*]   Let's go, Mikhailo Ivanych.

MIKHAILO.   What? A child, a silly kid!

MILASHIN.   Don't be sour, don't! I want to show you out because you are drunk. [MIKHAILO *stands, deep in thought.*]

MARYA.   [*Rises.*]   Stop, Ivan Ivanych.

MILASHIN.   Why on earth is he so sour? It irritates me, it does.

MIKHAILO.   Yes, it's terrible, terrible. Forgive me. What am I good for? Drunk in somebody else's home.

MARYA.   Oh, I feel sorry for him. Oh, dear Lord, how sorry I am!

MIKHAILO.   Marya Andrevna, don't despise me. I love you. I couldn't bear your answer. Of course, it was bad of me . . . mean . . . unworthy. But what could I do? I am a wretched man. You see, I love you, love you so very much.

MARYA.   I love you myself, Mikhailo Ivanych. I'm terribly sorry I found out about you too late. I am going to marry . . . Benevolensky. [*Weeps.*]

MIKHAILO.   Benevolensky! It's a sacrifice. Yes, a sacrifice. Well, then . . . nobly . . . nobly . . . tears.

MARYA.   [*Sits on a chair.*]   Oh, Mikhailo Ivanych, it's hard for me, very hard.

ANNA.   She is doing it for her mother. Maksim Dorofeich is a good man and with property.

MIKHAILO.   Yes, with property. Tears, tears . . . tears forever . . . wasting away, without ever living, never seeing the joy of living . . . Good-by. [*Falls on his knees, takes* MARYA's *hand and kisses it.*] I shall never live through it. [MARYA *faints. Everyone bustles around her.* MIKHAILO *weeps, leaning against the wall.*]

ACT FIVE

A small room is represented on stage. To the right of the audience is a door leading to the reception room. Nearer to the audience is a tall mirror (pier glass). Upstage center is the door leading to the hallway. To the left is a couch; in front of the couch, a round table. Farther away, another door. In the corner, an ordinary table, on which are cups and bottles. DARYA *is placing bottles on the table. A* WAITER *is placing cups on a tray; then he takes the tray and crosses to the door.* DOBROTVORSKY *enters.*

DOBROTVORSKY. What's that you're carrying, my boy?

WAITER. Tea, sir.

DOBROTVORSKY. How about rounding up some rum?

WAITER. First, we serve tea as it is, sir.

DOBROTVORSKY. Ekh, brother! You know who it is you're treating, don't you? See all those men of business we've pulled together. Look at them sitting around out there with those bright buttons.

WAITER. Darya Semenovna,[33] some rum, please, ma'am.

DARYA. What's wrong now? Oh, to hell with you! Rum, did you say?

WAITER. They're wanting rum, ma'am. [*Takes a bottle and puts it on the tray.*]

DOBROTVORSKY. Give some to me, and I'll just sit at the side here and drink my punch, free and easy like. [*Takes cup and sits on a couch. The* WAITER *exits, door to the right. A* WOMAN *enters, wearing a cloak and kerchief.*]

THE WOMAN IN THE CLOAK. Will there be dancing, dearie? My young miss sent me to ask. We have seven young ladies at our place, dearie. "Be sure and find out," she says, "if there'll be dancing, then we'll go look."

DARYA. There will, there will. Oh, to hell with you there. [*The* WOMAN *exits. Several persons enter and exit out the door to the right. A* COACHMAN *appears in the doorway.*] What are you here for?

COACHMAN. To look at the wedding.

DARYA. Oh, you lunkhead, you. Trying to crawl through here, are you!

COACHMAN. I suppose you think you're something, huh? A young lady, no less.

DARYA. Don't you go flapping back at me. What're you unraveling your tongue for, anyway?

COACHMAN. Now you just quiet down a bit or no doubt you'll scare me to death.

DARYA. I tell you beat it. Go on with you!

COACHMAN. I'm going. [*Exits.*]

DARYA. Oh, to hell with you. Oh, wouldn't I just like . . . [*Exits. Several people enter and look through the door, right. Among them are* TWO WOMEN, *rather well dressed; a* GIRL *wearing a kerchief;* TWO YOUNG MEN, *each dressed in a blue kaftan.*]

FIRST YOUNG MAN. [*To the* GIRL *wearing a kerchief.*] Mind pointing out which is the bridegroom, miss?

THE GIRL. There he is.

FIRST YOUNG MAN. Oh, that's the one, miss. And where's the bride, miss?

THE GIRL. There she is.

FIRST YOUNG MAN. Oh, that's the one, miss. And do you live far from here, miss?

THE GIRL. Only a hop, skip and a jump.

FIRST YOUNG MAN. I'm not too far away, myself, miss. Permit me to see you home.

THE GIRL. Oh, I know the way without you.

SECOND YOUNG MAN. [*To the* FIRST YOUNG MAN.] Oho! Looks like you grabbed the dipper and took off for the home-made booze. [*To* THE GIRL.] Why listen to him? Look, he's pretty well-known around us for things like that. [*To the* FIRST YOUNG MAN.] What're you pestering her for, anyway? Listen, brother, you're not about to pick up anything here. See, you flew right past and missed. [*To* THE GIRL.] The other day or so, he saw one home, all the way from town to Rogozhskaya Street. And when he got there the yardman scared him off with a broom. So he walked all the way there and back for nothing.

FIRST YOUNG MAN.   Enough of your lying, fellow.

SECOND YOUNG MAN.   What do you mean, lying? With a snout like yours, you should talk. You see what kind of a young lady she is, don't you? What do you say, miss, live around here? [*They continue to talk in whispers. Two young women,* DUNYA[34] *and* PASHA,[35] *come out of the crowd and cross downstage.*]

PASHA.   Really, aren't you sorry about him, Dunya?

DUNYA.   Look, there's nothing I'm sorry about. What I haven't gone through, living with him! It used to be he'd come in, drunk and raising Cain, just like he'd gone clean raving mad. I kept telling him, "Let me go free; if only you'd get married, maybe you'd settle down a bit." "If you'd get a pretty young lady," I said, "then maybe you'd turn out a decent person; as it is, you're just wasting yourself, somehow."

PASHA.   Don't tell me you said that!

DUNYA.   Sure I did. That way, too, Pasha.

PASHA.   Well, it's all dead and buried, now. Let's go look at the dowry.

DUNYA.   Let's go, Pasha.   [PASHA *and* DUNYA *exit through the door, left. Little by little, the crowd breaks up. Several old women remain.* DOBROTVORSKY *drinks punch.* MARYA *and* BENEVOLENSKY *enter.*]

BENEVOLENSKY.   You, young lady, have only to tell me what to do, and I'll carry it out, exactly.

MARYA.   You're going to listen to me in everything, Maksim Dorofeich?

BENEVOLENSKY.   Take the word of an honorable man.

MARYA.   I'll tell you frankly, I don't like one or two things about you. I'd like you to give up several habits. I'll marry you on those conditions. Will you listen to me?

BENEVOLENSKY.   Everything, whatever you like. Since I love you I'm ready for anything. You didn't like me drinking vodka, so I gave it up. You told me not to take snuff, so I don't any longer. Oh, Platon Markych, you're here. Come over to my place some time, and I'll make you a present of a silver snuffbox.

DOBROTVORSKY.   Thank you a lot, Maksim Dorofeich. I'll drop over some time.

BENEVOLENSKY. [*To* MARYA.] I am your humble servant for life. Permit me to kiss your little hand. Perhaps you'd like to stay here alone?

MARYA.   Yes, I must talk with Platon Markych.

BENEVOLENSKY.   I'll go then, ma'am. You see how I listen to you. [*Crosses to* DOBROTVORSKY.] What do you say, am I handling myself slick enough?

DOBROTVORSKY. [*Nodding his head with approval.*] Good enough. [BENEVOLENSKY *exits.*]

MARYA.   Am I a silly fool, Platon Markych? Tell me. You know it's true, don't you?

DOBROTVORSKY.   You're not serious. Who dares say that! You're our smart little girl.

MARYA.   Platon Markych, listen to me. I've just thought of something. Maybe it will seem funny to you. I was thinking, thinking . . . and do you know what I finally came up with? [DOBROTVORSKY *looks at her.*] Only, don't you laugh at me. It seemed to me I was marrying him to reform him, to make a decent person out of him. You know it's silly, Platon Markych? You know it's nonsense, it's impossible to do, hm? Platon Markych, isn't that so? It's all childish dreams?

DOBROTVORSKY.   Ferocious animals, and they tame them . . .

MARYA.   If I didn't think I could, Platon Markych, I don't believe I could live through it. It would be too hard. Right now I live for that one thought. Help me to see it through, Platon Markych.

DOBROTVORSKY.   You know, young lady, I'll tell you a Russian proverb. "What will be, will be; but what will be, God grants." But another proverb says, "You can't outrun the bridegroom, even on horseback." [MARYA *sits on a chair, near the tall mirror; she is deep in thought.* DARYA *enters and drives the spectators from the stage; the spectators exit through the upstage door.*]

DARYA.   Oh, to hell with you. Where do you think you're going? If you want to watch, then stand in the hallway. And what do you think you're going to see? Oh, that's something, isn't it? Really, something!

MARYA.   Fix up my hair, please. [DOBROTVORSKY *exits.*]

DARYA. [*Arranging her coiffure.*] Miss, Vladimir Vasilich is here in the garden.

MARYA.   Well, so what?

DARYA.   He wants permission to come in; he wants to talk to you.

MARYA.   Oh, what could he . . . ? Bolt the door. Call him in.
[DARYA *exits.*]   Why on earth has he come? I'll listen to what
he has to say. It's strange how soon I fell out of love with him.
Right now he looks like any other man. Here I am, waiting for
him, and I'm not the least bit upset. And before? [MERICH
enters. MARYA *does not turn around to him.*]   Why have you
come?

MERICH.   To look at you for the last time. Don't tell me you'll
refuse me even . . . ?

MARYA.   [*Turning around to him.*]   Am I beautiful?

MERICH.   Bewitching.

MARYA.   Good-by. It's time I went to the groom.

MERICH.   Oh, wait a bit, Marya Andrevna, for God's sake. Listen
to what I have to say. At least let me admire you a few moments
longer.

MARYA.   I'm listening. What do you want?

MERICH.   Don't be mad at me, Marya Andrevna.

MARYA.   I'm not mad at you.

MERICH.   You want to say I'm not even worth getting mad at.
Excuse me, but I think you don't understand me. I want to put
things straight in your eyes.

MARYA.   What do you want to put straight? I take all the blame,
myself. I thought you were a person capable of love, but I was
mistaken. I was looking for love, and you—for intrigues and
conquests. You and I are no match, no match at all.

MERICH.   I loved you sincerely, Marya Andrevna.

MARYA.   It's not true, Vladimir Vasilich. [*Having thought a
little.*]   Tell me, please, who is it you're deceiving? What do you
expect to gain? No doubt all your conquests are the same as it
was with me. The girl throws herself at you, and you run around
bragging of your conquest. Isn't that so? I would have fallen
out of love with you soon enough, no matter how far our love
might have gone. A little more suffering, repentance, shame,
perhaps . . . but all the same I would have fallen out of love
with you. I needed you to love me. It's the only thing I ever
wanted.

MERICH.   Priceless woman!

MARYA.   Before, you didn't want to listen to me at all. And now, you will listen to everything I have to say. How happy I would have been, if I had been born more of a coquette. I would have spent more time with dressing up, little intrigues, and everything would have been much easier, happier. I might have fallen in love and had a little fun, besides. Right now I look at life much differently. I am going to get married, and I want to be a good wife.

MERICH.   Dear God in heaven, what a mistake I made! I never really knew you, Marya Andrevna. I see now how vulgar and stupid[36] my behavior was . . .

MARYA.   I don't know whether you're saying these things straight from the heart or not. But I believe you. I don't want to hurt you. I'm not mad at you because of myself. I hope it will serve as a lesson to you. Let's say good-by as friends. [*Holds out her hand.*]

MERICH.   [*Kissing her hand.*]   I love you, Meri.

MARYA.   It's too late, Vladimir Vasilich, too late. A new path lies ahead of me, and I know what my future will be like already. I have much, so much for me to do—all cut out for a woman's heart. They say he is rude, uneducated, a bribe-taker. Perhaps it's because he's never had a decent person around him, no woman at all. They say a woman can do a lot, once she makes up her mind. There is my obligation. And I feel that I have the strength inside to do it. I shall force him to love, respect and obey me. And eventually—children. I shall live for the children. You smile. How honorable that is of you! Even if everything I've been saying to you were dreams alone, all the same I don't believe you should try to disillusion me. I need them desperately right now, to help me get through this difficult time. Oh, Vladimir Vasilich, never mind, never mind. You know it's difficult for me . . . very, very difficult, and no one on earth will ever realize it.

MERICH.   I wish you all the happiness in the world. As far as I'm concerned, I don't see how it's possible with a man like that.

MARYA.   No, Vladimir Vasilich, you'll never see the torment I'm going through. I'm not going to give you the pleasure of feeling sorry for me. I don't care what the circumstances are, I want to be happy. I want to, no matter what it may cost me. Why

should I suffer? Judge for yourself. Well, judge. Just because I
made a mistake, and you deceived me. Just because I'm carrying out my duty and saving my mother . . . No, no, no! I shall
be happy, I shall be loved. Isn't that so? Say it . . . Yes, yes
. . . tell me! I need it more than anything. Don't disillusion
me. . . .

MERICH.   [Having thought a little while.]   Yes.

MARYA.   Thank you with all my heart. Good-by. [Exits.]

MERICH.   [Alone.]   What a clever, clever girl! [37] I'd like to know
what she thinks of me. You don't suppose she considers me shallow, superficial, do you? Anyhow, thank the good Lord it's all
over and done with. If she'd been any sillier, I'd never have
known how to get free of her. Oh, reproaches would've been
going on forever, and I might have ended up marrying her.
[MILASHIN enters.]

MILASHIN.   What, you're here?

MERICH.   Yes, I came to say good-by to Meri. I loved her, Ivan
Ivanych. I won't hide it from you. You don't know how much it
hurts me to lose a woman like that. Oh, did she love me, too!
And you look at her right now. See how much will power she has,
how strongly she bears up under all the torment she's going
through. I alone know what she's going through. I won't say a
word about myself. I'm a man, after all. Are you here for the
whole affair?

MILASHIN.   Yes.

MERICH.   Do me a favor and see if she grieves a lot. Then comfort her. I'd be greatly obliged if you did. And, please, try to
do it so nothing will remind her of me. I put my hopes on you,
Ivan Ivanych. Good-by. [Exits.]

MILASHIN.   Oh, it's terrible, terrible. She hasn't said one word
to me the whole evening, but she came here to say good-by
to Merich. I've been going around, pining away three hours at
a time, and I don't get so much as a single glance. Boy, that
irritates the hell out of me. I hope my face shows how deep my
sorrow really is.[38]   [Looks at the mirror.]   Phew, now that's a
stupid expression, if I ever saw one. It's even funny. No, just
let her notice the evil irony in my eyes. [Looks at the mirror.]
But what if she doesn't want to look . . . Oh, why, why go on and
on, fussing around like this? Shall I leave? No doubt she'd never

even notice my absence. Oh, the devil take it, anyway. No, I'll stay. I shall be a cold-blooded spectator. I shall observe everything, coldly. Now that I come to think of it, what am I getting heated up for anyway? Oh, how beautiful, how very beautiful she is today. And the way she walks, and the way she looks, magnificent! No, the devil take it, it irritates me. Boy, does it irritate me. And look at the way the bulls and beasts dance around her. I suppose I'm just crabby today, must be my liver's acting up again. But that bridegroom, that bridegroom! Why, she's even making over him. No, she'll see, she will, the kind of looks I'll throw her way. [*Exits. Several persons cross the stage and exit door right.* BENEVOLENSKY *and* DOBROTVORSKY *enter, arm in arm.*]

BENEVOLENSKY.   I am grateful to you, Platon Markych, very grateful. You've made me obligated to you. Yes, very, very much so. Marya Andrevna is smart and educated. Exactly the kind of wife I need.

DOBROTVORSKY.   Hee, hee, hee, you old reprobate, you. No use talking now. They hooked a fine fellow, indeed. Whatever she is, there's no slipping back now! I'm joking, that's all, joking. . . .

BENEVOLENSKY.   Yes, sir, I tell you I'm not ashamed to show off a wife like that in society. [*Stops in front of the mirror and strokes his chin.*]   Tell me, do we match up pretty well? What do you think?

DOBROTVORSKY.   Oh, you joker, you. How do you like that? What silly nonsense will you come up with next!

BENEVOLENSKY.   What are you laughing at?

DOBROTVORSKY.   Enough of your silly jokes, now. I'm going to die laughing. Kiss me. [*They exchange kisses.*]

BENEVOLENSKY.   [*Aside.*]   What's he laughing at? [*To* DOBROTVORSKY.]   Listen, Platon Markych, I have a serious thing to talk over with you.

DOBROTVORSKY.   What's on your mind?

BENEVOLENSKY.   [*Takes him by the arm.*]   We were youngsters, once upon a time. [DOBROTVORSKY *nods his head as a sign of agreement.*]   Youth, as you know, has its own weaknesses. You know it very well, yourself. Otherwise, I'd never have brought it up.

DOBROTVORSKY.   All of us are sinners, and all of us are mortal. . . .

BENEVOLENSKY.   That's true, but it's not what I'm talking about.
Just listen to me. Mistakes like this are very peculiar to youth.
You see, I loved a certain girl. . . .

DOBROTVORSKY.   Hm! You don't say. Was the girl pretty?

BENEVOLENSKY.   Far from bad-looking. Well, of course, she came
from the lower classes, but far from bad-looking. The only
thing is that her nature doesn't quite match up with her appearance. She is jealous.

DOBROTVORSKY.   That appears surprising to you. Ekh, youth.
Wait till you're my age, and then you won't be surprised. Say,
I'll tell you a good story right now—only listen—it's not like
you and your girl friend, but then, just think of the things you
tell me. In fact, it was before the French came to . . .

BENEVOLENSKY.   Oh, you are a muddle-headed idiot, Platon
Markych. I'm scared to death she will show up here.

DOBROTVORSKY.   Who?

BENEVOLENSKY.   This girl, I mean.

DOBROTVORSKY.   Why? No, how come she'd show up here? Oh,
you can't be serious.

BENEVOLENSKY.   Understand me, Platon Markych. I tell you
she is jealous, and I'm scared to death she'll make a helluva row.

DOBROTVORSKY.   That's it. Ah! Now I get you.

BENEVOLENSKY.   Now then, you arrange it, brother, so they
won't let any outsiders in.

DOBROTVORSKY.   My boy, what on earth are you doing to my
Marya Andrevna? Why, you're going to kill her, the poor darling.
Now you let all this silly stuff alone, my boy.

BENEVOLENSKY.   Oh, what are you talking about? Look, I stopped
it a long time ago. Only, being careful won't harm a thing, all
the same. Do you understand me?

DOBROTVORSKY.   All right, sir. I understand now. [*Exits.*]

BENEVOLENSKY.   [*Alone.*] The important thing in life is brains
and foresight. What exactly was I, and what am I now? Here's
the story, all of it. It used to be I bowed to everyone I met,
just so I wouldn't get beaten for something or other. And now,
why nobody can touch me, nobody. I've got money, and I've
found a beauty of a wife. Oho, the devil take it! [*Clasps his
hands, then tugs his forelock.*] Oh, you, Maksimka[39] Benevolensky, you. And did you ever think about this kind of luck,

sitting there in school and wearing your shabby smock? No, sir, brother, not a bit of it. Here . . . [*taps forehead with his finger*] . . . Here's how I punched my way in. Necessity gives birth to brains, and brains give birth to money, and with brains and money you can do anything in the world. [*Deep in thought.*] Wonder if I should learn to dance? Yes, I will. Or do I need it? No, whatever for? It just isn't right for a man of business. But sometimes I feel so good, I want to break into a dance. [*Bobs up and down a little. Several persons enter from the reception room. He stops in a tolerable pose and stuffs his hand into his waistcoat. From the door, left, enter the* FIRST *and* SECOND WOMEN, PASHA *and* DUNYA.]

DUNYA.   Oh, Maksim Dorofeich, how do you do! My regards to you. [BENEVOLENSKY *turns aside.*]   Tell me, you recognize me, don't you? Well?

BENEVOLENSKY.   Oh, it's you, Dunya! What on earth are you . . .

DUNYA.   To take a look at your bride.

BENEVOLENSKY.   But how could you! You know I'd never have let . . .

DUNYA.   What wouldn't you let? You mean, you wouldn't have let me in. Oh, you shameless man, you. You, with your impudent eyes, you . . .

BENEVOLENSKY.   No, there's nothing I . . . I, well. All right, Dunya, go on, go on and look. Over there is the bride, and there is the dowry. . . .

DUNYA.   Oh, so that's it, is it? Go ahead and look. But I shouldn't look at you, I suppose. See, Pasha, he's sending me off to look at everything. Why, isn't he nice? He'll show me everything, himself. Tell you what, dearie, he's no stranger, you see. Oh, you sweet old bird, you.

BENEVOLENSKY.   You, Dunya, be a little more careful. Somebody might see, and that'd be too bad. [*Strikes a pose.*]

DUNYA.   Do you want me to cut loose and raise a rumpus, right now?

BENEVOLENSKY.   Oh, you fool, you fool, you. You're not serious, you can't be.

DUNYA.   Don't be afraid, don't. What are you scared to death of, anyway? I'm not in your class, you know.

BENEVOLENSKY.   No, Dunya, that will do. Yes, indeed. If you need anything, you'd be better off coming to my house.

DUNYA.   I'd never in my life go to you, don't worry.

BENEVOLENSKY.   But, Dunya, what are you doing here, then? All right, take a look at the bride, and then get out of here.

DUNYA.   I've seen her already. You know she's good-looking, Pasha. Yes, I can say she's good-looking. [*To* BENEVOLENSKY.] Only thing, do you know how to live with a woman like that? See you don't destroy her life for nothing. That would be sinful of you. Just settle down and live better than you used to. You weren't like that with me, you know. We lived and lived, and all of a sudden that was the last I saw of you. [*Wipes her eyes.*]

PASHA.   But you said you weren't a bit sorry.

DUNYA.   You know I loved him, then. Why, we had to part sometime or other. You can't go on living forever like that. Oh, it's good he's getting married. Maybe he'll live right and decent, now. But, all the same, Pasha, you know full well we lived together five years. Miserable, you know. Of course, I saw a little good out of him . . . but more, far more, tears. Oh, the shame I've had to put up with. And so, my youth went by, gone. Gone forever, and nothing ever came of it. Nothing.

PASHA.   What can you do, Dunya!

DUNYA.   But, you know, it used to be whenever he showed up, I was so happy, almost out of my mind with happiness. [*To* BENEVOLENSKY.]   Look, mind you live better than you used to. Right and decent, now.

BENEVOLENSKY.   Oh, sure. Of course.

DUNYA.   Just see that you do. That girl, you know, is yours forever, not at all like me. Well, good-by, think kindly of me; it's no good thinking otherwise. What was I doing, anyway, breaking into tears like that? What a fool I was, really. Oh, let's have done with it, Pasha, and hang our sorrow with a rope.

BENEVOLENSKY.   Good-by, Dunya!

DUNYA.   *Ade, muse!* [40] Let's go, Pasha. [DUNYA *and* PASHA *exit.*]

BENEVOLENSKY.   The crazy woman! It's even better it turned out this way. But, you know, I was scared to death. [*The* WAITER *enters.*]   Give me, brother, a glass of sherry, please. Phew! Like a mountain off my shoulders. [*The* WAITER *hands him the glass.*]   Thanks, fellow. [*Exits. Several persons appear on stage. Among them, two* WOMEN.]

FIRST WOMAN.   You know they say, "Don't be envious." How

can you help being envious, I'd like to know? Only one daughter, and see what they've hooked, a nice fellow, really something. And here I've got three daughters, and I can't get them off my hands. No matter how much I want to. But you know, I suppose they trapped the young fellow, somehow. Or why on earth marry her? You know there's nothing to her. Nothing at all.

SECOND WOMAN.   Well, dearie, you've come up with something to envy, all right.

FIRST WOMAN.   And why?

SECOND WOMAN.   Well, they say he's such a sweet old bird, that there'll be nothing but trouble. [*Two* OLD WOMEN *are heard.*]

FIRST OLD WOMAN.   The trunks have been hammered shut with iron, but no doubt they're empty.

SECOND OLD WOMAN.   Oh, no, they're full.

FIRST OLD WOMAN.   Where'd you get that, full? Anything good they've got, you could twist around your little finger.

SECOND OLD WOMAN.   Maybe you've been poking around other people's trunks?

FIRST OLD WOMAN.   I never poke around. Maybe somebody else did the poking.

SECOND OLD WOMAN.   Oh, you just like to backbite people, that's all. But what did he get with the girl, exactly?

FIRST OLD WOMAN.   A lot more than with you.

SECOND OLD WOMAN.   And who is it steals wood from other people's yards?

FIRST OLD WOMAN.   You're lying. I never steal.

SECOND OLD WOMAN.   Oh, yes, you steal.

FIRST OLD WOMAN.   Oh, you, you . . . [*The two* OLD WOMEN *disappear into the crowd. Out of the door, left, enter* ANNA, DOBROTVORSKY, *and* DARYA.]

ANNA.   Oh, I'm plain done in today. I don't have a bit of strength left. Let's sit down and rest a little. [*Sits on couch.*]

DOBROTVORSKY.   What of it, ma'am? You know it's your own doing. "You never feel a burden of your own making," as the proverb says. You fixed everything up, and it's a blessing for you.

ANNA.   You don't know how happy I am, Platon Markych, you just can't imagine. It's high time I knew a little peace. I'm a weak woman, dull and commonplace, and I had to deny myself in everything. But you know how I lived, when my husband—

now at rest—was alive. I was completely spoiled in every which
way.

DOBROTVORSKY. You were well cared for, even indulged, Anna
Petrovna.

ANNA. I tell you, Platon Markych, how much I've always loved
weddings. Don't give me a bite of bread, and I'll go to a wedding
any day. That's feast enough for me. Here, God has willed that
I marry off my little daughter. I never expected to live to see
happiness like this. How many times I've dreamed of this. Then
I dreamed again and again of dancing, dancing, and the way I
danced. You know, when I was young I could dance beautifully.
And once I dreamed I seemed almost drunk. Yes, fully and completely drunk, and I was swearing at you so much, it was simply
out of this world.

DOBROTVORSKY. To joy and happiness, ma'am.

ANNA. Well, yes. Thank the good Lord, everything is settled now.

DOBROTVORSKY. Thank the Lord, thank the Lord.

ANNA. Dasha, give us some kind of wine or other, please. Platon
Markych and I will drink to happiness. [DARYA *brings a bottle
and glasses on a tray and puts it on the table.*]

DOBROTVORSKY. [*Drinks.*] I have the honor to wish you the
best, Anna Petrovna. May God grant you life to see your grandchildren and great-grandchildren.

ANNA. Thank you with all my heart, Platon Markych. We are
obliged to you for everything, my dear. [MARYA *enters.*]

MARYA. Are you in here, mama? I was looking for you. [*Crosses
to her mother.*]

ANNA. What's wrong, darling, what's the matter?

MARYA. Oh, mama, I'm unhappy somehow, terribly unhappy.
[*Sits on couch and leans her head against her mother.*]

DOBROTVORSKY. [*Takes a glass.*] What can you do, young lady?
You must get used to it. To your health! Be rich, then don't
go and forget us. Hee, hee, hee. Your hand, please, young lady.
[*Kisses her hand.*]

ANNA. [*Drinks.*] Well, little one, be happy, and think kindly
of your old mother. You'll go on living for a while, then you'll
find out what children are like, exactly. [*Kisses her.*] Do you
like him? I must confess the thing was done a little fast. Who
knows him, really; you can't see inside him.

MARYA. [*In tears.*] Oh, I like him fair to middling, mama. Don't mind my crying. It's just I feel a little upset. I think I'll be happy. . . .

A VOICE IN THE CROWD. Some husbands, dearie,[41] are pretty willful and love to have you please them. You can take it for granted they'll come home drunk most of the time. Then, they love to have you wait on them yourself, and they'll never let anyone else close to them.

MARYA. But if I'm not happy, then it's not your fault, ever. You've done everything for me that you can, that you know how to. Thank you, mama, and you too, Platon Markych. [*From another room, music is heard.* BENEVOLENSKY *enters.* MARYA *crosses to meet him and holds out her hand.*]

DOBROTVORSKY. [*Giving his arm to* ANNA.] And you and I, ma'am, let's go dance the polka. [*They exit.*]

ONE OF THE CROWD. That one, I suppose, is the bride?

AN OLD WOMAN. That's the one, my dear, that's the one.

A WOMAN. How do you like that! Look at the way she is crying, poor thing!

AN OLD WOMAN. Yes, dearie, she is poor, that's for sure. He's taking her for her beauty.

THE STORM

THE STORM

I. COMPOSITION

Ostrovsky began writing *The Storm* in June or July of 1859, completed it the ninth of October, and published it the following January in the journal *Library for Reading*. In the same year a separate edition of the play was printed. The five-act tragedy was his fourteenth original play, and most critics have considered it his masterpiece. In keeping with his usual practice, Ostrovsky had worked out in his own mind the plot, characters, and even the language before he began to put the play down on paper. Nevertheless, he began the first draft as a comedy, but soon decided to write the play as a drama. In a comparison of the various drafts, A. I. Revyakin concluded that Ostrovsky repeatedly rearranged scenes, changed their content, shortened and enlarged the text, changed monologues to dialogues, strengthened the action, and individualized both character and language.

The major source of *The Storm* undoubtedly originated from a trip Ostrovsky made to the upper Volga region. The Maritime Ministry had organized an ethnological expedition in the summers of 1856 and 1857 and had selected the playwright as one of the observers. Concentrating on the economic conditions, work, mode of life *(byt)*, and language of the inhabitants, Ostrovsky collected materials, made careful notes, and kept a diary of his experiences and observations. By the end of the first summer, he had put together most of the information and, in the following summer, he added details and eventually wrote an article, "Journey Along the Volga from the Source to Nizhny-Novgorod." His journey provided background material for other plays as well as for *The Storm.*

As soon as the play appeared, it aroused controversy, and perhaps no other work by Ostrovsky provoked such divided opinion. Several viewed the play as little more than the simple story of a wife's treachery, her crime and repentance. Others greeted the play sympathetically, but felt it was limited artistically. One reviewer considered the action weak, based entirely on chance, its incidents adding up to potpourri.

Summing up the play as a melodrama, A. A. Fet called it unnatural and filled with French manners. Turgenev disagreed. Ostrovsky had given a reading in Turgenev's home, and the novelist sent a sharp note to Fet the next day.

> Where is your flair, your understanding of poetry, when you did not consider *The Storm* . . . as the most amazing, splendid Russian work, mighty, completely possessed by its own talent? . . . I absolutely don't understand, and for the first time I look at you . . . bewildered. Alack! How is it your mind has gone blank?

Harsh condemnation of the play was opposed by enthusiastic response. "The national character is felt," A. S. Gieroglifov wrote, "in every word, in every scene, in every personality of the drama." P. V. Annenkov believed *The Storm* reproduced "the Russian world in its whole simplicity and in its whole truth." In supporting the play for the Uvarov prize, I. A. Goncharov centered on its structure, its characters as typical of living people, and its essential poetry.

> As drama in our literature there has been no work similar to it. It undoubtedly occupies, and probably will long occupy, a first position by its lofty classical beauty. From whatever angle it is viewed—from the standpoint of construction, or dramatic action, or finally, its characters, everywhere it bears the mark of strong creativity, fine power of observation, and grace of completeness.

Even among critics who supported *The Storm*, however, there was disagreement. For example, A. A. Grigor'ev did not accept Dobrolyubov's argument expressed in "The Kingdom of Darkness." He pointed out that Ostrovsky did not depict life "with the evil humor of a satirist," but "with the naïve truth of a folk poet." There were no elements of satire in *The Storm*, nor was Ostrovsky indignant or making a protest. Grigor'ev published his long criticism in January and February 1860, and Dobrolyubov made his reply the following October in a famous article, "A Ray of Light in the Kingdom of Darkness."

In Dobrolyubov's opinion, *The Storm* marked a significant departure in Ostrovsky's "kingdom of darkness," for it introduced a new type of character—Katerina. Rooted in Russian reality and portraying the selfless nature of a Russian woman, Katerina was distinctive, complete, strong and heralded the destruction of the dark universe. To Dobrolyubov, Katerina was a folk character, truly national, and "a bright ray in the kingdom of darkness."

The nature of Katerina, as it is fulfilled in *The Storm*, made a step forward not only in the dramatic reality of Ostrovsky but also in all our literature. It corresponds to a new phase of our people's life; for a long time it demanded its own realization in literature; around it spin our best writers; but they have understood only its necessity without being able to comprehend its nature; this Ostrovsky tried to do.

Although the controversy and divided opinion continued in succeeding years, the criticism of Grigor'ev and Dobrolyubov formed the touchstone of subsequent response. Almost every first-rate Russian critic turned his attention to the play; and since *The Storm* became eventually Ostrovsky's best-known work abroad, the play has had its share of international criticism.

II. STAGE PRODUCTIONS

Shortly after completing *The Storm*, Ostrovsky submitted the play to the censorship office and received authorization for stage productions within three weeks. It was fortunate that the censor I. Nordstrem made the report of the play. In his recommendation for production, Nordstrem stressed the love story and neglected to mention the characters Dikoy, Kuligin, or Feklusha. *The Storm* was produced first at the Maly Theatre (16 November 1859) and next at the Aleksandrinsky Theatre (2 December). Both productions were rehearsed under the direction of the playwright.

Although Ostrovsky counted several actors among his close friends, he was particularly attached to the acting company at the Maly. His close association with the theatre dated from his youth when he became an avid playgoer. Moreover, the Maly often gave his plays their first productions and called on the dramatist for his assistance. Consequently, as soon as he had finished the play, Ostrovsky read *The Storm* aloud to the assembled Maly company at the home of the actress L. P. Kositskaya-Nikulina. N. V. Rykalova recalled that everyone was delighted, predicted immediate success for the play, and warmly congratulated the happy author.

In helping prepare the Maly production, Ostrovsky worked with the actors to reveal not only the outer appearance but also the inner action of the characters. He was especially interested in the spoken language and, as N. Efros observed, "he always wanted actors to give him the impression with the voice only, without the help of mimicry or gestures." Later in his career, Ostrovsky often listened to the productions of his plays, in place of viewing the performances. As a rule, Ostrovsky's plays were poorly designed, and the setting for *The Storm* at the Maly was no exception—simply a collection of old stock scenery. For example, the fourth act described "a narrow arched gallery of an ancient building," but the setting was a prison scene from an old melodrama. Costuming, however, was somewhat better than the settings. The actresses themselves prepared the costumes under the direction of the playwright. Ostrovsky had even brought back a fillet from his trip on the Volga, and the actress playing Varvara wore it. N. V. Rykalova, who performed the role of Marfa, discussed the première.

> The auditorium, of course, was filled, the success of the play took shape after my exit in the first act—loud applause resounded, which by the end of the play turned into a complete triumph directed both at the author and with respect to the cast members. And I must do justice—they performed the play "with hurrah."

Critics were especially pleased with the acting in the first production. The actor playing Boris, however, was considered incompetent for the role and was soon replaced. L. P. Kositskaya-Nikulina as Katerina, P. M. Sadovsky as Dikoy, and S. V. Vasil'ev as Tikhon were judged outstanding. Kositskaya-Nikulina's Katerina was particularly effective in the monologues. One reviewer noted that when she wept, all the spectators wept, too, and as the actress herself loved to say, "I know how to weep." In the scene with the key, as M. I. Pisarev observed, Kositskaya-Nikulina presented clearly "the inner battle between the direction of happiness and the thought of the crime." Ostrovsky felt that the actress was "an ideal Katerina."

In the role of Dikoy, P. M. Sadovsky produced still another splendid character in his gallery of Ostrovsky types. Critics pointed out his ability to create a rude provincial merchant without a trace of Moscow characteristics. S. V. Vasil'ev's Tikhon was judged his crowning achievement. He captured Tikhon's self-pity, weakness, and his joy at getting away from his mother in Act Two. "His very last shriek, 'Mama, you have killed her,'" Koropochevsky wrote, "was terrifying; it shocked the spectator and then for a long time haunted him." Of the remaining actors, N. V. Rykalova as Marfa was successful in a role she continued to play for the next forty years. Having been ill during rehearsals, she opened with only one special rehearsal, in which Ostrovsky gave her the blocking.

At the Aleksandrinsky in Petersburg, *The Storm* opened with huge success. At the end of the third act, and again at the end of the performance, Ostrovsky was called out several times before the audience. Nevertheless, the Petersburg production was inferior to the Moscow. Even though F. A. Snetkova III as Katerina enchanted the audience, she resembled a Petersburg young lady. A. E. Martynov as Tikhon, however, was judged almost as good as S. V. Vasil'ev, and several critics thought him superior in the last act. For example, thirty years later Stakhovich recalled Tikhon's final moments: "Even now . . . I am cold and terrified by that memory." Of the remaining actors, I. F. Gorbunov as Kudryash and Yu. N. Linskaya as Marfa were considered outstanding. As in the Moscow production, the settings were poorly designed. "We must realize," the reviewer in *Contemporary* wrote, "that inadequate scenery was the reason that the play lost much of the poetry on the stage."

In succeeding years *The Storm* was one of Ostrovsky's most popular plays. From 1875 to 1917 the play was performed 3,592 times in Russia, and since the Revolution the play has been produced numerous times. In 1937, for example, it was staged in more than twenty theatres. Since 1945 productions of *The Storm* have diminished, yet now and again theatres enter it into their repertories. It has remained in the repertory of the Mayakovsky in Moscow since 1953. *The Storm* has received productions abroad, and in recent years it has played in Hungary and Finland. The role of Katerina has challenged many actresses, and Fedotova, Ermolova, and Strepetova in the last century were outstanding in their interpretations. In this century *The Storm* has been staged in various styles by famous directors from Meyerhold in 1916 and Tairov in 1924 to Nemirovich-Danchenko in 1934.

III. NAMES OF THE CHARACTERS

In his study of the written versions, A. I. Revyakin noted that Ostrovsky made significant substitutions in the patronymics of Katerina and Dikoy. Katerina's patronymic was changed from Semenovna (the quality of being heard) to Petrovna (stone or jewel). About the same time the playwright changed Dikoy's patronymic from Petrovich to Prokofevich (*Prokof'evich*) which means making progress or getting on. The substitutions were apparently made to coincide with the nature of the characters. For example, Katerina as the daughter of stone exhibits the qualities of strength, resolution, steadfastness. The name Katerina means eternally pure; and even though her married name is

Kabanova, she is referred to only by her first name and patronymic. Moreover, in his cast of characters the playwright stated simply, "Katerina, his wife."

The last name Dikoy combines the meanings of savage, capricious, insane, and the character is called by his last name. His nephew Boris Grigorevich *(Grigor'evich)* has the same last name, but he is always called Boris Grigorevich, never Dikoy. Ostrovsky used the very same technique here as he did with Katerina's names and with Mikhailo's names in *The Poor Bride*. The last name of Marfa Ignatevna *(Ignat'evna)* Kabanova means wild boar, and she is referred to by her last name or its variant, Kabanikha. Her last name also derives from a word which meant block of ice in the upper Volga region. Her son's first name, Tikhon, meaning quiet or calm, suggests the qualities of obedience, meekness, mildness. Her daughter's first name, Varvara, means rough or coarse. Neither the son nor the daughter is called by his last name. The name Kuligin means virgin soil and suggests a clearing free from forests. Of the remaining characters, only Glasha's name was apparently linked semantically to bent or disposition. Her name derives from a word meaning facile or fluent and suggests the qualities of a sensible, reasonable girl.

The stress of the names is as follows: Savel (pronounced Savyól) Prokófevich Dikóy, Borís Grigórevich, Márfa Ignátevna Kabanóva (Kabaníkha), Tíkhon Iványch Kabanóv, Katerína Petróvna, Varvára, Kulígin, Ványa Kudryásh, Shápkin, Feklúsha, Glásha.

THE STORM

Groza

A Drama in Five Acts

CHARACTERS

SAVEL PROKOFEVICH DIKOY, *a merchant, an important person in the town.*

BORIS GRIGOREVICH, *his nephew, a young man, rather well educated.*

MARFA IGNATEVNA KABANOVA (KABANIKHA), *a rich merchant's widow.*

TIKHON IVANYCH KABANOV, *her son.*

KATERINA, *his wife.*

VARVARA, *Tikhon's sister.*

KULIGIN, *a tradesman,*[1] *a self-educated watchmaker, trying to find the secret of perpetual motion.*

VANYA KUDRYASH, *a young man who works in Dikoy's office.*

SHAPKIN, *a tradesman.*

FEKLUSHA, *a pilgrim.*[2]

GLASHA, *maid in the Kabanovs' house.*

A LADY, *an old woman in her seventies, half-mad, with two male servants.*

MEN AND WOMEN who live in the town.

[*All the characters except Boris are dressed in Russian costume.*]

The action takes place in the town of Kalinov,[3] *on the banks of the Volga, during the summer. Between the third and fourth acts, ten days elapse.*

ACT ONE

A public garden on the high bank of the Volga. A rural landscape beyond the Volga. Two benches and several bushes are on the stage. KULIGIN *sits on a bench and looks at the river.* KUDRYASH *and* SHAPKIN *are walking to and fro.*

KULIGIN. [*Sings.*]
> Mid the tranquil vale,
> On the silken upland plains . . . [4]

[*Stops singing.*] Magnificent! Yes, I can truly say it's magnificent. Kudryash! You know, brother, I've been looking at the Volga every day for fifty years, and I can never see enough of it.

KUDRYASH. See what, exactly?

KULIGIN. The marvelous view. The beauty of it all. The joy I find in my heart just to look.

KUDRYASH. Nothing so special!

KULIGIN. It's a sheer delight! But all you can say is "Nothing so special." Why, you've seen it so much you've grown used to it. Or maybe you don't understand the beauty and joy of nature.

KUDRYASH. Oh, why should I talk to you! Around here everybody knows you're a crackpot, a chemist.

KULIGIN. A mechanic, a self-taught mechanic.

KUDRYASH. It's the same thing. [*Silence.*]

KULIGIN. [*Pointing to one side.*] Take a look, my dear Kudryash, who's that waving his arms over there?

KUDRYASH. That one? Why, that's Dikoy swearing at his nephew.

KULIGIN. A nice spot for it!

KUDRYASH. For him any spot is nice. You know, don't you, there's nobody he's afraid of. It just happens he's cornered his nephew, Boris Grigorich.[5] So now Dikoy is riding roughshod over him.

SHAPKIN. Try and find another sorehead like Savel Prokofich[6] round here. You won't! Why, Dikoy'll rip into a person for nothing at all.

KUDRYASH. Loud-mouthed peasant!

SHAPKIN. Think he's bad—old Marfa Ignatevna Kabanova is even louder.[7]

KUDRYASH. Well, at least the old woman runs everything through the odor of sanctity. But Dikoy? Why, he acts as though he's just broken his chain.

SHAPKIN. There's no one to calm him down. So he's ready to fight at the drop of a cap.

KUDRYASH. If there were more fellows like me around, we'd break his bad habits for him.

SHAPKIN. And what d'you think you'd do?

KUDRYASH. Why, scare the hell out of him.

SHAPKIN. How'd you do that?

KUDRYASH. Why, four or five of us would have a little talk with him in an alley somewhere, face-to-face. That'd soften him up, fine as silk. And he wouldn't say a peep about our lesson, either. From then on he'd walk the straight and narrow, for sure.

SHAPKIN. Oh, he'd have reason enough for wanting to ship you off to the army.

KUDRYASH. He might, but he wouldn't. So nothing would ever come of it. He won't ship me off. With that nose of his, he's sharp enough to know I'll never sell out that cheap. He may scare fellows like you, but I know how to talk his language.

SHAPKIN. Oh, is that so!

KUDRYASH. What d'you mean, is that so? Everybody knows I'm pretty tough. So, why does he hang on to me? No doubt he needs me. Well, that means I'm not scared of him. So, let him get scared of me then.

SHAPKIN. You mean to say he doesn't curse you?

KUDRYASH. How can he help it? He can't breathe without cursing. But I don't let him get very far. For every word of his, I give him ten in return. So he spits and clears out, that's what. No, you'll never catch me crawling on my knees before him.

KULIGIN. I suppose you think he's a good example to follow? You'd be better off if you put up with his swearing.

KUDRYASH. Well, if you're so bright, why don't you teach him how to be decent first? Then you can teach us. It's too bad his daughters are so young—not one of them's big enough yet.

SHAPKIN.   What'd happen then?

KUDRYASH.   I'd fix him up, that's for sure. When it comes to girls, I know what to do. [DIKOY *and* BORIS *walk past.* KULIGIN *takes off his cap.*]

SHAPKIN.   [*To* KUDRYASH.]   Let's get out of here. No doubt he'll latch on to us next. [*They cross away from* DIKOY *and* BORIS.]

DIKOY.   I suppose you've come to town just to waste time. You lazy good-for-nothing, you. Go to hell!

BORIS.   Today's a holiday. What can I do at home?

DIKOY.   You can find enough to do if you want to. Listen, you. If I've told you once I've told you twice: don't you dare get in my way. Seems I can't escape—you're always in the way. Can't you find somewhere else to go? Wherever I turn, here you are. Tphew![8] Damn it, you. Why're you standing around like a dumb cluck? Are you being talked to, or not?

BORIS.   I'm listening. What else can I do?

DIKOY.   [*Having looked at* BORIS.]   Go to hell! I won't say another word, you Jesuit, you. [*On his way off stage.*]   You pain-in-the-neck, you! [*Spits and exits.*]

KULIGIN.   Why do you even bother with him, sir? Looks like we'll never understand it. Why do you want to live with him and put up with insults?

BORIS.   What do you mean, want to, Kuligin? There's nothing else I can do.

KULIGIN.   Why nothing else, sir, if you'll permit me to ask? If you want to, sir, then tell me why.

BORIS.   Don't see why I shouldn't. You knew my grandmother, Anfisa Mikhailovna,[9] didn't you?

KULIGIN.   Yes, I knew her, of course.

KUDRYASH.   Yes, of course.

BORIS.   Well, she hated my father since he married into the no-bility.[10] That's the reason my father and mother lived in Moscow. Mama used to say she couldn't stand three days with father's relatives. They seemed savage, even insane to her.

KULIGIN.   Savage, even insane. I'm not surprised. You must get used to their ways, sir, to stand it.

BORIS.   In Moscow our parents gave sister and me an excellent education. They spared no expense. I was sent to the Academy of Commerce; [11] my sister, to a first-rate boarding school. Then our parents suddenly died of cholera, and sister and I were left alone. We heard then that grandmother had died here and had set aside a share of her estate, which my uncle will pay to us when we come of age. There's one condition, though.

KULIGIN.   What is the condition, sir?

BORIS.   That we treat him with respect.

KULIGIN.   That means, sir, you shan't see a kopek of your inheritance.

BORIS.   No, that isn't all, Kuligin. First, he'll ridicule sister and me, insult us in every way he can find, till we can scarcely stand it. And when it's all said and done, he won't give us a single kopek. Or at best, the least amount he can get away with. And then he'll say he gave it out of charity, that he certainly wasn't bound to give it.

KUDRYASH.   That's the usual way merchants act around here. Let's say you did treat him with respect. But who will stop him from saying that you didn't?

BORIS.   Of course. Do you know that even now he's been saying, "I have my own children. Why should I give money to outsiders? If I did, I'd ruin my whole family."

KULIGIN.   I'd say, my dear sir, the thing's pretty far gone.

BORIS.   If it were up to me, I shouldn't care at all. I'd throw it all away and simply leave. But it's my sister I think about. My uncle insisted that she come, too. Thank God, my mother's family wouldn't hear of it. They wrote him that she was ill. How could she possibly live through it here? Just imagine how terrified she'd be.

KUDRYASH.   I think you're absolutely right. You can't expect Dikoy and his kind to know how people really feel.

KULIGIN.   What kind of standing do you have in his business, sir?

BORIS.   None, whatsoever. "You can live," he said, "at my place, and you'll do what I tell you. As to your salary, I'll assign that later on." Of course, what he meant was that after a year he'd give me whatever he chooses.

KUDRYASH.   I'd say that's typical. It's the usual way he acts around here. Not one of us at his place can make a peep about salary.

Otherwise, he'll start raising hell with us. "I suppose," he'll say, "you know what I've got in mind? You'll never know what I'm thinking, do you hear! I suppose you think I'm in the mood to hand over five thousand rubles to you." Try and talk to him! He's never once been in the right mood, in his whole life.

KULIGIN.   What can you do about it, sir? I suppose you must try to please him in some way.

BORIS.   That's the whole point, Kuligin, it's impossible. If his own family can't please him, what can I possibly do?

KUDRYASH.   Since his whole life is one brawl after another, who on earth can please him? It's about money, most of all. He can't settle a single account without quarreling over it. Some people are happy to hand everything over to him, just to shut him up. If someone gets him started in the morning, then watch out. He spends the rest of the day pick, pick, picking on everyone he meets.

BORIS.   Every single morning, my aunt, with tears in her eyes, begs everybody: "Saints in heaven, don't get him started. Oh, my darlings, please don't."

KUDRYASH.   What chance does anyone have, really? Let him go to the bazaar, and all hell breaks loose. He raises Cain with all the peasants. Even if you let him have something at a loss, he still won't walk away without swearing a blue streak. And then he's off for the whole day.

SHAPKIN.   In short, he's a scrapper!

KUDRYASH.   A scrapper. You can say that again.

BORIS.   But, you know, the real trouble starts if he's insulted by someone he doesn't dare curse in return. Then the people at home had better watch out.

KUDRYASH.   Oh, good Lord! I just remembered something funny. Dikoy was crossing the Volga once when a hussar cursed him out. Was that something to see! Magnificent!

BORIS.   And what about the people at home after that? For two whole weeks, everybody kept hiding out in the attics or storerooms.

KULIGIN.   [*Looking offstage.*]   What's this? Surely people aren't leaving vespers already?   [*Several people pass by upstage.*]

KUDRYASH.   Let's join the party, Shapkin, and have some fun. No use hanging around here, is there?   [KUDRYASH *and* SHAPKIN *bow and exit.*]

BORIS.   Oh, Kuligin, it's pretty hard for me here. I'm not used to it at all. Everyone looks at me strangely, as though I were unnecessary, as though I were disturbing them in some way. I don't understand the customs here. I know it's our native Russian way; but all the same, I don't believe I'll ever get used to it.

KULIGIN.   You'll never get used to the ways here, sir.

BORIS.   Why do you say that?

KULIGIN.   In our town, sir, the ways are cruel, brutal. Among the townspeople,[12] sir, those of us who work for a living, you'll see nothing but coarseness and poverty beyond belief. And there's no way out, sir. None at all. We can never escape the skin that binds us. However much we may work, however honest we may be, we can never make more than our daily bread. The one who has money is the one who will do everything possible to enslave the poor man. Yes, bind him to his daily labor, just to make even more money. You know, don't you, what your uncle, Savel Prokofich, said to the mayor, when the peasants complained to him? They came to the mayor because your uncle hadn't paid them a single kopek. So the mayor talked to your uncle. "Listen, Savel Prokofich," he said, "just pay the peasants what you owe them. They're at my place every day with complaints." Well, your uncle patted the mayor on the shoulder and said, "It's not worth our breath, your honor, to chat about little things like that. You know I hire hundreds of peasants every year. Now you can see, if I slip a kopek or two away from each one, then I can make a thousand or more in the deal. In that way I can keep the wheels greased and running." That's the way it goes around here, sir, "greased and running." How do the big shots operate among themselves, sir? You must see it to believe it. In business they cut each other up. And they do it out of jealousy, sir, more than for the money. They quarrel, feed one upon the other, and trap drunken clerks in their tall mansions. Clerks without one trace of humanity—even their appearance of humanity has been used up. But for the slightest favor granted, these clerks scribble away on official documents, writing vicious scandal sheets against their fellow men. From there, the law takes over, sir. And there's no end to the suffering once the lawyers get their hands on a fat lawsuit. First, it's suit after suit in our local courts, and then on to the District

Court. There, of course, lawyers are waiting for them, too, just clapping their hands for joy. Remember the old proverb: "A fairy tale but quickly told is quickly gone. But a case in court drags on, and on, and on." So it goes, the lawsuit passing from one court to the next; shuffled here, shuffled there. And all the time the contestants click their heels, overjoyed by the dangling and wrangling. That's exactly what they want, exactly what they deserve. "I may spend some money," the big shots say, "but it's costing him a pretty kopek, too." Someday I'd like to put it all down into verse. . . .

BORIS.   Don't tell me you know how to write poetry?

KULIGIN.   The older type, sir, that's all. I've read a lot from the old poets, Lomonosov, Derzhavin.[13] A wise man, Lomonosov. He understood the ways of nature. You know he was one of us, a man from the common class.

BORIS.   You must write your verses. I would enjoy reading them.

KULIGIN.   I don't think I could, sir. Why, I'd be eaten up, swallowed alive, if I did. I'm always catching it for too much talk. I can't help it, though. I love talking to everyone I meet. I'd like to tell you about family life here, sir, but some other time perhaps. It's worth listening to. [FEKLUSHA *and another woman enter.*]

FEKLUSHA.   Nothing gra-ander, dearie, nothing gra-ander on earth. A land of milk and . . . Sweetie, I just don't know how to put it in words. Well, you've made it to the promised land, that's for sure. And the merchants here . . . Well, they're a God-fearing lot, all right. Just brimming over with virtue. Generous, too. And can they dole out the money. I'm so happy, sweetie, so happy I could shout for joy. They really take care of you here. May their bounties increase and multiply. Especially to the house of the Kabanovs. [*The two women exit.*]

BORIS.   The Kabanovs?

KULIGIN.   The old woman there, Marfa Ignatevna Kabanova, is something of a bigot, sir. Self-righteous and overbearing. Gives plenty to the beggars passing by, but swallows up her own family. [*Silence.*]   If only I could find the answer to *perpetu-mobil!*[14]

BORIS.   And what would you do then?

KULIGIN.   What wouldn't I do, sir! The English, you know, would give a million for it. I'd spend it all to help the people, to give

them support. For example, the townspeople here need employment. They're ready and willing, but there's nothing for them to
do.

BORIS.   And you hope to find the answer to *perpetuum-mobile?*

KULIGIN.   Yes, I do, sir. If I could only raise some money for the
models. Good-by, sir. [*Exits.*]

BORIS. [*Alone.*]   God help you, old fellow. I'd never disillusion
you. A splendid person, as good as they come in this life. He
can still dream, a truly happy man. But me? Why, I'll no doubt
destroy my youth in this god-forsaken place. Here I am then,
weary unto death, and yet . . . Oh, I shouldn't even think it.
Probably no more than a schoolboy crush. Forget it, then! I'm
hemmed in, there's no way out, so forget it. And yet . . . Oh,
I'm an idiot to think of falling in love. And with whom? With
a woman I can scarcely say "hello" to, let alone talk to. [*Silence.*]
I can't get her out of my mind. However much I try, I can't
do it. Oh, dear God! There she is. And her husband and mother-
in-law are with her. I know I'm a fool, but I must see her, if
only for a moment. A glance, no more.[15] Then off you go, home.
[BORIS *exits. From the opposite side of the stage enter* MARFA
KABANOVA, KABANOV, KATERINA, *and* VARVARA.]

MARFA.   If you listen to your mother, when you get there, you'll
do exactly what I told you.

KABANOV.   But, mama, I wouldn't think of disobeying you.

MARFA.   Nowadays, parents don't get the respect they used to.

VARVARA. [*Aside.*]   Respect you. Fat chance of that!

KABANOV.   But, mama, it seems I scarcely take a step without
your permission.

MARFA.   I'd believe you, dear boy, if I didn't see with my own
eyes, or hear with my own ears, the way children respect their
parents these days. If they only knew how much suffering and
pain their own mothers go through for them.

KABANOV.   But, mama, I . . .

MARFA.   If your mother treats you badly now and then, just
realize you bring it on yourself. You and your pride. Seems to
me, you could take it better than you do. Well, what'd you
want to say?

KABANOV.   When was it, mama, I didn't know how to take it?

MARFA.   I know, you don't have to tell me. Your mother is old and stupid. But you! Oh, yes, you youngsters think you're smart, don't you? Well, then don't go around demanding so much from old fools like us.

KABANOV.   [*Sighing. Aside.*]   Oh, God in heaven, help me!   [*To* MARFA.]   How could we ever dream up something like that, really, mama?

MARFA.   You know why parents are strict with youngsters like you, don't you? Because they love you. Why do they pick on you? Because they love you. Everything parents do comes from wanting to teach you what's right and good. Nowadays, of course, children won't take one bit of it. Oh, no. Instead, they run from one person to the next, whispering stories about their own mothers. Saying that mother is an old grouch, that mother won't give them an ounce of freedom, that mother squeezes the life right out of them. And God help us, if something we say doesn't please our daughter-in-law. Then watch out for all the whispering, the rumors, the griping. Oh, yes. Mama has just swallowed up her own daughter-in-law, once and for all.

KABANOV.   Come now, mama, who'd ever talk about you?

MARFA.   I didn't hear anything like it, dear boy. No, I didn't. I don't want to lie. But if I ever did, son, don't on your life think we'd ever skip it.   [*She sighs.*]   Oh, it's a heavy load we carry. And you can't help sinning, either. Get into a conversation close to your heart, and before you know it, you lose your temper. And that's a sin. No, dear boy, say what you want about me. No one can stop gossiping. If they don't tell it to your face, then they'll tell it behind your back.

KABANOV.   God in heaven, may my tongue wither . . .

MARFA.   Stop, my boy, stop. Don't swear before the Lord like that. You know it's a sin! I've seen for some time that your wife means more to you than your own mother does. From the day you married, I could see you've never cared for me like you did before.

KABANOV.   What do you mean, mama, in what way?

MARFA.   In everything you do, dear boy. What a mother can't see with her own eyes, she knows in her heart. In her heart of hearts, a mother can feel everything. Or is it your wife pulling you away from me, maybe? I don't know if that's it or not.

KABANOV.   No, mama, no. What do you mean, for pity's sake?

KATERINA.   Please, mama. I care for you just as if you were my own mother. And you know Tikhon loves you, too.

MARFA.   Seems to me, you ought to keep still until somebody asks you. Don't take sides, my dear. And don't be afraid I'll hurt him, either. I won't. He's my own son, after all, and don't you ever forget it. Why jump in and make a fuss in front of everyone? I suppose you want people to see how much you love your husband? Well, we all know it. Yes, we do. Why wouldn't we? The way you show off in front of everybody and his brother.

VARVARA.   [*Aside.*]   A nice place to give a lecture.

KATERINA.   You've no right, mama, to say that. I'm the same anywhere, in front of people or alone. And I don't try to show off, either.

MARFA.   I didn't mean to talk about you, especially. It just came to mind, that's all.

KATERINA.   Even if it did, why on earth do you want to hurt me?

MARFA.   Look at her, will you? Ruffled her feathers, no less, and got hurt right off.

KATERINA.   No one likes to hear silly and false stories.

MARFA.   I know, don't think I don't. Anything I say rubs every one of you the wrong way. How can I help it, I'd like to know? You can't call me an outsider, can you? My heart aches for you, it does. I've known for some time you want your own way. Well, you'll get your own way, if you wait a little while. You'll get it soon enough when I'm dead and gone. Then, go ahead and do what you like. Nobody will be around then to tell you what to do. You'll see. And maybe you'll remember me then.

KABANOV.   But, mama, we pray to God day and night for you. We pray, mama, that God may grant you health, happiness, and success in business.

MARFA.   Come now, stop it, please do. When you were single, perhaps you loved your mother then. But now you have a young wife. You don't give me the time of day.

KABANOV.   One thing doesn't prevent another, ma'am. My wife is my wife, but at the same time I respect my mother.

MARFA.   Don't tell me you'd exchange a wife for your own mother? As long as I live I'll never believe it. No, never.

KABANOV.   Why should I give up one for the other, ma'am? I love my wife and my mother.

MARFA.   Oh, yes, yes, just as I thought! Spread it on thick, son, while you're at it. I know only too well I'm in your way. Yes, and your wife's way, too.

KABANOV.   Think what you want. Yes, have it all your own way. I'm the unhappiest man ever born on this earth. Why did it happen to me, I'd like to know? Nothing I do, nothing I say, will ever please you. Nothing.

MARFA.   Oh, stop pretending you're alone, helpless, and so unhappy. What are you sniveling for? Well, what kind of husband are you? Just look at yourself! And you expect your wife to be afraid of you after that? No backbone, no backbone at all.

KABANOV.   And why should she be afraid? It's enough for me that she loves me.

MARFA.   Afraid! Why should she be afraid? Don't tell me you've lost your mind? If she isn't afraid of you, how can she be afraid of me then? If that happens, there'd be no sense of order in the house. You married her lawfully, didn't you? Or I suppose the law means nothing to you? If you've such silly ideas in your head, then don't blow off in front of her, at least. Or in front of your sister, either. She's not married yet, but she's going to be. If she takes up your nonsense now, her husband will have you to thank later on. You can see, can't you, how smart you are now? And you want to go your own way, all alone, without any help.

KABANOV.   No, mama, I don't want to go my own way. I know I couldn't do it by myself.

MARFA.   You think, I suppose, you must treat your wife with kindness? Never raise your voice to her, or threaten her? Is that it?

KABANOV.   But, mama, I only . . .

MARFA.   [*Heatedly.*]   Do you want to send her off to another man, to a lover? Is that it? I suppose that wouldn't mean a thing to you, would it? Well, answer me.

KABANOV.   Oh, mama, really and truly, I don't see . . .

MARFA.   [*Fully composed; in a cold, calm way.*]   Fool! [*Sighs.*] There's no use in talking to a fool. I'd commit a sin, if I did. [*Silence.*]   I'm going home.

KABANOV.   And we'll go, too, pretty soon. We'll just walk around the boulevard once or twice.

MARFA.   Well, it's up to you. Only see that I don't have to wait for long. You know I don't like it.

KABANOV.   No, mama. God help me if I did.

MARFA.   See that you don't. [*Exits.*]

KABANOV.   There, you see. Because of you I'm always catching it from mother. Oh, God in heaven, this is no way to live.

KATERINA.   Why do you blame me?

KABANOV.   I don't know who's to blame.

VARVARA.   You couldn't be. I'm sure of that!

KABANOV.   When I was single she never stopped saying, "Get married, that's what you should do, get married. If only I'd see you married." And now she never lets up, never gives me a minute's peace. And all because of you.

VARVARA.   Why is Katerina to blame, really! Mother jumps on her, and you do, too. And yet you say you love your wife. I'm fed up just looking at you. [*Turns away.*]

KABANOV.   Oh, what's the use of talking. All right, what can I do?

VARVARA.   Know your place, that's all. And shut up if you can't think of anything better to say. What are you doing, shuffling from one foot to the next like an idiot? Oh, I can see from the look in your eyes what you've got in mind.

KABANOV.   All right, what?

VARVARA.   It's pretty obvious. You want to see Savel Prokofich, have a drink with him. That's it, isn't it?

KABANOV.   You guessed it, sister.

KATERINA.   Tishka,[16] please hurry back, or mama will begin all over again.

VARVARA.   And be quick about it, or you know what'll happen!

KABANOV.   As if I didn't!

VARVARA.   We don't want to catch it, just because of you.

KABANOV.   Be back in a flash. Wait for me! [*Exits.*]

KATERINA.   You're sorry for me then, aren't you, Varya?[17]

VARVARA.   [*Looking to one side.*]   Of course I am.

KATERINA.   Then you love me, don't you? [*Kisses her affectionately.*]

VARVARA.   Of course. Why shouldn't I love you?

KATERINA.   Oh, thank you, my dearest. I love you with all my heart. [*Silence.*] Do you know what came to mind just now?

VARVARA. What?

KATERINA. Why is it people don't fly? [18]

VARVARA. I don't know what you mean.

KATERINA. I mean, why is it people don't fly like birds? You know, sometimes I imagine I am a bird. When I stand on a hill, I want . . . I long to fly. I feel as if I could run, lift my arms, and then . . . fly away. Would you like me to try it now? [*She is about to run.*]

VARVARA. How did you ever come up with something like that?

KATERINA. [*Sighing.*] Oh, I used to be alive, happy, not a care in the world. But living in your house I feel I've lost everything, everything worth living for.

VARVARA. Do you think I haven't seen it happen?

KATERINA. I was never like this before.[19] I just lived. Nothing to worry about, completely free, like a bird simply let free of its cage. Mama adored me, dressed me up like a doll, and never made me work hard. I used to do whatever I wanted to. Do you know how I lived before I married? If you like, I'll tell you about it. I used to get up early. In summer I'd go down to the spring, bathe, and then take water back to sprinkle all the flowers in the house. Every single one. Then mother and I would go to church. Yes, and the holy women—the pilgrims—would go with us, too. Our house used to be filled with holy women. When we came home from church, we'd sit down to sew, mostly gold thread on velvet. Then the holy women would begin to tell where they'd been, what they'd seen, or the lives of the saints. Sometimes they'd sing spiritual verse. We spent our time like that until dinner. Later on the older women would take a nap, but I would walk through the garden. Then we all went to vespers, and in the evening there'd be more stories and songs. Everything was lovely. Lovely and beautiful.

VARVARA. But we do the very same things at our house.

KATERINA. Yes, but there is no freedom here. It's as if you're forced to do everything. How I loved going to church when I lived at home. I felt as though I were in heaven. I didn't see a single person, and time passed so quickly that I didn't know when the service ended. I felt as though everything passed by in one brief moment. Mother said that everyone used to look at me, wondering what'd happened to me. But you know, on sunny days, a bright pillar of light shone down from the dome. And then smoke from the incense burner swirled into the bright pillar and drifted like clouds high in the sky. Sometimes I thought I saw angels appear, flying throughout the bright pillar, all singing in one beautiful chorus. Sometimes I used to wake up at night and see the lamps burning brightly before the icons throughout our house. Then I would get up, kneel before one of the icons, and pray until morning. Sometimes I would go out into the garden, just as the sun began to come up, fall on my knees and pray and weep. I never knew why I felt as I did. But there they would find me. What I prayed for, or what I sought from God, I really don't know. I had everything I wanted, don't you see? My life was full, perfect. And my dreams, Varenka, were wonderful and beautiful. Golden temples and lovely gardens where beautiful songs by unseen choruses merged with the scent from cypresses.[20] The mountains and trees in my dreams could never be found in nature, for they looked exactly like those painted on our holy images. Sometimes I felt as though I were flying, surrounded by the beauty I saw in my dreams. I have dreams now at times, but very seldom, and never like the ones I used to dream.

VARVARA.   What kind of dreams do you have now?

KATERINA.   [After a pause.] I shall die soon.

VARVARA.   No, don't! Think what you're saying!

KATERINA.   No, I know I shall die soon. Oh, my dear, something terrible is happening to me. I don't know what it is. But something strange . . . perhaps, miraculous. I never felt anything like this before. I feel as if I'm beginning my life all over again. As if . . . Oh, I don't know.

VARVARA.   What's the matter? Tell me.

KATERINA.   [Takes VARVARA's hand.] I know what it is, Varya. Something terrible is going to happen. Oh, I'm afraid, my dear, so afraid. It's as if I were standing on a cliff, and someone were ready to push me off. And I have nothing to hold on to. Nothing, nothing at all. [Clutches her head.]

VARVARA.   Oh, my darling, what is it? You're not sick, are you?

KATERINA.   No, it's all right. I'd be better off if I were sick. I know something is wrong. Strange thoughts keep coming back, and I can't escape them. I try to get rid of them. I try to think of something else, but I can't. I try to pray, but I can't. Oh, the words come easily, Varya, but my mind is filled with other thoughts. I can't escape it. It's as if the devil himself were whispering in my ears, whispering something evil. And then I imagine terrible things, so terrible I'm ashamed of myself. What's the matter with me? I know something dreadful will happen, I know it will. I can't sleep at night, Varya. Someone whispers to me, speaking softly, tenderly to me—it's like a caress, like the murmuring sound of a dove. I no longer dream as I used to, of beautiful heavenly trees and mountains. It's as if someone were holding me closely, passionately. As if he were taking me away with him. . . . And I go willingly . . . yes, willingly. I can't stop myself.

VARVARA.   And then?

KATERINA.   No, I shouldn't tell you. You are an unmarried girl.

VARVARA.   [*Glancing around.*]   Tell me. I'm much, much worse than you.

KATERINA.   Well, what can I say? I'm so ashamed.

VARVARA.   Tell me. You've nothing to be ashamed of.

KATERINA.   I feel hemmed in at home, so guarded and restrained that I want to run away forever. I sometimes think that if I were free I could go sailing on the Volga. Free to sing wonderful songs, free to ride in a beautiful troika, lying in the arms of . . .

VARVARA.   Someone. But not your husband.

KATERINA.   How did you know?

VARVARA.   Why shouldn't I know!

KATERINA.   Oh, Varya, why do I have evil thoughts? You don't know how terrible I feel, how much I've wept and struggled to rid myself of the temptation. But I can't escape it. There's no place to go. It is a sin, isn't it, Varenka? A terrible sin for me to love another man.

VARVARA.   Don't ask me to judge you, I can't. I know what I've done myself.[21]

KATERINA.   What can I do? I don't have the strength to stop now. I have no place to go, no place to hide. I feel so terrible I could kill myself.

VARVARA.   Oh, don't talk like that. Please, don't. Only wait for a little while. My brother is going away tomorrow. Then we'll think of something. Perhaps you'll be able to see each other then.

KATERINA.   No, I shan't, I must not. How can you even think it! Oh, God in heaven, help me.

VARVARA.   Why are you so frightened?

KATERINA.   If I see him even once, I'll run away from home. And I'll never come back. Never as long as I live.

VARVARA.   Just wait, and we'll see.

KATERINA.   No, don't say another word, don't. I won't listen, I won't.

VARVARA.   And why on earth do you want to waste away? Even if you died of despair, who do you think would care? No one! So don't expect it. And there's no use tormenting yourself, either. [*Enter an* OLD LADY,[22] *with a cane, followed by two servants in three-cornered hats.*]

OLD LADY.   Well, my pretty things. What are you doing here? Waiting for young men to show up, your boy friends? Are you happy? Is that it? Glad that you're beautiful? Well, that's where beauty leads, there. [*Points toward the Volga.*] There, right into the whirlpool. [VARVARA *smiles.*] You can laugh about it, can you! Don't be too pleased with yourself. [*Raps with her cane.*] You will burn forever in the eternal fire. You will seethe forever in fires of damnation. [*Leaving.*] There, that's where beauty leads, there. [*Exits.*]

KATERINA.   Oh, she frightened me to death! I'm trembling all over, just as if she'd told me what will happen in the future.

VARVARA.   [*To* OLD LADY.] I hope it happens to you, you old witch!

KATERINA.   What was it she said? Do you remember? What was it?

VARVARA.   A lot of nonsense. Why listen to her? It's the way she is, always saying the same thing to everybody she comes across. Frankly, it's because she's done plenty herself. And she started sinning as soon as she was old enough to. Ask around, and anybody will tell you all about her. Turns out she's growing old now, and she's afraid to die. Why shouldn't she be afraid? So she goes around frightening others with what she's afraid of herself. Even the little boys in town hide when they see her coming. Shakes her cane at them and shouts [*mimics the* OLD LADY], "You'll burn forever in the eternal fire!"

KATERINA.   [*Closing her eyes.*]   Oh, stop it! Please, do. My heart's stopped beating.

VARVARA.   What's there to be afraid of? She's a stupid old woman.

KATERINA.   I'm frightened, frightened to death. I can't put her out of my mind.   [*Silence.*]

VARVARA.   [*Glancing around.*]   Why doesn't Tikhon show up? Look, Katerina, a storm's coming.

KATERINA.   [*Terrified.*]   A storm! Oh, dear God. Let's run home. Hurry!

VARVARA.   What's wrong with you? Have you lost your mind? We can't show up at home without Tikhon.

KATERINA.   No, let's go home. Let's go, please. Never mind about Tikhon.

VARVARA.   Look, there's no reason to be so frightened. The storm is still far off.

KATERINA.   If it's far off, maybe we can wait a little while. But really it'd be better to go. We'd better go now.

VARVARA.   If you think something's going to happen, you can be sure you won't be safe—even at home.

KATERINA.   All the same, it'd be better, more peaceful there. At home I can pray to God. I can kneel before our holy icons.

VARVARA.   I never knew a storm could frighten you so much. Look, I'm not afraid.

KATERINA.   How is it you're not afraid? Everyone should be afraid, Varya. It's not so terrible to be killed by lightning. I'm not afraid of that at all. Only that death may come all of a sudden. Just as I am now with my sins and evil thoughts. I am not afraid to die. But when I think I might come before God now, as I stand here with you and after all I've told you . . . that's what I'm afraid of. Oh, dear God, what am I thinking? It's evil and wicked! I can't, I must never even say it.   [*Sound of thunder.*]   Oh!   [KABANOV *enters.*]

VARVARA.   Here comes Tikhon now.   [*To* KABANOV.]   Come on, hurry up!

KATERINA.   Oh, hurry! Please, please hurry!

ACT TWO

A room in the Kabanovs' house. GLASHA *is collecting clothing into bundles and* FEKLUSHA *enters.*

FEKLUSHA. Oh, my sweetie, you're working all the time! Yes, all the time. What are you doing, dearie?

GLASHA. Collecting clothes for the master's trip.

FEKLUSHA. You don't mean our boy's going on a trip?

GLASHA. Yes, he is.

FEKLUSHA. Going to be gone long, dearie?

GLASHA. No, not too long.

FEKLUSHA. Well, let him have a good trip! Say, what do you think? Will his wife start moaning and wailing or not? [23]

GLASHA. I don't know what to say, exactly.

FEKLUSHA. But she does moan and wail, doesn't she?

GLASHA. I've never heard anything like it.

FEKLUSHA. There's nothing I love so much, dearie, as hearing somebody moan and wail real good. [*Silence.*] Say, girlie, you better keep an eye on that beggar woman. Or she'll swipe something before you know it.

GLASHA. I can't figure you out, Feklusha. You folks slander each other so much, I don't see how you can live together. Seems to me you pilgrims get along pretty well here—plenty of food and drink—but you never stop fighting and squabbling. And you don't seem afraid of sinning, either.

FEKLUSHA. If you live in this world, my dear, you're going to live in sin. And that's all there is to it. Now I'm going to tell you something, sweetie, and you'd better believe it. You, and by you I mean you simple folks, have only one devil each to tempt you. While we, and by we I mean us holy women, some of us

have six devils apiece. And then there are a few of us who're
stuck with twelve devils. And all twelve are just aching for
us to make a wrong step. So we've got to move and move fast
to whip every last one of them. And it ain't easy, sweetie. No,
it ain't.

GLASHA.   Why is it you have so many?

FEKLUSHA.   Simply because the devil hates us for leading a righteous life, my dear. But you won't find me quarrelsome, sweetie,
so that's one sin we can forget when it comes to me. But I
do have at least one sin, you can be sure of that. Even I know
what that one is. I love to eat dessert, don't you think I don't.
So you see what happens. The Lord sends me off to a house
where the cooking's good, the dessert's piled high, and here I
am face-to-face with my weakness.

GLASHA.   Feklusha, have you traveled far and wide?

FEKLUSHA.   No, dearie, I haven't. You see, I haven't gone very
far or wide because of my weakness. But I've heard a lot of
stories. You can bet your life, I have. They say there are countries, sweetie, where orthodox tsars can't be found. Instead, sultans
govern those lands. In one country the Turkish Sultan Maknut [24]
sits on the throne, but in another—the Persian Sultan Maknut.
And talk about the way they judge everybody, sweetie. Why,
they do as they darn well please. It's all wrong, too. They can't
pass a single thing that's righteous. That's for sure. And do you
know why? Because the good Lord has put His limit on them.
Now take our country. Why, we have righteous laws. But in
those other countries, dearie, theirs are all wrong. Whatever
comes out one way with our laws, will come out the opposite
with their laws. And the judges in those other countries are
crooked, too. In fact, they're so crooked that when they write
up petitions, they always put down: "Judge me, oh, you crooked
judge, you." And then there's another land where all the people
have dogs' heads. [25]

GLASHA.   What do you mean, dogs' heads?

FEKLUSHA.   Why, because they are infidels. Well, sweetie, I'm
off to visit the merchants. Maybe they'll have a little something
for the poor people. Good-by for now.

GLASHA.   Good-by. [FEKLUSHA *exits*.] Now that's something.
Oh, what countries there are! And what miracles there are in

the world! Why, we just sit here and never know about them, either. It's a fine thing there are good people around; sometimes even you hear what's going on in the world. Otherwise, we'd end up fools the rest of our lives. [KATERINA *and* VARVARA *enter.*]

VARVARA.   [*To* GLASHA.]   Take the bundle to the kibitka,[26] Glasha, the horses are ready. [*To* KATERINA.] They married you off too young, and you never had a good time, the way a girl should before marriage. That's why you're all stirred up—you've never had a chance to settle down. [GLASHA *exits.*]

KATERINA.   And I never shall. I know it only too well.

VARVARA.   Why, for heaven's sake?

KATERINA.   Because I was born that way. I mean, doing things on impulse, passionately. I remember once, when I was only six years old, and do you know what I did? Someone at home hurt my feelings, so I ran away. I remember it was evening at the time, already dark outside. But I ran to the Volga, got into a boat, and pushed it into the river. They found me the next morning, almost ten versts[27] away from home.

VARVARA.   Tell me, did the boys ever go for you?

KATERINA.   Of course they did.

VARVARA.   And you? Did you ever fall in love?

KATERINA.   No, I only laughed at them.

VARVARA.   You know something, Katya?[28] You don't love Tikhon.

KATERINA.   No! Of course I love him. I feel sorry for him, very sorry.

VARVARA.   No, you don't love him. If you're sorry for him, then you don't really love him. Besides, there's no reason you should, to tell the truth. So don't try to hide it, either. I've seen it for a long time now, you are in love with another man.

KATERINA.   [*Frightened.*]   How could you ever have seen it?

VARVARA.   Oh, my darling, how silly can you be! Perhaps you think I'm still a child? Do you know what the first sign is? Whenever you see him, everything about you changes. Your face, the expression in your eyes, everything. [KATERINA *drops her eyes.*]   And that's not all . . .

KATERINA.   [*Keeping her eyes lowered.*]   Well, who is he then?

VARVARA.   But you know yourself. Why should I tell you his name?

KATERINA.   No, say it. Tell me his name.

VARVARA. Boris Grigorich.

KATERINA. Oh, yes, it's he, Varenka. It's he. Please, Varenka, for the love of God, don't ever . . .

VARVARA. Don't be silly! I won't even mention it. But you're the one who should be careful. Don't let anything slip out.

KATERINA. I don't know how to fool anyone. I'm not very good at hiding what I feel.

VARVARA. Well, you'd better learn, and learn soon. Just remember where you live. Everything at home is threaded with lies, with deceit. Once upon a time I believed in truth, too. But I soon learned what I had to do to get along, just to survive. So I learned to lie, to cheat, to deceive. I took a little walk last night, ran into Boris Grigorich, and I talked to him.

KATERINA. [*Following a short pause, her eyes still lowered.*] Well, what happened then?

VARVARA. He wanted to be remembered to you. "I'm sorry," he said, "there's no place we can see each other."

KATERINA. [*Lowering her eyes even more.*] Where could we see each other! Besides, why . . .

VARVARA. He's unhappy, bored to death. . . .

KATERINA. Don't talk about him anymore. Please, please don't. I don't want to know him, I don't. Ever. I shall love my husband. Tisha,[29] my darling, I shall never give you up, not for anyone in the world. Oh, Varenka,[30] I don't want to think about it. Please don't go on. You're getting me all mixed up.

VARVARA. Then don't think about him. No one's forcing you to, are they?

KATERINA. You don't care at all, do you? Oh, Varya, please help me. You say don't think about him, and then you turn right around and remind me of him. It's true I don't want to think about him. But what can I do? I can't get him out of my mind. I try to think of something else, but it doesn't work. All I can think of, all I can see is him. I want to get hold of myself, see things straight again, but I can't. I can't. And do you know what happened last night? The devil himself tempted me again. I almost ran away from home.

VARVARA. Oh, you're being silly and difficult. God help you, if you aren't. Take my advice and do what you want to. Go on, just as long as no one on earth knows about it.

KATERINA.   I can't, I know I can't. Besides, what good would
it do! No, the best I can do is to go on as I am, hanging on as
long as I can.

VARVARA.   And when you can't stand it any longer, what will
you do then?

KATERINA.   What will I do?

VARVARA.   Yes, what will you do then?

KATERINA.   I shall do exactly what I want to.

VARVARA.   Go ahead and try it. You know they'll simply eat you
alive.

KATERINA.   I don't care, Varenka, I don't. I'll go away and
they'll never see me again.

VARVARA.   And where do you think you'll go? After all, you
are married.

KATERINA.   Oh, Varya, you don't understand me at all. God
help me, I pray it won't happen. But if it should, if everything
presses in on me, then no power in the world can stop me. I'll
throw myself out the window or drown in the Volga. If I don't
want to stay here, then I shan't. Never, never. Even if they cut
me to pieces. [Silence.]

VARVARA.   Know what, Katya! As soon as Tikhon goes on his
trip, we'll stay in the garden, sleep in the summerhouse.

KATERINA.   But why should we, Varya?

VARVARA.   Why not? Shouldn't make any difference, should it?

KATERINA.   I'm afraid to spend the night in some strange place.

VARVARA.   Afraid? Why be afraid? Glasha will be with us.

KATERINA.   I wouldn't feel right, somehow. Well, maybe I will
anyway.

VARVARA.   I'd never have asked you, but you know mama would
never permit me to stay there alone. But I must.

KATERINA.   [Looking at her.]   Why must you?

VARVARA.   [Laughing.]   We'll tell each other's fortunes there.

KATERINA.   You're joking, aren't you?

VARVARA.   Of course, I'm joking. You don't think I meant it,
do you?   [Silence.]

KATERINA.   What's Tikhon doing? He's been gone a long time.

VARVARA.   Do you want him for something?

KATERINA.   No, I . . . no special reason. You know he's leaving
soon.

VARVARA.   He's with mama. Locked up while she tells him what to do. Wearing him down, bit by bit, the way rust eats into iron.

KATERINA.   What for?

VARVARA.   For nothing, except to drive some sense into his head. He'll be on the road for two weeks away from her and out of her sight. Isn't that enough? Figure it out yourself. Her heart will be pining away the whole time, because he'll be on his own and doing what he likes. So now she's putting down all sorts of rules and regulations, each one more ferocious than the last. And then she'll take him to the holy icon, force him to swear obedience, and make him do exactly as she ordered.

KATERINA.   So, even on his own, it's just as if he were still tied to her.

VARVARA.   That's what you think! As soon as he leaves here, he'll start in drinking. And he'll keep it up till he comes back. I'd guess that right now, even though he's listening to her, he's thinking to himself about getting away as soon as possible. [*Enter* MARFA *and* KABANOV.]

MARFA.   Well, do you remember everything I told you? See that you do. Cut it into your skin and keep it there.

KABANOV.   I remember, mama.

MARFA.   Well, everything's ready now. The horses have come. Only say good-by, and God be with you.

KABANOV.   Yes, ma'am. It's time to leave, mama.

MARFA.   Well!

KABANOV.   What is it, ma'am?

MARFA.   Why are you standing there, like you don't know what to do? Tell your wife how to behave while you're gone. [KATERINA *has dropped her eyes to the ground.*]

KABANOV.   But I think she knows that herself.

MARFA.   Don't be silly. Well, go on. Tell her yourself. And I want to hear exactly what you tell her to do. Then, when you come back, you will ask her if she has done everything you said.

KABANOV.   [*Standing next to* KATERINA.] Do as mama says, Katya.

MARFA.   Tell her not to be rude to her mother-in-law.

KABANOV.   Don't be rude.

MARFA.   To respect her mother-in-law like her own mother.

KABANOV.   Katya, respect mama like your own mother.

MARFA.   Tell her she can't sit around all day with her hands folded, like a lady.

KABANOV.   Do some work while I'm gone.

MARFA.   Tell her she can't look out the window all the time.

KABANOV.   But, mama, when has she ever . . .

MARFA.   Well, go on.

KABANOV.   Don't look out the window.

MARFA.   Tell her not to stare at the young men when you're gone.

KABANOV.   Oh, mama, that's foolish, really and truly.

MARFA.   [*Sternly.*]   Don't be difficult. Do as you're told.   [*With a smile.*]   Your mother knows what's best for you. Then tell her what to do.

KABANOV.   [*Confused and ashamed.*]   Don't stare at the men. [KATERINA *looks at him sternly.*]

MARFA.   Now, go ahead and talk a little together if you want to. Let's go, Varvara.   [MARFA *and* VARVARA *exit.* KATERINA *stands as if frozen.*]

KABANOV.   Katya!   [*Silence.*]   Katya, you're not mad at me, are you?

KATERINA.   [*After a short pause, she shakes her head.*]   No!

KABANOV.   But why are you like that? Forgive me, please.

KATERINA.   [*Still in the same position, gently shaking her head.*] God help you!   [*Having covered her face with her hands.*]   She insulted me!

KABANOV.   If you take everything to heart, you'll worry yourself to death. Don't even listen to her. You know she has to say something. Well, let her say it. As for you, let it go in one ear and out the other. Well, good-by, Katya.

KATERINA.   [*Throwing herself on her husband's neck.*]   Tisha, don't go! For God's sake, don't go! Darling, I beg you.

KABANOV.   No, Katya, I must go. If mama sends me, I have to go.

KATERINA.   Then take me with you. Please, take me with you.

KABANOV.   [*Freeing himself from her embrace.*]   No, I can't.

KATERINA.   Why can't you, Tisha, why?

KABANOV.   What fun would I have with you around? All of you have just about torn me apart here. I can hardly wait to get out, and you're trying to latch on to me.

KATERINA.   What is it, Tisha? Don't you love me?

KABANOV.   Of course, I love you. But the way things are around here—no freedom at all—any man would run away from the most beautiful wife in the world. Don't you see? Call me what you like, but I'm still a man. You know what it's like around here. You can see for yourself what I have to endure. I must get away from it, if only for two weeks. When I think of two whole weeks away from storms and threats of storms, two whole weeks without being chained down, unable to move, why should I think of my wife now?

KATERINA.   How can I love you when you talk like that?

KABANOV.   Talk, why shouldn't I talk like that? What do you want me to say? What are you afraid of, for God's sake? You won't be alone, you know. You'll stay with mama.

KATERINA.   Don't talk about her to me. Don't torment me like that. Oh, God help me, help me. [*Weeps.*] What can I do? I feel so worthless. What can I hold on to? Oh, God, dear God. I am lost, lost.

KABANOV.   Stop it, Katya, stop.

KATERINA.   [*Crosses to her husband and holds on to him.*] Tisha, my darling, please stay here with me. Or if you must go, take me with you, please. I shall love you, my darling, care for you and love you every moment. [*Caresses him.*]

KABANOV.   I can't figure you out at all, Katya. You don't give me a moment's thought, to say nothing of a caress, but now you can't stop hanging on to me.

KATERINA.   Tisha, think who it is you're leaving me with! Something terrible will happen, I know it will.

KABANOV.   Well, you know I can't take you. There's nothing we can do about it.

KATERINA.   If that's so, then do this for me. Make me swear . . . Make me swear a solemn oath . . .

KABANOV.   What kind of oath?

KATERINA.   Like this, I mean. Make me swear, while you're gone, that I should never dare, never once dare, speak with any stranger, never see anyone, nor even think of anyone except you.

KABANOV.   Why on earth should I do that?

KATERINA.   To help me, my darling, and set my soul at rest. Do this favor for me, my darling.

KABANOV.   How can you guarantee something like that? I don't see it. Anything at all might cross your mind.

KATERINA.   [*Falling on her knees.*] Oh, make me swear, please. That I should never see my father or mother, that I should die without repentance, if I even . . .

KABANOV.   [*Raising her up from the floor.*]   Oh, don't talk that way, don't. Stop it. You know it's sinful to talk that way. I won't listen to you. [*The voice of* MARFA: "It's time to go, Tikhon." *Then* MARFA, VARVARA *and* GLASHA *enter.*]

MARFA.   Well, Tikhon, it's time to go. May God be with you. [*Sits.*] Sit down, all of you. [*All sit down. Silence.*] [31] Well, good-by. [*She rises and all rise.*]

KABANOV.   [*Crosses to his mother.*]   Good-by, mama.

MARFA.   [*Points to the ground.*]   Bow down to me, bow down. [KABANOV *bows down. Then he kisses his mother.*]   Say good-by to your wife.

KABANOV.   Good-by, Katya. [KATERINA *throws herself on his neck.*]

MARFA.   Why are you hanging on his neck, you shameless hussy! You're not saying good-by to your lover. He is your husband, your master. Don't you know how to behave? Bow down to him at once.   [KATERINA *bows down to* KABANOV.]

KABANOV.   Good-by, sister. [*Kisses* VARVARA.]   Good-by, Glasha. [*Kisses* GLASHA.]   Good-by, mama. [*Bows to* MARFA.]

MARFA.   Good-by. Now, go at once. Long farewells give useless tears. [KABANOV *exits, followed by* KATERINA, VARVARA, *and* GLASHA. MARFA *is alone on stage.*]   Oh, look at these young people today, will you! It makes me laugh just to watch them. If they didn't belong to me, I'd cut loose and have a good laugh. They don't know anything or even how to behave properly. They don't know the way to see somebody off on a journey. It's a good thing older people are around the house. As long as older people are alive, some kind of order is held on to. And yet the youngsters want their freedom, want to handle everything themselves. If the silly things get their own way, they make fools of themselves and bring reproach and laughter on the heads of good people. Of course, there are those who'll be sorry, but most people will just laugh. And you can't help laughing, either. They invite guests to the house but can't seat them properly, and what's more, they'll forget one of their own relatives to boot. It's laughable, I have to admit it. That's the way our customs die out. Even now there are some houses you don't want to go into. If you do go, you're ready to spit and leave as soon as possible. What'll happen when the old folks die off, how the world will stand it, I really don't know. Well, maybe it's even good I won't live to see it. [KATERINA *and* VARVARA *enter.*] You were boasting not so long ago how much you love your husband. Well, I can see pretty clearly how much you care. You don't behave the way a good wife does when she sees her husband off. Any good wife would've fallen on the porch floor and wailed and moaned for a good hour or more. But you, I see, you don't love him at all.

KATERINA.   Why should I carry on like that? Besides, I don't know how. Why should I make people laugh?

MARFA.   It's not difficult. If you loved him, you'd learn soon enough. Even if you don't know how to behave the right way, at least you could've made an attempt and pretended that you did. It would have looked better anyway. But, no, all you can do is say you care for him. Just words. Well, it's time for me to say my prayers; don't disturb me.

VARVARA.   I'm going outside.

MARFA.   [*With affection.*]   I don't care. Go ahead. Have fun while you can. Time will come soon enough when you're married and have to sit around home.   [MARFA *and* VARVARA *exit.*]

KATERINA.   [*Alone. Pensively.*]   At last peace will come again to our house, deathly peace and quiet. How terribly, terribly tired I am now. If only there were some children. Oh, dear God in heaven, I pray, pray for children. I should love them so, just to sit and play with them. How much I love talking to them. Lovely, beautiful children. [*Silence.*] I think . . . I know it would've been better to have died young. Far, far better. I'd look down from heaven and see the beauty of the earth. And I'd be happy. Maybe I could fly wherever I wanted, and no one could see me. I could fly into a field and let the wind carry me from flower to flower, like a butterfly. [*Deep in thought.*] I know what I must do. I'll start work on something as I promised. I'll go to the shops, buy some linen, make clothes and give them to the poor. They will pray to God for me. Varvara will help me. We'll sit together and sew, we won't even notice how time passes, and soon Tisha will come back. [VARVARA *enters.*]

VARVARA. [*Puts on a kerchief before the mirror.*]   I'm going out now. Glasha will make up our beds in the garden, since Mama has decided it's all right. There's a gate back of the raspberry bushes in the garden. Mama always locks the gate, then hides the key. I have it here, and I've put another in its place so she'll never notice it. Here, take it. Maybe you'll need it. [*Gives her the key.*]   If I see him, I'll tell him to come to the gate.

KATERINA. [*Pushing the key away, frightened.*]   Here, I don't want it. I don't. I'll never use it, never.

VARVARA.   If you won't use it, I shall. Take it. It won't bite you.

KATERINA.   Please, Varya, don't do this. You're trying to tempt me, don't! Did you think I would . . . Oh, don't, Varya, don't.

VARVARA.   Well, I'm not going to stand around talking about it. I don't have the time. I must go now. [*Exits.*]

KATERINA. [*Alone, holding the key in her hands.*]   Oh, why is she doing this? What can she be thinking of? She's mad to do it. Yes, mad to give me this key. Oh, I'm lost, lost. I must throw it away. Far, far away. Deep in the river where it can never be found. Dear Lord God in heaven, it burns my hands, burns like a live coal. [*After a moment's thought.*]   I see now what destroys us forever, what kills every moment of happiness. It can happen to any woman, just as it's happening to me. Shut in as we are, away from the world, why shouldn't we get all sorts of ideas? Any woman imprisoned as I am would do it. Given the chance, she would take it and find happiness. And she wouldn't even think about it. But I must think, I must think it over carefully. It's easy to get into trouble. And if I do, I can spend the rest of my life in tears, torturing myself forever because of one brief moment. My life then would be even worse than it is now. And more bitter. [*Silence.*]   Oh, dear God, how bitter it is to live as I do. Bound hand and foot, no chance of freedom at all. Why shouldn't a person cry over it? Above all, a woman. What is there for me now? I go on living, just existing. And I can see no way out. There is no escape, none at all. The longer I live the worse it gets. And now this . . . this terrible thing I may do. [*Deep in thought.*]   If only my mother-in-law were different. She has ruined my life, crushed me to the point I can't stand living in this house. Even the walls make me shudder from hate. [*Looks at the key, thoughtfully.*]   Must I throw it away? Of course I must. Why did I ever get it? It must have been to tempt me, to destroy me. [*Listens.*]   Oh, someone is coming. My heart's stopped beating.   [*Hides the key in her pocket.*]   No, it's no one. Why was I so frightened? And I hid the key. Well, that's where it should be. It's fate, I can see that now. But why shouldn't I look at him from a distance? It's no sin to do that. And even if I talk to him a little, there's no harm in that. But I promised my husband . . . And yet he never insisted himself. A chance like this may never come again. Not in my whole life. I know I'd be sorry then. And I'd never forget it, either. You had your chance, but you never took it. Oh, dear God, why do I stand here talking? I'm only deceiving myself. Even if I should die for it, I know I must see him. Why do I pretend anymore? Throw away the key! No, never, not for anything on earth. The key is mine now. . . . Come what may, I know I shall see Boris. Oh, if only night would come as soon as possible!

ACT THREE

SCENE ONE

A street. The gates of the Kabanovs' house. A bench in front of the gates. MARFA *and* FEKLUSHA *are sitting on the bench.*

FEKLUSHA. It's the end of the world, Marfa Ignatevna. According to all the signs, my dear, it's the end. Finally and forever. Not here in your town, naturally. It's like a paradise on earth here, so quiet and easy. But other places? Why, every other town is simply another Sodom, my dear. You can't get over the noise or all the running about that people do. Going here, flying there, it never stops. Everybody scurries around. First one place; then another. You have to see it to believe it.

MARFA. We don't have places to run around to, dear. We can take our time and live a peaceful life.

FEKLUSHA. No, my dear, that's not the reason at all. You live a peaceful life because there are so many people like you in town, virtuous and righteous. That's the reason. Take you, for example. Why, you're covered with virtues like flowers in a field. Because of people like you, everything goes along peacefully, calmly. You know what scurrying around leads to, don't you, my dear? Right to vanity, that's what. Now you take Moscow. That's something to see, if you haven't. In Moscow people run to and fro. And nobody knows why. So there you have it. Vanity, nothing but vanity. The people in Moscow are vain, my dear Marfa Ignatevna. That's why they run around like they do. I'll give you an example. Take the man who thinks he's running after business. Poor old thing. He's in such a hurry he doesn't even recognize the people he runs by. He lives in a dream world of his own. He thinks someone is waving to him, urging him on. And so he hurries on until he finally gets there. And

know what? Nothing is there, nothing. Only a dream. So off
he goes, overcome with grief. Another fellow dreams he's going
to pass somebody he knows, leave him right in his own dust. And
does he? Why, ask anybody else on the way. Ask anybody else
seeing him rush by, who it is that's up ahead. And he'll answer
at once, nobody. Nobody at all. But the poor old thing rushing
along, overcome with his vanity, really thinks he's going to pass
someone he knows. You know, vanity is like being in some kind
of fog. Anyone in it will never get out. In this town it's different.
People here seldom come outside their own gates and sit a
little while on a beautiful evening. But in Moscow right now
people are having a gay old time. Parties, dancing, card-playing,
things like that. And along the streets, you can't hear yourself
think. The noise goes on and on, till you think the streets themselves are groaning. And know something else, sweetie? They're
starting to harness up a fiery serpent,[32] right in Moscow. You
see, it's all for the sake of going even faster than they are.

MARFA.   I've heard about it already, dear.

FEKLUSHA.   Well, my dear, I've seen it with my own eyes. And
just let me tell you. Some people, because of their vanity, don't
really know what they've seen. They think it's an engine. And
do you know, they even call it an engine. But I've seen it, and
it runs around on its own paws, just like this. [*Spreads apart
her fingers.*] And it groans, too, you know. Of course, only
people who live upright lives can hear those kind of groans.

MARFA.   Go ahead and call it whatever you want. If you like,
call it an engine. I don't care. Some people are stupid enough
to believe anything. As far as I'm concerned, you can cover
me with gold, but I'd never go riding on one.

FEKLUSHA.   No one's forcing you to, my dear. May God keep
you safe from disaster like that. But you know, my dear Marfa
Ignatevna, I must tell you about a vision I had in Moscow once.
Early one morning I was walking along. In fact, it was just
starting to get light. I happened to look up, and then I saw
somebody. He was standing on the roof of a tall, and I mean
tall, building. His face was as black [33] as the ace of spades.
And you can just guess who it was. He was doing something
with his hands, just as if he was throwing something about. But
nothing was being thrown, nothing at all. All at once I guessed

what he was doing. He was throwing weeds, throwing them down early in the morning. So that during the day people would pick them up. The weeds were invisible, of course. But people picked them up because of their vanity. That's the reason they run around so much. That's the reason Moscow women are so thin. You know their bodies never fatten up at all. That's why they look as if they had just lost something, or as if they were looking for something. You look at their faces and they seem so sad, you end up feeling sorry for them.

MARFA. I don't doubt it at all, my dear. No, I don't. The way things are these days, I'm not a bit surprised anymore.

FEKLUSHA. Oh, my dear Marfa Ignatevna, times are hard. Yes, you can say that again. And what's more, time itself is getting shorter, too.

MARFA. How's that, dear? What do you mean, shorter?

FEKLUSHA. Of course, we wouldn't notice it, caught up as we are in our vanity. But wise men have seen that our time grows shorter and shorter. It used to be that summer and winter dragged on and on until you guessed it would never end. These days you don't see how time flies by. Both the days and the hours have stayed the same. But time itself, because of our sins, is getting shorter and shorter. At least that's what wise men keep saying.

MARFA. If you think this is bad, dear, just wait. It'll get worse.

FEKLUSHA. If only we don't live to see it.

MARFA. Maybe. But then again, we may live to see it. [DIKOY enters.] What's this, old friend, why are you roaming around so late?

DIKOY. And who do you think will stop me?

MARFA. Who? Why, who wants to?

DIKOY. All right, then. Why discuss it? I suppose you think somebody's bossing me around, is that it? Just what do you think you're doing here, I'd like to know? What the devil are you fishing around for, anyway?

MARFA. Now just hold up there. Let up on all that yelling. Go find someone a little cheaper than me, 'cause I'm too rich for your yipping. Better get on your way. Feklusha, let's go home. [Rises.]

DIKOY. Wait a minute, old friend, wait. Don't get mad. Time enough for you to get home. Can't say it's beyond the mountains. Take a look. There, you see it.

MARFA.   If you're here on business, then don't shout. And start talking some sense.

DIKOY.   I'm not here on business. Don't see how I can be. I'm a little drunk, that's all.

MARFA.   What do you expect me to do, praise you for it?

DIKOY.   No, I don't. I don't want your praise, and I don't want you to raise Cain, either. Just like you to know I'm a little drunk. So we can stop right there. Until I sleep it off, there's not a damn thing anybody can do.

MARFA.   Then get going and start sleeping.

DIKOY.   Where is it I should go?

MARFA.   Home. Where do you think!

DIKOY.   But if I don't want to go home? What then?

MARFA.   And why not, may I ask?

DIKOY.   Because there's a battle going on at home.

MARFA.   And who's fighting this time? I thought you were the only fighter there.

DIKOY.   Well, so what if I am? What difference does it make? Well?

MARFA.   Oh, no difference at all. But you don't get much credit out of it, because you've spent your whole life fighting with women. That's what.

DIKOY.   Well, they ought to give in to me then. If I ever start giving in to them, that'll be the day.

MARFA.   I'm pretty surprised at you. With all the people in your house, you'd think there might be at least one person who could please you.

DIKOY.   That'll be the day!

MARFA.   Well, what can I do for you?

DIKOY.   Just this, talk to me till I cool off. You're the only one in the whole town who knows how to talk to me.

MARFA.   Go along, Feklusha, and order something to eat. [FEKLUSHA *exits.*] Let's go inside.

DIKOY.   No, I don't want to go inside. I'm worse inside.

MARFA.   What was it, exactly, that made you so angry?

DIKOY.   It's been going on all day, ever since morning.

MARFA.   No doubt they were asking for money.

DIKOY.   Seems like they ganged up on me, damn it. Been after me all day. First one, then another.

MARFA.   If they kept after you like that, no doubt they really wanted something.

DIKOY.   I know it, don't think I don't. But what the hell can I do with myself? You know how upset I get. Oh, I know I have to pay up, but I can't do it on my own. Now you, for example, are a friend of mine and say I had to give you some money I owed you. But if you came and asked me for it, I'd start calling you names. Oh, I'd pay up, but I couldn't help raising all kinds of hell at the same time. Because if you so much as mention money to me, everything inside starts flaring up. I get boiling mad, and I can't stop. And right then and there, I'm all set to curse a man for nothing, nothing at all.

MARFA.   Well, your trouble is you have no one older to sit on you. That's the reason you bully everybody in sight.

DIKOY.   No! Now shut up for a minute, old friend, and just listen. I'll tell you some things that happen to me all the time. During Lent I was fasting, but then the devil goes and slips a lousy grubbing peasant under my nose. He'd come for his money since he'd hauled some wood for me. And here he showed up at the worst possible time, as if on purpose. That did it, so I went and committed a sin. I let him have it. I swore, I cursed. I raised more hell than you'd think possible. In fact, I almost gave him a good beating. There you are, that's how upset I get. Afterward I begged his forgiveness. I got down on my knees. Yes, heaven help me, I did. I'm telling you the truth, I got down on my knees before a peasant. That's where my temper leads me. There, in the yard, on my knees in the mud. Begging his forgiveness, right in front of everybody.

MARFA.   How come you get heated up so much on purpose? That's not good, old friend, not good at all.

DIKOY.   What do you mean, on purpose?

MARFA.   I've seen it often enough, so I know what you're up to. Whenever you see that somebody wants something, you know what you do? You jump on someone in your own family, one of the kids or your wife. And you do it on purpose, just so you can get angry. Why do you do it? Because you know no one, absolutely no one, will ever come near you when you're mad.

Nobody will ask you for a thing. That's the reason, old friend.

DIKOY.   Well, so what? Why can't a body feel sorry if he has to give up something of his very own? [GLASHA *enters.*]

GLASHA.   Marfa Ignatevna, the table's been set, please.

MARFA.   There it is, old friend. Won't you come in and have a bite of what the Lord has sent us?

DIKOY.   Maybe I will.

MARFA.   Come in, please. [*She lets* DIKOY *pass ahead of her, then exits after him. With folded arms,* GLASHA *stands by the gates.*]

GLASHA.   It looks like Boris Grigorich is on his way here. Has he come for his uncle or just out for a walk? He must be taking a walk. [BORIS *enters.*]

BORIS.   Is my uncle here?

GLASHA.   Yes, he is. I suppose you've come for him?

BORIS.   They wanted me at home to find out where he is. But if he's here, then let him stay. Who wants him around, anyway? At home they're dancing for joy because he's gone out.

GLASHA.   If only our mistress were to marry him, she'd soon put an end to his nonsense. But why am I standing here like a fool? I must go at once. Good-by. [*Exits.*]

BORIS.   Oh, God in heaven, if I could only get one look at her! I can't just walk into her house. No one goes in there unless he's been invited. What a terrible way to live! Here we are in the same town, practically next door to each other, yet we see each other about once a week. And when we do, it's either in church or on the street. And that's all there is to it. In this town when a woman gets married, she might as well go to her grave. It's the same thing. [*Silence.*] It'd be a lot easier for me if I never see her again. The truth of the matter is I only see her now and again, anyway. And when I do, it's in front of everybody with a hundred eyes staring at you. It almost breaks my heart. I can't seem to get hold of myself anymore. Whenever I go out for a walk, I always end up here, standing outside her gates. Why come here at all? I can never see her. Besides, people very likely will start talking. If that happened, it could really get her into trouble. Oh, what a town I'm stuck in! [*He begins walking;* KULIGIN *meets him halfway.*]

KULIGIN.   Oh, there you are, sir. Taking a walk?

BORIS.   Yes, taking a walk. Beautiful weather today, isn't it?

KULIGIN.   Very beautiful, sir, for a walk. It's quiet and serene, and the air so perfect, we can smell the flowers in the meadows beyond the Volga. The sky above is clear, pure . . .

> Opening wide, abyss on high;
> See countless stars, our infinite sky. [34]

Let's take a walk on the boulevard, sir. You won't find a soul there now.

BORIS.   Let's go.

KULIGIN.   You can see the kind of town we have, sir. It's all there, on the boulevard. We've built the boulevard, but no one goes for walks on it. Of course, you'll see people walking there on holidays. But they're only pretending to walk, just to show off their best clothes. Oh, now and again you'll see a drunken clerk weaving his way home from the tavern. But you'll never see the poor people taking a walk, sir, never. They're always at work, and if they get three hours sleep out of twenty-four, they're lucky. And the rich people? What do they do? You'd think they would have time for a walk, time to get a breath of fresh air, but they don't. Instead, long before dusk, they've bolted their gates and untied their dogs. I suppose you'd think they were hard at work or repeating their prayers. No, sir, that's not it at all. And they haven't locked their doors because of thieves, either. It's simply they don't want people to see the way they browbeat their servants. Yes, and the way they ride roughshod over their own family. And the tears that are shed behind those locked doors—tears that no one sees, cries that no one hears. But why tell you, sir? You know it only too well, yourself. But think what happens behind some of those locked doors. The worst kind of debauchery and drunkenness. But it's all done on the sly, so that no one will ever see or know it. God alone sees it. "Go ahead," they say, "look at me in public, and look as much as you like; but what I do at home doesn't concern you at all." "That's the reason," they tell you, "I have my doors locked and bolted and vicious dogs running loose." "Family life," they go on, "should be kept to one's self, a secret." Well, we know only too well what secrets they mean. It's the husband alone who gets any pleasure from secrets like that. As for the rest of the family, they can only howl like wolves. And what is it, exactly, the secret of family life? Who doesn't know precisely what it is! To rob orphans, relatives, nephews. To start beating anyone at home, children or servants, if they so much as threaten to squawk about what he does there. That's the secret of family life. No more and no less. Well, leave him to God! Do you know, sir, who likes to take walks in the evening? The young men and their girls. Stealing an hour or two from sleep, so they can stroll around together. Look, there's a couple now. [KUDRYASH *and* VARVARA *appear. They kiss.*]

BORIS.   They're kissing.

KULIGIN.   Never mind. [KUDRYASH *exits.* VARVARA *crosses to the gates and beckons to* BORIS. *He crosses to her.*]   I'm going to the boulevard, sir. No reason for me to bother you here. I'll wait for you over there.

BORIS.   All right, I won't be a minute. [KULIGIN *exits.*]

VARVARA.   [*Covering her face with her kerchief.*]   Do you know the ravine behind the Kabanov garden?

BORIS.   Yes, I do.

VARVARA.   Be sure to go there later on this evening.

BORIS.   Why?

VARVARA.   Don't be silly! Just be sure to go, and you'll find out. All right, you'd better hurry. You know they're waiting for you on the boulevard. [BORIS *exits.*]   I'm sure he didn't recognize me. Well, let him try to figure it out. When the time comes, I know Katerina won't hold back. I know she will slip out to see him. [*Exits through the gates.*]

SCENE TWO

Night. A ravine, covered with bushes. Above, the fence of the Kabanovs' garden and wicket gate. A path leads down from above.

KUDRYASH.   [*Enters with guitar.*]   Nobody here. What can she be doing now? Wish she'd hurry. Well, nothing to do but sit

down and wait a while. [*Sits on a stone.*] Guess I'll sing a
song, just to pass the time. [*Sings.*]

> *Oh, Don Cossack, lead thy horse to water,*
> *Then ride, brave Lord, to thy home for slaughter;*
> *Wait at the gate, and think, Oh, why*
> *Thy wife must kill, thy wife must die;*
> *Watch as she throws herself at thy feet,*
> *For mercy she prays, for time must entreat:*
> *'Oh, dear my Lord, sweet love of my life!*
> *Do not kill me now, my friend, I pray;*
> *Till midnight comes, our babes do lay*
> *Fast asleep in their beds; our neighbors, too;*
> *Then to thy task; kill me then, pray do.'*

[BORIS *enters.* KUDRYASH *stops singing.*] What do you know?
Don't tell me our good little boy's going to raise a little hell
tonight.

BORIS.   Oh, it's you, Kudryash?

KUDRYASH.   It sure is, Boris Grigorich.

BORIS.   What are you doing here?

KUDRYASH.   Me, fellow? If I'm here, Boris Grigorich, you can
bet I'd better be here. I'd never have come, if I didn't have
something going for me. But where are you off to?

BORIS.   [*Glancing around at the place.*] Wait a minute,
Kudryash. You see I have to stay here. If you wouldn't mind,
maybe you could go somewhere else?

KUDRYASH.   No, I won't, Boris Grigorich. I can see you're here
for the first time. But you may as well know I've been here so
much I've worn this seat out. In fact, that path over there was
made by me. I like you, sir, and I'd be happy to do a good turn
for you anytime. But I'll warn you now. Better not let me see
you on that path at night. Or so help me God, you'll get something coming you'd never expect. Remember what I've told you.
It's a hell of a lot better than money.

BORIS.   What's the matter with you, Vanya?

KUDRYASH.   Oh, come off it. What's this Vanya business? I know
I'm Vanya. But you'd better move over to your side of the
road, and that's all there is to it. Get your own girl, have a
good time with her, and nobody will care one way or the other.
But better not touch another fellow's girl! That's not the way

we do things around here. Otherwise, the boys in town will break your legs for you. If anybody'd try something with my girl . . . Well, I don't know what I'd do. No doubt I'd slit his throat, that's for sure.

BORIS.   Forget it, you're getting mad over nothing at all. I'm not about to take her away from you. It's the last thing I'd think of. If you want to know something, I wouldn't even be here now if someone hadn't told me to come.

KUDRYASH.   Who told you to?

BORIS.   I couldn't see who it was. It was dark. Some girl stopped me on the street and said I should come here. Behind Kabanovs' garden, where I'd find a path.

KUDRYASH.   Who on earth could it be?

BORIS.   Listen, Kudryash, I'd like to speak frankly if I could. You won't give it away, will you?

KUDRYASH.   Speak up, don't be afraid. You can talk to me as if I were dead.

BORIS.   I'm at a loss about what to do. You see, I don't know much about the way things are done around here. Your customs and what's acceptable. All this business here tonight, for example . . .

KUDRYASH.   You've fallen in love with someone, haven't you?

BORIS.   Yes, Kudryash.

KUDRYASH.   Well, that's nothing to worry about. Things are pretty free and easy around here. The girls go out whenever they want to, and their fathers and mothers don't make any fuss. Of course, the married women are kept locked up.

BORIS.   Well, that's just the trouble.

KUDRYASH.   Don't tell me you've gone and fallen in love with a married woman?

BORIS.   Yes, a married woman, Kudryash.

KUDRYASH.   Oh, Boris Grigorich, you must give her up.

BORIS.   It's easy to say give her up. I suppose it wouldn't make much difference to you. You could give her up, then find another. But I can't do that. When I've fallen in love . . .

KUDRYASH.   I suppose you realize that if you keep it up, Boris Grigorich, you can only destroy her.

BORIS.   God forbid. So help me God, I won't. No, Kudryash, how could I? I'll never want to destroy her, never. If I could only see her somewhere, that's all. Nothing more. Just to see and talk with her.

KUDRYASH.   And how can you ever guarantee that, sir? You know the way people are around here. You know it yourself. If they find out, they'll swallow her up, drive her to her grave.

BORIS.   Oh, don't say that, Kudryash! I beg you, don't frighten me.

KUDRYASH.   But does she love you?

BORIS.   I don't know.

KUDRYASH.   But you've seen each other, haven't you?

BORIS.   I was in her house once, together with my uncle. I see her in church, and we meet on the boulevard. Oh, Kudryash, if you could only see her when she prays. She has the smile of an angel, and her face shines with a sacred light.

KUDRYASH.   Then it's the young Kabanov woman, isn't it?

BORIS.   Yes, Kudryash.

KUDRYASH.   Oh, I see, that's the way it is. Well, I'd like to congratulate you.

BORIS.   For what?

KUDRYASH.   Don't you see what it means? It's simple. Everything's going pretty well if you were told to come here.

BORIS.   So you think it was she who told me?

KUDRYASH.   Who was it then?

BORIS.   No, you're joking. It couldn't have been she. [Clasps his head.]

KUDRYASH.   What's the matter with you?

BORIS.   I'm so happy I could lose my mind.

KUDRYASH.   Oho, you'll have something to lose your mind over, don't think you won't. If you aren't careful, you'll find yourself in a helluva mess, and you'll take her right along with you. We all know her husband is a silly fool, but watch out for the mother-in-law. Get her started, and she'll rip you apart. [VARVARA enters through the gate.]

VARVARA.   [Stands by the gate, sings.]
    Beyond the river, ever so swift, my Vanya is walking,
    There my sweet Vanya is walking . . .

KUDRYASH.   [Continues.]
    Buying good wares as he's walking. [Whistles.]

VARVARA.   [Comes down the path, and having covered her face

with her kerchief, she crosses to BORIS.]   Wait right here, fellow.
I think you'll be surprised. [*To* KUDRYASH.]   Let's go to the
Volga.

KUDRYASH.   What took you so long? You've kept me waiting.
You know I don't like it. [VARVARA *embraces him with one
arm, and they exit.*]

BORIS.   I must be dreaming! A night like this, songs, and sweet-
hearts who meet. And now, walking off, arm-in-arm. It's all so
new to me, but it's beautiful, and I'm happy, really happy. And
here I am, waiting for something, waiting for . . . Oh, I don't
know. I can't believe it's happening to me. My heart is beating
so fast, and every nerve seems to tremble. I can't even think
what to say to her. I don't know if I can even talk to her. I
feel like I'm losing my breath, and I can scarcely stand up. If
I can just get my courage up, then I know I can talk to her.
There, I see her now. [KATERINA *slowly walks down the path,
her head covered with a large white kerchief, her eyes looking
at the ground. Silence.*]   Is it you, Katerina Petrovna? [*Silence.*]
I don't know how to thank you, I don't. [*Silence.*]   If you
only knew, Katerina Petrovna, how much I love you! [*Wants
to take her hand.*]

KATERINA.   [*Frightened, but doesn't raise her eyes.*]   Please.
Please, don't touch me. Please.

BORIS.   Don't be angry.

KATERINA.   Oh, dear God, please go away, please. If you only
knew what you've done to me, you'd leave now. Oh, God in
heaven, if you only knew. Never in all my prayers can I rid
myself of this sin. Never, never. It lies in my heart forever like
a dull, heavy ache.

BORIS.   Don't send me away, I beg you.

KATERINA.   Why have you come? Oh, why? Why do you destroy
me? You know I'm married. You know I must live with my
husband till the day I die.

BORIS.   But you told me to come . . .

KATERINA.   Till the day I die. Listen carefully to me, you are
my enemy. Understand? My enemy.

BORIS.   Then it would be better for me never to see you again.

KATERINA.   [*Agitated.*]   You know, don't you, what will become
of me? You know what I'm headed for, don't you?

BORIS.   Calm yourself, please.   [*Takes her hand.*]   Sit down.

KATERINA.   Why do you want to destroy me?

BORIS.   I don't want to destroy you. I love you more than anything in the world, more than life itself.

KATERINA.   No, no! You have destroyed me.

BORIS.   Do you really think I'm that evil?

KATERINA.   [*Shaking her head.*]   Destroyed me, destroyed, destroyed me!

BORIS.   No, God help me, no! I would rather die than hurt you in any way.

KATERINA.   But you have, don't you see? The moment I left my home and came to you in the night.

BORIS.   But you came freely, didn't you? Of your own will?

KATERINA.   I have no will of my own. If I had, I should never have come here to you.   [*She raises her eyes and looks at* BORIS. *A short pause.*]   Whatever you want, I am yours. Now and forever. Don't you see?   [*Throws herself on his neck.*]

BORIS.   [*Embraces* KATERINA.]   My love, my life.

KATERINA.   Do you know? I should like to die. Now, at this moment.

BORIS.   Why should you die when life for us means happiness?

KATERINA.   No, I know I shall not live for long. I know I shall die soon.

BORIS.   Don't, my darling, don't say things like that! Please, I can't bear to hear you. . . .

KATERINA.   Yes, I know. You don't want to feel unhappy, I know. But it's different for you. You are a man, you are free, but I . . .

BORIS.   No one will ever know of our love, no one. I'd never hurt you, never.

KATERINA.   Oh, why shouldn't you? No one is to blame. I came here myself. Please don't spare me, for heaven's sake, destroy me. Let everyone see what I'm doing.   [*Embraces* BORIS.]   If I were not afraid of sin for your sake, why should I fear how people may judge me? They tell you it's better to suffer here and now for what you've done on this earth.

BORIS.   Well, don't think about it. Let's keep the happiness we have now.

KATERINA.   Yes, I believe you. Yes, time will come when I must think, when I must weep.

BORIS. I was afraid, you know. At first, I mean. I was afraid you would send me away.

KATERINA. [Smiling.] Send you away! How could I ever? How? I love you with all my heart. If you hadn't come to me, I think I should have gone to you.

BORIS. I never realized that you loved me.

KATERINA. I've loved you for a long time. It's almost as if you had come to our town just to destroy me. From the first moment I saw you, I was no longer the same woman. Had you so much as beckoned that first moment, I would have followed you. Had you gone to the end of the world, I would have followed you and never once looked back.

BORIS. Will your husband be away long?

KATERINA. Two weeks.

BORIS. Oh, we must make every moment count. There is plenty of time.

KATERINA. Yes, we shall make every moment count. And then . . . [Deep in thought.] When they lock me up, I know I shall die. If they don't, then I'll find a way to see you. [KUDRYASH and VARVARA enter.]

VARVARA. Well, what'd you say? Everything set? [KATERINA hides her face on BORIS' chest.]

BORIS. All set.

VARVARA. Go ahead and go for a walk then. We'll wait here. If it's necessary, Vanya will call you. [BORIS and KATERINA exit. KUDRYASH and VARVARA sit on the stone.]

KUDRYASH. Say, that's a good trick you thought of, to go through the garden gate. Works pretty well for us fellows.

VARVARA. I thought it up myself.

KUDRYASH. You're the one to come up with tricks, all right. Won't your mother miss you?

VARVARA. How could she, really! The idea won't even enter her mind.

KUDRYASH. What happens if it does? Guess we've had it, then?

VARVARA. When she falls asleep, that's it. Of course, toward morning, she starts to wake up.

KUDRYASH. Well, you can't be sure, can you? You know the devil might get her up.

VARVARA.   Suppose he does! We've locked the door to the court-yard from the garden side. She'll knock, knock some more, and then go away. In the morning, we'll just tell her we were sleeping so soundly we didn't hear her. What's more, Glasha is watching out for us. If something happens, she'll let us know at once. And it might. You can't do anything without some danger. You never know, really. At any moment, the roof can cave in. [KUDRYASH *strikes several chords on the guitar.* VARVARA *leans on his shoulder.* KUDRYASH *pays no attention to her, playing quietly on the guitar.* VARVARA *yawns.*]   Do you know what time it is?

KUDRYASH.   Past twelve.

VARVARA.   How do you know?

KUDRYASH.   The watchman just struck the hour.[35]

VARVARA.   [*Yawning.*] It's time to go. Call to them now. We'll come out earlier tomorrow. Then we'll have more time.

KUDRYASH.   [*Whistles and sings in a loud voice.*]
> Time to go home. Everybody home!
> But who wants to? I sure don't.

BORIS.   [*Behind the setting.*]   I hear you!

VARVARA.   [*Rises.*] Well, good-by. [*She yawns, then kisses* KUDRYASH *coldly like an old friend.*] Be sure you come earlier tomorrow. [*Looks in the direction where* BORIS *and* KATERINA *have gone.*] Say, let's go. You're supposed to say good-by and stop acting like you're parting forever. You'll see each other tomorrow. [*Yawns and stretches.* KATERINA *runs in, followed by* BORIS.]

KATERINA.   [*To* VARVARA.]   Let's go then. Let's go.   [*They cross up the path.* KATERINA *turns back.*]   Good-by.

BORIS.   Till tomorrow.

KATERINA.   Yes, till tomorrow. Remember to tell me your dream. [*Crosses to gate.*]

BORIS.   I will.

KUDRYASH.   [*Plays guitar and sings.*]
> Oh, little girl, stroll on and on;
> Be sure to return well before dawn;
> Ai-leli, ai, well before dawn,
> And don't stay out till morn.

VARVARA.   [*At the gate.*]
> *Oh, I'm the girl to stroll on and on;*
> *And you won't see me till after dawn;*
> *Ai-leli, ai, till after dawn,*
> *And I'll stay out past morn.*

[VARVARA *and* KATERINA *exit.*]

KUDRYASH.
> *When the sun next day broke through,*
> *There I was, strolling homeward, too . . .*

ACT FOUR

In the foreground a narrow arched gallery of an ancient building which is beginning to fall into ruin. Here and there grass and bushes. Through the arches may be seen the bank and a view of the Volga. Several MEN *and* WOMEN *stroll to and fro, crossing downstage of the arches.*

FIRST MAN. It's drizzling now. A storm isn't coming, is there?
SECOND MAN. Looks like it.
FIRST MAN. It's a good thing we've shelter here. [*All cross under the arches.*]
A WOMAN. Look at all the people on the boulevard, will you? It's a holiday today, so everybody has come out for a walk. Even the merchants' wives are all dressed up.
FIRST MAN. Drizzling like it is, they'll be running for shelter somewhere or other.
SECOND MAN. Wait and see if they all don't run in here.
FIRST MAN. [*Examining the walls.*] Take a look, old fellow, this has been painted at one time or other. Some of the spots still show through.
SECOND MAN. Well, of course. Stands to reason it was painted once. Right now, you can see for yourself it's been left deserted. It's gone to pieces and overgrown. Nobody fixed it up after the fire. Doubt if you remember that fire. Why, it must have been forty years ago.
FIRST MAN. Look, old fellow, can you make out what's painted there? It's hard as the devil to figure out.
SECOND MAN. That's the hell fire itself.
FIRST MAN. You don't say, old fellow!

SECOND MAN.   And everybody and his brother is on his way there.

FIRST MAN.   Yes, sure enough. I see it now.

SECOND MAN.   People of every rank.

FIRST MAN.   Even the blacks?

SECOND MAN.   Even the blacks.

FIRST MAN.   And this, old fellow, can you make this out?

SECOND MAN.   Oh, that's the Lithuanian destruction.[36] It's a battle! See? It shows how we beat the Lithuanians.

FIRST MAN.   What do you mean by this Lithuania?

SECOND MAN.   Just Lithuania, that's all.

FIRST MAN.   You know, old fellow, they tell us that it fell on us from the sky.

SECOND MAN.   I can't tell you exactly. Maybe from the sky, maybe from somewhere else.

A WOMAN.   You don't know what you're talking about. Everybody knows they fell from the sky. And where the battle was you'll find burial mounds piled up as a memorial.

FIRST MAN.   That's it, old fellow. That's exactly how it happened.

[DIKOY enters, followed by KULIGIN without a cap. Everyone bows and assumes respectful positions.]

DIKOY.   How d'you like that! Soaked to the skin.   [To KULIGIN.] Get away from me. Leave me alone. [Angrily.] Stupid old man!

KULIGIN.   Savel Prokofich, you know it's so, your honor. Everyone in town will find use for it. It's a benefit for all the people in general.

DIKOY.   Get out of here. What do you mean, a benefit? Who wants to use it?

KULIGIN.   Why, even you, your honor, might find use for it, Savel Prokofich. You know, sir, it could be set up on the boulevard in some open spot. And there'd be no expense to speak of. A stone pillar [indicates with gestures the size of each thing], a copper plate, a round one like this, and a needle, one that's straight [indicates with gesture], nothing special at all. I'll do it all myself. Even carve out the figures myself. Then, your honor, whenever you happen to be out for a walk, or anyone else for that matter, why you can go over and see what time it is. And the spot for it is beautiful, and so is the view and everything. Now, of course, the place seems empty without it. And you know, your honor, many travelers come to our town just to take a look at our beautiful sights. And this would be one of them, an ornament everyone could see how perfect it is.

DIKOY. Why come crawling to me with this nonsense? What if I don't want to talk to you about it? You should have found out first if I was ready to listen to a fool like you. I suppose you think you're as good as me, maybe. Equal to me, maybe. How d'you like that? Oh, you think you've found something pretty important, don't you? And right off you poke your nose in and start talking to me.

KULIGIN. If I'd come to you with something for myself, then you'd have every right in the world to push me aside. But this is for general benefit, your honor. What do a few rubles mean when it's for the whole town? And, sir, the cost will be no more.

DIKOY. But what if you want to steal them? How do we know you won't do that?

KULIGIN. But I'm giving my own work for nothing, your honor. How could I ever steal anything? Everybody in town knows me. Nobody has ever said a thing against me.

DIKOY. I don't give a damn if everybody and his brother knows you. The point is, I don't want to know you.

KULIGIN. But Savel Prokofich, sir, why insult an honest man?

DIKOY. If you think I'm going to give you an account of what I do, you are mistaken. Why, I wouldn't do it for someone who's more important than you. Whatever I want to think about you, I'll say it. You may be an honest man to other people around here, but as far as I'm concerned you're a thief. And that's all there is to it. If that's what you wanted to hear, then go ahead and listen. I'll say it again. You are a thief, a damned thief, finally and forever. I suppose you'll want to sue me for saying it? Go ahead, but you'd better understand that you are a worm. That's all, a worm. If I feel like it, I may let you crawl away. If I don't, then I'll step on you.

KULIGIN. God forgive you, Savel Prokofich. It's true, sir, I'm not very important. So it's not hard to insult me and get away with it. But I must tell you this, your honor: "Even in rags virtue must be respected."

DIKOY. Don't you dare insult me! Understand? Don't you dare!

KULIGIN. I wouldn't think of insulting you, sir. I'm only talking to you because you may want to do something for the town someday. You have the power to do it, your honor. I pray you may find the will for good works. For example, here's something you might do. We have a lot of thunderstorms, but we don't have any lightning conductors.

DIKOY. [*Arrogantly.*] Stuff and nonsense! They'd never work.

KULIGIN. How can you say nonsense, when there've been experiments?

DIKOY. What kind of lightning conductors do you have in mind?

KULIGIN. Steel ones.

DIKOY. [*Angrily.*] Well, go on! Anything else?

KULIGIN. Steel rods.

DIKOY. [*Growing angrier each moment.*] I've heard there are rods, you silly fool, but is there anything else? You've said they were steel. Anything else, for heaven's sake?

KULIGIN. Nothing more.

DIKOY. And what are thunderstorms in your opinion? Huh? Well, speak up.

KULIGIN. Electricity.

DIKOY. [*Having stamped his foot.*] So here you go again with electricity! Well, if you're not a thief, what are you then? You know damn well storms are sent to us as a punishment, so that we will repent. But you, God help us, you want to defend ourselves against them with rods or some kind of sticks. What are you, a Tartar,[37] maybe? Are you a Tartar? Well, speak up. Are you a Tartar?

KULIGIN. Savel Prokofich, your honor, remember what Derzhavin said:

> Though my body die, return to dust;
> Whilst I live, my mind over storms entrust.[38]

DIKOY. When you talk like that, I ought to drag you off to the mayor. He'd take care of you, don't think he wouldn't. Listen here, all you good people, just listen to the way he talks.

KULIGIN. I see I can't do a thing, so I'd better give in. If I ever get my million, you'll have to listen to me then. [*Having waved his hand hopelessly, he exits.*]

DIKOY. Go on, try to get your million. I suppose you'll steal it from somebody? Better grab him now. He's nothing but a cheating, lousy, grubbing peasant! What can you do with people like him? What can you do, I'd like to know! [*Turning to the crowd.*] Damn you, damn you all, anyway. I've lost my temper just because of you. I didn't want to get mad today, but then that damned fellow showed up. And wouldn't you know it, he's made me furious. Let him go to hell! [*Angrily.*] Don't tell me it's still raining?

FIRST MAN. Looks like it's stopped.

DIKOY. What do you mean, looks like it? You fool, go on out and look. Wouldn't you know it, looks like it!

FIRST MAN. [*Coming out from under the arches.*] It's stopped!

[DIKOY *exits, followed by the others. The stage is empty for a short while.* VARVARA *runs in quickly under the arches. Then, having hidden herself, she looks around.*]

VARVARA. I think it's he! [BORIS *crosses upstage.*] Psst! [BORIS *looks around.*] Come here. [*Waves hand.* BORIS *crosses to her under the arches.*] What are we going to do with Katerina? Tell me, for heaven's sake.

BORIS. Why? What's happened?

VARVARA. Plenty, that's for sure. Her husband has returned, haven't you heard? We never expected him now. But he is here all the same.

BORIS. No, I didn't know.

VARVARA. She's simply frantic, lost all control of herself.

BORIS. Good Lord, only ten short days of true happiness. And now he's come home. I know I shall never see her again.

VARVARA. What kind of person are you, anyway? Can't you think of anyone but yourself! Now you listen to me. Something has happened to Katerina. She's trembling all over as if she had a bad fever. She's terribly pale and wanders around the house as if she were searching for something. Her eyes have the look of someone insane. This morning she began weeping, sobbing as if she wanted to die. God in heaven, what can I do with her?

BORIS. Oh, I think she'll get over it.

VARVARA. Well, I don't think she will. She doesn't dare look at her husband. And mama has started to notice it. She goes around looking at Katerina out of the corner of her eyes. Mama looks like a snake just ready to strike. Of course, this makes

Katerina only worse. It's simply terrible to look at her. And I'm scared, scared to death.

BORIS.   What are you afraid of, for heaven's sake?

VARVARA.   Oh, you don't know her like I do. Katerina is different, you know, strange. She might do anything, anything at all. She might do something that would . . .

BORIS.   Oh, dear God, what can we do? You'd better have a good talk with her. Try to persuade her to settle down, can't you?

VARVARA.   I've tried to, and she won't listen to a thing. It's better to stay away from her.

BORIS.   Well, what do you think she might do?

VARVARA.   I'll tell you right now what I'm afraid of. She'll throw herself at her husband's feet and tell him everything. That's exactly what I'm afraid she'll do.

BORIS.   [Frightened.] God in heaven, she wouldn't do that. She couldn't.

VARVARA.   Listen, she might do anything.

BORIS.   Where is she now?

VARVARA.   At the moment she's gone walking with her husband on the boulevard, and mama is with them. Go on and see her if you want to. Wait a minute! No, better not go. Otherwise, she may go all to pieces if she saw you. [In the distance, thunderclaps.] That's a storm coming, isn't it? [Looks around.] Yes, and here comes the rain. Look, people are starting to come here. Hide over there somewhere. I'll stand here, where everybody can see me, and no one will suspect a thing. [Enter several persons of both sexes and of various classes; among them is KULIGIN.]

FIRST MAN.   That young woman must be pretty frightened, to run as fast as she is to hide from the storm.

A WOMAN.   Well, you can't hide from it. Whatever fate has in store for you, you can never escape from it.

KATERINA.   [Running in.] Oh, Varvara! [Grabs VARVARA'S hand and holds it tightly.]

VARVARA.   Stop it! What's wrong with you?

KATERINA.   I know I'm going to die.

VARVARA.   Get hold of yourself. Think what you're saying.

KATERINA.   No, I can't! I can't do anything. My heart is breaking.

MARFA. [*Entering, followed by* KABANOV.]   As far as I'm concerned, a body ought to live so as to be always prepared for anything. If you did, then you wouldn't be so frightened.

KABANOV.   But, mama, what kind of sin could she have committed? The same as the rest of us do all the time. Seems to me, Katerina gets frightened simply because it's her nature.

MARFA.   How do you know? Someone else's soul is a mystery. No one knows what goes on inside.

KABANOV. [*Jokingly.*]   Well, maybe there was something when I was gone, but I know nothing's happened while I've been here.

MARFA.   Maybe there was something when you were gone.

KABANOV. [*Jokingly.*]   Better confess, Katya my girl, if you've done something you shouldn't have. You know you can't hide anything from me. None of your tricks now. I know everything.

KATERINA. [*Looking into* KABANOV's *eyes.*]   My darling.

VARVARA.   Why are you worrying her, anyway? Can't you see it's hard enough for her to put up with your joking? [BORIS *comes out from the crowd and exchanges bows with the Kabanovs.*]

KATERINA. [*Cries out.*]   Oh!

KABANOV.   Why are you frightened? Do you think he's a stranger? Why, he's someone we know. Is your uncle well?

BORIS.   Yes, he is, thanks to God.

KATERINA. [*To* VARVARA.]   What more can he want from me? Doesn't he know I can barely stand it?   [*Clings to* VARVARA *and sobs.*]

VARVARA. [*In a loud voice, so her mother can hear.*]   We've done everything on God's earth with her. I don't know what else to do. And I've no idea why strangers should crowd around now. [*Signals to* BORIS, *who crosses to the far side of the stage, nearest the exit.*]

KULIGIN. [*Crosses to the center of the stage, turns to the crowd.*]   Well, what are you afraid of? Tell me, for heaven's sake. Right now every blade of grass, every single flower is rejoicing. But we are hiding, scared to death, as if some kind of disaster were going to fall upon us. To you the storm will slay. This is not a storm, but a blessing. Yes, a blessing! To you it's always a storm, always. If the northern lights shine in the sky, you ought to adore them and marvel at God's wisdom. "From the midnight lands does the dawn appear!"³⁹ But you are terrified and imagine it means war or the plague. If a comet appears, don't turn away from it. Good Lord, it is beauty itself flashing through the sky! You're not afraid to look at the stars. Why? Because they never change. But a comet? This is something new, different, wonderful. You ought to look and admire it. You're afraid to look up to the sky. Instead, you shake from fear. Every beautiful, gracious event in the heavens you turn into a thing of terror. What kind of people are you, I'd like to know! Look at me now. I'm not afraid.   [*To* BORIS.]   Let's go, sir.

BORIS.   Let's go. It's even more frightening here.   [KULIGIN *and* BORIS *exit.*]

MARFA.   Listen to that, will you? Talk about a sermon. Who wants to listen, I'd like to know? Well, you can see where things are going now when teachers like him sprout up. If an old man carries on and on, then what can you expect from young people?

A WOMAN.   Take a look. The whole sky is clouded over just as if it's been covered by a cap.

FIRST MAN.   I can't believe it, old fellow. See how that storm cloud turns and tosses like a ball in the sky. Why, it looks as if there was something alive whirling about inside. See how it flies right at us as if it were alive.

SECOND MAN.   You remember my words, that storm's not going to pass without doing something. No, sir, I'm telling you the truth. I know what I'm talking about. It's going to kill somebody, or else it's going to burn down a house. Wait and see. Look at the sky. Have you ever seen a color like that before?

KATERINA.   [*Listening.*]   Do you hear what they're saying? They're saying the storm will kill someone.

KABANOV.   Don't worry about it. They're just talking, saying whatever pops into their heads.

MARFA.   Better not judge those older than you! They know far more than you do. Old people know what every sign means. So you'd better listen to them. An old person never talks just to hear himself think.

KATERINA.   [*To her husband.*]   Tisha, I know who's going to be killed.

VARVARA.   [*To* KATERINA, *softly.*]   Don't say any more. Be still, please!

KABANOV. How do you know?

KATERINA. I shall be killed. When it happens, pray for me. [*Enter the* OLD LADY *with the* TWO SERVANTS. KATERINA *cries out and hides herself.*]

OLD LADY. Why are you hiding? It's no use trying to hide. Why, you're frightened, aren't you? You don't want to die, you want to go on living. Of course, you do. Why shouldn't you when you're as beautiful as you are? Ha, ha, ha. Beautiful! Better pray to God to take away your beauty. You know beauty is our ruin. You will destroy yourself, you will entice men. Then see if you can enjoy your beauty. You will lead men into sin. Yes, many, many men. Empty-headed fools will fight duels, killing each other with swords. All because of your beauty. You'll be happy then, won't you? And the old men, the respectable men, will forget all about the grave, enticed by your beauty. Who must answer for it? You will. Yes, you must answer for everything. Better destroy yourself than so many. Into the river with your beauty. Yes, at once, at once. [KATERINA *hides herself.*] Why are you hiding, you silly girl? You know you can't escape from God. [*A thunderclap.*] All of you shall die. Yes, and burn in the ever-lasting fire. [*Exits.*]

KATERINA. Oh, I am dying.

VARVARA. Stop tormenting yourself, stop it. Go over there and pray. Things will seem better then.

KATERINA. [*Crosses to the wall, falls on her knees, then jumps up quickly.*] Oh, it's hell itself. The burning fire of hell! [MARFA, KABANOV, *and* VARVARA *surround her.*] My heart is breaking. I can't stand it any longer. Mama! Tikhon! I've sinned before God and before you. Didn't I fall on my knees before you? Didn't I promise never to look at anyone while you were gone? Remember? Remember what I swore to you? Do you know what I did when you were gone? God in heaven, I have sinned. The very first night I left the house . . .

KABANOV. [*In confusion and in tears, pulls* KATERINA *by her sleeve.*] Don't, don't say anything, don't. Not another word. What are you doing? Mama is here.

MARFA. [*Sternly.*] Well, go ahead, speak up. Better finish what you've started.

KATERINA.   And all ten nights I went out with . . .   [*She sobs.*
KABANOV *wants to embrace her.*]

MARFA.   Let her alone. With whom?

VARVARA.   She's lying. She doesn't know what she's saying herself.

MARFA.   Shut up, you. So that's it. Well, who was it, then?

KATERINA.   Boris Grigorich. [*A thunderclap.*] Oh! [*Faints
and falls into her husband's arms.*]

MARFA.   There, son. See where freedom leads now. I told you,
but you didn't want to listen. Well, it's happened, and you never
expected it, did you? I hope you're pleased with yourself.

ACT FIVE

The same setting as in Act One. Twilight. KULIGIN *sits on a bench.* KABANOV *is walking along the boulevard.*

KULIGIN. [*Sings.*]
> *The heavens enclosed by the night so deep,*
> *And men find peace with eyes fast asleep.*[40]

[*Seeing* KABANOV.]   Good evening, sir. Are you going far?

KABANOV.   Home. I suppose you've heard, old friend, what's happened? The whole family's upset, completely lost.

KULIGIN.   Yes, I've heard, sir. Yes, I have.

KABANOV.   I suppose you know I went to Moscow? Before I left, mama gave me a good talking to. But wouldn't you know it? As soon as I got on the road, I started raising Cain. You see, I was so happy to get away from it all and call my soul my own. So I drank all the way to Moscow and kept it up the whole time I was there. In short, I had one helluva good time, don't you think I didn't. Well, I had a whole year to make up after all. I didn't give a single thought to what was going on at home. And even if I had, it would never have entered my mind about what was going on here. I suppose you've heard?

KULIGIN.   Yes, I've heard, sir.

KABANOV.   Dear Lord in heaven, I'm unhappy now. So damn unhappy, old friend. It's killing me. And I know I didn't do a thing to cause it, not one single thing.

KULIGIN.   Your mother is pretty severe, don't you think?

KABANOV.   Yes, she is. She's the one who's responsible for everything. But why should I suffer for what she has done? Tell me, for heaven's sake. I dropped by to see Dikoy just now, and we had a drink. I thought maybe that would help. But it didn't,

Kuligin. No, it's worse now. I can't get over what my wife has done to me, I can't. Nothing could be worse, nothing.

KULIGIN.   It's difficult to figure out, sir. It's difficult to say who's responsible.

KABANOV.   No, wait a minute! What on earth could be worse than this? It's not enough simply to kill her for what she's done. Mama says that she should be buried alive to pay for her sin, but I love her. It tears me up even to lay a hand on her. I beat her a little and I'm sorry I did, but mama said I had to. I'm sorry to see her the way she is. Can you understand that, Kuligin? Mama keeps after her, won't let her alone for a minute. And she, poor thing, walks around like a shadow and can say nothing at all. She cries and cries, wasting away moment by moment. It breaks me up inside seeing her the way she is.

KULIGIN.   Why couldn't you try to work things out, sir? You ought to forgive her and never say another word about it. After all, you are partly to blame, aren't you?

KABANOV.   Yes, I am. Yes, indeed.

KULIGIN.   Well then, forgive her, and try not to accuse her when you're drunk, either. She will make you a good wife, sir. In fact, better than anyone else.

KABANOV.   Don't you understand, Kuligin? I'd be glad to forget it, but mama . . . Well, I'd never be able to convince her, never.

KULIGIN.   It's about time, sir, for you to live your own life, to make up your own mind.

KABANOV.   But how can I? I can't become somebody I'm not. I don't have a mind of my own, or so they say. That means go on and live the way somebody else has figured it out for you. Well, what's left for me then? Nothing but to take what little mind I have and put it in on hard drinking. Then let mama take care of me, nurse me like the fool I am.

KULIGIN.   Oh, sir, what can I say? The whole thing's pretty hopeless, hopeless. But what about Boris Grigorich? What's to become of him?

KABANOV.   The scoundrel's on his way to Tyakhta [41] on the Chinese border. His uncle's shipped him to some merchant friend there to work in the office. He'll be gone for three years.

KULIGIN.   How is he taking it, sir?

KABANOV.   He's in bad shape, too. Mopes around and cries. His uncle and I jumped on him the other day and raised Cain. But he didn't say a single word, not one. He looks like a wild animal. "Do whatever you want to me," he says, "only don't torment her anymore." Even he feels sorry for her.

KULIGIN.   He is a good man, sir.

KABANOV.   He is all set to leave. Even the horses are harnessed. He's all torn up inside. I know he wants to say good-by to her. Well, I don't care. He can go to hell, as far as I'm concerned. You know he's my enemy, Kuligin. He should be ripped to pieces, so he'd realize . . .

KULIGIN.   We ought to forgive our enemies, sir.

KABANOV.   Go and tell my mother that. Then see what she'll have to say to you. Our whole family life, my dear Kuligin, has been smashed, torn apart. We are no longer close to one another. Instead, we've become enemies. Mama nagged and picked at Varvara until she couldn't stand it anymore. So she's gone and left the house for good.

KULIGIN.   Do you know where she went?

KABANOV.   Who knows for sure? They say she's run off with Kudryash. He's nowhere to be found, either. And I can say right off, Kuligin, that mama's to blame, because she started bossing her and locking her up. "Don't lock me up," Varvara said, "or it will be worse." And it turned out it was. Tell me what I can do now. Tell me how I'm supposed to live now. I'm sick and tired of the house. I'm ashamed to see people. I try to do something at work, and my hands start shaking. Right now I'm going home, but what happiness can I ever find there?   [GLASHA *enters.*]

GLASHA.   Tikhon Ivanych, sir!

KABANOV.   What is it?

GLASHA.   Something's gone wrong at home, sir.

KABANOV.   Good Lord! One thing after another. Tell me, what's happened there?

GLASHA.   It's your wife . . .

KABANOV.   Come now, what is it? Has she died, is that it?

GLASHA.   Oh, no, sir. She's gone away somewhere, and we can't find her. We've worn ourselves out looking for her.

KABANOV.   Let's go, Kuligin, old friend! We must try and find her. Do you know what I'm afraid of? She is so grief-stricken I'm afraid she may kill herself. Dear God, how upset she is! Terribly, terribly upset! My heart breaks whenever I look at her. [*To* GLASHA.] Why didn't you watch her? Has she been gone for long?

GLASHA.   Not very long, sir. It's my fault she's gone. But I don't see how I could've taken care of her every minute.

KABANOV.   Well, don't stand around here. Run, look for her. [GLASHA *exits.*] Let's go, Kuligin. [*They exit. The stage is empty for a short time.* KATERINA *enters from the opposite side and walks slowly across the stage. Throughout this monologue and in the succeeding scenes,* KATERINA *speaks pensively and as if she were unconscious, drawling and repeating her words.*]

KATERINA.   [*Alone.*] No, I can't find him anywhere. Oh, the poor darling, what's he doing now? I only wanted to say good-by to him, and afterward . . . afterward I am ready to die. Oh, why did I do this to him, why? And it isn't any easier for me, either. Oh, better, far better to die alone. But now I've ruined myself, and I've ruined him. I've brought disgrace to myself and eternal shame to him. Oh, dear God, yes. Disgrace to myself, eternal shame to him. If I could only remember what he used to say. How was he sorry for me? What were his words to me. [*Holds her head.*] I don't remember. I've forgotten everything. Night time is the worst for me. Yes, night time. Everyone goes to bed, and I go to bed, too. They fall asleep, but I . . . I feel as if I were in my grave. I'm so afraid of the dark. There are noises everywhere. And I think I hear people singing . . . singing as if they were burying someone. Singing so quietly that I can hardly hear them. As though they were far, far away. I'm happy, so very happy when light comes. But I don't want to get up, because it's the same thing all over again—the same people, the same kind of talk, the same torture. Why do they keep looking at me like that? Why don't they kill people like me nowadays? Why do they want to be different now? Before they used to kill you. Yes, take you and throw you in the Volga. Oh, dear God, I'd be happy if they would. "If we punish you," they say, "then you would be forgiven; but you must live and suffer for your sins." Haven't I suffered enough? How long must I go on suffering? What can I live for now? What is left for me? I've nothing to live for, nothing to care for, nothing in God's world to hope for. Yet death does not come. I cry out for death to take me, but death does not come. No matter what I see, no matter what I hear, I can only feel pain. [*Points to her heart.*] If I could only have lived with him, then perhaps I would have been happy. . . . But it's all the same now. I've destroyed my heart and soul. Oh, dear God, I long, how I long, to see him. My dearest Boris, if I can't see you, then listen to my voice from afar. Wild winds, please carry my sorrow and longing to him. Oh, dear God in heaven, I feel weary, so very weary. [*Crosses to the bank and cries in a loud voice.*] My joy, my darling, light of my life, I love you! Answer me! [*Weeps.* BORIS *enters.*]

BORIS. [*Not seeing* KATERINA.]   My God! That was her voice, I know it was. Where is she? [*Looks around.*]

KATERINA. [*Runs to him and falls on his neck.*]   At last I've found you. [*Puts her head on his chest and weeps. Silence.*]

BORIS.   Well, now we have wept together, and God has brought us together again.

KATERINA.   You didn't forget me?

BORIS.   How could I ever forget you? How could I?

KATERINA.   No, I didn't mean it that way, no. You're not angry, are you?

BORIS.   Why should I be angry?

KATERINA.   Then, forgive me. I didn't mean to hurt you. I couldn't help myself. I was so upset I didn't know what I said or did.

BORIS.   It's all right. Don't think about it, darling, don't.

KATERINA.   Well, what about you? What are you going to do now?

BORIS.   I am going away.

KATERINA.   Where?

BORIS.   Far away, Katya. To Siberia.

KATERINA.   Take me away with you.

BORIS.   I can't, Katya. I'm not going because I want to. My uncle is sending me away. Everything's set, even the horses are ready. Only I begged my uncle for a moment or two. I wanted to say good-by to the place where we used to see each other.

KATERINA.   God be with you, Boris. Don't worry about me. I imagine you'll miss me at first, my poor darling, but soon you will forget.

BORIS.   Don't talk about me. I'm free, completely free. But you, how is it with you? What about your mother-in-law?

KATERINA.   She torments me, keeps me locked up all the time.
She tells everyone, even my husband, "Don't believe her; she's
a sly wench." Everybody follows me around all day, laughing
right in front of me. They keep reproaching me with you at
every word.

BORIS.   And your husband?

KATERINA.   One moment he is affectionate, the next he is angry.
And he drinks all the time. I am sick of him, sick to death. His
kindness is worse than his beatings.

BORIS.   It's hard for you, isn't it, Katya?

KATERINA.   Yes, it is. So hard I'd rather be dead.

BORIS.   Who'd have known the suffering we've been through,
just because we love each other? I should have run away long
before we met.

KATERINA.   It all started the first moment I saw you. I've known
so little happiness and so much bitterness and sorrow. Oh, how
much, how very much lies ahead for me. But why think of the
future? I have seen you, my dearest, and they can't take that
away from me. You know there's nothing I wanted more, nothing
I needed more than to see you once again. I feel better now, as
if a great weight had been lifted from my shoulders. I kept thinking you were angry with me, that you cursed me . . .

BORIS.   Oh, my dearest, how could you ever think that? How
could you?

KATERINA.   No, that wasn't what I meant, what I wanted to say.
I have longed for you, longed for you to hold me in your arms.
That's what I wanted to say. And at last I have seen you once
more.

BORIS.   I hope no one finds us here.

KATERINA.   Wait, please wait. I wanted to tell you something.
And I've forgotten what it was. I must tell you something. I'm
so confused I can't remember it.

BORIS.   It's time for me to leave, Katya.

KATERINA.   Wait, please wait!

BORIS.   Well, what is it you wanted to tell me?

KATERINA.   I'll tell you in a moment.   [*Having thought a little.*]
Oh, yes, yes! As you go on your way, don't pass by a single beggar; give him something and ask him to say a prayer for my sins.

BORIS.   Oh, if people only knew how hard it is for me to say good-by. Oh, dear Lord in heaven! God grant it's as pleasant for them as it is for me now. Good-by, Katya. [*Embraces her and starts to go.*]   You scoundrels. It's monstrous what they're doing to us. Oh, if I only had the power!

KATERINA.   Wait, please wait. Let me look at you for the last time. [*Looks into his eyes.*]   Well, you must go now. God be with you. Go, my dearest, go quickly.

BORIS.   [*Walks a few steps and then stops.*]   Katya, something's wrong, isn't there? You're not planning to do something wrong, are you? I know I shall worry on the way, just thinking of you.

KATERINA.   It's nothing, my dearest. Nothing. God be with you! [BORIS *starts to cross to her.*]   Don't, my darling, don't. It's enough.

BORIS.   [*Sobbing.*]   God be with you, Katya. The only thing to pray for is that she may die as soon as possible. God in heaven, don't let her suffer long. [*To* KATERINA.]   Good-by. [*Bows.*]

KATERINA.   Good-by. [BORIS *exits.* KATERINA *follows him with her eyes, then stands for a short time, deep in thought. Alone.*] Where can I go now? Home? No, to go home is like going to the grave. Yes, home, or to the grave . . . to the grave. It is better in the grave. A little grave under a tree . . . How beautiful. The sun warms it, the rain washes it. In the spring the grass will grow over it . . . soft, soft grass. The birds will fly to the tree, they will sing, raise their young. The flowers will blossom, yellow, red, blue . . . all kinds . . . [*deep in thought*] all kinds . . . How quiet, how beautiful everything will be. I feel better, much better. I don't want to think anymore about life. To live again? No, no, I don't want to. It's not worth it anymore. I despise the people, I despise the house, I despise every wall in it. I won't go there. No, I'll never go there, never. If I went back, all they would do is talk, and I can't stand that. Oh, it's growing dark. And I hear people singing somewhere. What is it they're singing? I can't make out. . . . If only I could die now. What is it they're singing? What does it matter if death comes to me, or if I go to . . . I can't go on living, I can't. I know it's a sin, but will they pray for me? Those who love me will pray. . . . They place your hands crossed . . . in the coffin. Yes, like this . . . I remember. But they will catch me and take me home by force. Oh, hurry, hurry. [*Crosses to the bank. Loudly.*]   My darling. My joy. Good-by. [*Exits. Enter* MARFA, KABANOV, KULIGIN, *and* A WORKMAN *with a lantern.*]

KULIGIN.   It was here, they say, she was seen.

KABANOV.   Are you sure it's here?

KULIGIN.   They're certain it was she.

KABANOV.   Well, thank the Lord. They saw her alive at least.

MARFA.   You're in a fine state, aren't you? Frightened and crying like that. There's nothing for you to cry about. Don't worry, she will be a burden to all of us for a long time to come.

KABANOV.   Who would have thought she'd come here? People are here all the time. Who'd think of hiding here?

MARFA.   Can't you see what she's doing? It's just like her, the wench. She wants to show everybody the kind of person she is. [*From different directions people gather with lanterns.*]

ONE MAN IN THE CROWD.   Have you found her?

MARFA.   No, not yet. Seems to have disappeared completely.

SEVERAL VOICES.   How's that! Sounds funny. Pretty strange. Where could she have gone off to?

ONE MAN IN THE CROWD.   She'll be found.

ANOTHER.   Yes, of course she will.

A THIRD.   You'll see, she'll come back herself.

A VOICE.   [*Behind the setting.*]   Hey, there. Bring a boat!

KULIGIN.   [*From the bank.*]   Who is shouting? What's going on?

A VOICE.   A woman has thrown herself into the water!   [KULIGIN *and several men run off.*]

KABANOV.   Oh, God in heaven, I know it was she. [*Starts to run.* MARFA *holds him back by the hand.*]   Mama, let me go! I can't stand it. I'll pull her out, or else I'll go myself. I can't go on living without her.

MARFA.   I won't let you. And don't even think about it. You can't kill yourself because of her. She isn't worth it. Hasn't she caused us shame enough? And see what she's doing to us now.

KABANOV.   Let me go!

MARFA.   They don't need you; there are plenty of others. If you go, I shall curse you.

KABANOV.   [*Falls on his knees.*]   If only I can look at her.

MARFA.   Let them pull her out. Then you can see her.

KABANOV.   [*Rises. To the crowd.*]   Can you see anything at all, folks?

FIRST MAN.   Pretty dark down there, nothing to see.   [*A noise behind the setting.*]

SECOND MAN.   Sounds as if they're shouting something, but I can't make out what it is.

FIRST MAN.   That's Kuligan's voice.

SECOND MAN.   There they are, with the lanterns, walking along the bank.

FIRST MAN.   Here they come. They're bringing her here.   [*A few people return.*]

ONE OF THOSE WHO HAVE COME BACK.   Kuligin's pretty good! He's the one who found her. She was in a pool, close to the bank. You could see deep down in the water with a light. He caught a glimpse of her dress, then pulled her out.

KABANOV.   Is she alive?

ANOTHER.   No, she is dead. She jumped from the cliff and probably hit her head on an anchor or something. Cut herself, poor thing. Only a little cut on her temple, just a small drop of blood showing. She looks as if she were alive.   [KABANOV *starts to run, but is met halfway by* KULIGIN *and others who carry in* KATERINA.]

KULIGIN.   Here is your Katerina. Do with her what you want to now. Her body is here, take it. But her soul is no longer yours. She is now before a judge who is more merciful than you.   [*Places her body on the ground and exits, running.*]

KABANOV.   [*Rushes to* KATERINA.]   Katya! Katya!

MARFA.   That's enough. You know it's a sin to weep for her.

KABANOV.   Mama, you have killed her! You, you, you . . .

MARFA.   What do you mean? Have you lost your senses? Remember who it is you're talking to.

KABANOV.   You have killed her! You, you!

MARFA.   [*To her son.*]   Listen, I'll talk to you when we get home.   [*Bows low to the crowd.*]   Thank you, good people, for all your help.   [*All bow.*]

KABANOV.   It's all right now, Katya, it's all right now. But what can I do? Why, dear God, why must I go on living, yes, living and suffering . . .   [*Falls on his wife's body.*]

THE SCOUNDREL

THE SCOUNDREL

I. COMPOSITION

Ostrovsky began working on *The Scoundrel* in the summer of 1868. By the end of August he had started the actual writing and promised F. A. Burdin that the five-act comedy would be finished in time for the actor's benefit in Petersburg. The writing took longer than Ostrovsky anticipated, and Burdin was worried that the play might arrive too late. "The plot is so serious," the playwright explained to his friend, "that it is impossible to hurry; especially important is the last act, which must be finished properly."

Ostrovsky completed the play on the seventh of October, submitted it to the censorship office, and received authorization in less than two weeks. The play was produced at the Aleksandrinsky the first of November, and in that same month it was published in the journal *Home Notes*. It was his twenty-seventh original play.

In 1912 N. P. Kashin suggested that Sheridan's *The School for Scandal* may have been one of Ostrovsky's sources for his comedy. Certainly the Russian playwright had the language ability to read the English original; and even though Sheridan's play was also available in three translations, Albert Kaspin noted that Ostrovsky's source may have been Druzhinin's 1854 monograph of *The School for Scandal* which had been reissued in 1865. Other major sources of the play were Gogol's *Inspector General (Revizor)*, the controversial period of reforms which was drawing to its close in 1868, and comic devices that date back to the classic theatre of Greece and Rome.

Critical response to the play ranged from censure to high praise. Some critics considered the play as little more than a vaudeville, containing gross caricature. Others commended it as a superb comedy, filled with clever satire. One reviewer judged its form as crude and exaggerated, while the next lauded its artistic depiction of "the true surroundings of our society." A. S. Suvorin had mixed feelings. A serious error had been made, he suggested, by encircling the atypical Glumov with typical fools. Nevertheless, the play was significant.

There are scenes, very well written, brilliant dialogue, often breathing of wit; the action moves quite lively and naturally. [The comedy] left far behind itself a crowd of dramatic wares of other Russian writers.

To E. I. Utin, the chief merit of the play was that the author had shifted from the merchant *byt* and domestic relations to the nobility circle and social relations. "A picture of our contemporary society," he wrote, "is reflected with complete clarity." Much of his criticism centered on the character Glumov. A false chord was struck, Utin pointed out, when Glumov—exhibiting integrity and nobility—wrote his "chronicle of human vulgarity *(poshlost')*." Dissatisfied with the introduction of vaudeville devices, Utin believed that the plot was artificial and that too many events were governed by chance. Nekrasov, on the other hand, saw "inclinations of the true comic" in the play, and Saltykov-Shchedrin was so pleased with Glumov that he added the character to his own gallery of types.

In succeeding years critics debated the merits of the play. Discussing Ostrovsky's works in 1899, the critic A. Kugel' summed up the play as "perhaps the most profound in conception." He added that the play was seldom produced simply because few people understood its form. To A. Yu. Yur'ev a decade later, *The Scoundrel* was delightful, "a highly-talented piece, containing a whole gallery of splendid, vital figures." Its dialogue was brilliant, "literally saturated with humor and wit," he concluded and praised the play as "a witty satire with wide social application everywhere."

II.   STAGE PRODUCTIONS

The first performance of *The Scoundrel* at the Aleksandrinsky was well received, and critics praised several actors. For example, F. A. Burdin as Mamaev, A. M. Chitau as Kleopatra, and Yu. N. Linskaya as Glafira were judged excellent. N. V. Samoilov caught the mirror-like quality of Glumov, reflected the tone of each character he flattered, and at the same time preserved the feeling of superiority and irony. V. V. Samoilov as Gorodulin was noted for his "simplicity, undue familiarity, naturalness, vitality," and one reviewer suspected that the actor "imitated some sort of real person."

P. V. Vasil'ev as Krutitsky received mixed notices. Complimenting Vasil'ev for his excellent image of an old general, one reviewer singled out his scene with Turusina in Act Three and noted his change "from the government official . . . to the voluptuous old man." D. V. Aver-kiev, on the other hand, felt Vasil'ev was inadequate and rarely showed more than the importance of the gentleman. The production as a whole was considered superior and well designed, which attracted "the mass of the public." Ostrovsky was absent for the performance, but Burdin wrote to him immediately.

I'll tell you that the actors have done their parts (completely in all conscience); the play was very well appreciated; they called for the actors and you countless times; the debut had great success.

In Moscow the production opened at the Maly on the sixth of November, scarcely a month after Ostrovsky had finished the play. It was judged completely successful, and D. A. Koropchevsky observed that S. V. Shumsky as Krutitsky was outstanding.

Shumsky was a general without official duties, convinced of his own worldly wisdom and experience. His passion for precepts and schemes was not the eccentricity of an unoccupied old man, but the result of a deep conviction of his own righteousness, his desire to direct everyone to the true path. In this way Krutitsky was the most interesting person in the play.

Ostrovsky was delighted with the performance and wrote to Burdin, "My play went off in Moscow with fantastic success." The press concurred. "The public accepted the new play with extreme favor," one reviewer wrote, "they repeatedly called for the author as well as the performers." G. N. Fedotova was there playing the role of Mashenka and later recalled the occasion.

At the first performance an unprecedented event took place. After Glumov's monologue and exit [in Act Five], Ostrovsky was called for several times . . . in the presence of the characters on stage. In my whole life I don't recall such an event [like this].

In later years several productions of *The Scoundrel* brought forth outstanding actors and new interpretations of the play. For example, in 1876 A. P. Lensky played Glumov at the Maly and created something of a theatrical legend. E. D. Turchaninova was enchanted with his interpretation.

I never saw such a complete disclosure of character, beginning from the first moment. His Glumov was intelligent, evil, ironic; he knew with whom he had dealings, knew how it was necessary to speak with them, and all the time he followed his own line of action. It was completely amazing.

Ten years later at the Maly, critics praised a new production of the play and noted especially the interpretations of O. O. Sadovskaya as Glafira, N. A. Nikulina as Kleopatra, and M. P. Sadovsky as Golutvin. In 1910 the Moscow Art Theatre featured Kachalov as Glumov and Stanislavsky as Krutitsky.

From 1875 to 1917 there were only 627 performances of the play in Russia, but in succeeding years there have been numerous productions in the Soviet Union as well as abroad. In the twenties *The Scoundrel* was given an experimental production by Eisenstein, who later achieved recognition as a film director. In his production, some characters were eliminated, new ones were substituted, at times the actors literally balanced on a tightrope, and a film showing the theft of Glumov's diary was inserted. Perhaps the most brilliant production, according to Russian critics, occurred in the thirties at the Maly. Something of the 1935 interpretation is revealed by A. A. Yablochkina who played Kleopatra.

> The interest of the [former] actresses concentrated on her love relationship with Glumov . . . I was striving . . . to disclose the typical in her character, to show in all her improper actions the reflection of the typical qualities of the parasitical class.

III. NAMES OF CHARACTERS

Several names in the play reveal the disposition or bent of the character. Like the name Gurmyzhskaya in *The Forest*, the name Mamaev is of Tartar origin. Mamaev's wife Kleopatra is associated by name with the Egyptian queen's passion, while her patronymic suggests daughter of a young lion. The name Gorodulin derives from *goroduli*, a word in Ostrovsky's own dictionary, which the playwright defined as "nonsense, idle talk, fibbing." Closely associated to the name Gorodulin is the name Turusina, which derives from a word meaning gossip, nonsense, twaddle. The name Krutitsky comes from the verb *krutit'*, to twist, twirl, roll up, have on leading strings. The name Golutvin, on the other hand, suggests cutting down, opening up, beggar, poor, etc. Finally, the name Glumov is derived from the verb *glumit'sya*, to mock, jeer, scoff, make game of.

The stress of the names is as follows: Egór Dmítrich Glúmov, Glafíra Klímovna Glúmova, Nil Fedóseich Mamáev, Kleopátra Lvóvna Mamáeva, Krutítsky, Iván Ivánovich Gorodúlin, Sófya Ignátevna Turúsina, Máshenka, Egór Vasílich Kurcháev, Golútvin, Manéfa, Matrésha, Anfísa, Grigóry.

THE SCOUNDREL

Na vsyakogo mudretsa dovol'no prostoty*
A Comedy in Five Acts

CHARACTERS

EGOR DMITRICH GLUMOV, *an impoverished young nobleman.*

GLAFIRA KLIMOVNA GLUMOVA, *his mother.*

NIL FEDOSEICH MAMAEV, *a rich gentleman and distant relative of Glumov.*

KLEOPATRA LVOVNA MAMAEVA, *his wife.*

KRUTITSKY, *an old general, very influential.*

IVAN IVANOVICH GORODULIN, *a young nobleman, influential.*

SOFYA IGNATEVNA TURUSINA, *a rich widow and lady; by birth, of the merchant class.*

MASHENKA, *her niece.*

EGOR VASILICH KURCHAEV, *a hussar.*

GOLUTVIN, *a man without a profession.*

MANEFA, *a woman engaged in fortune-telling and predictions.*

MATRESHA, *parasite and companion to Turusina.*

ANFISA, *parasite and companion to Turusina.*

MAMAEV'S SERVANT.

KRUTITSKY'S SERVANT.

GRIGORY, *Turusina's servant.*

*A literal translation of Ostrovsky's title is "Enough Stupidity in Every Wiseman."

ACT ONE

GLUMOV's *apartment. Morning. A neat, well-furnished room. A writing desk. A mirror. One door leads to the inner rooms. On the right side of the stage, a second door leads to the street.* GLUMOV *and* GLAFIRA *are behind the setting.*

GLUMOV. Well, I like that. Necessary? It's essential. If you stop now, we've had it. [*Entering through the side door.*] Do as you're told, and don't argue.

GLAFIRA. [*Entering through the side door.*] Why do you insist on me writing these letters? It's hard for me, really.

GLUMOV. Keep writing, my dear, keep writing!

GLAFIRA. What's the use? You know they won't let her marry you. Turusina has a dowry of two hundred thousand, position in society, connections. Why the girl's set for a prince or a general,[1] at least. And they won't give her to Kurchaev, either. So why should I saddle him with such cock-and-bull stories? The poor boy.

GLUMOV. Whose side are you on, mine or the hussar Kurchaev? Why should he get the money? He'd only throw it away at cards. And you're forever whimpering, "I carried you next to my heart."

GLAFIRA. If only my writing letters will work!

GLUMOV. You let me worry about that.

GLAFIRA. Do you really have some kind of chance?

GLUMOV. Yes, I have.[2] Mama, my dear, you know me. I'm clever, ruthless, and envious—just like you. What have I done up till now? I've only lost my temper and written epigrams about everyone in Moscow. In other words, I've been twiddling my thumbs. Well, enough of that. What's the use of laughing at fools, when you ought to know how to profit by their weaknesses? Naturally you won't make a career here. Petersburg is the place for careers and business, while here they can only talk. Of course, you can get a cushy job and a rich wife here. And for me, that's enough. How do you get into society? Not so much through deeds, but more often through the art of glibness. And do we love to talk in Moscow! So why shouldn't I become a success in this vast land of tittle-tattle. Why not? I'll worm my way in with the big shots. I'll become their toady. Just wait and see. It's foolish to annoy them, so I'll flatter and fawn and truckle. Therein lies the whole secret of success. I'll begin with the less influential, with Turusina's circle, squeeze everything out of them that I need, and then move on—higher and higher and . . . Off with you now, start writing! We'll chat about this later on.

GLAFIRA.   May God help you!   [*Exits.*]

GLUMOV.   [*Sits at the desk.*]   Away with epigrams! This sort of poetry can only lead to trouble. We'll take up panegyrics.   [*Takes a notebook from his pocket.*]   Into this diary I'll pour all the rancor in my soul, while words sweet as honey from my lips shall come. Alone, at night, I'll write the chronicle of all that is tawdry, cheap, and trivial.[3] This manuscript is not meant for the public, for I alone shall be both author and reader. Although it's possible in time—once I've strengthened my position—to extract a section here and there.   [KURCHAEV *and* GOLUTVIN *enter.* GLUMOV *rises and hides the notebook in his pocket.*]

KURCHAEV.   Bonjour!

GLUMOV.   Pleased to see you, Kurchaev. What brings you here?

KURCHAEV.   [*Sitting at the desk in* GLUMOV's *place.*]   We're here on business.   [*Pointing to* GOLUTVIN.]   See the fellow standing over there. I'd like to put in a good word for him.

GLUMOV.   Yes, I've known Golutvin a long time. Why put in a good word for him?

GOLUTVIN.   I don't like your tone of voice. No, sir, I don't.

GLUMOV.   You said it, I didn't. No doubt, gentlemen, you've had a decent breakfast.

KURCHAEV.   Let's say, we've eaten.   [*Takes a pencil and paper and begins drawing.*]

GLUMOV.   Uh-hm, that's obvious. Gentlemen, I don't have much time to spare.   [*Sits,* GOLUTVIN *also.*]   What's the trouble?

KURCHAEV.   You don't have any verses, do you?

GLUMOV.   What kind of verses? No doubt you've come to the wrong place.

GOLUTVIN. No, my dear fellow, to the right place.

GLUMOV. [*To* KURCHAEV.] Please stop scribbling on that paper!

KURCHAEV. Look here, Glumov, we need epigrams. I happen to know you're loaded with them.

GLUMOV. No, not one.

KURCHAEV. Oh, come off it! Everyone knows you've satirized the whole town. This gentleman here would like to contribute to the comic newspapers.

GLUMOV. [*To* GOLUTVIN.] So that's it. Have you written before?

GOLUTVIN. I have.

GLUMOV. What?

GOLUTVIN. Everything. Novels, stories, dramas, comedies . . .

GLUMOV. And so?

GOLUTVIN. And so nobody will publish them. Not for anything, however much you beg. Why they don't even want my pieces as a gift. I'd like to take up gossip and scandal now.

GLUMOV. They won't publish that, either.

GOLUTVIN. I'll try.

GLUMOV. It's dangerous, you know.

GOLUTVIN. Dangerous? You don't mean that they might beat me?

GLUMOV. Perhaps.

GOLUTVIN. Well, you may get beaten for it in other cities, but I've never heard tell of it in Moscow.

GLUMOV. In that case, write.

GOLUTVIN. But what do I write about? I don't know anyone.

KURCHAEV. You have some kind of diary, they say, in which you've picked everybody to pieces.

GOLUTVIN. Well, let's have it. Give it to us.

GLUMOV. Whatever is there to give!

GOLUTVIN. And we'll publish it.

GLUMOV. But I don't have a diary.

KURCHAEV. Stop joking. They've seen you with it.

GOLUTVIN. Oh, just look how he's pretending—you can see he belongs in our little group.

GLUMOV. No, I don't.

GOLUTVIN. And could we make money with your diary!

KURCHAEV. You can bet your life he needs the money. "I've done," he says, "with drinking at the expense of others; now I want to work." And he calls this—working. What do you say to that?

GLUMOV.   I'm listening.

GOLUTVIN.   I have no material. How can I write a scandal sheet, if I have no material?

KURCHAEV.   There, you see, he has no material. Give him material, then he'll go to work.

GLUMOV.   [*Rises.*]   Will you stop dabbling on that paper!

KURCHAEV.   Oh, come now, what does it matter?

GLUMOV.   Why, you're drawing roosters of some sort or another.

KURCHAEV.   You're mistaken. They're not roosters, but my dear respected uncle, Nil Fedoseich Mamaev. There! [*Finishes the drawing.*]   Looks very much like him, topknot and all.

GOLUTVIN.   Say, could I use him in my scandal sheet? I mean, is there anything special about him?

KURCHAEV.   Is there! In the first place, he thinks of himself as the cleverest man in the world. In the second, he considers it his duty to lecture everyone he meets. He'd rather give advice than eat.

GOLUTVIN.   Well, then, put a caption under the rooster—"The latest how-to-do-it-yourself book." [4]   [KURCHAEV *writes it.*]   Now let's get it printed.

KURCHAEV.   No, let's don't. After all, he is my uncle. Besides, I'm the only one named in his will.[5]   [*Puts the paper to one side.* GLUMOV *takes it and hides it in his pocket.*]

GOLUTVIN.   You don't say! Anything else!

KURCHAEV.   Plenty! The past three years he's been looking for an apartment. He doesn't really need an apartment. He's simply making the rounds in order to chatter. And of course, it looks like he's busy. He starts out in the morning, looks over ten apartments, babbles with the landlords, even the doormen. Then he runs from shop to shop, sampling caviar, sturgeon, and plopping down to start a discussion. The shopkeepers don't know how to get rid of him. And at the same time, he's so pleased that he hasn't shot the whole morning.   [*To* GLUMOV.]   Well, what do you know, I forgot to tell you. His wife is madly in love with you.

GLUMOV.   You don't say?

KURCHAEV.   Yes, aunt Kleopatra saw you at the theatre. Her eyes popped out. Her neck twisted around. She asked everything. Who is he? What's his name? Where does he live? You know you shouldn't joke about this!

GLUMOV.   I'm not joking. You're the one who likes to joke.

KURCHAEV.   Well, it's up to you. If I were in your spot . . . Are you going to hand over those verses?

GLUMOV.   No.

GOLUTVIN.   What's the use of talking to him! Let's go to dinner!

KURCHAEV.   Let's go! Good-by!   [*Bows and starts to leave.*]

GLUMOV.   [*Stopping* KURCHAEV.]   Why are you running around with him?

KURCHAEV.   I like clever people.

GLUMOV.   Is he the best you can find?

KURCHAEV.   The best we can do. Why should really clever people get to know fellows like you and me?   [*Exits.*]

GLUMOV   [*Following him.*]   Better watch out! Mama, my dear! [GLAFIRA *enters.* GLUMOV *shows her the picture of* MAMAEV.]   Take a look at that, will you. That's the one I start with. That's the man I must butter up first.

GLAFIRA.   Who is he?

GLUMOV.   Our distant relative, my dear uncle, Nil Fedoseich Mamaev.

GLAFIRA.   And who's the artist?

GLUMOV.   His nephew, that very same hussar, Kurchaev. We must save this drawing—to be on the safe side.   [*Hides it.*]   The whole trouble is that Mamaev can't stand relatives. Out of some thirty nephews, he plucks one and makes him his sole heir. He won't give the others the time of day. When he becomes bored with one pet, he throws him out, latches on to another nephew and immediately rewrites his will. At the moment Kurchaev happens to be in his good graces.

GLAFIRA.   If only you could . . .

GLUMOV.   It's difficult, but I'm going to try. Mamaev doesn't even suspect that I exist.

GLAFIRA.   If only you could meet him. First of all, the inheritance; then a beautiful house, influential friends, connections.

GLUMOV.   Right! But there's more. My aunt likes me—Kleopatra Lvovna[6]—she saw me somewhere. Keep that in mind! My first job is to meet Mamaev. It's the first step to my career. My uncle will introduce me to Krutitsky and to Gorodulin. In the first place, they are influential people. In the second, they are close friends of Turusina. Once I gain entrance to her house, I will certainly marry her niece.

GLAFIRA.   Of course, dear boy, but the first step is the most difficult.

GLUMOV.   Don't worry, I've already taken it. Mamaev is coming here.

GLAFIRA.   How did you manage that?

GLUMOV.   No trouble at all! I set it up ahead of time. Mamaev loves to look at apartments. So, I threw out the line and he snapped up the bait.   [MAMAEV'S SERVANT *enters.*]

SERVANT.   I've brought Nil Fedoseich.

GLUMOV.   Excellent! Here, take this.   [*Gives him some money.*] Bring him in here.

SERVANT.   Well, I'll bet you he's going to be angry. I told him it was a nice apartment.

GLUMOV.   I'll take the responsibility. Trot off to your room, Mama dear. When the time comes, I'll call you.   [MAMAEV'S SERVANT *exits.* GLUMOV *sits at the desk and pretends that he is working.* MAMAEV *enters, followed by his* SERVANT.]

MAMAEV.   [*Doesn't remove his hat; looks around the room.*]   This is a bachelor apartment.

GLUMOV.   [*Bows and continues to work.*]   Yes, it is.

MAMAEV.   [*Not listening.*]   It's not bad, but it's a bachelor apartment.   [*To* SERVANT.]   Where have you brought me, brother?

GLUMOV.   [*Indicates a chair and again starts to write.*]   Won't you sit down?

MAMAEV.   [*Sits.*]   Thanks!   [*To* SERVANT.]   Where have you brought me, I ask you?

SERVANT.   Sorry, sir.

MAMAEV.   Is it possible, brother, you don't know the kind of apartment I need? You must understand that I'm a Councillor of State; [7] that my wife, and your mistress, likes to live well. We need a drawing room, and not only one. Where is the drawing room, I ask you?

SERVANT.   Sorry, sir.

MAMAEV.   Where is the drawing room?   [*To* GLUMOV.]   You will excuse me?

GLUMOV.   Of course, sir. You're not bothering me.

MAMAEV.   [*To* SERVANT.]   You can see, can't you, that a man is sitting over there, writing? Perhaps we're bothering him. Naturally he's too considerate to admit it. All the same, you fool, you're to blame for this.

GLUMOV. Don't scold him. He's not to blame, I am. On the stairs he asked about an apartment. I pointed to mine and told him it's a nice one. I didn't know you're a family man.

MAMAEV. Do you rent this apartment?

GLUMOV. I do.

MAMAEV. Why are you leasing it?

GLUMOV. I can't afford it.

MAMAEV. Then why are you renting it, if you can't afford it? Is someone forcing you to keep it? Did someone grab you by the collar, shove you in here and demand, "Rent, rent!" And now, no doubt, you're deep in debt? Behind the cart, are you? Why, of course, of course. So now you must move from a big apartment and live in a single room. How do you like that?

GLUMOV. No, I'm planning to rent a much larger apartment.

MAMAEV. A larger apartment? You don't have the money to live here, but you're renting a larger apartment. What kind of reasoning is that, I'd like to know.

GLUMOV. It's not reasoning at all. Only my stupidity.

MAMAEV. Your stupidity? What nonsense!

GLUMOV. Oh, yes, what nonsense it is! I am stupid.

MAMAEV. Stupid! That's odd. How do you mean, stupid?

GLUMOV. Very simple. No brains. What's so surprising about that? You don't think it happens? Oh, but it happens a lot.

MAMAEV. No, you don't say. Oh my, this is interesting! There's a man who tells you himself that he's stupid.

GLUMOV. What would you have me do—wait until others tell me? What's the difference, really? You can't keep it a secret, you know.

MAMAEV. But, of course. It's very difficult to keep something like that secret.

GLUMOV. So I'm not going to hide it.

MAMAEV. I am sorry.

GLUMOV. I thank you, humbly.

MAMAEV. I suppose there's no one to teach you, to give you a little advice?

GLUMOV. No, no one.

MAMAEV. There are teachers—you might say intelligent teachers —but no one listens to them nowadays. Well, you can't expect anything from old people. Every one of them thinks that if he's old, then he's wise. And if youngsters don't want to listen, then what can you expect from them? I'll tell you what happened to me recently. A boy was running—almost flying—out of school. So naturally I stopped him; and, as a joke, you know, I began to deliver a lecture: "With creeping pace to school each day, but homeward bound he runs to play." "My boy," I said, "it's quite the reverse." You know anyone else would have been thankful if a respectable person had stopped him and given advice. Yes, even kissed my hand, but not that young puppy!

GLUMOV.   You know, instruction nowadays is . . .

MAMAEV.   "In school," he says, "we are sick and tired of all this lecturing!" "If you," he says, "like to lecture, then try for the job of supervisor." "Right now," he says, "I'm going to eat, so let me go." Can you imagine any brat talking to me like that!

GLUMOV.   Oh, that boy's on a dangerous road. I feel sorry for him.

MAMAEV.   But where do dangerous roads lead? You know, don't you?

GLUMOV.   I know.

MAMAEV.   What's the reason for bad servants nowadays? Because they are free from the duty of listening to our instructions. In the old days, I taught each and every one of them, from the smallest to the biggest. I would give two-hour lectures to each one. Oh, how I used to reach the highest spheres of thought. My serf would stand before me, little by little overcome with emotion. And, now and again, fainting dead away. It was beneficial to him, and a noble calling for me. Nowadays, after all this . . . You understand, after what, don't you?[8]

GLUMOV.   I understand.

MAMAEV.   Try that with your servant nowadays! Read metaphysics to him two or three times, and that's the last you see of him. "Oh, I'm in for it," he says. Yes, that's what he says, "Oh, I'm in for it."

GLUMOV.   Wicked, that's what it is. Wicked.

MAMAEV.   You know I'm not strict at all. Everything I do is with words. But shopkeepers here have an idiotic habit. Like grabbing a person by the hair and, at every word, tugging and tugging. "By doing this," they say, "it's stronger and clearer." Now, that's something, isn't it? Everything I do is with words, but no one likes that nowadays.

GLUMOV.   Yes, sir. After all that tugging and pulling, I'd think it must be unpleasant for you.

MAMAEV.   [*Sternly.*]   Let's don't talk about it, I beg you. It was just like someone stabbed me right here   [*points to his chest*] and I still feel it somehow . . .

GLUMOV.   Is this the place?[9]

MAMAEV.   Higher.

GLUMOV.   About here?

MAMAEV.   [*Testily.*]   Higher, I tell you.

GLUMOV.   I'm sorry. Please don't be angry! I've already told you I'm stupid.

MAMAEV.   Yes, sir, you are stupid. That's pretty bad. That is, it's not really bad, if you have an elderly, experienced relative, or friend.

GLUMOV.   Unfortunately, there's no one. I have mother, but she's more of an idiot than I.

MAMAEV.   Your situation is bad. I feel sorry for you, young man.

GLUMOV.   I do have an uncle, they say, but it really doesn't make any difference.

MAMAEV.   For what reason?

GLUMOV.   He doesn't know me, and I don't want to meet him.

MAMAEV.   I won't praise you for that, young man. No, I won't.

GLUMOV.   Oh, for pity's sake! If my uncle were poor, I believe I would see him, maybe kiss his hand; but he's rich. If I go to him for advice, he might think I'm after his money. If it were only possible to let him know that I don't need a single kopek— that I long for advice, crave direction, like manna from heaven. They say he's a man of splendid intelligence. I'd be ready to listen day and night.

MAMAEV.   You're not as stupid as you think.

GLUMOV.   There are times a lucid moment will come across me, suddenly, like everything is clearing up; but only now and again. Most of the time I don't understand a thing I'm doing. That's when I need advice.

MAMAEV.   And who is your uncle?

GLUMOV.   You know, I nearly forgot his name. Mamaev, I believe. Nil Fedoseich.

MAMAEV.   But who are you?

GLUMOV.   Glumov.

MAMAEV.   The son of Dmitri Glumov?

GLUMOV.   The very same, sir.

MAMAEV.   Well, then, I am Mamaev.

GLUMOV.   Oh, good lord! Can it be! No, it's not possible. Give me your hand! [*Almost in tears.*]   But, uncle, I heard you can't stand relatives. Don't worry, we can be as distant as before. And you'll never see me again, unless you request it. It's enough for me to have seen you. To have reveled in the words of such a clever man.

MAMAEV.   Look here, young man. Whenever you need advice about anything, just come by and see me.

GLUMOV.   Whenever I need it! I constantly need it, every minute. I know I'll die without an adviser.

MAMAEV.   Then come by this evening.

GLUMOV.   How can I ever thank you? Permit me to introduce my dear old mother. She's none too clever; but kind, a very kind woman.

MAMAEV.   Why not? I wouldn't mind.

GLUMOV.   [*Loudly.*]   Mama, my dear! [GLAFIRA *enters.*]   Mama, dear! Look! [*Pointing to* MAMAEV.]   Only don't cry! Good fortune has brought us dear uncle Nil Fedoseich. You've wanted so much to see him.

GLAFIRA.   Yes, dear cousin. I've prayed a long time for this moment. But I've heard you can't stand relatives.

GLUMOV.   That's enough, mama dear, that will do. Dear uncle has his own reasons.

MAMAEV.   There are relatives, and then there are relatives.

GLAFIRA.   Let me look at you, dear cousin. But, sonny boy, there's no resemblance at all!

GLUMOV.   [*Pulls at her dress.*]   That will do, mama dear, now please stop it!

GLAFIRA.   What do you mean, stop it? There's no resemblance, absolutely no resemblance at all.

MAMAEV.   [*Sternly.*]   What are you whispering about? Who is it I don't look like? I resemble myself, that's who.

GLUMOV.   [*To Mother.*]   I suppose you think it's important to keep up this nonsense.

MAMAEV.   Since you've already started, why don't you finish it?

GLAFIRA.   I tell you the portrait doesn't resemble him.

MAMAEV. What portrait? Where did you find a portrait?

GLAFIRA. Well, you see, sometimes Kurchaev comes to visit us. I think he's one of your relatives, too, isn't he?

GLUMOV. What an excellent, happy-go-lucky fellow!

MAMAEV. Well, what about it?

GLAFIRA. He's drawing pictures of you all the time. Show him, sonny boy.

GLUMOV. You know, I don't know where I put it.

GLAFIRA. Keep looking! I'm sure he drew one recently. Don't you remember? He had with him . . . Oh, what do you call them? You know, critics who write those verses. Kurchaev was saying, "I'll draw a picture of uncle, and you write the caption!" I heard him say it myself.

MAMAEV. Show me the portrait! Show it to me at once!

GLUMOV. [*Giving the portrait.*] Never, mama dear, never talk about things that might hurt someone else.

MAMAEV. Now don't teach your mother to be a hypocrite. Don't listen to him, cousin. Let simplicity be your guide. Simplicity is much better. [*Scrutinizes the portrait.*] Oh, dear Lord God in heaven! Wouldn't you know it? My own nephew.

GLUMOV. Oh, forget it, uncle! There's absolutely no resemblance, and the caption doesn't fit, either: "The latest how-to-do-it-yourself book."

MAMAEV. Yes, there is a resemblance, and the caption does fit. Anyway, it's not your concern, it's mine. [*Returns the portrait and rises.*] Are you planning to draw caricatures of me?

GLUMOV. Oh, for pity's sake. What do you take me for? As if I'd . . . Oh, silly, silly!

MAMAEV. Don't forget, you're coming to see me this evening, for sure. [*To* GLAFIRA.] And you're welcome, too.

GLAFIRA. Well, you know me . . . I might pester you with my stupidity. [MAMAEV *and* SERVANT *exit.* GLUMOV *escorts* MAMAEV.] I believe things are looking up. But sonny boy still faces so many difficulties. Oh, how hard and frustrating it is—to get somewhere in this life! [GLUMOV *returns.*]

GLUMOV. Mama, my dear, Manefa is coming. Be courteous to her, do you hear! Yes, be more than courteous. In fact, toady and truckle as much as you can.

GLAFIRA. Do you expect me to humiliate myself in front of that old woman?

GLUMOV.   You'd like to play the grand lady, wouldn't you? But where's the money? If it weren't for my ingenuity you'd be little more than a beggar right now. Then help me, I tell you, help me. [*Hearing steps, runs into the hall and returns with* MANEFA.[10]]

MANEFA.   [*To* GLUMOV.] Forswear all worldly vanity, forswear!

GLUMOV.   [*With pious expression and sighing.*] I forswear. I forswear.

MANEFA.   Think not of yourself!

GLUMOV.   That sin—I know not of.

MANEFA.   [*Sits down and pays no attention to* GLAFIRA, *who is bowing to her repeatedly.*] I was flying, I fluttered, and flipped at last to you.

GLUMOV.   Oh, we could feel it. We could feel it.

MANEFA.   I was in a certain God-fearing house. They gave me ten rubles for charity. They offer up alms through my hands. The way is opened more easily through holy hands than through sinful ones.

GLUMOV.   [*Taking out some money.*] Please accept fifteen rubles from your slave Egor.

MANEFA.   A blessing for those who give.

GLUMOV.   Don't forget me in your prayers!

MANEFA.   In that very same God-fearing house I drank tea and coffee.

GLAFIRA.   If you please, *matushka*,[11] it's ready right now. [MANEFA *rises; they escort her arm-in-arm to the door.* GLAFIRA *and* MANEFA *exit.* GLUMOV *returns and sits at the desk.*]

GLUMOV.   Let's jot this down! [*Takes out diary.*]   To Mamaev's servant, three rubles; to Manefa, fifteen rubles. And at the same time—the whole conversation with uncle. [*Writes.* KURCHAEV *enters.*]

KURCHAEV.   Now look here! Was uncle just here?

GLUMOV.   He was.

KURCHAEV.   Did he say anything about me?

GLUMOV.   Well, now, why should he? He scarcely knew where he was. He dropped by to look at the apartment. It's a habit with him, you know.

KURCHAEV.   It's a plot, that's what it is, a hellish damn plot!

GLUMOV.   I'm listening. Go on!

KURCHAEV.   Just imagine, uncle met me on the way and . . .

GLUMOV.   And . . . what?

KURCHAEV.   And ordered me to keep out of his sight. Just think of that!

GLUMOV.   I'm thinking.

KURCHAEV.   I arrive at Turusina's. They won't let me in. They send out some kind of slovenly old woman to say they can't receive me. Do you hear me?

GLUMOV.   I hear you.

KURCHAEV.   Then, please tell me what's going on?

GLUMOV.   How can I tell you?

KURCHAEV.   At least you're clever and understand things better than I.

GLUMOV.   Very well, you asked for it! Just look at yourself. What kind of life are you leading?

KURCHAEV.   What kind? What do you mean, what kind? I'm only doing what everyone else is doing, so why pick on me? For that, they rob me of my inheritance, take away my fiancée, smash my reputation.

GLUMOV.   And look at the people you run around with. Golutvin, for example.

KURCHAEV.   What about Golutvin?

GLUMOV.   Nothing but a pest and a parasite! Why, you can't trust him out of your sight. That's your explanation! And why did you bring him here, of all places? When it comes to choosing friends, I'm very careful. I like to do it myself. I ask you, therefore, never to come here again.

KURCHAEV.   Have you gone out of your mind?

GLUMOV.   Uncle chased you out, and I want to copy that worthy gentleman in every respect.

KURCHAEV.   Aha! I think I'm beginning to understand.

GLUMOV.   Well, thank the Lord for that.

KURCHAEV.   Now see here, my dear sir, are you responsible for all this? If my suspicions are right, then watch out! You'll pay for this. Just wait and see!

GLUMOV.   I'll wait and see . . . if it's necessary. At the moment there's no serious danger. Good-by.

KURCHAEV.   Good-by.   [*Exits.*]

GLUMOV.   Uncle has chased him out. The first step has been taken.

ACT TWO

MAMAEV's *house. Evening. A week later.*[12] *A spacious, main room. An entrance door and two side doors.* MAMAEV *and* KRUTITSKY *enter through a side door.*

MAMAEV. Well, we're on our way to some place. They're leading us somewhere. But neither we, nor those who are leading us, know the place. And how will it all end?

KRUTITSKY. I look upon all this as a frivolous experiment. But, you know, I don't see anything evil in it. Our century, for the most part, is a frivolous century. Everyone is young, so inexperienced; let's try this, let's try that; let's alter this, let's change that. It's easy to change. Look, I could take all the furniture and stand it upside down, and that's a change for you. But where, I ask you, is the age-old wisdom, the age-old experience demanding that furniture should stand, to wit, on its legs? Here's a table standing on four legs. And does it stand well, firmly?

MAMAEV. Firmly.

KRUTITSKY. Sturdily?

MAMAEV. Sturdily.

KRUTITSKY. Suppose someone turns it upside down. All right, let's say it's upside down.

MAMAEV. [*Having waved his hand.*] All right, it's upside down.

KRUTITSKY. Now they'll see.

MAMAEV. But will they see, my dear Krutitsky, will they?

KRUTITSKY. Oh, you're not serious, surely? What an odd thing to say. Well, if they don't see it, then others will point it out. We have the right men.

MAMAEV. We have. Yes, we do. You can be sure of that. I

tell you there are many, but nobody's listening. Nobody's listening. That's the whole trouble nowadays. Nobody is listening to the intelligent people like us.

KRUTITSKY.   It's our own fault. We don't know how to speak, to express our own opinions. Who's doing the writing? Who's doing the shouting nowadays? Only the brats. We keep silent and even gripe that no one is listening to us. We must write, write . . . and then write some more.

MAMAEV.   It's easy to say: just write! You must have practice in it. There's a kind of trickiness to it. Of course, it's nothing but nonsense, but all the same, you need it. Look at me. I could talk all night, but if I took up writing, only God knows what would come out. I believe you know I'm no fool. Now let's look at you. Well, can you write?

KRUTITSKY.   No, don't start talking about me! I write. Of course, I write. I write a lot.

MAMAEV.   You don't say? You write? I didn't know. But surely you don't expect that out of everyone.

KRUTITSKY.   Time marches on, my dear Nil Fedoseich, time marches on. If you want to be useful, you must know how to wield a skillful pen.

MAMAEV.   That doesn't come easy to everyone.

KRUTITSKY.   Say, by the way, you don't happen to know a young man, unassuming and educated, of course. Someone who can easily state on paper various thoughts, theses, and so on?

MAMAEV.   I do. I know just the man.

KRUTITSKY.   He isn't a tattle-tale, or one of these up-to-date scoffers?

MAMAEV.   No-no-no! You have only to say so, and he'll follow the bait, like a fish.

KRUTITSKY.   Well, you see, I've written a very serious thesis, or report—whatever you want to call it. But, as you well know, I'm a man of the old school . . .

MAMAEV.   Oh, it was much stronger, much stronger.

KRUTITSKY.   I agree with you. I really use an old style. What do you call it? Well, it's close to the style of the great Lomonosov.

MAMAEV.   The old style was stronger. The one nowadays is way off.

KRUTITSKY.   I agree. But, all the same, as you know, to write nowadays in the style of Lomonosov, or Sumarokov[13]—well, you know they might ridicule me. Do you think he might give my work . . . what do you call it? Yes, a little polish.

MAMAEV. He could, he could, he could.

KRUTITSKY. Now I'll pay him for it. Well, what's right and proper.

MAMAEV. You'll insult him. He'd love to do it, just for the honor of doing it.

KRUTITSKY. You don't say! Why should I be obligated to him? Just who is he?

MAMAEV. A nephew, a dear nephew. Yes, sir.

KRUTITSKY. Then tell him to drop in to see me. At some early hour; say, around eight.

MAMAEV. Of course, of course. You may rest assured.

KRUTITSKY. Better tell him, mum's the word! I don't want any talk about it for the time being. It would weaken the effect.

MAMAEV. Oh, good heavens. I understand. I'll insist upon it, insist.

KRUTITSKY. Good-by!

MAMAEV. I'll bring him over tomorrow myself.

KRUTITSKY. You're always welcome. [*Exits;* MAMAEV *escorts him.* KLEOPATRA *and* GLAFIRA *enter.*]

KLEOPATRA. He is young, good-looking, well-educated, a dear boy! Ah!

GLAFIRA. Isn't he though! Yet, even so, Kleopatra Lvovna, he might have withered away. Alone, forgotten, unknown.

KLEOPATRA. And just who told him to wither away, forgotten and unknown? Isn't it enough that he's young and good-looking?

GLAFIRA. As far as that goes, it isn't what you are, but who you know. And if you don't know the right people, how can you ever find a patron?

KLEOPATRA. Ah, but the right people would have found him. He shouldn't have escaped our attention. Oh, my, no. Society would have discovered him. Yes, we would.

GLAFIRA. In order to be discovered, you must be especially brilliant. But it's hard for ordinary people. Oh, how hard it is.

KLEOPATRA. You do your son an injustice. Why, he's really quite clever. And why should he need a brilliant mind, especially when he's so good-looking? What would he do with brains?

He's not going to be a professor. Believe me, a handsome young man will always find people to help him, and they'll do it out of sympathy—to help him get on in the world, and to live quite comfortably. If you happen to see a clever man poorly dressed, living in an ugly apartment, riding in second-rate cabs—why this doesn't startle you, or set your teeth on edge. It's as it should be. It's rather becoming to a clever man, and there's no obvious contradiction. But, on the other hand, if you happen to see a young, good-looking man, poorly dressed—now that's painful. You know it mustn't be, that it won't be, and never shall be!

GLAFIRA.   Oh, you have the heart of an angel!

KLEOPATRA.   It won't happen! We just won't tolerate it, we women. We shall rouse our husbands, our friends. We'll go to the highest authority. We shall fix it for him. Nothing must stop us from feasting our eyes on him. Poverty! Fie! We shall spare nothing, in order to . . . It shan't be! It shan't! Beautiful young men are so rare. . . .

GLAFIRA.   If only everyone would think like you . . .

KLEOPATRA.   Everyone does, everyone. As a matter of fact, we are bound to sympathize with poor people. It's our duty, responsibility; there's nothing to discuss here. But who could have the heart to bear the sight of a handsome man in poverty—a young man. Sleeves threadbare or too short, a dirty collar. Oh, my, that's terrible. Terrible! Besides, poverty murders sprightliness, somehow humiliates and destroys that triumphant look, that audacity which is so pardonable and so becoming a handsome young man.

GLAFIRA.   Oh, you can say that again, Kleopatra Lvovna! [14]
[MAMAEV enters.]

MAMAEV.   How do you do.

GLAFIRA.   I'm going to lodge a complaint against you, Nil Fedoseich!

MAMAEV.   What's all this?

GLAFIRA.   You have completely stolen my son. He has stopped loving me entirely. He raves constantly about you. Yes, everything about your mind and conversation simply astounds him.

MAMAEV.   He's a good boy. Yes, good.

GLAFIRA.   As a baby, he was simply a marvel.

KLEOPATRA.   Oh, but he's practically a baby, still.

GLAFIRA.   Such a gentle, quiet baby—it was amazing.[15] Never once did he forget to kiss his father's hand, or his mother's. Nor did he forget all the grandmothers and all the aunts. It turned out that we had to forbid him doing it. Otherwise, they might think we taught him to do it on purpose. And then, on the sly, when no one was looking, he would go up and kiss their hands. But one time, when he was five years old, he really astonished us! He came in one morning and said: "What a dream I had! Angels flew down to me in my little bed and said:— Love your papa and mama, and obey them in everything! And when you get bigger, love your superiors. I told them: 'Angels! I shall obey everyone!'" He surprised us by this dream, made us so happy. I can't tell you how much. I'll always remember this dream, always.

MAMAEV.   Good-by, now, I'm going, my business is a little more important than yours. I'm pleased with your son. So you may tell him that I'm pleased.   [*Putting on his hat.*]   Oh, I almost forgot. I know you're just getting on, and you don't know how to live. Why don't you drop in some time in the morning? I'll give you . . .

GLAFIRA.   How can we ever thank you . . .

MAMAEV.   No, it's not money. In fact, it's better than money. I'll give you advice concerning your budget.   [*Exits.*]

GLAFIRA.   He is satisfied, thank the Lord for that! There's no one who can show his gratitude like my sonny boy.

KLEOPATRA.   I'm very pleased to hear that.

GLAFIRA.   Not only is he grateful, but he adores his benefactors.

KLEOPATRA.   Adores? That's a bit too much.

GLAFIRA.   No, not too much. Such character, such feeling. Of course, it won't do when a mother praises her son so much. And, what's more, he doesn't like me to talk about him.

KLEOPATRA.   Oh, do me the favor. I won't tell him a thing you say.

GLAFIRA.   He is simply blinded by his benefactors. As far as he's concerned, there's no one better in the whole world. With regard to intellect, he says, Nil Fedoseich has no equal in Moscow. And your beauty, he says, must be described in words— to believe it.

KLEOPATRA.   Do go on, please.

GLAFIRA.   Oh my, the things he compares you to!

KLEOPATRA.   You don't say so?

GLAFIRA.   He's seen you before, hasn't he?

KLEOPATRA.   I don't know. I saw him at the theatre.

GLAFIRA.   Oh, he must have seen you.

KLEOPATRA.   Why do you say that?

GLAFIRA.   Yes, why do I? He knows you such a short time, and suddenly, this . . .

KLEOPATRA.   Come, come! This what?

GLAFIRA.   And suddenly this great fascination for you.

KLEOPATRA.   Ah, the dear boy!

GLAFIRA.   I just don't understand it. His uncle, he says, is so clever, so very clever. But his aunt, he says, is an angel, simply an angel, yes . . .

KLEOPATRA.   Please, please, go on! I'm simply bursting with curiosity.

GLAFIRA.   Then you won't be angry for my talking so openly, so stupidly.

KLEOPATRA.   No, no.

GLAFIRA.   An angel, he says, an angel. And he falls on my breast, and what's more, in tears . . .

KLEOPATRA.   Come now, that's . . . You don't mean it? How strange.

GLAFIRA.   [*Having changed her tone.*]   He's so overjoyed by the great kindness you've shown him—an orphan—that he cries out of gratitude.

KLEOPATRA.   Of course, the boy's all heart, all . . .

GLAFIRA.   You can say that again! How hot-blooded he is.

KLEOPATRA.   At his age it's understandable and . . . forgivable.

GLAFIRA.   Forgive him then. Please forgive him. He's so young.

KLEOPATRA.   Why should I forgive him? What's he done?

GLAFIRA.   Well, you know, don't you, perhaps for the first time in his life, he's seen such a beautiful woman—what could he do? She is sweet to him, indulgent . . . as a relative, naturally . . . He's such a hot-head, you'll drive him wild.

KLEOPATRA.   [*Thoughtfully.*]   What a dear boy. What a darling.

GLAFIRA.   Of course, his whole feeling is that of a relative. But you know, don't you . . . the very closeness of such a charming woman to a boy of his age . . . You know, he doesn't sleep nights. When he comes home from your place, he turns and tosses.

KLEOPATRA.   He tells you everything? He doesn't hide his feelings from you?

GLAFIRA.   Of course he doesn't. But you know his feelings. . . . Well, he's still a child.

KLEOPATRA.   But of course he is. He still needs direction in everything. Under the direction of an intelligent woman, with time he might . . . Yes, he might . . .

GLAFIRA.   Oh, do direct him! His future demands it. You are so kind.

KLEOPATRA.   [*Laughs.*]   Yes, yes, kind. But you know, don't you, that it's really dangerous. It's possible I might even . . . get carried away myself.

GLAFIRA.   You are really and truly kind.

KLEOPATRA.   I see you love him very much.

GLAFIRA.   He's my only one. Why shouldn't I love him!

KLEOPATRA.   [*Languidly.*]   Then let's love him together.

GLAFIRA.   You make me envy my own son. Yes, I see he has found happiness in your family. But it's time for me to go. Don't be angry with my jabbering on so. What trouble there'd be if my son finds out! Please don't give me away. Sometimes he gets ashamed because I'm so brainless. Sometimes he'd like to say, "Mama, dear, what silly things you do." But, you know, he never says it. He avoids such words out of respect for his mother. If only it would stop me from foolish mistakes in the future, I'd forgive him if he did say it. Good-by, Kleopatra Lvovna.

KLEOPATRA.   [*Embraces her.*]   Good-by, my dear Glafira Klimovna. I'll see you one of these days, and we shall talk again about your sonny boy. [*Escorts her to the door.* GLAFIRA *exits.*]   What a chatterbox! If the son ever heard her, he'd never thank her. He is so proud, cold, respectful around me, and listen to the way he acts at home. It looks as though I'm still capable of inspiring real passion in a young man. That's the way it ought to be. Lately, of course, I've noticed a severe shortage of admirers. That's because the people around me have had their day and are all played out. Well, here you are, at last. Oh, the dear boy! I'm going to look after you now. However timid he may be, true passion must burst forth. How very exciting, when you know in advance that a person's in love with you. [GLUMOV *enters, bows and stands in a respectful pose.*] Come, come here. [GLUMOV *timidly approaches.*]   What are you doing now? Don't tell me nephews behave this way?

GLUMOV.   [*Kisses her hand.*]   Good evening, Kleopatra Lvovna.

KLEOPATRA.   Bravo! How did you ever find the courage! At last! You surprise me!

GLUMOV.   I'm very shy.

KLEOPATRA.   Don't be upset! What are you afraid of? I'm just as human as anyone else. You should be more frank and open with me. Trust me with the secrets of your heart! Don't forget, I'm only your aunt.

GLUMOV.   I would be more frank with you, if only . . .

KLEOPATRA.   If only what?

GLUMOV.   If only you were an older woman.

KLEOPATRA.   Oh, don't be silly! I don't want to be old.

GLUMOV.   Nor do I want it, either. May God grant you the full bloom of youth, as long as possible. I only said "older" because if that were true, I wouldn't be so shy and I'd feel more natural.

KLEOPATRA.   But why? Sit down next to me and tell me quite frankly. Why would you feel more natural if I were an older woman?

GLUMOV.   [*Takes chair and sits near her.*]   A young woman has her own affairs, her own interests. How could she find time to worry about poor relatives? But that's the only worry an older woman has.

KLEOPATRA.   Why shouldn't a young woman want to look after her relatives?

GLUMOV.   She might, but a person would be ashamed to ask her, ashamed to pester her. She thinks of gaiety, sports, amusements. And suddenly here's the boring sight of a nephew, with his favors, his eternal whimpering. An older woman, on the other hand, would delight in all this. She would bustle about Moscow, pleading his case. It would be preoccupation for her, and a good thing for him. Of course, she could boast about it afterward.

KLEOPATRA.   Well, if I were an older woman, what would you ask me to do?

GLUMOV.   Oh, if you only were! But you're not old. Quite the contrary, you are a very young woman. You're trying to trap me.

KLEOPATRA.   It doesn't matter. Go on! Go on!

GLUMOV.   Yes, it does matter. Now, I know, for example, that one word to Ivan Ivanych[16] Gorodulin, and I'd have a very good position.

KLEOPATRA.   Well, I think it would take more than one word.

GLUMOV.   All the same, I wouldn't bother you with a favor like this.

KLEOPATRA.   Why not?

GLUMOV.   Because it would be simple coercion. He's completely fascinated by you.

KLEOPATRA.   Are you sure?

GLUMOV.   I'm certain of it.

KLEOPATRA.   How infinitely wise you are. Well, and I?

GLUMOV.   Really, that's your affair.

KLEOPATRA.   [*To herself.*]   He's not jealous. That's strange.

GLUMOV.   He can refuse you nothing. Then, too, he would welcome a request from you. Forcing you to ask him is just like giving him a bribe.

KLEOPATRA.   All this is nonsense, just fantasy! Don't you want me to ask him for you?

GLUMOV.   I do not, absolutely. Besides, I don't want to be indebted to you. How could I ever repay you?

KLEOPATRA.   How would you repay an older woman?

GLUMOV.   By constantly playing up to her. I'd carry her lapdog around, put a footstool at her feet. I'd always be kissing her hand and wishing her "happy returns" on every possible occasion. All this, of course, the old lady would value most highly.

KLEOPATRA.   Oh, yes, of course.

GLUMOV.   Then, if the old lady were really kind, I might become somewhat attached to her, come to love her.

KLEOPATRA.   You don't think you could fall in love with a young woman?

GLUMOV.   I could, but I wouldn't dare.

KLEOPATRA.   [*To herself.*]   At last!

GLUMOV.   And just what would it all lead to? Little more than useless suffering. [SERVANT *enters.*]

SERVANT.   Ivan Ivanych Gorodulin, ma'am.

GLUMOV.   I'll go to uncle's study. I have some work there. If you please, ma'am. [*Bows with great respect and exits.*]

KLEOPATRA. [*To* SERVANT.] Ask him in! [SERVANT *exits.*
GORODULIN *enters.*] [17]

GORODULIN.   I have the honor to present myself.

KLEOPATRA. [*Reproachfully.*] You are a nice one! Sit down.
What wind, what storm brings you here?

GORODULIN. [*Sits.*]   The wind that is in my head, and the gale
of passion that rages in my heart.

KLEOPATRA.   I thank you. It's sweet of you to remember me,
deserted and forsaken.

GORODULIN.   Where is he? Where is that wretch who has forsaken you? Just show him to me! I'm in a warlike temper, at
the moment.

KLEOPATRA.   You're the wretch, you're precisely the one who
should be shot, drawn-and-quartered, or taken care of in some
way or other.

GORODULIN.   I'd prefer some way or other.

KLEOPATRA.   I've already invented a punishment for you.

GORODULIN.   Permit me to know. Announce the verdict. For
without the verdict there can be no execution. If you've decided
to smother me in your embrace, I shall never appeal the verdict.

KLEOPATRA.   No, I wish to appear as petitioner before you.

GORODULIN.   You mean you want to switch roles with me?

KLEOPATRA.   Are you really a petitioner? Aren't you almost a
judge some place or other?

GORODULIN.   Just so, ma'am. But among the ladies I'm always . . .

KLEOPATRA.   Let's stop all this nonsense. I have a serious matter
to discuss.

GORODULIN.   I'm listening, ma'am.

KLEOPATRA.   My nephew needs . . .

GORODULIN.   Just what does your nephew need? A jacket,
trousers?

KLEOPATRA.   You're going to upset me. Just listen and don't
interrupt! My nephew certainly isn't a child. He's a very dear
young man, quite good-looking, clever, well-educated.

GORODULIN.   So much the better for him. So much the worse for
me.

KLEOPATRA.   He needs a position.

GORODULIN.   Say the word! What kind?

KLEOPATRA.   A good one, of course! He's a boy of splendid
ability.

GORODULIN.   Splendid ability? Sorry. Right now those with splendid ability have no place to go. Something like a glut on the market. Such positions are already filled. One by Bismarck, the other by Beist.

KLEOPATRA.   Listen, I'm going to lose my patience. Then we shall quarrel. Tell me, do you have a position in mind?

GORODULIN.   For an ordinary mortal we can turn up something.

KLEOPATRA.   Excellent.

GORODULIN.   [*Tenderly.*]   We need people. Permit me at least one quick glance at this phenomenon. Then, I can tell you precisely what he's good for, and the kind of position I can recommend.

KLEOPATRA.   Egor Dmitrich! Sonny boy! Come here! [*To* GORODULIN.]   I'll leave you two alone. Come see me later! I'll be waiting for you in the drawing room. [GLUMOV *enters.*] May I present my nephew: Egor Dmitrich Glumov. [*To* GLUMOV.]   Ivan Ivanych would like to get to know you. [*Exits.*]

GORODULIN.   [*Offering his hand to* GLUMOV.]   Are you in service?

GLUMOV.   [*With poise.*]   I was in service, but no longer.[18] And I really don't care to be.

GORODULIN.   Why?

GLUMOV.   God didn't grant me the knack. There are certain necessary qualifications, but I just don't have them.

GORODULIN.   It seems to me you'd require only intelligence and a desire to work.

GLUMOV.   Let's assume there's no objection on that count. But what's the sense? However much you may work, you end up as the office boy. If you want to make your mark, and if you're without patronage, then you need something else.

GORODULIN.   And what's that, exactly?

GLUMOV.   First of all, don't use your brains unless you're forced to do so. Second, laugh only when the chief takes it into his head that he's come up with a joke. Third, you must do all the thinking as well as all the work of your superiors in the department. And, at the same time, convince them with all sorts of bowing and scraping that I—and I quote—"am only stupid, whatever please you, your Excellency, was really ordered by you, your Excellency." In addition to all this, you must qualify as something of the lackey—combined, of course, with that well-known grace. For example, when the chief enters, you must know how to leap up and stretch to attention in such a way that it's both subservient, and not subservient, but something like "as your Excellency wills." At the same time, demonstrating your gentility, rigidity, and grace. Whenever the chief sends you on an errand, you must know how to execute a rather facile, fluttering step. Something between a gallop, march time, and the usual gait. I've scarcely told you half the things you need to know, if you want to make your mark in the service.

GORODULIN.   Splendid. That is, all this smells badly, but you say it so beautifully. That's the important thing. Then, too, all that you've said is somewhat old-fashioned. Nowadays, it's quite a different matter.

GLUMOV.   I haven't seen the difference. And besides, it all comes from the same mold. There are whole walls, whole fortresses created out of red tape. And out of these fortresses fly bombardments of dry circulars and instructions.

GORODULIN.   Oh, this is good! First-rate, superb! What talent!

GLUMOV.   I'm very pleased you sympathize with my ideas. Very few people really do!

GORODULIN.   Ideas? What are ideas to us! Who doesn't have the very same ideas? It's the words, phrases, that make the difference. You know, you could do me a great favor.

GLUMOV.   Whatever you say.

GORODULIN.   Jot all this down on paper!

GLUMOV.   Of course, I'd love to. Why do you need it?

GORODULIN.   I shall be frank with you. We're both rather honest men, and we should speak openly. I've a bit of a problem. To-morrow I must deliver a speech at dinner, and I have absolutely no time to think.[19]

GLUMOV.   Of course, certainly!

GORODULIN.   [*Squeezing* GLUMOV's *hand.*] Do this for me, as one friend to another.

GLUMOV.   Don't mention it, for pity's sake! Yes, give me the sort of position wherein I might be face to face with the race of man. Give me the opportunity to see for myself his urgent needs and to satisfy them quickly and with compassion.

GORODULIN.   Excellent, excellent! Now write this down, too! Do I understand you to mean that, according to your honest manner of speaking, that you need a post as inspector, or executive, or . . .

GLUMOV.   Whatever you say. I don't mind having a position, and I'll work assiduously, to my full capacity. But there is one condition. My work must be of some real use, something to improve the well-being of the people. To beat the air, call it service, and receive a decoration—I wouldn't care for that.

GORODULIN.   Now that's right to the point: "to improve the well-being . . ." Oh, I like that!

GLUMOV.   Would you like me to write out the whole speech?

GORODULIN.   You don't say! As you can see, it doesn't take long for two honest men to agree! They exchange a few phrases, and suddenly they're friends. My, how you can talk! Our country needs people like you, my boy. Yes, we desperately need them! [*Having looked at his watch.*]   Come see me tomorrow, around twelve. [*Shaking hands with* GLUMOV.]   Oh, I'm pleased, very pleased. [*Exits to the drawing room.* MAMAEV *enters.*]

MAMAEV.   Oh, there you are! Come here! [*Mysteriously.*] Recently Krutitsky dropped by to get advice about a certain matter. A kindly old fellow! He's written something that he wants dressed up. You know, press out a few syllables here and there. I mentioned you. In our circle, we don't consider him too intelligent. And no doubt he's written some sort of nonsense. But when you see him remember to butter him up a bit.

GLUMOV.   My dear uncle, what are you teaching me?

MAMAEV.   You shouldn't flatter people all the time, but a little butter now and again is quite permissible. Praise a bit here, a bit there, and it will please the old fellow. He might come in handy later on. Don't worry, we'll take him to task. He won't escape us. You're still a youngster, so you must praise him, all the same. I'll take you over to see him tomorrow. Well, there's a rather delicate situation I'd like to discuss with you. How are you and your aunt getting on?

GLUMOV.   I'm a person of good breeding. You don't need to teach me courtesy.

MAMAEV.   Now, that's stupid. Really, quite stupid. She is still rather young, pretty. She doesn't need your courtesy. What do you want to do, make her your enemy?

GLUMOV.   My dear uncle, I don't understand.

MAMAEV. If you don't understand, then listen and learn! Thank the Lord you have someone to teach you. Women will never forgive the man who doesn't notice their beauty.

GLUMOV. Yes—yes—yes! Go on, I'd never thought of that!

MAMAEV. That's the idea, brother! Although you're a second cousin twice removed, you're a relative all the same. Therefore, you possess a little more freedom than a mere acquaintance. Sometimes you might—a bit absentmindedly, you know—kiss her hand a little more than necessary. Then, of course, there's that special something with your eyes. I think you know how?

GLUMOV. No, I don't.

MAMAEV. Where've you been, brother? Well, now, something like this. [*Rolls his eyes upward.*]

GLUMOV. No! Go on with you! Why, that's impossible.

MAMAEV. Well, you can learn it, if you use the mirror. Now and again you must sigh with a languid air. All this will tickle her vanity a bit.

GLUMOV. I certainly thank you.

MAMAEV. And I certainly feel better now. You do understand, don't you?

GLUMOV. No, I don't.

MAMAEV. She's a woman of passion. She's a hot-head. She could very easily fall for some kind of dandy, the devil knows who. Get trapped by some engineer, perhaps. Someone quite unbearable. Leeches like that have no conscience. Now where would that get us? But, you see, here you are. Wouldn't you like to be our own responsible man? If the wolves are satisfied, the lambs are safe. Ha, ha, ha! You understand now?

GLUMOV. What brains you have, my dear uncle.

MAMAEV. I hope so.

GLUMOV. But there's still a problem! In order to stop any gossip—you know how vicious people can be—you must introduce me to Turusina. Then I can openly court her niece, and if you like, I can even ask her to marry me. In that way we shall really satisfy the wolves and save the lambs.

MAMAEV. That's it, that's it. You've got the idea!

GLUMOV. Of course, we won't say a word about Turusina to Kleopatra Lvovna. No question of jealousy, but you know how sensitive women can be.

MAMAEV.   You're telling me! I know, I know. No—no—no! No need to mention it.

GLUMOV.   When will we visit Turusina?

MAMAEV.   Tomorrow afternoon. You know what to do now, don't you?

GLUMOV.   What to do? I'm amazed by your cleverness.   [KLEO-PATRA *and* GORODULIN *enter.*]

GORODULIN.   [*Softly to* KLEOPATRA.]   In two weeks he shall be assigned.

KLEOPATRA.   In two weeks I shall kiss you.

MAMAEV.   Ah, Ivan Ivanych! I stopped by to see you today. I wanted to give some advice about the club.

GORODULIN.   Excuse me, Nil Fedoseich, there's no time now. [*Shakes hands with* GLUMOV.]   I'll be seeing you.

MAMAEV.   Then we can go together. I'll tell you on the way. I must go to the Senate.   [GORODULIN *and* MAMAEV *exit.*]

KLEOPATRA.   [*Sits in armchair.*]   You may kiss my hand. Your business has been settled.

GLUMOV.   I didn't ask you to do it.

KLEOPATRA.   Never mind, I guessed it myself.

GLUMOV.   [*Kisses her hand.*]   And I thank you.   [*Takes hat.*]

KLEOPATRA.   Where are you going?

GLUMOV.   Home. I'm so happy. I must share my good fortune with mother.

KLEOPATRA.   Are you happy? I don't believe you.

GLUMOV.   I'm as happy as I can be.

KLEOPATRA.   You mean, not completely so; meaning, you haven't achieved everything you want.

GLUMOV.   Everything that I can only dare hope for.

KLEOPATRA.   No, tell me quite frankly. Have you achieved everything?

GLUMOV.   What more is there? I shall receive a position.

KLEOPATRA.   I don't believe you, I don't. You want to prove yourself—at your young age—a materialist. You want to convince me that you think only about work and money.

GLUMOV.   Kleopatra Lvovna . . .

KLEOPATRA.   You want to convince me that your heart never quickens. That you never dream, never weep, that you love no one.

GLUMOV.   Kleopatra Lvovna, I'm not saying that.

KLEOPATRA.   And if you love, don't you want her to love you?

GLUMOV.   I'm not saying that.

KLEOPATRA.   You say you have achieved everything.

GLUMOV.   Yes, everything possible. Everything I might venture to hope for.

KLEOPATRA.   That means, you can't risk hoping for her love in return. In that case, why do you waste your feelings? You know they are the pearls of the soul. Tell me, who is this cruel woman?

GLUMOV.   But you know this is torture, Kleopatra Lvovna.

KLEOPATRA.   Tell me, you scalawag, tell me at once. I know, I can see in your eyes that you're in love. Poor boy! Are you suffering so very, very much?

GLUMOV.   You don't have the right to resort to such measures. You know I can hide nothing from you.

KLEOPATRA.   Who is it you love?

GLUMOV.   Have pity!

KLEOPATRA.   Is she worthy of you?

GLUMOV.   Good Lord, what are you doing to me?

KLEOPATRA.   Can she appreciate your passion, your sensitivity?

GLUMOV.   If you beat me, I shan't tell you.

KLEOPATRA.   [In a whisper.]   Courage, my friend, courage!

GLUMOV.   Whom do I love?

KLEOPATRA.   Yes.

GLUMOV.   [Falling on his knees.]   You.

KLEOPATRA.   [Shrieks softly.]   Ah!

GLUMOV.   I am your slave for life. Punish me for my impudence, but I love you. Forbid me to speak, forbid me to look at you, to stop admiring your beauty, or, worst of all, send me away. But don't be angry with me! You are to blame. If you had not been so charming, so indulgent to me, perhaps I would have kept my passion within the bounds of decency. Whatever the cost to me. But you—my angel of goodness—you, my beautiful one, have turned me—a sensible man—into a raving idiot. Yes, I am mad! It seemed to me that bliss was beckoning me, and I flung myself—unafraid—into the abyss. There, I might perish, never to return. Forgive me.   [Bows his head.]

KLEOPATRA.   [Kisses his head.]   I forgive you.   [GLUMOV, having bowed respectfully, exits. KLEOPATRA follows him with her eyes.]

ACT THREE

TURUSINA'S *country home. The following afternoon. A drawing room, richly furnished, in the country home in Sokolniky. A door in the center, another at the side.* MASHENKA *and* TURUSINA *enter through the center door.*

MASHENKA. Let's go, *ma tante!*[20] Let's go. Come, please, let's go!

TURUSINA. No, my dear, no! Not for the world! Besides, I've had the horses unharnessed.

MASHENKA. For pity's sake, *ma tante,* I've never seen anything like it! We've been planning to go for simply ages. What a short drive, too. We get no more than ten steps from the gate, and now—here we are again.

TURUSINA. [*Sits.*] My dear, I know very well what I'm doing. Why should we expose ourselves to danger, when it's possible to escape it?

MASHENKA. But why should anything harm us?

TURUSINA. I don't understand why you even question it. You saw it yourself. At the very gates a certain woman crossed the road in front of us. I wanted to stop then and there, but I reluctantly drove on, and suddenly, this omen . . .

MASHENKA. Oh, what do you mean? What omen?

TURUSINA. Yes, if it had come from the left side, but it was from the right . . .

MASHENKA. Come now, left or right. What's the difference?

TURUSINA. Don't talk like that. I don't like it. I can't stand freethinking in my own home.[21] I hear quite enough blasphemy from our guests. I can't stop them, but I can stop you. We must be careful with our lives. It's a sin, of course, to worry too much about ourselves, but we are obliged to protect ourselves. Don't be obstinate! We see so many accidents: horses running away, carriage broken down, the coachman getting drunk and driving into the ditch. Thank the Lord, Providence takes care of its own. If we are told bluntly: don't go there, you'll expose yourself to danger—then who's to blame if you don't listen to good advice, and break your neck?

MASHENKA.   No one told us don't go!

TURUSINA.   Are actual words necessary? An evil omen is far more eloquent than all the words in the world. If we had been going for some useful purpose . . . well, that had nothing to do with it. But just to be going—the Lord knows why—in order to spend the whole evening in empty chatter and gossip about our neighbors. And all this—just to ignore the highest of instructions, to expose ourselves to obvious danger! No, I thank you. I know only too well why you want to go! You think you're going to meet Kurchaev there, that unrepentant atheist. Why, I shall never allow him in my house again. That's why you're forcing your poor aunt to go. You're thinking only of yourself, and you're forgetting that I might break my leg or arm.

MASHENKA.   I don't understand, *ma tante*, why you're set against Kurchaev.

TURUSINA.   Against Kurchaev? Why he dares to laugh at the most sacred things—right in front of me, too.

MASHENKA.   Now really, *ma tante*, whenever did that happen?

TURUSINA.   All the time. He constantly ridicules my pilgrims, my *yurodivy*.[22]

MASHENKA.   You say he ridicules sacred things.

TURUSINA.   Why, of course. I told him once, "Just look, my Matresha's face is beginning to glow with holiness." And he said, "Not with holiness, with grease." I shall never forgive him. You can see what freethinking leads to, how young people forget their place today! I can prove what kind of person he really is. Yesterday I received two letters. Read them, if you like.

MASHENKA.   Can you really trust anonymous letters?

TURUSINA.   I'd have my doubts if there were only one. But suddenly there are two, and from different people. [GRIGORY *enters and gives* TURUSINA *a letter.*]

GRIGORY.   Some stray people have wandered in, ma'am.

TURUSINA.   What he's talking about, the Lord only knows. Well, they're probably pilgrims. [*To* GRIGORY.] Let them be fed. [GRIGORY *exits.* TURUSINA *reads the letter.*] Here is another letter. Obviously a reliable lady wrote it. [*Reads aloud.*] "My dear madam, Sofya Ignatevna,[23] although I do not have the pleasure . . ." [*Reads to herself.*] Here's something! "Your choice of such a person as Egor Vasilevich[24] Kurchaev compels me to shed tears for the fate of poor Mashenka . . ." Well, and so on.

MASHENKA.   That's strange! I don't know what to think of it.

TURUSINA.   You don't mean to quarrel with me, do you? Nevertheless, my dear, if you certainly want to, then marry him. [*Sniffs spirits.*] I don't care to be called a tyrant. Only you ought to know that you'll distress me if you do, and that you'll scarcely have the right to complain, if I should . . .

MASHENKA.   If you should not give me any money . . .

TURUSINA.   But, more important, my blessing.

MASHENKA.   No, *ma tante,* have no fears! I was born and raised in Moscow. So I won't marry without money, or the permission of relatives. Kurchaev pleases me very much, but if he displeases you, I won't marry him. And I shan't die of consumption because of it. But, *ma tante,* take pity! I have money, thanks to you. I would really like to live a bit.

TURUSINA.   I understand, my dear, I understand.

MASHENKA.   Find me a fiancé who pleases you—only a decent sort of fellow—and I shall marry him without one single objection. I want to glitter, show off a little. Living as we do, in this humdrum way, bores me to death.

TURUSINA.   I sympathize with you. Vanity at your age is excusable.

MASHENKA.   When I get older, *ma tante,* I'll probably live very much the same as you—it runs in our family.

TURUSINA.   May God grant it. I hope and pray with all my soul. It's the true and right way.

MASHENKA.   Yes, *ma tante,* but first of all I must get married.

TURUSINA.   I won't try to hide that I'm somewhat at a loss. Nowadays young men are so spoiled. It's quite difficult to find the sort of man who would please me. You know my requirements.

MASHENKA.   Oh, *ma tante,* if he can't be found in Moscow, what's the use of looking somewhere else! Everything worth having is here. You know so many people. It's possible to turn to this person, or to that. Krutitsky, Mamaev, Gorodulin will help you. They will find precisely the sort of fiancé you'd like. I'm convinced of it.

TURUSINA. Krutitsky, Gorodulin. You know they are only human, my dear. They might trick us, or be deceived themselves.

MASHENKA. But what can we do?

TURUSINA. We must wait for a sign. Without a special sign I can decide nothing.

MASHENKA. A special sign? What kind of sign?

TURUSINA. You will know soon enough. It shall appear today.

MASHENKA. *Ma tante,* please don't refuse Kurchaev admission to our home. Please let him come.

TURUSINA. Very well. But remember, you shan't marry him.

MASHENKA. I shall depend completely on you, *ma tante.* I am your obedient, your most obedient niece.

TURUSINA. [*Kisses her.*] You are a sweet child.

MASHENKA. I shall be rich, I shall be happy—and life: so many adventures, so much to do. You used to play the game, *ma tante,* didn't you? [25]

TURUSINA. How did you find that out?

MASHENKA. I know. I know that you were once playful as a . . . [26]

TURUSINA. Yes, you know a thing or two; but you don't, and you shouldn't, know everything.

MASHENKA. It doesn't matter. You are the best woman I know, and I'll take you any day as my model. [*Embraces her.*] I also want to play the game. [27] If I should sin, then I shall repent. I shall sin, and I shall repent, exactly like you.

TURUSINA. What nonsense, Mashenka! What nonsense!

MASHENKA. [*Having folded her hands.*] I am guilty.

TURUSINA. Yes, you are, and I've heard enough. I'm tired, let me rest a little. [*Kisses* MASHENKA; *she exits.*] What a sweet girl! I can't be angry with her. I don't think she understands a thing she says. How could she understand? Such prattle. I shall do my best to make sure that she's happy. She richly deserves it. How sensible and obedient she is! You know, I almost cried— what childish devotion. It's true, she's nearly ruffled me. [*Sniffs spirits.* GRIGORY *enters.*]

GRIGORY. General Krutitsky.

TURUSINA.   Show him in!   [GRIGORY *exits, and* KRUTITSKY *enters.*]

KRUTITSKY.   [*Takes* TURUSINA's *hands.*]   What is it, nerves? Hmm?

TURUSINA.   Nerves.

KRUTITSKY.   That's bad! What cold hands you have. You're much too . . .

TURUSINA.   Too, what?

KRUTITSKY.   Much too, that is, diligent. . . . Well, to overwork yourself so much. . . . You mustn't do so very much. . . .

TURUSINA.   I've already asked you not to speak to me about that.

KRUTITSKY.   Very well, I won't.

TURUSINA.   Sit down.

KRUTITSKY.   No, it's nothing. I'm not tired. Well, I was taking a walk, and you know, I thought I'd drop in to visit an old acquaintance, an old girl friend. . . . Hee, hee, hee. Remember, you know we . . .

TURUSINA.   Ah, don't remind me! I am now . . .

KRUTITSKY.   Now what's this! Why not remind you? There was a great deal of good in your past. But if there was in your opinion a little something sinful, no doubt you've already repented—a long time ago. To tell you the truth, I always look back with great pleasure, and I have absolutely no regrets, that we . . .

TURUSINA.   [*With a pleading look.*]   Stop it!   [GRIGORY *enters.*]

GRIGORY.   Ma'am, the hollow man has arrived.

KRUTITSKY.   What's this?

TURUSINA.   Grigory, aren't you ashamed of yourself! What do you mean, hollow man? Hallowed! Holy! [28] Let him be fed. [GRIGORY *exits.*] Servants are so stupid. They can't pronounce the most common of names.

KRUTITSKY.   Well, I won't say that nowadays holy men are too common. Other than in your home, you scarcely meet them. I'd like to return to our previous discussion. You will excuse me, I only wanted to say that in the old days, when you were leading a different kind of life, you were healthier.

TURUSINA.   Healthier in body, yes; but not in soul.

KRUTITSKY.   Well, I don't know much about that. It's not really my line of business. Generally speaking, you looked healthier. You are still quite young. It would still be possible to live as you ought.

TURUSINA.   I'm living now as I ought.

KRUTITSKY.   Well, that is, it's too early to play the hypocrite.

TURUSINA.   I asked you . . .

KRUTITSKY.   Well, I'm sorry. I'm sorry. I won't go on.

TURUSINA.   You're a strange man.   [GRIGORY *enters.*]

GRIGORY.   Ma'am, a strange man has arrived.

TURUSINA.   Didn't you ask him where he comes from?

GRIGORY.   He says, "from countries unknown . . ."

TURUSINA.   Let him be seated at the table, together with the others.

GRIGORY.   Yes, ma'am, precisely, together they very likely will . . .

TURUSINA.   Go, go!   [GRIGORY *exits.*]

KRUTITSKY.   You ought to ask those who come "from countries unknown," if they have passports.

TURUSINA.   But why?

KRUTITSKY.   Because with people like that you're only asking for trouble. One time at a certain house there were also three pilgrims who were seeking their salvation.

TURUSINA.   So, what happened?

KRUTITSKY.   Well, it turned out that all three were excellent engravers.

TURUSINA.   What's the matter with that?

KRUTITSKY.   You see, it's something of a bad trade.

TURUSINA.   In what way is it a bad trade—engraving?

KRUTITSKY.   They don't engrave portraits in mud-huts.

TURUSINA.   [*Softly.*]   Icons?

KRUTITSKY.   How could it be icons! Silver rubles.

TURUSINA.   [*Frightened.*]   Ah, you don't say so?

KRUTITSKY.   [*Sits.*]   There, now you understand! Virtue is its own reward, but it wouldn't hurt to be careful. You especially should be on your guard. It's a well-known fact that if a lady goes in for virtue on a grand scale, then she's ripe for plucking by swindlers! You see, my dear, you're just asking for trouble.

TURUSINA.   Goodness is as goodness does. By the way, I wanted to ask your advice concerning a very important matter.

KRUTITSKY.   [*Having moved a little closer.*]   What is it? Go on! I should be happy, quite happy, to serve you in any way I can.

TURUSINA.   You know that Mashenka is now at the age, that . . .

KRUTITSKY.   Yes, yes, I know.

TURUSINA.   You don't happen to know a young man, do you? You know the kind I need?

KRUTITSKY.   The kind you need? Well, that's the hitch. There are plenty of young men. . . . Wait a minute. There is, that is, there's just the sort of man you need.

TURUSINA.   You don't mean it?

KRUTITSKY.   I'm telling you. Unassuming beyond his years, intelligent, nobleman by birth, assured of an excellent career. Generally speaking, a first-rate fellow . . . a fellow who's . . . first-rate. He's been recommended to me for a little work. Well, you know, I put him through his paces, you might say, to see what sort of bird he is! A solid young man! He will go far. Wait and see.

TURUSINA.   But who is he?

KRUTITSKY.   Now what do you call him! Oh, Lord, help me think! Wait a minute, he gave me his address. I don't need him at the moment, Lord knows. [*Takes out paper.*] Here! [*Reads.*] "Egor Dmitrev Glumov!" My, how he writes! Neat, exact, beautiful! You can recognize a man's character immediately by his handwriting. Exact—that means accurate; round, without flourishes, now that means he's no freethinker. Here, take it; perhaps you'll find use for it.

TURUSINA.   [*Takes address.*]   I thank you.

KRUTITSKY.   Thanks for what? Well, I like that. It's our duty! [*Rises.*] Good-by. May I drop by again, what do you think? Or are you angry with me?

TURUSINA.   Oh, how can you say that! It's a pleasure, always.

KRUTITSKY.   That's right. I'm affectionate, you know. Too bad!

TURUSINA.   Come again.

KRUTITSKY.   For old times' sake? Hee, hee, hee! Well, good-by. [*Exits.*]

TURUSINA.   What an old man he is, and how silly! How can you possibly trust him? [*Hides address in her pocket.*] But all the same it may be necessary to look up this Glumov. [GRIGORY *enters.*]

GRIGORY.   Mr. Gorodulin.

TURUSINA.   Show him in. [GRIGORY *exits.* GORODULIN *enters.*] I'm very pleased to see you. Aren't you ashamed! What's been keeping you away so long?

GORODULIN.   Duties, duties. Here—a dinner; there—a railroad opening.

TURUSINA.   I can scarcely believe it, somehow. It's simply that you're bored with us. Well, I'm thankful that you visit us now and again. What's the latest in that little matter of ours?

GORODULIN.   What little matter of ours?

TURUSINA.   So you've forgotten already? That's just wonderful! How can I ever thank you. It was foolish of me to entrust you with it. A man occupied with important affairs—when could you find time to help the poor, unhappy and oppressed! How could you sacrifice your time for this trifle!

GORODULIN.   Oppressed, I believe you said, madam. I can recall nothing about the oppressed. Oh, but of course, I remember now. You asked me, didn't you, to find out about a fortune-teller?

TURUSINA.   Not a fortune-teller, but a prophet. There's quite a difference. You know I should never have gone to a fortune-teller.

GORODULIN.   Excuse me! I confess my ignorance. Subtlety of detail is not one of my strong points. In a word, this widow of the collegiate registrar, Ulita Shmygaeva . . .[29]

TURUSINA.   Whatever her rank may have been, it makes no difference, in any case. She's a lady of a respectable and strict life, and I'm proud to have enjoyed her special favor.

GORODULIN.   It's quite evident from the investigation—that her special favor was enjoyed by a retired soldier.

TURUSINA.   Don't talk like that. It's all nonsense, slander! She was successful; she was acquainted with the best people. Obviously someone was envious and slandered her. I just hope she's been acquitted. Innocence will triumph.

GORODULIN.   No, ma'am, she must go to Siberia.

TURUSINA.   [Having risen.] What? So here is your vaunted court! To send away an innocent woman! And for what? Because she was of benefit to others?

GORODULIN.   Surely you don't think she was tried for fortune-telling.

TURUSINA.   No, don't tell me! It was all done to please those fashionable unbelievers of today.

GORODULIN.   They tried her for deliberately harboring stolen goods, for giving shelter to criminals, and for poisoning some merchant.

TURUSINA.   Oh, dear God! What are you saying?

GORODULIN.   The sacred truth. A merchant's wife asked her for a potion. The wife wanted it for her husband so he might love her even more. Well, they cooked the love-potion, according to all the rules, in Madeira—only they forgot one item. To get authorization from the Board of Health.

TURUSINA.   And the merchant?

GORODULIN.   It had an effect. He almost died, but not from love.

TURUSINA.   You think all this is funny, I see. Lawyers and doctors have no heart. And was there no one who would take the part of this poor woman?

GORODULIN.   For pity's sake, one of our best lawyers defended her. Oratory flowed, swirled, overflowed the banks, and at last subsided to a barely audible babble. Nothing could be done. They confessed everything. The soldier who enjoyed her special favor confessed first, then she.

TURUSINA.   I didn't expect this. How easy to be mistaken. It's impossible to live in this world.

GORODULIN.   I wouldn't say, impossible; but faced with a vague understanding of things, you must split hairs. Nowadays, the science of mental disorders is pushing ahead quite a bit, and hallucinations . . .

TURUSINA.   I've asked you never to talk to me about this.

GORODULIN.   Sorry. I forgot.

TURUSINA.   Let's say I'm mistaken about people. Let's say they deceive me. But to help people, to petition for the unfortunate— for me this is my only blessedness.

GORODULIN.   Blessedness is certainly no laughing matter. Nowadays it's rare to meet a blessed[30] person.   [GRIGORY enters.]

GRIGORY.   A blessed man has just arrived.

GORODULIN.   You don't mean it?

TURUSINA.   And who is he?

GRIGORY.   An Asiatic, I think, ma'am.

TURUSINA.   Why do you think he's Asiatic?

GRIGORY.   He's really terrifying, ma'am. It's horrifying just to look at him, ma'am. If it's near evening, ma'am—then God help us all.

TURUSINA.   What do you mean "terrifying"? Don't be silly!

GRIGORY.   It's an unusual kind of "ferocious," ma'am. He's covered all over with hair—you can only see his eyes, ma'am.

TURUSINA.   He's probably a Greek.

GRIGORY.   Not likely that he's Greek, ma'am, his color's not ripe enough. But there is something of the Hungarian in him, ma'am.

TURUSINA.   What kind of Hungarian? Don't be silly!

GRIGORY.   The kind that sell mouse traps.

TURUSINA.   Take him in, feed him, perhaps he needs something.

GRIGORY.   I think he's a bit peculiar, ma'am.

TURUSINA.   That's enough, stop your babbling!

GRIGORY.   Yes, ma'am.   [*Exits.*]

TURUSINA.   I have a favor to ask, Ivan Ivanych.

GORODULIN.   I'm all ears.

TURUSINA.   I'm thinking of Mashenka. You don't happen to have someone in mind, do you?

GORODULIN.   A fiancé? Oh, spare me that! What took it into your head to ask me? Do I look like a Moscow matchmaker to you? My job is to break knots, not to tie them. I'm opposed to all sorts of chains, even matrimonial ones.

TURUSINA.   But you're chained yourself.

GORODULIN.   That's why I wouldn't wish it on a Tartar.

TURUSINA.   All joking aside, do you happen to know a young man?

GORODULIN.   Just a minute, I saw someone a couple of days ago, and he had written all over him: a good catch. Keep an eye on him—at any moment he'll marry a rich heiress.

TURUSINA.   Tell me, do you remember his name?

GORODULIN.   Yes, yes . . . Glumov.

TURUSINA.   Is he a good match?

GORODULIN.   He's an honest fellow. I know nothing more than that. All joking aside, he's an excellent man.

TURUSINA.   Just a minute, what's his name?   [*Takes paper out of her pocket.*]

GORODULIN.   Glumov.

TURUSINA.   Egor Dmitrich.

GORODULIN.   Yes.

TURUSINA.   Why, he's the very one Krutitsky told me about.

GORODULIN.   Well, I'd say he's the one. You know, as I said: a good catch. Good-by.   [*Bows and exits.*]

TURUSINA.   What kind of a person is this Glumov? I've heard his name twice today. Although I trust neither Krutitsky nor Gorodulin, there must be something in it all the same. Especially if two people of completely opposite convictions praise him.]*Rings.* GRIGORY *enters.*] Go to your mistress and say that everyone should come here. [GRIGORY *exits.*] What a loss for Moscow that Ivan Yakovlich[31] died! Life with him was so simple and easy in Moscow. Now I can't sleep at nights. I'm always thinking how to settle Mashenka's affairs. But if Ivan Yakovlich were alive, I'd have nothing to worry about. I'd just see him, ask his advice, and there'd be no thinking. You see, we don't know the true value of a person until he's no longer with us! I don't know if Manefa can take his place, but there is a great deal of the supernatural about her. [MASHENKA *enters;* MATRESHA *with pack of cards, which she carries in front of her like a book;* MATRESHA *sits at table,* ANFISA[32] *sits on footstool at feet of* TURUSINA *with a lapdog in her arms.*]

MATRESHA.   Say the word, ma'am, and I'll deal 'em up.

TURUSINA.   One moment! Now, Mashenka, I spoke to Krutitsky and Gorodulin about you.

MASHENKA.   [*Excited.*] Tell me. Please do. I've promised you obedience, and now I can scarcely wait for your decision.

TURUSINA.   They both recommended the same man, as if they had agreed beforehand.

MASHENKA.   Wonderful. That means he's a worthy man. But who is he?

TURUSINA.   But I don't trust them.

MATRESHA.   Say the word. Do you want me to . . . ?

TURUSINA.   Lay out the cards! Let's see if they spoke truthfully. [*To* MASHENKA.] I don't trust them, they might be mistaken.

MASHENKA.   By why, *ma tante?*

TURUSINA.   They are only human. [*To* ANFISA.] Don't drop the dog!

MASHENKA.   But whom will you trust, *ma tante?* An oracle? I'm terrified somehow.

TURUSINA.   It's quite natural. That's the way it ought to be. Probably you should feel terrified. We can't, we shouldn't lift the veil of the future without fear. For there, behind this veil, may be found both happiness and unhappiness, both your life and your death.

MASHENKA.   Who will lift the veil for us?

TURUSINA.   The one who has the power. [GRIGORY *enters.*]

GRIGORY.   Manefa, ma'am.

TURUSINA.   Here is the one. [*Rises, goes to meet* MANEFA. *The others follow.* MANEFA *enters.*] Welcome, welcome. Please come in!

MANEFA.   And so I come. The *shabala*[33] went, and the *shabala* came.

MATRESHA.   [*With tender emotion.*] Oh, I just know something's going to happen. I just know it.

TURUSINA.   [*Sternly.*] Be quiet!

MANEFA.   [*Sitting down.*] I came and sat down like a kneading trough.

ANFISA.   [*With a sign.*] Oh, oh, oh, ah! Ah, what wisdom!

MATRESHA.   Praise be to God that we have lived to see this!

MANEFA.   [*Quietly.*] Don't goggle at me so wall-eyed!

TURUSINA.   We are overjoyed that you honored us with your coming.

MATRESHA.   Oh, so honored!

ANFISA.   Everyone is honored!

TURUSINA.   We are waiting, mother Manefa, what will you say?

MANEFA.   We are waiting! We expected him in socks; he's come in shoes of bark.

MATRESHA.   Oh, it's sacred, you just know it's sacred! Listen and learn, that's what it is, you gotta listen and learn!

ANFISA.   I'm listening, I'm listening.

TURUSINA.   I wanted to ask you . . .

MANEFA.   Don't ask. I know beforehand. He who knows, runs; he who knows not, suns. A little girl, less; then an old woman, more.

ANFISA.   It's true, you just know it's true.

TURUSINA.   We need to know the man, precisely. Won't you even tell your little slave? Maybe you've had a dream, or a vision . . .

MANEFA.   It was a vision, it was. Down from the mountains, and up to the door, throw off the blankets, and you'll see—Egor.

ANFISA.   Did you hear that, did you! Egor!

MASHENKA.   [*Quietly to* TURUSINA.] Kurchaev is Egor, you know.

TURUSINA.   Wait! What sort of person is he?

MANEFA.   How can I tell? Once you see him, then you know him.

TURUSINA.   But when shall we see him?

MANEFA.   A welcome guest arrives with the blest.

MATRESHA.   Hey, get that, did you hear that, did you?

TURUSINA.   Tell us at least what he looks like.

ANFISA.   First of all, you've got to ask the color of his hair. You always ask that, so you'll know it.

TURUSINA.   Just you keep silent! What's the color of his hair?[34]

MANEFA.   Toward some he's a bear, but to you, he's fair.

MASHENKA.   That means, he's a blond. Kurchaev is a blond, you know. Perhaps it's he?

TURUSINA.   Now you just heard—she's had a vision. Is it possible for a hussar to appear in a vision to God-fearing people? How silly you are.

MATRESHA.   Oh, it's happened, it's happened!

ANFISA.   I knew it, I knew it.

MATRESHA.   It's in the cards, it's Egor.

TURUSINA.   How shallow you've become! [To MASHENKA.] How could she see a name in the cards?

MATRESHA.   [To ANFISA.] Wouldn't you know it! A bit of a slip. I mean the cards turn out "blond."

TURUSINA.   [To MANEFA.] To you all is known, while we sinful creatures remain in doubt. There are many Egors and plenty of blonds.

MANEFA.   All alien ones have met their fate, but the intended husband is at the gate.

TURUSINA AND THE OTHERS.   At the gate?

MANEFA.   Let all be garbed, assemble all; guests are coming, down the hall.

TURUSINA.   When?

MANEFA.   This very hour, this very moment. [All turn to the door. GRIGORY enters.] Here they have come, here they have come, with Sinament and Ginger, Nutmegs and Rum. [Rises.]

GRIGORY.   Nil Fedoseich Mamaev.

TURUSINA.   Alone?

GRIGORY.   A young gentleman is with him, a blond gentleman.

MATRESHA.   Ah! Are we really alive?

ANFISA.   Is it possible we're dreaming?

TURUSINA.   Ask   them   in!   [*Embracing*   MASHENKA.]   Now,
Mashenka, my prayers have been heard! [*Sits down, sniffs
spirits.*]

MASHENKA.   This is so unusual, *ma tante.* I'm trembling all over.

TURUSINA.   Go, calm yourself, my dear. Come back later.
[MASHENKA *exits.*]

MANEFA.   If in trouble, never drown. Virtue ends with the bridal
crown.   [*Goes to the door.*]

TURUSINA.   [*To the companions.*]   Let each of you accompany
her and she needs some tea . . . tea.

MANEFA.   Whoever drinks tea is desperate.

TURUSINA.   Then give her anything that pleases her.   [*The companions take* MANEFA *by her arms and go to the door. At the
door they stop.*]

MATRESHA.   If only we can get a glimpse of him.

ANFISA.   I'll just die if I don't see this miracle.   [MAMAEV *and*
GLUMOV *enter.*]

MAMAEV.   Sofya Ignatevna, allow me to present my nephew, Egor
Dmitrievich Glumov.

MATRESHA.   [*At the door.*]   Ah, it's Egor!

ANFISA.   [*At the door.*]   Ah, he's a blond.

MAMAEV.   Be good to him.

TURUSINA.   [*Rises.*]   I thank you! I shall love him like my own
son.   [GLUMOV *respectfully kisses her hand.*]

ACT FOUR

SCENE ONE

Reception room at KRUTITSKY'S. *Two days later.*[35] *An entrance door. A door on the right, leading to the study. A door on the left, to the drawing room. A table and one chair.* GLUMOV *enters. A* SERVANT *stands at the door.*

GLUMOV. Announce me.

SERVANT. [*Glancing through the door to the study.*] He will be here in a moment, sir. [KRUTITSKY *enters.* SERVANT *exits.*]

KRUTITSKY. [*Nodding his head.*] Ready?

GLUMOV. Ready, your Excellency.[36] [*Hands him note pad.*]

KRUTITSKY. [*Takes note pad.*] Legible, beautiful, excellent. Bravo, bravo! "Treatise." Why don't you say, "project"?

GLUMOV. You use project, your Excellency, whenever you suggest something new. Your Excellency, on the contrary, repudiates anything that is new . . . [*with ingratiating smile*] and with complete justification, your Excellency.

KRUTITSKY. So you say "treatise."

GLUMOV. "Treatise" is better, sir.

KRUTITSKY. "Treatise"? Well, very likely. "A treatise on the harm of reforms in general." Isn't the phrase, "in general," a bit superfluous?

GLUMOV. Your Excellency's main thought is that all reforms in general are harmful.

KRUTITSKY. Yes, absolutely, radical ones. But if insignificant ones are changed, or improved, I'm certainly not opposed to this.

GLUMOV. In that event, they won't be reforms, but readjustments, a little repair here and there.

KRUTITSKY. [*Tapping his forehead with a pencil.*] Yes, of course, that's true. Clever, clever. You have something up there, young man. Yes, you do. I'm very pleased. Keep it up!

GLUMOV. With all my thanks, your Excellency.

KRUTITSKY. [*Putting on his glasses.*] Let's go on. I'm curious to know how you begin the explanation of my chief purpose. "Article one. Every reform is harmful by its very essence. What does a reform contain? A reform contains two movements: (1) the abolition of the old and (2) the introduction of something quite new in its place. Which of these movements is harmful? Both are equally harmful. (1) Discarding the old, we give dangerous inquisitiveness of the mind full play to penetrate into reasons why one or the other is being discarded, and to create such conclusions: something useless is being discarded; such-and-such an institution is being discarded; that means, it is useless. But it must not be, for this stimulates freethinking and makes it a challenge to discuss that which should never be subject to discussion." Well-rounded, sensible.

GLUMOV. And completely justified.

KRUTITSKY. [*Reads.*] "(2) Introducing the new, we seem to be making concessions to the so-called spirit of the times, which is little more than a concoction of empty minds." Clearly stated. I hope it will be clear to everyone. That is to say, popular.

GLUMOV. It's hard to give an account of sophisms, but undeniable truths . . .

KRUTITSKY. Do you think these are undeniable truths?

GLUMOV. I'm completely convinced of it, your Excellency.

KRUTITSKY. [*Glances around.*] Why don't they put another chair in here?

GLUMOV. It's nothing, sir. I can stand, your Excellency.

KRUTITSKY. Of course, you can't allow everyone to sit down. Very likely someone would sprawl about . . . A shopkeeper bustling about with his bill, or the tailor will arrive . . .

GLUMOV. Please don't trouble yourself, your Excellency. I must ask the forgiveness of your Excellency.

KRUTITSKY. What is it, my boy, what is it?

GLUMOV. I left unchanged several words and phrases in your treatise.

KRUTITSKY. Why?

GLUMOV. Our language today is too weak to express the complete gracefulness of your thoughts.

KRUTITSKY. For example?

GLUMOV. In the twenty-fifth article, when you discuss minor officials in the civil service . . .

KRUTITSKY. Well?

GLUMOV. Your Excellency put it quite strongly that absolutely no pay raises should be granted to minor officials, and, in general, no improvements in their living conditions. On the contrary, however, significant salary increases should be made to chairmen and executive officials.

KRUTITSKY. I don't recall saying that. [*Turns pages of pad.*]

GLUMOV. I learned it by heart, your Excellency, and not only this paragraph but the whole treatise.

KRUTITSKY. I believe you, but I'm amazed. Why on earth did you do that?

GLUMOV. I have, as you know, my whole life before me. I must lay in a supply of wisdom. I don't often find a chance like this. But when I do, then I want to use it. You can't learn horse sense like this by reading magazines.

KRUTITSKY. I should say not!

GLUMOV. It's easy for a young man to go astray.

KRUTITSKY. Splendid, splendid! I'm pleased to see this kind of thinking in a young man. No matter how much they harp on it, loyalty is a good thing.

GLUMOV. The greatest, your Excellency.

KRUTITSKY. Well, now what do I have there in article twenty-five?

GLUMOV. Article twenty-five. "Salary increases in the civil service, if for any reason such increases are demanded, should be granted with extreme discretion, and then only to chairmen and executive officials, but by no means to minor officials. Salary increases to executives should be granted in order that the image of the government be maintained in all its outward and inherent brilliance. On the other hand, if a minor official gets too well-fed and contented, he takes on that picture of self-respect and dignity which doesn't match his condition in life. Whereas, for a successful and harmonious flow of work, the minor official must be timid and constantly trembling."

KRUTITSKY.   Yes, that's right. Quite right.

GLUMOV.   That word "trembling," your Excellency, completely charmed me.

KRUTITSKY.   [*Absorbed in reading, now and again glances at* GLUMOV. *Cursorily.*]   If you'd like to smoke, please do. Matches are on the fireplace.

GLUMOV.   I don't smoke, your Excellency. Nevertheless, I will, if you'd like me to.

KRUTITSKY.   What's that! What does that matter to me? Did your uncle see this work?

GLUMOV.   How could he? I wouldn't have the courage.

KRUTITSKY.   Well, now you understand. He only thinks he has brains, but you know he's a complete idiot.

GLUMOV.   I dare not argue with your Excellency.

KRUTITSKY.   He's forever giving instructions, but just let him try to write—then we'd see. His wife is a splendid idiot, too, you know.

GLUMOV.   I shan't defend her, either.

KRUTITSKY.   How you get along together—I don't understand.

GLUMOV.   It's a matter of necessity, your Excellency.

KRUTITSKY.   Are you in service?

GLUMOV.   I'm planning to enter soon. As a favor to my aunt, Ivan Ivanych Gorodulin promised to get me a place.

KRUTITSKY.   There now, you've found the man. He'll get you in. You should look for something more durable. All these Gorodulin positions are quickly closed out. Just wait and see. We consider him a dangerous person. Mark my words.

GLUMOV.   I don't agree with the new establishment . . .

KRUTITSKY.   Oho, I see. But I really thought . . . Well, go on, take the position. Loafing around is worse than working. Then if you like, I can give you letters to Petersburg—you might be transferred—you'd make a bigger splash there. Your past is in good shape, completely clean? Is it possible to recommend you?

GLUMOV.   I was a bit lazy as a student, your Excellency.

KRUTITSKY.   Well, what of it? It's not important. It would've been worse if you'd studied too much. Don't you have anything more important than that?

GLUMOV.   I'm ashamed to confess before your Excellency.

KRUTITSKY.   [*With a serious expression.*]   What is it? You'd better tell me straight out.

GLUMOV.   When I was young, there were indiscretions, passions . . .

KRUTITSKY.   Go on, talk. Don't be afraid.

GLUMOV.   As a student, your Excellency . . . I kept more to the old customs.

KRUTITSKY.   What old customs? I hope you weren't a dissenter?

GLUMOV.   I mean I didn't conduct myself like students today.

KRUTITSKY.   How is that?

GLUMOV.   I had my fling, your Excellency. Some stories are told of ungodly hours, little encounters with the police.

KRUTITSKY.   Is that all?

GLUMOV.   Nothing more, your Excellency. I swear to God, there isn't.

KRUTITSKY.   You know, this is even better. It's as it should be. When you're young, you must drink, have your fling, run amuck a bit. Why should you be ashamed? You're not a girl, you know. Well, that means I'm completely at ease concerning your record. I won't be ungrateful. I liked you from the beginning. I've already put in a good word for you at a certain house.

GLUMOV.   Sofya Ignatevna told me. I can't find the words to thank your Excellency.

KRUTITSKY.   Did you propose, perhaps? You know, there's a good deal of money there.

GLUMOV.   I'm something of a fool about money, your Excellency. But the girl is quite good-looking.

KRUTITSKY.   Well, I can't tell you about that. They all look the same to me, my boy. The aunt, I know, is something of a hypocrite.

GLUMOV.   Nowadays, love is unacceptable, your Excellency. But I know from experience what an exalted feeling it is.

KRUTITSKY.   Then let them repudiate love. He who repudiates knows neither passion, nor despair, but he whom it possesses, then he knows. It happened to me in Bessarabia, about forty years ago. I almost died of love. Why are you looking at me like that?

GLUMOV.   Tell me, please, your Excellency.

KRUTITSKY.   A fever seized me. You can't repudiate it then. Well, God bless you, my boy, God bless you. I'm very pleased. You shall be a capitalist. We'll find you a good safe appointment. We need men like you. Will you really be one of us? We need support now, since the greenhorns are beginning to overpower us. But tell me, my dear boy, how much I should pay you for your work?

GLUMOV. You will offend me, your Excellency.

KRUTITSKY. You will offend me.

GLUMOV. If you want to compensate me, then there is something you could do that would make me happy, your Excellency!

KRUTITSKY. What is it? What's the trouble?

GLUMOV. Marriage is such a significant matter, such an important step in life. Please don't refuse me! The blessing of such a high-minded personage of morality would serve as security. Just knowing your Excellency gives me happiness, and to some degree the kinship, although it's only spiritual, would even for the sake of future children . . .

KRUTITSKY. You want me as a sponsor at your wedding, is that it? I don't understand, somehow or other.

GLUMOV. You would make me so happy, your Excellency?

KRUTITSKY. Glad to, glad to. You should have spoken right up. The thing's not so difficult.

GLUMOV. I'll share the happy news with Sofya Ignatevna.

KRUTITSKY. Share it with her. Please do.

GLUMOV. Your Excellency no longer needs me?

KRUTITSKY. No.

GLUMOV. I have the honor to take my leave.

KRUTITSKY. Not a word about my scribbling, mind you. It will soon be printed. Without my name, of course. An editor asked me. Although it's rather strange, he's a very honest fellow; and he wrote so courteously, "Your Excellency would make me so happy," well, and so on. If you hear any gossip about the author's identity, just act as though you don't know.

GLUMOV. I understand, your Excellency! [*Bows and exits.*]

KRUTITSKY. Good-by, my dear boy! Why do we always blame the younger generation? Glumov's a good example, and he's a boy with brains and heart. Of course, he's a bit of a hypocrite when it comes to flattery, and he's too independent. But perhaps it will pass. If he's basically mean, that's bad; but if it's only a mannerism, then there's no great problem. With money and rank it will disappear little by little. His parents no doubt were poor, and his mother a bit of the sponger: "Kiss this one's hand, kiss that one's." Well, it's all a part of him now. Nevertheless, for all that, it's better than rudeness. [SERVANT *enters.*]

SERVANT.   Mrs. Mamaev. She's in the drawing room, sir. I announced that her Excellency is not at home, sir.

KLEOPATRA.   [*Behind the door.*]   Will I disturb you?

KRUTITSKY.   No, no!   [*To* SERVANT.]   Bring an armchair!   [SERVANT *exits, returns with armchair.* KLEOPATRA *enters.* SERVANT *exits.*]

KLEOPATRA.   Oh, my, there you sit—up in your study—so busy, busy. You ought to pay some attention to the girls! But no, you're forever glued to your desk. What an ungracious little old man you are!

KRUTITSKY.   It's all over for me. What a colt I once was. Yes, always on the go! Hee, hee, hee! It's time to give way to the youngsters.

KLEOPATRA.   [*Sits.*]   Nowadays the youngsters are worse than the old.

KRUTITSKY.   Are you complaining?

KLEOPATRA.   Isn't it really true?

KRUTITSKY.   It's true, true. Nowadays there's no poetry, absolutely no feeling of grandeur. And do you know why? Because they no longer give tragedies at the theatre. If they would only bring back Ozerov,[37] why the youngsters would acquire these ticklish, delicate feelings. They ought to present tragedies more often; say, every other day. Yes, and there's Sumarokov, too. Why, I put together a treatise once about the improvement of morals in the younger generation. For the nobility, the tragedies of Ozerov; for the common people, the legal sale of home-made booze. In my day, we knew all the tragedies by heart, but nowadays, what a waste! Why, they don't even know how to read. That's why in my day there was chivalry, yes, and integrity; but nowadays, there's nothing but the drive for money.   [*Declaims.*]

   Must I wait for fate to break off the days' coursing,
   When melancholic days do bring me grief and cursing?
   I will break off.
Do you remember?

KLEOPATRA.   Why shouldn't I remember? You know, I suppose, it's no more than fifty years old. So why shouldn't I remember?

KRUTITSKY.   Sorry, sorry! I think of you as around my age. Oh, I almost forgot to tell you! I'm very pleased with your relative. A splendid young man.

KLEOPATRA.   Don't you think he's a dear boy?

KRUTITSKY.   Yes, yes. You know that you're pampering him.

KLEOPATRA.   In what way, exactly?

KRUTITSKY.   Allow me, I just remembered some more!   [*Declaims.*]

> *Oh, gods! not art of speech from you I pray,*
> *But give me tongue of heart and soul today!*

Oh, how charming!

KLEOPATRA.   In what way do we pamper him?

KRUTITSKY.   As if you don't know! He's getting married. What a bride you've found . . .

KLEOPATRA   [*Startled.*]   Bride! Oh, you're mistaken.

KRUTITSKY.   [*Declaims.*]

> *Oh, mother, that flow of tears, if you can, please stop!*
> *And, you, daughter, the despondency of soul, please drop!*

KLEOPATRA.   Who is she? Who's the girl?

KRUTITSKY.   Oh, good lord! Turusina. As if you don't know. A dowry of two hundred thousand.

KLEOPATRA.   [*Rises.*]   It can't be! It can't be, I tell you.

KRUTITSKY.   [*Declaims.*]

> *In the presence of such news your spirit died;*
> *The painful sighs in your bosom you hide,*
> *But dismal sorrow on your features is seen!*

KLEOPATRA.   Oh, you bore me to death with your poetry.

KRUTITSKY.   But the boy has a good heart, it seems. "Your Excellency," he says, "don't think I'm after the money." He wanted me as sponsor at the wedding. "You will honor me," he says. As if I wouldn't be his sponsor! "I don't want the dowry," he says, "I like the girl." "She's an angel, an angel," he says, with such feeling. Well, now, that's splendid! God bless him. Here you are, something from Donskoy.[38]   [*Declaims.*]

> *When Russians with their word do pledge,*
> *Not without shame would they ever hedge.*

KLEOPATRA   Oh!

KRUTITSKY.   What's wrong?

KLEOPATRA.   A migraine. Ah, I'm really sick.

KRUTITSKY.   Well, that's nothing. It'll soon pass.   [*Declaims.*]

> *Don't you know, that this union is entrusted to those . . .*

KLEOPATRA.   Oh, why don't you stop! Tell your wife that I wanted to wait for her, but I can't, that I feel so terrible. Ah! Good-by!

KRUTITSKY.   But it's nothing. What's wrong? You look the picture of health.   [Declaims.]

> Before her rival she exposes his unfaithfulness,
> And jealous-driven she poisons all his cheerfulness.[39]

KLEOPATRA.   Goody-by, good-by!   [Exits quickly.]

KRUTITSKY.   What's biting her? To hell with these old women! It's worse to manage them than a whole division.   [Takes pad.] To work on this at leisure. Don't let anyone in!   [Exits to the study.]

SCENE TWO

Same room as in the first act. An hour later. With his diary,
GLUMOV *enters through the side door.*

GLUMOV.   At last I've finished it. The whole interesting conversation with Krutitsky has been put down. A curious memorial for posterity! No doubt I laid it on a bit too thick when talking to him. I'm probably too young for this sort of thing. I get carried away. Oh, do I get carried away! Well, it won't harm anything—you can't spoil the porridge with butter. And what a delight my uncle is! To think he taught me himself how to chase after his own wife. And I overdid that a bit, too. That's no laughing matter, either! However much we keep our matchmaking a secret, she will undoubtedly find out. Oh, could she make a fuss. If not out of love, then out of jealousy. Women are envious. Not all of them know how to love, but each and every one of them is a past master when it comes to jealousy.   [GLAFIRA enters.] My dear mama, are you on your way to Turusina's?

GLAFIRA.   Yes, I'm on my way.

GLUMOV.   [Looks at watch. Sternly.]   You are a little late, mama dear. You should go there as soon as you get up. And that means every day. You should practically live there.

GLAFIRA.   It is possible to bore them to death, you know.

GLUMOV.   Well, there's nothing you can do about it. Remember to get in with the servants, the fortune-tellers, and the leeches. And don't spare the gifts. In fact, on your way, buy two snuff-boxes, silver, and not too large. All these leeches take snuff with a passion, and they really love gifts.

GLAFIRA. All right, all right!

GLUMOV. Most important, watch all entrances and exits, so that absolutely nothing questionable can get into the house. In order to do this, humor the servants. You know servants have a way of sniffing things out. Well, good-by! Try to speed up the announcement of our engagement.

GLAFIRA. They say it's impossible to do it any sooner than a week. [*Exits.*]

GLUMOV. Whew! That's a long time! I'll be exhausted. Wealth is swimming straight into my grasp. To let an opportunity like this slip through my fingers would be a pity. No, an unpardonable sin. [*Sits at desk.*] What is it I wanted to add to my diary? Yes, jot down the expenses. [*Writes.*] Two snuffboxes for the leeches. [*Hearing sound of a carriage, crosses to the window.*] Now who's this? Kleopatra Lvovna. What the hell! Does she know, or doesn't she know? We'll see soon enough. [KLEOPATRA *enters.*] You know, I didn't expect such good fortune! If all the Olympian gods were to descend from the skies . . .

KLEOPATRA. Don't get excited. I haven't come to see you. I dropped in to chat with your mother.

GLUMOV. [*To himself.*] She doesn't know. [*Aloud.*] She just left.

KLEOPATRA. I'm sorry.

GLUMOV. [*Indicating a chair.*] Please sit down. You bring happiness to my hut. You illuminate it with your proximity.

KLEOPATRA. [*Sits.*] Yes, we bring happiness. But what do you give us in return? Nothing but unhappiness.

GLUMOV. Unhappiness? Don't you really know what a crime that would be?[40] I could never cause you the slightest distress.

KLEOPATRA. Come, now, am I to believe that?

GLUMOV. Yes, you should!

KLEOPATRA. All right, I will believe you.

GLUMOV. [*To himself.*] She doesn't know. [*Aloud.*] How could I ever cause you distress! I, a passionate, timid youth, have searched long for a girlish heart. With passionate yearning, I sought the eyes of that woman who would command me to be her slave. I would call her my goddess, I would give her my whole life, all my dreams and hopes. But I was poor, unknown, and they all turned away from me. Then you appeared before me. You did not push me aside. You descended to the unfortunate sufferer. You warmed the poor heart without misgivings, and I'm happy. I'm happy, infinitely happy. [*Kisses her hand.*]

KLEOPATRA.   Are you getting married?

GLUMOV.   What! No . . . yes . . . but!

KLEOPATRA.   Are you getting married?

GLUMOV.   I mean, your husband wants me to marry, but I don't think I do. And I certainly have no intention, no desire to marry.

KLEOPATRA.   How my husband loves you, you can see that! He wants to make you happy against your own will.

GLUMOV.   He wants me to marry for money.[41]

KLEOPATRA.   For money? Then you don't care for the bride-to-be?

GLUMOV.   Of course, I don't care for her. How could I possibly . . .

KLEOPATRA.   Then you don't love her?

GLUMOV.   How could I? Really, whom could I deceive: her, or you?

KLEOPATRA.   Maybe a little of both.

GLUMOV.   Why are you tormenting me with your suspicions? No, I see I must stop this.

KLEOPATRA.   How will you stop it?

GLUMOV.   Let uncle get as angry as he wants. I'll tell him in no uncertain words that I don't want to marry.

KLEOPATRA.   Are you sure?

GLUMOV.   I'll tell him today.

KLEOPATRA.   Splendid. What is marriage without love!

GLUMOV.   How could you even think that of me? And aren't you ashamed of yourself?

KLEOPATRA.   Now that I see you really don't care, of course I'm ashamed.

GLUMOV.   [*Ardently.*]   I am yours. Yours, forever yours. Only remember—not a word about this. Not to uncle, not to anyone. I'll arrange everything myself. It's possible you might give yourself away.

KLEOPATRA.   Of course, of course.

GLUMOV.   Now you can see what shyness can lead to. I was afraid to tell uncle right out that I didn't want to marry. I kept cutting him short: "Let's wait and see; what's the hurry?" And now you see how it all turned out. I gave you reason enough to suspect me of misconduct. [*Door bell.*] Now who can that be? As though we need that! [*Goes to door.*]

KLEOPATRA.   [*To herself.*] He is deceiving me. It's clear. He wants to calm me down, so I won't stop the marriage.

GLUMOV.   Kleopatra Lvovna, please go into mama's room. There's someone here to see me. [KLEOPATRA *exits.* GOLUTVIN *enters.* GLUMOV *glances intently at* GOLUTVIN.] Well, sir?

GOLUTVIN.   In the first place, you don't receive guests like this. In the second, I'm tired because I walked all the way here. [*Sits.*]

GLUMOV.   What do you want from me?

GOLUTVIN.   It's nothing. At least twenty-five rubles, and as much more as you'd like. I won't be offended in the least.

GLUMOV.   Oh, so that's it! For charity? Now who told you I'd be willing to donate such a lavish gift?

GOLUTVIN.   I'm not asking for a gift. I'm to be paid for my work.

GLUMOV.   For what?

GOLUTVIN.   I've followed you, watched, gathered information about you and what you've been doing. I've written your biography and added your portrait. I have carefully described your recent activities. Wouldn't it please you to buy the original, or should I sell it to a magazine? You can see, I'm not asking much. I don't price my work too high.

GLUMOV.   You don't frighten me. Get it published! Who will read it?

GOLUTVIN.   Now, you know, I'm not asking a thousand rubles. I know I can't harm you too much; but, all the same, it'd be rather unpleasant, if there's scandal. It's really better for you if nothing were said. Come, now, and hand over the money!

GLUMOV.   You know what they call this, don't you?

GOLUTVIN.   I know. The knack of using circumstances.

GLUMOV.   But would you call it honest?

GOLUTVIN.   I don't know. It's probably more honest than sending anonymous letters.

GLUMOV.   What letters? Can you prove that?

GOLUTVIN.   Don't get excited! It's better to pay. That's my advice.

GLUMOV.   Not one kopek.

GOLUTVIN.   Come, now, you're planning to marry a rich girl. What would happen, if she read it. "Aha!" she would say. Don't quarrel. Just pay! It's bread to me, and peace to you. Come, now, it's really cheap.

GLUMOV.   To pay for what? If you get the habit now, you'll come another time, perhaps.

GOLUTVIN.   Word of honor. What do you take me for?

GLUMOV.   [*Pointing to door.*]   Good-by.

GOLUTVIN.   But I'll go to the next place.

GLUMOV.   Wherever you like!

GOLUTVIN.   Let's have five rubles then. Money isn't everything.

GLUMOV.   I won't give you five kopeks.

GOLUTVIN.   Have it your way. You don't happen to have a cigarette, do you?

GLUMOV.   No. Just get out of my house.

GOLUTVIN.   Pretty soon. I'd like to rest a bit.

GLUMOV.   Did Kurchaev send you?

GOLUTVIN.   No, we've quarreled. He's an honest goose, a bit like you.

GLUMOV.   All right, I've heard enough.

GOLUTVIN.   [*Rises and peeps through door.*]   What is it you have in there?

GLUMOV.   What vulgarity! Go on. Beat it!

GOLUTVIN.   I'm a little curious.

GLUMOV.   Beat it, I tell you.

GOLUTVIN.   [*Leaving.*]   You can't value honor, my dear sir, because you haven't any yourself.   [*Exits into hall.*]

GLUMOV.   If that doesn't take the cake. Well, let him publish it! [*Goes after* GOLUTVIN.]

GOLUTVIN.   [*At the door.*]   Two words only.   [GLUMOV *follows him into hall and closes door.* KLEOPATRA *enters.*]

KLEOPATRA.   No one's here. Where on earth did he disappear? [*Crosses to desk.*]   What's this! It's his diary. Ai, ai! What a devil! This is terrible! Here's a passage about his fiancée. Oh, my God, I knew it was true. He's deceiving me. What an idiot! Here's a little something about me. I feel so terrible I'm going to faint. He's a devil. That's what he is, a devil! [*Dries tears. Thinks for a moment.*] That's an idea! He'd never dream it was I. [*Hides diary in her pocket and walks away from desk.*] Oh, can I make him grovel! How I'll love to see him begging! When everyone turns away, when they all chuck him out like the good-for-nothing he is, then he'll come crawling back to me, meek as a lamb. [GLUMOV *enters.*]

GLUMOV.   Boy, that does it!

KLEOPATRA.   Who was it came by?

GLUMOV.   People like that[42] . . . He wrote a sickening article about me and then came for money. Otherwise, he says, "I'll publish it."

KLEOPATRA.   It's terrible. But what can you say? Why, the man's no more than a hired killer. Who is he, I'd like to know?

GLUMOV.   Why do you want to know?

KLEOPATRA.   Well, I'd like to be on my guard.

GLUMOV.   Golutvin.

KLEOPATRA.   Where does he live?

GLUMOV.   Here one day, there the next. You can get his address at the newspaper office. But why do you ask?

KLEOPATRA.   If someone wants to hurt me, then that's my revenge. A woman has no other course to take. We certainly can't fight duels.

GLUMOV.   You're joking?

KLEOPATRA.   Of course I'm joking. Did you give him any money?

GLUMOV.   A little. He's not expensive, you know. Besides, it's safer. Scandal of any kind is bad.

KLEOPATRA.   What would happen if someone gave him more money?

GLUMOV.   Why should someone? I have no enemies.

KLEOPATRA.   Ah, my poor boy![43] He's upset you, hasn't he? Then you really plan to break your engagement?

GLUMOV.   I do.

KLEOPATRA.   You know, don't you, what you're giving up?

GLUMOV.   Money. Why should I give up paradise—just for money?

KLEOPATRA.   But it's so much money, you know. Two hundred thousand.

GLUMOV.   I know.

KLEOPATRA.   Whoever could do such a thing?

GLUMOV. One who truly loves.

KLEOPATRA. Don't tell me such people exist.

GLUMOV. Here is proof that they do.

KLEOPATRA. What a hero you are. Yes, a hero! Your name shall go down in history. Come to my arms. [*Embraces him.*] Now, good-by, soul of my soul! I'll be waiting for you this evening. [*Exits.*]

GLUMOV. [*Alone.*] Whew! What a load off my mind. And now, to my bride-to-be. [*Takes hat and looks in mirror.*] Of course, all this is really nothing, but in games of chance, better watch your hand. What right have I to the girl, or more important, to the dowry? Absolutely none at all. Guts, that's what it is, sheer guts. A whole castle is swinging in the air—and there's no foundation. At any minute it may fall, smash to bits. You can't help but feel scared. Yes, and be careful. Come, now, there's nothing to frighten me at the moment. I've taken care of Kleopatra Lvovna. I've paid off Golutvin. For the time being I've settled everything. [*Sings.*] Everything's settled, everything's settled. All my troubles have scattered. My hat, my gloves . . . Where are my gloves, where are my gloves? Here they are. [*Crosses to desk.*] In this pocket my wallet, in that my diary. [*Without looking, he fumbles with one hand at the desk, then puts the other in his back pocket.*] My handkerchief is here. [*Turns around to desk.*] What's this? Where is it? [*Opens drawer.*] Where have I put it? What could I have done with it? Boy, wouldn't you know it! Oh, no, it can't be! I know I put it here. I just saw it. Augh! Now where is it? It can't be, it . . . [*Stands silently.*] To pieces, everything's going to pieces . . . and I'm dropping. Yes, dropping into a deep pit. Why did I ever get the habit of a diary? Whatever did I jot down in it? Oh, no! If you do something like I've done, absolutely nothing should be written down! Well, I've just given the public "Diary of a Scoundrel, Written by Himself." But why should I curse myself? Oh, there will be others to do it for me. Who could have taken it? He or she. If he took it, I'll buy it back. He'll be after the money. No trouble here. But what if it were she? In that case, the answer is simply eloquence. A woman's soft-hearted. Yes, gentle and kind. But, you know, there's nothing more vicious in the world than a woman who thinks she's been had. At that moment she's the devil incarnate.

She will devise the most horrifying revenge. She will think up the dirtiest trick possible—something that'd never, ever, enter a man's head. Well, what's to be done? I must do something. To do nothing is the worst thing of all. I shall go straight into the jaws of—the hyena.   [*Exits.*]

ACT FIVE

TURUSINA'S *country home. The same evening. A large terrace at the summer home. A garden in front. Doors at the sides.* KURCHAEV *and* MASHENKA *enter from the drawing room.*

KURCHAEV. How quickly everything has happened.

MASHENKA. I just don't understand it. It's either the most subtle of plots hatched, or . . .

KURCHAEV. A miracle, do you think?

MASHENKA. I don't know. I simply lost my head.

KURCHAEV. I've known him a long time, and there's nothing very special about him. I suppose he's a good man.

MASHENKA. Suddenly he appeared like the irresistible prince in a fairy story. Everyone's excited about him. All auntie's friends recommend him without the slightest hesitation. The spongers see him every night in their dreams. They tell my fortune, and there he is—right in the cards. The fortune-tellers say that he's the one, and so do the pilgrims. At last, Manefa—whom my aunt looks upon almost as a saint—and although Manefa had never seen him, she described his appearance and predicted the very moment he would arrive. How could I object? Auntie holds my fate in her hands, and she is completely charmed by him.

KURCHAEV. That means he gets you and the money. Virtue is rewarded, vice punished. You can't object, and I can't say a thing. So I must beat a retreat in silence. If it were anyone but he, I'd challenge him to a duel. But when I meet a virtuous man, I've had it. I've never gone in for virtue.

MASHENKA. Shush, please! They're coming. [TURUSINA *and* GLUMOV *enter.* TURUSINA *sits in armchair;* GLUMOV *stops at her left and puts his hand on the back of the armchair.* KURCHAEV *stands at the right, eyes slightly downcast, in the most respectful of poses.* MASHENKA *is at the desk, leafing through a book.*]

GLUMOV.   When at last I felt the temptation of hearth and home, I considered the matter most seriously. To marry for money is foreign to my principles. It would have been a business deal, not a marriage—that institution of sacred trust. To marry for love . . . but love, you know, is a transient feeling—an itch of desire. I knew that selecting a mate for life meant something special; something out of fate, if the marriage is to hold fast. I had to find a girl of gentle heart, with whom I could unite with inseverable bonds. I said, "Fate, show me that heart, and I shall resign myself to your commands." I tell you, I expected something of a miracle! There are many miracles in the world, only we don't want to fool around with them.

TURUSINA.   I've said the very same thing myself, but no one listens to me. [*Looks at* KURCHAEV, *who clicks his heels and bows.*]

GLUMOV.   I expected a miracle and the miracle finally came.

TURUSINA.   You don't say! And it came. Oh, that's marvelous.

GLUMOV.   I went to a certain pious woman.

KURCHAEV.   It wasn't Manefa, was it?

GLUMOV.   No, to another. I don't know Manefa. Just as I entered, and before I could utter a sound, the pious woman—even before she saw my face, she was sitting with her back to me—the pious woman spoke, "It's not you who seek a wife; it's she who seeks you. Go, close your eyes, and you will find her." Where do I go, I said, point the way. "As you enter," she said, "the first unfamiliar house, where you've never visited before, seek you there, and there they know you." At first, I was amazed, don't you know, as though I couldn't quite believe it. She told me all this in the morning, and that very afternoon uncle brought me to you. Here there's a bride-to-be, and here they knew me.

TURUSINA.   To be sure, there are many miracles, but few are chosen . . .

KURCHAEV.   When we were stationed in Little Russia, we had a case just like this with a certain Jew . . .

TURUSINA.   I think you ought to take a little walk in the garden. [KURCHAEV *clicks his heels and bows.*][44]

MASHENKA.   [*To* KURCHAEV.]   I'll go with you.   [*They go into the garden.*]

GLUMOV.   Doesn't it strike you as predestination? I haven't even had time to inquire about my fiancée's thoughts and feelings. I was completely satisfied, when she consented.   [GRIGORY *enters.*]

TURUSINA.   Nothing more is really needed.

GRIGORY.   Ivan Ivanych Gorodulin.   [GRIGORY *exits.*]

TURUSINA.   I shall go and dress in something warmer. It's getting damp here.

GLUMOV.   Perhaps if I don't quite appeal to her now, then I will later on. A marriage like ours ought to prove happy and prosperous. A marriage arranged by fate cannot be marred by human error.

TURUSINA.   Those are principles! Everyone should know them by heart, if he wants to know how to live.   [TURUSINA *exits;* GLUMOV *crosses to garden;* GORODULIN *enters.*]

GORODULIN.   How do you do! How much money are you making?

GLUMOV.   I think it's two hundred thousand.

GORODULIN.   How did you ever manage that?

GLUMOV.   Why, you really recommended me yourself. Sofya Ignatevna told me.

GORODULIN.   You don't mean it! When could that have been? Yes, yes, I remember. How did you happen to get on so well with Turusina, especially since you're a freethinker?

GLUMOV.   I don't quarrel with her.

GORODULIN.   But if she talks nonsense?

GLUMOV.   It's impossible to reform her. So why make the effort?

GORODULIN.   Oh, so that's the way it is! Very good. You'll soon have plenty of money. I shall get you into our club.

GLUMOV.   [*Softly.*]   One of these days Krutitsky's treatise will be printed.

GORODULIN.   You don't say? Wouldn't I like to give him a good dressing down!

GLUMOV.   That's quite easy.

GORODULIN.   I should think so, especially with your talent. But it's a bit awkward for you. You're still a very young man, and you might hurt yourself. Someone else ought to speak for you. Let's see. Yes, you will do the writing, and I—there's no other way—and I will sacrifice myself. I'll give it out as my own. Together we can give the old boys a good dressing down.

GLUMOV. We can, we can. You should see what they write.

GORODULIN. We must ridicule everything they write. I'd like to do it myself, but there's really no time. I'm very happy for your good fortune. I congratulate you. We need men like you. Yes, we do. I must confess I've felt the shortage. Oh, there are those who can get the job done, but there's no one who can speak out. The old boys might attack us by surprise. And then, we'd be in for it. Some of our youngsters have brains enough; but they're so very young, you can't allow them to speak out. No one would pay them the slightest attention. We have a chorus, but absolutely no soloists. You, however, could set the tune, and we could all join in. Where's Mashenka?

GLUMOV. Over there. She's walking in the garden.

GORODULIN. I'll go and chat with her. [*Exits.*]

GLUMOV. [*Following.*] I'll catch up with you in a moment. [*To himself.*] It seems that the Mamaevs have just arrived. I've certainly made her see the light! Not only did she consent to my marriage, but she's come here herself. That's really sweet of her. [MAMAEV, KRUTITSKY, *and* KLEOPATRA *enter;*[45] MAMAEV *and* KRUTITSKY *cross to the garden;* KLEOPATRA *stops when she sees* GLUMOV.]

MAMAEV. [*To* KRUTITSKY.] I agree with you in principle, but not in the details.

KRUTITSKY. And why not?

MAMAEV. Why do you always insist on tragedies, why not comedies?

KRUTITSKY. For the simple reason that comedies depict the low, while tragedies portray nobility; and we need precisely nobility.

MAMAEV. Yes, but allow me! Let's examine this issue from all sides. [MAMAEV *and* KRUTITSKY *go into the garden.*]

KLEOPATRA. Well, now, did you find it?

GLUMOV. No. Golutvin swore to God he didn't take it. You know, he even cried.

KLEOPATRA. But who could have taken it? Maybe you lost it somewhere.

GLUMOV. I just can't imagine doing that.

KLEOPATRA. Someone will find it and throw it away.

GLUMOV. It'd be wonderful if they did.

KLEOPATRA. But what are you afraid of? Is it possible there's something there that shouldn't be?

GLUMOV. Nothing special! Effusions of the heart, love notes, passionate tirades, verses on eyes and curls. In short, everything you write for yourself, that if someone else reads it you feel ashamed.

KLEOPATRA. So your diary contains verses on eyes and curls. Well, then don't worry. No one will pay the slightest attention to it. You find diaries like that the world over. What are you doing here alone? Where's your fiancée?

GLUMOV. She's strolling in the garden with young men. There's proof for you. You can see I'm certainly not marrying because I feel like it. Listen, I need the money. And I need position in society. I don't want to be a dear, young boy forever. It's time I became a man. Wait and see the splash I'll make. Oho, what horses I shall drive! No one even knows I'm around now, but suddenly they'll be saying, "Ah, what a handsome man!" Exactly as though I'd just arrived from America. And everyone will envy you.

KLEOPATRA. And why me?

GLUMOV. Because I am yours.

KLEOPATRA. That would be fine, if you could take the money without the bride. But you'll have a young wife, you know.

GLUMOV. That won't stop me. To the girl, my hand. To the money, my pocket. But to you, my heart.

KLEOPATRA. You are a dangerous man. If a girl listens long enough, yes, she may begin to believe you.

GLUMOV. Wait till you see the beautiful trotters I shall drive. Right up to your door.

KLEOPATRA. And I shall be waiting. But now you must run to your fiancée. You shouldn't leave her alone. If you don't like her, then for the sake of appearance, for the sake of propriety, you must pay some attention to her.

GLUMOV. Remember, you're sending me to her yourself.

KLEOPATRA. Run along, run along. [GLUMOV *exits*.] Oh, my, how exultant he looks! Just wait, my friend, mind you don't rejoice too early. [KURCHAEV *enters*.] Where are you going?

KURCHAEV. Home, ma'am.

KLEOPATRA. Home, with such a sad face? Wait. Let me guess

what it is. [KURCHAEV *bows.*] Wait, I tell you. [KURCHAEV *bows.*] Oh, how contrary you are! Wait, I tell you. I need you. [KURCHAEV *bows and remains.*] Are you in love? [KURCHAEV *bows and wants to leave.*] Don't you know anything at all?

KURCHAEV. Permit me to withdraw.

KLEOPATRA. I'm going home early, alone, you may escort me. [KURCHAEV *bows.*] Why are you always silent? Listen. Be frank with me. I'm ordering you, as your aunt. You're in love, I know. Does she love you? Well, answer me! [KURCHAEV *bows.*] I'm convinced that she does. Don't lose hope. Little do you know what surprises may take place.

KURCHAEV. In any other case I would . . .

KLEOPATRA. But why not here and now?

KURCHAEV. Turusina demands such requirements . . .

KLEOPATRA. What requirements?

KURCHAEV. I never in my life expected this. And besides, it just doesn't go with my profession.

KLEOPATRA. What doesn't go?

KURCHAEV. And my upbringing didn't prepare me for . . .

KLEOPATRA. I don't understand you.

KURCHAEV. For the sake of her niece, Turusina is looking for . . .

KLEOPATRA. Well? Go on.

KURCHAEV. How could I have expected it? It rarely happens . . .

KLEOPATRA. What, what?

KURCHAEV. In fact, I've never heard of . . .

KLEOPATRA. Come now, let's have it out.

KURCHAEV. She is looking for a virtuous man.

KLEOPATRA. Well, what about it?

KURCHAEV. I have no virtues.

KLEOPATRA. What do you mean, you don't? I suppose you have only vices.

KURCHAEV. I have no vices, either. I'm simply an ordinary man. It's a weird thing to look for a virtuous man. Well, if it weren't for Glumov, where could she possibly find him? There's no one like him in all Moscow. You'd think miracles would be enough for him. But, no! He sees visions, too. If you don't mind my asking, how on earth can Turusina expect that of everybody?

KLEOPATRA. Now, hold on. Just a moment. It's probably better to possess neither virtues nor vices. [MASHENKA *enters from the garden.*]

MASHENKA.   Good evening, Kleopatra Lvovna.

KLEOPATRA.   I congratulate you! You're getting prettier every day. I'm so glad for your good fortune.

MASHENKA.   Mr. Glumov has so many qualities that I'm terrified. I'm really not worthy of such a husband.

KLEOPATRA.   Where can you possibly look for virtue, if not in your own home? And your aunt, you know . . .

MASHENKA.   I'm so very thankful for her! To tell the truth, it's a good thing to be virtuous, but I can only boast of one: obedience. [TURUSINA *enters.*]

TURUSINA.   [*To* KLEOPATRA.]   It seems quite fashionable nowadays to believe in nothing. I constantly hear, "Why do you allow Manefa in your home! You know, she's a fraud." Would I like to invite these non-believers and show them the kind of fraud she is. I'm very happy for her. Now she will become all the rage, and she'll get a huge practice. Moreover, the city will probably thank me for finding such a woman. You know, I've done a lot for Moscow.

KLEOPATRA.   But where is your fiancé? I don't see him.

TURUSINA.   Mashenka, where is Egor Dmitrich?

MASHENKA.   He's in the garden with Gorodulin. [MAMAEV *and* KRUTITSKY *enter from the garden.*]

TURUSINA.   With all the recommendations of my friends and for several other reasons, I expected to meet an exemplary young man. But when I came to know Egor Dmitrich, he surprised me by surpassing all my expectations.

MAMAEV.   [*Approaching her.*]   Who surpassed all your expectations?

TURUSINA.   Your nephew.

MAMAEV.   I knew you'd thank me for him. I know what's what, I do. I didn't try to marry him off to someone else. I brought him straight to you.

TURUSINA.   It would've been sinful if you hadn't. You know, I'm all alone.

KRUTITSKY.   Yes, Glumov is certain to go far.

MAMAEV.   Of course, with our help.   [GRIGORY *enters.*]

TURUSINA.   And why should I deserve such good fortune? Except for my . . . [*to* GRIGORY.] What do you want? Except for my good works! [SERVANT *hands her an envelope.*] What's this? [*Breaks the seal.*] Some sort of newspaper! It's probably not for me.

KLEOPATRA. [*Takes envelope.*] No, it's for you. As you can see, here's your address.

TURUSINA. It's probably a mistake. Who brought it?

GRIGORY. The postman, ma'am.

TURUSINA. Where is he?

GRIGORY. He left sometime ago, ma'am. [GRIGORY *exits.*]

MAMAEV. Give it here. I'll sort it out and explain it to you. [*Takes envelope and removes a printed page.*] First of all, it's a newspaper. And yet it's not a newspaper, but only one page from a newspaper. In fact, it's one article.

TURUSINA. But isn't it from the newspaper office?

MAMAEV. No, someone who knows you probably sent it.

TURUSINA. Let's hear what you have.

MAMAEV. We'll see soon enough. The article is entitled, "How to Get on in Society."

TURUSINA. That doesn't concern us. Throw it away.

MAMAEV. Why should we? We ought to examine it. Here's a portrait with the inscription, "The sort of husband you don't meet every day." Ba, ba, ba! Why, it's Egor Dmitrich!

KLEOPATRA. Show it to me. My, how interesting. [MAMAEV *gives her the newspaper.*]

TURUSINA. This is some kind of wicked intrigue. He probably has many enemies. [MAMAEV *looks obliquely at* KURCHAEV.]

KURCHAEV. You don't suspect me, do you? I'm no artist. I can only draw pictures of you.

MAMAEV. [*Sternly.*] Yes, yes, I know.

KLEOPATRA. The person who wrote this article must know Egor Dmitrich quite well. You find all the small details of his life. The article may be an invention, though.

MAMAEV. [*Removes notebook from envelope.*] Why, here's something else.

KRUTITSKY. It's his handwriting. I know his writing well. It's his, it's his! If you like, I'll answer for it.

MAMAEV. Yes, it is his handwriting, but here's a note written by someone else. "To prove that everything in the article is true, this diary is enclosed." What should we read—the article or the diary?[46]

KRUTITSKY. Better take the original.

MAMAEV. We'll begin with the page that's been marked. It's a series of expenses. "Manefa, twenty-five rubles, she gets another twenty-five . . . She's an utter fool, but she takes up fortune-telling. Teaching her is like pouring water through a sieve. She barely got it right. Finally had to send her a bottle of rum. She got fifteen more rubles at home. It's unfortunate that such a lucrative trade is taken up by stupid people. Curious to know what she takes from Turusina. Remember to ask later on! To the two leeches at Turusina's, for telling fortunes by cards and for repeating dreams in which they see me every night: seven and a half rubles to each; silver snuffboxes, ten rubles for the pair."

TURUSINA. [Sniffs spirits.] I'll get rid of them all, each and everyone. To be evil is sinful, but to be kind is stupid! How can I live after this?

KLEOPATRA. Don't complain. You're not the only one who's been deceived.

MAMAEV. "For three anonymous letters to Turusina, fifteen kop . . ."

MASHENKA. So that's where the letters came from, ma tante!

TURUSINA. I see, my dear. Forgive me. I was mistaken to take the trouble to arrange your life. I see that I lacked the intelligence and the strength. Do as you want. I shan't stop you.

MASHENKA. [Softly.] My choice is already made, ma tante.

TURUSINA. That's splendid. He won't deceive you, because he's promised you absolutely nothing. [KURCHAEV bows.] And I certainly plan to send Anfisa and the others away.

KRUTITSKY. And replace them with others?

TURUSINA. I don't know.

MAMAEV. Do you want me to continue?

TURUSINA. Go on if you like. It makes no difference to me now.

MAMAEV. "To Mamaev's servant, for delivering to me his master by fraud, having taken advantage of his weakness for apartment hunting—to this benefactor of mine, three rubles. I feel it's much too little." Following this is a long conversation with me, really quite uninteresting. "The first visit to Krutitsky. Oh, Muse! Let us sing of the valiant man and his projects. My admiration for you is limitless, venerable old boy! Reveal to us and to the world, how you managed—having lived to the ripe old age of sixty—how you managed to preserve, in all its virginity, the brain of a six-year-old child?"

KRUTITSKY.   Now, that's enough! Stuff and nonsense . . . Who cares to hear that?   [GORODULIN *enters.*]

MAMAEV.   [*Doesn't notice* GORODULIN's *arrival.*]   If you please, I see here a few words about Gorodulin. "Once during some sort of stupid quarrel about horse racing, a certain gentleman called Gorodulin a liberal. Gorodulin was so overjoyed with the name, that for three days he ran all over the city telling everyone he was a liberal. So nowadays he's considered a liberal." You know, that's a good description.

KRUTITSKY.   A good description! You should read about yourself. Let's see if his description resembles you.

GORODULIN.   So you consider it a good description?

MAMAEV.   Ah, Ivan Ivanych, I didn't know you were here. Just see how we've all been painted.   [*Gives diary to* GORODULIN.]

GORODULIN.   And who is this modern Juvenal?

MAMAEV.   My nephew, Glumov.

TURUSINA.   Please, Ivan Ivanych, please return this manuscript to its author and ask him to leave here inconspicuously.   [GLUMOV *enters.* GORODULIN *respectfully hands him the diary.*]

GLUMOV.   [*Accepting the diary.*]   And why inconspicuously? I don't plan either to explain or to justify myself. I'll only say that you will soon regret having ordered me out of your circle.

KRUTITSKY.   My dear sir, our circle is made up of honest, decent people.

ALL.   Yes, yes, yes.

GLUMOV.   [*To* KRUTITSKY.]   And when did you, your Excellency, suspect that I was a dishonest man? [47] Perhaps, with your penetrating mind you became convinced of my dishonesty the moment I began to polish up your treatise? After all, what kind of educated person would undertake that sort of work? Or, you discovered my dishonesty that moment in your study when I, with all servility, raged wildly over your sentences and cringed slavishly before you? No, then you were quite prepared to kiss me. And if this unfortunate diary hadn't fallen into your hands, you'd have believed me an honest man forever.

KRUTITSKY.   But, of course, yet . . .

GLUMOV.   [*To* MAMAEV.]   You, my dear uncle, also suspected it yourself, didn't you? Was it the day you taught me to flatter Krutitsky? Or was it when you taught me how to chase after your own wife, in order to divert her from other admirers—when I minced and made excuses, said I didn't know how, and seemed ashamed? You saw I was pretending, but you were pleased because I let you have full range to teach me some kind of sense. I have far more brains than you, and you know it. Yet when I pretended to be an idiot and asked you for all sorts of advice, you were overjoyed and prepared to swear that I was the most honest fellow alive.

MAMAEV.   Well, that doesn't count. It's all in the family.

GLUMOV.   You, Sofya Ignatevna, I deceived you, and I feel guilty about it. That is, I feel guilty about Mashenka, but I'm not sorry to have deceived you. You pluck some sort of half-drunk peasant off the street, and you take her word when it comes to choosing a husband for your own niece. Whom does your Manefa know, whom could she possibly have named? Of course, the person who gave her the most money. It's a good thing I dropped by. Manefa might have proposed some sort of fugitive, and you would have given in to whatever happened.

TURUSINA.   I know one thing for certain. There's no truth on this earth, and I'm convinced of it more and more with each passing day.

GLUMOV.   Well, what about you, Ivan Ivanych?

GORODULIN.   There's nothing to say. You are the most delightful of men! Here's my hand on it. And everything you've said about us, that is, about me—I really don't know about the others—is the complete truth.

GLUMOV.   You need me, ladies and gentlemen. You can't get on in the world without a person like me. If I weren't around, there'd be someone else like me. You'll find someone worse than me, and you'll say, "Ah, this one's worse than Glumov, but all the same he's a good fellow." [*To* KRUTITSKY.]   You, your Excellency, have position in society, rather urbane, we might say. But in your study, when you're alone with a young man standing at attention and humbly repeating "yes, sir" and "your Excellency" after every word, then—at that moment—you're in seventh heaven. To an honest man, you'll refuse your patronage, but to that capering jackass in your study, you'll bustle about and break your neck doing him a good turn.

KRUTITSKY.   You are abusing our lenience, sir. You've overstepped yourself.

GLUMOV.   Excuse me, your Excellency! [*To* MAMAEV.] My dear uncle, you also need me. Even your servants refuse to listen to your instructions, not for all the money in the world. But I listen free-of-charge.

MAMAEV.   That's enough! If you don't understand . . .

GLUMOV.   I understand. And you, Ivan Ivanych, you need me.

GORODULIN.   I need you. Yes, I need you.

GLUMOV.   To borrow clever phrases for your speeches . . .

GORODULIN.   To borrow clever phrases for my speeches.

GLUMOV.   To write criticisms together.

GORODULIN.   To write criticisms together.

GLUMOV.   And you, aunt, you need me.

KLEOPATRA.   I certainly won't quarrel with you, and I don't blame you for anything.

KRUTITSKY.   [*To* MAMAEV.] Don't you know, I noticed immediately . . .

MAMAEV [*To* KRUTITSKY.] So did I at once. There was something about the eyes.

GLUMOV.   You both saw absolutely nothing. My diary tipped you off. How it fell into your hands, I don't know. There's enough stupidity in every wiseman. But please know, ladies and gentlemen, that from the moment I entered your circle, I was only honest when I was writing in this diary. What was it in my diary that offended you? Did you find anything new about yourselves in it? You constantly say the same things about each other. Only you don't say them face-to-face. If I had read to each of you separately exactly what was written about the others, you all would have cheered me on. If someone has the right to feel offended, to be angry, raise hell, then I'm the one. I don't know who, but one of you honest people stole my diary. You've taken everything from me: money and reputation. You're driving me away, and you think that's it. That the whole matter is over. You think that I'll forgive you. No, ladies and gentlemen, there'll be plenty to pay for this. Good-by. [*Exits. Silence.*][48]

KRUTITSKY.   But you know, ladies and gentlemen, whatever you might say, he is, all the same, a business-like fellow. We must punish him; but, I suggest, that in a little while, we might invite him back into our little circle.

GORODULIN.   Absolutely, without fail.

MAMEV.   I agree.

KLEOPATRA.   Leave it all to me.

THE FOREST

THE FOREST

I. COMPOSITION

In the spring of 1870 Ostrovsky began working on *The Forest*. Since *The Scoundrel*, he had published two new plays, *An Ardent Heart* (1869) and *Wild Money* (1870). In the first he had returned to the scene of *The Storm*, his fictional town of Kalinov in the upper Volga region. In *Wild Money* he brought back Glumov, less powerful than before but still trying to make his mark in the world. As he worked on his thirtieth original play, he turned again to Kalinov, but in place of the provincial townspeople and merchants he concentrated on the landed nobility. In place of the role-playing Glumov, he introduced two traveling professional actors who shatter the tedious *byt* of those living in the backwoods.

Ostrovsky began *The Forest* early in May, stopped long enough to make a translation of a play from the French, and then continued his work until the last of September. "I am diligently writing a play," he wrote to F. A. Burdin, "but I can scarcely finish it by October." He worked sporadically on *The Forest* throughout the fall and finally completed it about the middle of December. It was too late in the season, he decided, to try for a production in either Moscow or Petersburg. In January 1871, *The Forest* was published in the journal *Home Notes*.

The first draft of *The Forest* differed from the final version. The play was originally conceived as essentially a domestic comedy. Neschastlivtsev and Aksyusha were brother and sister, children of Gurmyzhskaya's brother. The plot revolved primarily around the love relationship of Gurmyzhskaya and Bulanov. Aksyusha appeared only in the fourth act, in which Bulanov declared he loved her so much it was driving him out of his mind. Neschastlivtsev was simply a professional actor who delighted in playing roles in life situations. For example, when he persuaded Vosmibratov to hand over the money, Neschastlivtsev said, "What an excellent role I played today."

In the development of *The Forest*, Ostrovsky changed the plot by making the love story of Aksyusha and Petr primary and by subordinating the love story of Gurmyzhskaya and Bulanov. He added elements to increase the social *byt* and eliminated details to decrease the family *byt*. For example, Vosmibratov as the rising power in the community was given greater significance, while Neschastlivtsev was given qualities, as Albert Kaspin noted, which approximated those of the *raznochintsy* in the seventies. In short, Ostrovsky changed the play from a domestic to a social comedy.

As soon as he finished the play, he sent a copy to his brother M. N. Ostrovsky in Petersburg. Within a week a reading of the play was given there, and the playwright received word of an enthusiastic reception. In January 1871, the playwright himself read *The Forest* aloud to an audience in Petersburg assembled to support the Literary Fund. The play was also submitted to the Fifteenth Uvarov Competition. Although Ostrovsky had received the Uvarov Prize twice, *The Storm* in 1860 and *Sin and Sorrow are Common to All* in 1863, the jury rejected *The Forest*. Upset by the decision, P. V. Annenkov—in a letter to M. N. Ostrovsky—concluded that the jury was composed of those who exhibited "not a crumb of taste, not a spark of poetic feeling, not a sign of understanding masterly constructions in literature . . ."

The negative response by the Uvarov jury was echoed by other critics. N. Starkhov, for example, was displeased with the satirical treatment of Gurmyzhskaya, Bulanov, Milonov, and Bodaev. The characters of the first two had been only sketched, whereas the dialogue of the last two at times brought laughter.

> But this laughter did not contain the true comic; this comic of the lowest sort, which ought rather be called pockmarked . . . [especially] in the relation to the district council *(zemstvo)*, which is glimpsed at the end of the comedy when Bulanov intends to enter *zemstvo* activities.

The Forest soon found support. Naturally, the editors Nekrasov and Saltykov-Shchedrin of *Home Notes* judged the play favorably. Nekrasov called it "a splendid piece," and P. M. Sadovsky liked it so much he wanted his son Mikhail to play Bulanov. "How charming it is!" Turgenev wrote Ostrovsky, "The character of the 'tragedian'—one of your most successful." In 1880 the poet A. N. Pleshcheev saw an amateur production of *The Forest*, called it "an excellent piece," and pointed out that Neschastlivtsev was a "bright ray" in "the kingdom of darkness."

> You are not able not to fall in love with this unfortunate ragamuffin, who is alone in this dark environment, in this thick forest, where he has found himself, appearing as the bearer of human, noble, elevated ideas.

Subsequent criticism of *The Forest* has generally followed the response of Nekrasov, Turgenev, and Pleshcheev. The play today is considered one of Ostrovsky's masterpieces.

II. STAGE PRODUCTIONS

The first production of *The Forest* at the Aleksandrinsky (1 November 1871) was unsuccessful. Ostrovsky was personally unable to assist in its preparation, and Burdin as Neschastlivtsev was wrong for the part. The playwright's brother felt that Samoilov should have played the role, but Ostrovsky had promised it to Burdin for his benefit performance. The first production at the Maly (26 November 1871), on the other hand, received an enthusiastic reception. In 1885, a year before his death, Ostrovsky recalled the occasion.

> This production clearly showed that the Moscow public loves and values me: when after the fifth act . . . I came on stage, the whole audience in the theatre stood up; I alone of all Russian writers was awarded this honor.

In the Maly performance N. M. Medvedva, S. V. Shumsky, and S. P. Akimova created brilliant interpretations of Gurmyzhskaya, Schasetlivtsev, and Ulita.

The Forest immediately entered the Russian repertory, but not until 1880 at Brenko's theatre in Moscow was there an outstanding performance of Neschastlivtsev. M. I. Pisarev played the role and, together with V. N. Andreev-Burlak as Schastlivtsev, set high standards which not only enthralled audiences but also served as models for subsequent productions. Andreev-Burlak found elements of humor which even Shumsky had missed, while Pisarev gave a fully rounded interpretation of Neschastlivtsev. Ostrovsky himself came backstage after the performance, S. V. Maksimov recalled, "completely emotional, in tears." "What have you done to me?" the playwright questioned Pisarev. "You have broken my heart! [The performance] is extraordinary. . . . It is highly artistic." Pisarev wrote to Ostrovsky and explained that the greatest share of the success belonged to the playwright. "*The Forest* ran two seasons with such success," Ostrovsky later wrote, "that it was impossible to get a single seat the day before [any performance]."

The Forest was the most popular of Ostrovsky's plays. From 1875 to 1917 the comedy was performed 5,106 times in Russia. After the Revolution, *The Forest* continued its record. For example, in 1939 there were 514 performances; in 1940, 588 performances. Even today in

362   FIVE PLAYS OF ALEXANDER OSTROVSKY

Russia *The Forest* may be counted among Ostrovsky plays which remain in repertory.

After the Revolution, the stage productions of *The Forest* at the Maly (1918, 1936, 1937) and those (1918, 1936, 1948) at the Pushkin, formerly the Aleksandrinsky, have been judged outstanding. The Moscow Art Theatre production, opening 11 May 1948, received high praise by Russian critics. The production stressed certain characteristics of Vosmibratov and thereby created a new interpretation of the play. "The merchant is unable to break the chief precept of his life: grab, loot, circle, squeeze, filch, but—store up the ruble," one reviewer pointed out and concluded, "And there is no power that will stop him!" *The Forest* has received experimental productions, such as Meyerhold's 1924 version, and it has also been staged in countries outside Russia.

III.   NAMES OF THE CHARACTERS

Several names indicate the attitude or bent of the characters. Like Mamaev in *The Scoundrel*, the name Gurmyzhskaya is of Tartar origin. In his plays Ostrovsky used names of Tartar origin only for characters of the nobility. Neschastlivtsev incorporates a word meaning unfortunate, unhappy, unlucky, while his fellow actor's name means the opposite—fortunate, happy, lucky. The young heroine is named Aksinya (Aksin'ya), but she is called Aksyusha throughout the play. The former name approximates the feeling of hardship; the latter name suggests unspoiled sincerity. The name Vosmibratov suggests the following combinations: eight brothers; take or seize the brothers; you—we—brothers.

The stress of the names is as follows: Raísa Pávlovna Gurmýzhskaya, Aksínya Danílovna (Aksyúsha), Evgény Apollónych Milónov, Uár Kirílych Bodáev, Iván Petróv Vosmibrátov, Petr (pronounced Pyotr) or Pétya, Alekséy Sergéevich Bulánov, Gennády Neschastlívtsev, Arkády Schastlívtsev (Arkáshka), Karp, Ulíta, Terénka.

THE FOREST

Les

A Comedy in Five Acts

CHARACTERS

RAISA PAVLOVNA GURMYZHSKAYA, *a widow in her early fifties; very wealthy landowner. She is dressed in an unpretentious manner, almost as though she were in mourning, and she always has a workbox in her hand.*

AKSINYA DANILOVNA (AKSYUSHA), *her distant relative; a poor girl of about twenty; dressed neatly but poorly, a little better than a housemaid.*

EVGENY APOLLONYCH MILONOV, *a rich neighbor, about forty-five, neatly groomed hair; fastidiously dressed with a rose-colored necktie.*

UAR KIRILYCH BODAEV, *another rich neighbor, about sixty, retired cavalry officer; closely clipped gray hair, with a large mustache and whiskers. He wears a black frock coat, tightly buttoned, with military crosses and medals; a crutch in his hand. He is a little deaf.*

IVAN PETROV VOSMIBRATOV, *a merchant, dealing in timber.*

PETR (PETYA), *his son.*

ALEKSEY SERGEEVICH BULANOV, *a young man who has failed to complete his education at the gymnasium.*

GENNADY NESCHASTLIVTSEV, *a traveler on foot.*

ARKADY SCHASTLIVTSEV (ARKASHKA), *another traveler on foot.*

KARP, *Raisa's lackey.*

ULITA, *the housekeeper.*

TERENKA, *a boy, servant of Vosmibratov.*

ACT ONE

The Gurmyzhskaya country estate, about five versts¹ from the district town. A large drawing room. Directly upstage are two doors: one leading outside; the other, to the dining room. A window and a door, leading to the garden, are to the right of the audience. To the left are two doors: one leading to inner rooms; the other, to the corridor. Expensive, antique furniture. Trellises and flowers. Near the window is a small work table. To the left are a round table and several armchairs. KARP *stands by the door leading to the garden. Enter* AKSYUSHA.

AKSYUSHA. Has Raisa Pavlovna called me?

KARP. That she did, miss. The guests have just come, so they're still in the garden.

AKSYUSHA. [*Having taken a letter from her pocket.*] Listen, Karp Savelich,² would you be able to . . . ?

KARP. What can I do for you, miss?

AKSYUSHA. Deliver this. You know the one I mean.

KARP. Yes, but how young lady? You know it's . . . well . . . a little awkward now. It's true, isn't it, that your aunt would like to marry you off to the young master?

AKSYUSHA. Well, it makes no difference. Do as you please. [*Turns away toward the window.*]

KARP. Oh, all right. I'd like to. Since it's you, no reason why I . . . [*Takes the letter.*]

AKSYUSHA. [*Gazing out the window.*] Has Raisa Pavlovna sold the forest?

KARP. Sold it to Ivan Petrov. We're selling everything, miss, but what for?

AKSYUSHA.   She doesn't want to leave anything for the heirs. And the money can always be given away, even to outsiders.

KARP.   I think that must be it, miss. Pretty sharp idea.

AKSYUSHA.   I hear she wants the money for my dowry.

KARP.   May God grant it.

AKSYUSHA.   [*Very earnestly.*]   Oh, don't ask God, Karp Savelich!

KARP.   Well, it's up to you, miss. I only meant it's much better to let the money go for the dowry, than where it usually goes, like where the other money went.

AKSYUSHA.   Where the other . . . and where exactly did the other go?

KARP.   Well, young lady, I don't think you'd even understand, and I'm not about to twist my tongue around to explain it. Aleksey Sergeich[3] is coming here.   [*Walks away from the door.* AKSYUSHA *looks out of the window. Enter* BULANOV.]

BULANOV.   [*To* KARP.]   What do you say, have you rolled my cigarettes?

KARP.   No, not yet, sir.

BULANOV.   And why haven't you? You know I told you.

KARP.   You told me to do all sorts of things. So when could I?

BULANOV.   You don't because you spend too much time prancing around. That's the trouble. Keep it up, and I'll tell Raisa Pavlovna.

KARP.   No, you won't tell her. Why, you're even afraid to smoke in her presence.

BULANOV.   Afraid? Look here, just roll those cigarettes! I'm not going to tell you again.   [*Having seen* AKSYUSHA, *he crosses to her and, presumptuously, puts his hand on her shoulder. His manner is impudent and casual.*]

AKSYUSHA.   [*Quickly turns around.*]   What are you doing? Are you out of your mind?

BULANOV.   [*Taking offense.*]   Oh, my! Excuse me, please. Think you're some kind of duchess, staring at me like that? You pretty thing, you.

AKSYUSHA.   [*Almost through tears.*]   Why do you insult me? I've done nothing to you. What am I here, a plaything for anyone who walks by? I am a human being, the same as you.

BULANOV.   [*Indifferently.*]   No, listen to me. If you want to know the truth, I like you. A lot.

AKSYUSHA.   Oh, as if it matters. You think that gives you the right to touch me?

BULANOV.   How can you be angry at something you know nothing about? Big deal! So you're not about to be touched, hmm? You belong to me, and I can't touch you. And who do you think will stop me?

AKSYUSHA.   [*Sternly.*] Suppose I'm not yours, but somebody else's? What will you do then?

BULANOV.   Stop this silly nonsense. I'm sick and tired of it. Keep it up, and you'll spoil the whole affair.

AKSYUSHA.   What affair?

BULANOV.   What? What do you mean, what? As if you don't know. All right, I'll tell you. Raisa Pavlovna would be tickled to death if I married you. And whatever tickles Raisa Pavlovna . . .

AKSYUSHA.   Ought to turn out?

BULANOV.   Now you've got it. Look, you and I are poor people. Think we should hang around till they ship us off somewhere? No, thanks. Where could I go? Back to mama again? Become a magpie outside some stranger's courtyard?

KARP.   Be careful, sir. Ulita is coming. [*Enter* ULITA *who is looking for something.*] What are you doing here?

ULITA.   Seems I've forgotten . . .

KARP.   You haven't forgotten a thing. So don't try that story around here. You have your own department, and you don't see us walking in on you. [ULITA *exits.*] Well, that's better now. Damned old woman!

BULANOV.   What do you say? A straightforward business deal. Think you understand now?

AKSYUSHA.   Yes, I understand.

BULANOV.   Why not stop being so stubborn? I'm not impressed with your playing the high and mighty lady around here. You know Raisa Pavlovna promises to give a lot of money. What more do I want? If I get it, I'll make the sign of the cross with both hands.

AKSYUSHA.   You might buy some people with money, but you can't buy everyone.

BULANOV.   [*Smiling contemptuously.*] Moral platitudes! [*Seriously.*] You don't know what money can buy, or you'd talk differently. Obviously, you've never seen poverty? Look here, right now we could look forward to a life of comfort. . . . Don't you know people sell their souls to the devil for money? They don't turn around and refuse it. [ULITA *appears.*]

KARP. Why are you darting back and forth? We've seen too much of you. We try to keep the place clean, you know.

ULITA. Don't tell me I can't come in!

KARP. Why don't you take a little rest? You're rushing around like a cat on fire. If they call you, then that's another matter. [ULITA *exits.*]

AKSYUSHA. You won't get kindness by force, Aleksey Sergeich.

BULANOV. Well, I'll get what I want. You won't wriggle away from me. As for anyone better than me, you know you won't find him around here.

AKSYUSHA. [*Calmly and quietly.*] You are mistaken. If I wanted to look, then I'd find him. And, perhaps, I've already found him. [*To* KARP.] If Raisa Pavlovna asks for me, I'll be in my room. [*Exits.*]

KARP. [*Crossing to* BULANOV.] Oh, master, master!

BULANOV. Yes, Karp, what is it?

KARP. You are young, sir, very young.

BULANOV. I know I'm young.

KARP. And everything is going badly.

BULANOV. What can I do about it?

KARP. It doesn't speak well for you. But you must try . . .

BULANOV. However much I may try, I can't suddenly add on years. I've just come out of the gymnasium.

KARP. To the devil with the gymnasium. There are people who've never been inside a gymnasium, and they're pretty clever.

BULANOV. Clever? Clever about what?

KARP. About everything, especially at snatching up whatever swims by. [ULITA *appears in the corridor.*] Again? Tphew![4] Go along, scat, you damned old woman.

ULITA. [*Stealing away.*] Smart aleck!

BULANOV. [*Deep in thought.*] Yes, it may be? Well, so what?

KARP. Aha, there you are, with your "yes, it may be." Why do you worry the young lady? What advantage is there in it?

BULANOV. All the same . . .

KARP. You must be more careful, sir. Ulita doesn't creep around here for nothing. Everything she sees or hears, she carries off to

the mistress. And do you think the mistress will like what she
hears? No one knows what Raisa Pavlovna has in mind for you.
She may be the grand lady, but you know she acts like a woman
in everything. You'll never know for certain what goes on in her
mind. First, one thing; then, another. Think she changes her mind
seven times a week? More than likely, seven times a day. And
here you are, talking about getting married—when she may force
you to do something quite different. Don't think you can do what
you'd like to. You were brought here to be taken care of, because your mama has nothing, nothing at all. But here you want
. . . Tell you one thing you ought to do—keep looking in her eyes.
BULANOV.   In her eyes?
KARP.   Yes, that's what I said. Go and look at her, and keep
looking, because you're completely dependent on her. Then, after
a while, from something she may say or do, you'll know what
she has in mind. Wait, the mistress is coming here. [*Exits.*
BULANOV *smoothes out his hair and gently twists his mustache.*
Enter RAISA, MILONOV, *and* BODAEV.]
RAISA.   I was saying to you, gentlemen, and I'll repeat it again.
No one understands me, no one at all. The only ones who do are
our governor and Father Grigory.⁵
MILONOV.   And I, Raisa Pavlovna.
RAISA.   Perhaps.
MILONOV.   Raisa Pavlovna, believe me. Everything is grand, and
everything is marvelous . . .
RAISA.   I believe you. Indeed, I do. Sit down, gentlemen.
BODAEV.   [*Clearing his throat.*]   I'm sick and tired of this.
RAISA.   What was that?
BODAEV.   [*Rudely.*]   Nothing.   [*Sits down some distance apart
from the others. Aloof.*]
RAISA.   [*Having seen* BULANOV.]   Aleksis, Aleksis!⁶ Are you dream-
ing? Gentlemen, I'd like to present a young nobleman, Aleksey
Sergeich Bulanov.   [BULANOV *bows.*]   His life makes a very in-
teresting story, and I'll tell you all about him soon. Aleksis, take
a walk in the garden, my dear. [BULANOV *exits.* RAISA *and*
MILONOV *sit down at the table.*]
MILONOV.   He's your relative, no doubt?
RAISA.   No, he's not a relative. But why should relatives have
the only right to our compassion? All people belong in the same

family. Gentlemen, why should I live only for myself? Everything that I have, all my money belongs to the poor. [BODAEV *starts to listen attentively*.] I happen to be a sort of clerk for my money. The real owners are every poor man, every unlucky man on this earth.

BODAEV.   As long as I live, I will not pay a single kopek. Let them take my estate and sell it.

RAISA.   You're not going to pay whom?

BODAEV.   I said, the District Council.[7]

MILONOV.   Oh, Uar Kirilych, nobody's said a word about the District Council.

BODAEV.   They don't do a damn thing except rob people.

RAISA.   [*In a loud voice*.]   Come over a little closer. You can't hear what we're saying.

BODAEV.   Yes, I can't hear. [*Sits at the table*.]

RAISA.   This young man, gentlemen, is the son of one of my friends. I met her last year in Petersburg. Before that, some time ago, we knew each other so well we were like sisters. Later on, we parted. My husband died, and she married. I told her not to do it. Having experienced it myself, I felt a distinct loathing for matrimony.

BODAEV.   For matrimony, but not for men?

RAISA.   Uar Kirilych!

BODAEV.   Now, how should I know? I'm only asking. You know there's a difference.

RAISA.   [*Jokingly*.]   And for men, especially men like you.

BODAEV.   [*Rises, leans on his crutch, and bows*.]   Oh, I must really thank you for that one.

MILONOV.   By the severity of her life, Raisa Pavlovna lights up our whole district. Indeed, our moral atmosphere, if you'll permit me to say, smells sweetly with her virtues.

BODAEV.   About six years ago, when the rumor started that you were coming to live in the district, we were all scared to death of your virtues. Why, all the wives started to make peace with their husbands; all the children, with their parents. And in many homes, they even started to speak more gently.

RAISA.   Oh, you're joking. Yes, you are. And do you think they gave me this respect without a battle? But we're wandering away from the point. When we met in Petersburg, my girlhood friend had been a widow a long time. And, to be sure, she deeply regretted that she hadn't followed my advice. She wept as she introduced me to her only son. A boy, as you can see, who's grown into manhood.

BODAEV. Looks good enough to be a soldier.

RAISA. You shouldn't judge him by his outward appearance. You know, the poor thing's in bad health, and you can imagine the unhappiness he's been through. Because of this he lagged behind his companions. When I met him, he was still in school, and I think he had about a couple of years to go. You know, he had a little mustache. And his thoughts, well, they were certainly quite different from those of his companions. Indeed, women were beginning to get interested in him. And there he was, going to school with boys, naughty little boys. He felt humiliated, bored to death. He kept away from people and walked alone on god-forsaken streets.

BODAEV. Sure it wasn't on the Nevsky?

RAISA. He was suffering, and his mother was suffering, too. But she had no means to lift the weight from their shoulders. Their estate was completely squandered. The son had to go to school in order to care for his mother. Yet both time and desire for study had long disappeared. Well, now, gentlemen, think what you like of me. I made up my mind to do three good deeds at once.

BODAEV. Three? That's curious.

RAISA. Soothe the mother, give money to the son, and settle affairs for my niece.

BODAEV. I'll be damned. Three.

RAISA. I invited the young man here for the summer. I thought, let them get to know each other. And then I'll let them marry, giving my niece an excellent dowry. Well, now, gentlemen, I am satisfied that you know my intentions. I am above suspicion, as you know. But if you chance to hear evil gossip, you will be able to explain what's going on.

MILONOV. All that is noble and all that is marvelous will find its own valuation, Raisa Pavlovna. Who on earth would dare . . .

BODAEV. Well, why on earth shouldn't a person dare? You can't stop a person, can you? There's no censorship for that.

RAISA. I care very little about public opinion, though. I'm doing something worthwhile, and I shall go on doing it. So let them say whatever they like. Lately, gentlemen, some sort of strange presentiment has been torturing me. The thought of an early death never leaves me for an instant. Gentlemen, I shall die soon. I even desire to die. Yes, I do.

MILONOV.   You're not serious, you can't be! Live. Yes, live!

RAISA.   No, no. And don't beg me, please.

MILONOV.   You know there will be tears, bitter tears.

RAISA.   No, gentlemen, if I don't die today or tomorrow, it will be soon, in any case. I must do my duty for my heirs. Gentlemen, help me with a little advice.

MILONOV.   Hear, hear!

RAISA.   My only close relative is my husband's nephew. As for my niece, I hope to settle her affairs while I'm still alive. I haven't seen my nephew for fifteen years, and I haven't received a bit of news about him, either. But he is alive, I know. I hope there is nothing to stop me from naming him as my sole heir.

MILONOV.   Don't see why you can't.

BODAEV.   Then, why are we going on and on and on about it?

RAISA.   Thank you. I thought as much myself. He hasn't forgotten me, either. He sends me presents every year, but he never writes letters. Where he is, nobody knows; so I can't write to him. And I owe him something, too. One of his father's creditors paid off an old debt. Although the sum isn't too large, it still troubles me. It's as if he were hiding from me. I've received his presents from every corner of Russia. This one from Arkhangelsk, that one from Astrakhan, another from Kishinev, one from Irkutsk.

MILONOV.   What kind of work does he do?

RAISA.   I don't know. I had him trained for the army. When his father died, he was just a boy of fifteen, almost without any money at all. At the time I was a young thing, but I had pretty firm ideas about life. And I brought him up according to my own method. I prefer a tough education for youngsters, tough and simple—what they call copper-money training. I didn't do it out of stinginess. No, but out of principle. I am convinced that simple people, ignorant people, live much happier lives than we do.

BODAEV.   Nonsense! You can't buy anything good with copper money, especially happiness.

RAISA. But you know, he didn't complain about his education. In fact, he even thanked me. Gentlemen, I am not against education, but I am not for it, either. Corruption of morals comes about from two extremes. From ignorance and from excessive education. Good morals lie in between.

MILONOV. Hear, hear!

RAISA. I wanted this boy to go through the tough school of life. I prepared him for soldiering and then let him work it out in his own way.

BODAEV. That's the simplest.

RAISA. Sometimes I sent him money. But I confess, it was little, very little, indeed.

BODAEV. And he started stealing, no doubt.

RAISA. You're mistaken. Just see what he wrote to me. I always carry this letter with me. [*Takes letter from her pocket and gives it to* MILONOV.] Read it, Evgeny Apollonych!

MILONOV. [*Reads.*] "My auntie and benefactress, Raisa Pavlovna. This statement as to my conformity with the circumstances of my life, I write in a letter to you, with chagrin in the presence of shortages, but not without despair. Oh, fate, fate! Under the burden of my own ignorance, put to shame in front of my comrades, I predict failures in my career for successes achieved."

BODAEV. Up to now, scarcely flattering for you or for him.

RAISA. Keep on listening.

MILONOV. "But I'm not scared. I see glory ahead for me, glory! Although your meager charity more than once brought me to the very edge of poverty and utter ruin, I still kiss your hand. From my youthful years as a minor until I reached adulthood, I was in complete ignorance as to what lay in store for me. But now everything before me is pretty clear."

BODAEV. Aren't you ashamed that your nephew, a nobleman, writes like a soldier's bastard son? [8]

RAISA. The point cannot be found in the words alone. Oh, no! As far as I'm concerned, it is beautifully written. I see here a pure, unspoiled feeling. [KARP *enters.*]

KARP. Ivan Petrov Vosmibratov has come with his son, ma'am.

RAISA. You will excuse me, gentlemen, if I receive a peasant in your presence.

BODAEV.   Only you'd better be careful when he's around. He can swindle you with one hand tied behind his back.

RAISA.   You know, don't you, he's a good family man. That's the important thing.

BODAEV.   Family man or not, he can strip you clean before you know it.

RAISA.   I don't believe it. No, I don't. It can't be true.

MILONOV.   It looks as if you and I are in perfect agreement. I, too, am a hot-tempered defender of family men and family relations. [*To* BODAEV.] Uar Kirilych, when were people really happy? [9] Under tents. Isn't it too bad that we have traveled so far away from primeval simplicity, that our paternal relations and our paternal measures in application to our lesser brothers have been severed? Severity in treatment, yes. But love in our souls. Oh, what harmony and grace! But today we are separated by a law. Yes, a law has come about, but with it came coldness. In the old days, they say there was absolute rule, but at the same time there was warmth. Why so many laws? Why try to legislate relationships? Let the heart legislate them. Let everyone recognize his own duty. The law is written in the souls of men.

BODAEV.   That might work if there were fewer scoundrels. As it is there are too many, more than we can handle.

RAISA.   [*To* KARP.] Tell Ivan Petrov to come in. [KARP *exits.* VOSMIBRATOV *and* PETR *enter.*] Sit down, Ivan Petrovich.

VOSMIBRATOV.   [*Bows and sits.*] Petr, sit down. [PETR *sits on the edge of the chair, next to the door.*]

MILONOV.   Do you want me to go on reading?

RAISA.   Go ahead. He won't bother us.

MILONOV.   [*Reads.*] "Oh, necessity, thou inscrutable! I thank you. Yes, I do. Soon my name will be covered with immortality, and with it yours will never die for the sake of posterity, children and grandchildren. Once more I thank you for everything. Yes, indeed. Your humble and obedient nephew, child of nature, fostered with unhappiness, Gurmyzhsky."

RAISA.   [*Taking the letter.*] Thank you, Evgeny Apollonych! Let's ask a simple man. He will tell the truth. Ivan Petrovich, isn't that letter well written?

VOSMIBRATOV.   First rate, ma'am! Say you wanted to turn in a petition, where'd you find a better?

MILONOV.   But you know this letter is twelve years old. What's going on now with your nephew and his celebrated glory?

RAISA.   I tell you I don't know.

BODAEV.   He'll surprise you, all of a sudden.

RAISA.   No matter what happens, I am proud of this letter. And I am very pleased to have found gratitude among people. To tell the truth, I'm very fond of him. I beg you, gentlemen, please come to dinner here day after tomorrow. You won't refuse to witness my will, I hope? I think it shall be ready then. Be that as it may, please come anyway.

BODAEV.   I'll be here.

MILONOV.   Believe me. All that is noble and all that is marvelous...

RAISA.   Of course, should you wish to judge me harshly, I'm somewhat to blame when it comes to my heir. You see, I've already sold part of the estate.

VOSMIBRATOV.   I'd go so far as to say, ma'am, quite a bit. Especially since you've taken to living in Moscow and St. Petersburg.

RAISA.   I am generous to a fault. You won't find me stingy with my neighbors.

VOSMIBRATOV.   That's so, ma'am. And you sure aren't stingy with yourself, either. And why not? You're the owner. We're all human, after all.

RAISA.   But for the last seven years I've been living quite differently.

VOSMIBRATOV.   You can say that again, ma'am. Not a smidgen of gossip about something or . . . Well, you've been keeping to the straight and narrow, ma'am.

RAISA.   Oh, but you know that even before . . . Well, there's no use talking about it. I must say that I live very economically.

BODAEV.   Excuse me. And don't think I'm talking about you. I'm not. So don't get angry, please. But really, we've had so many of our noble estates completely ruined by old women. If a man throws his money away, there's usually some sort of reason in his extravagance. But there's no limit to an old woman's stupidity.[10] Say the old woman wants to give her lover a dressing gown. Why, she'll sell the grain right out of her fields, at the wrong time of the year, and for next to nothing. Or, say the old woman wants to give her lover a skullcap and tassel, she'll sell a whole forest of high-grade timber to the first swindler who comes by.

VOSMIBRATOV. You can say that again, your Excellency. Give women the freedom to do what they like, and not much good will come out of it.

BODAEV. Is that what you think?

MILONOV. [To VOSMIBRATOV.] Oh, Vanya, Vanya,[11] how rude you are!

VOSMIBRATOV. I hear that all the time, sir.

MILONOV. All the same, Vanya, you must be more careful, my friend. And you are mistaken on this point. The estates have been ruined, not by the ladies, but because there is too much freedom.

BODAEV. What freedom? Where is it, I'd like to know?

MILONOV. Oh, Uar Kirilych, I'm for freedom myself. But I am against embarrassing measures. Well, of course, for the sake of the people, for those who are morally immature, it is necessary that . . . But, you must admit what it is we are coming to! Merchants going bankrupt, noblemen spending all their money. You must admit that in the end it will be necessary to limit everybody's expenses by law, to set up a standard according to ranks, classes, jobs.

BODAEV. Well, what are you waiting for? Go ahead and submit your project. It's the time for projects nowadays. Everybody's doing it. You won't surprise anyone. Don't be afraid, either. I'm sure that sillier ones than yours have been turned in. [Rises. MILONOV rises, too. BODAEV and MILONOV bow. VOSMIBRATOV and PETR rise.]

RAISA. [Conducting BODAEV and MILONOV to the door.] Gentlemen, I shall expect you day after tomorrow. [MILONOV and BODAEV exit.] Sit down, Ivan Petrovich!

VOSMIBRATOV. [Sitting.] Petr, sit down! [PETR sits.] You sent for me, my lady?

RAISA. Yes, I had to see you. It means a lot to me. Did you bring the money?

VOSMIBRATOV. No, ma'am, I must confess I didn't take it with me. If it's necessary, just say the word, and I'll drop it by tomorrow, for sure.

RAISA. If you would, please. Won't you have some vodka?

VOSMIBRATOV. Beg your pardon! It's not the right time for us . . . Well, why not? We're all human, after all.

RAISA. Remember to bring everything that we mentioned in our agreement.

VOSMIBRATOV. I will, ma'am.

RAISA. I don't remember exactly, but it seems . . .

VOSMIBRATOV. Now don't you go on worrying about it.

RAISA. It seems to me fifteen hundred rubles. [*Digging into her workbox.*] Where is the note? Don't tell me I dropped it somewhere? I can't find it anywhere.

VOSMIBRATOV. Better look for it real good, ma'am.

RAISA. Well, at any rate, it's not enough money for me. You'll buy another section of the forest from me, won't you?

VOSMIBRATOV. Why don't you just go ahead and sell the whole forest? Don't really see why you're hanging on to it. You know, with a forest, ma'am, it's just one sin after another. Believe it, or not. The peasants go in and steal, and you end up taking them to court. In that part of the forest next to town, why every fugitive, every hobo, finds shelter in it. And as for the servants, I mean the female servants, they go into the forest for mushrooms and berries. But they come out with something a lot different than mushrooms or . . .

RAISA. No, I won't sell the whole forest.[12] Why, an estate just isn't an estate without a forest. It isn't pretty at all. Perhaps, later on . . . But you buy that section which is nearest to town.

VOSMIBRATOV. Though I don't have the money now, why shouldn't I buy it, if you'll sell it at the right price? But I must confess I came about some other goods.

RAISA. I don't understand.

VOSMIBRATOV. You have a relative, a young girl, not exactly rich . . .

RAISA. What's that got to do with this?

VOSMIBRATOV. It seems he saw her, or met her here. My boy, I mean. [PETR *rises.*]

RAISA. Your boy?

VOSMIBRATOV. Petr, ma'am. I tell you the boy's a lamb, he is. Because of his silliness or lack of gumption, he took a liking to her, ma'am. Well, of course, he and I don't cost a lot. But if God will let you do a good deed and give him, say, four thousand rubles worth of forest to chew on . . . Well, we'd both be satisfied. With your help, he'll be able to get a good start and make a living.

RAISA.   I'm very much obliged to you, but excuse me, my friends. You see, the girl has a suitor already. In fact, he's living in my home now. Perhaps you've heard all kinds of nonsense in town about it. But I can say right now that he is the girl's suitor.

VOSMIBRATOV.   [To PETR.]   Hear that? Fallen right on your nose, haven't you! Only you've made a fool of your father. Just wait till I get you alone.

RAISA.   And don't think I'm snubbing you, either. Your son would be an excellent choice for her. It's only because of my good graces that she happens to have a nobleman as a suitor. She really isn't worthy of him.

VOSMIBRATOV.   We understand, ma'am.

RAISA.   The matter is already settled, so let's drop the subject. We'll talk a little about the forest. Buy it, Ivan Petrovich, please.

VOSMIBRATOV.   I don't have the money. No, I don't, ma'am.

RAISA.   It's not possible.

VOSMIBRATOV.   If the price won't hurt me, then it's possible, ma'am.

RAISA.   And what exactly would you give for it?

VOSMIBRATOV.   [Having thought about it.]   Will five hundred rubles, ma'am, be about right for you?

RAISA.   You're not serious, you can't be. You paid fifteen hundred for that other piece, and you offer five hundred for this. You know this piece is larger and much better.

VOSMIBRATOV.   That's so, ma'am. Excuse me. It just slipped out without thinking. I really don't feel like taking the matter up right now. Well, what price did you have in mind?

RAISA.   Well, at least two thousand. Somebody offered me that price.

VOSMIBRATOV.   My advice. Take it.

RAISA.   Well, I didn't want to insult you.

VOSMIBRATOV.   I'm very much obliged to you for that. But I'll say right off, it's not worth fussing about.

RAISA.   Ivan Petrovich, for shame! Here I am, an orphan. When it comes to business, I'm only a woman. It's a sin to harm an orphan. You shouldn't go against God in this.

VOSMIBRATOV. If we went against God, our merciful creator, ma'am, there'd be no place to hide, when our time comes. It's impossible to go your own way without God. For us He is our only refuge.

RAISA. Well, there you are then. You know yourself I need the money for a good purpose. The girl is fully grown, she's not very bright, and I would like to settle her affairs while I'm still alive. What good would it do her if I weren't around to look after her? You know what sort of people there are nowadays! You're a father yourself, and you have a daughter, too. So just figure out whether you'd like to see your own . . .

VOSMIBRATOV. Well, if she starts playing around . . .

RAISA. Ivan Petrovich, watch your language. You know I don't like it. Now, listen carefully. Since it's you, I'll drop my price five hundred rubles and let you have it for fifteen hundred.

VOSMIBRATOV. There won't be a bit of profit.

RAISA. Well, I don't want to talk about it. But you ought to be ashamed. Yes, you should.

VOSMIBRATOV. Too much money, but you're welcome to it, ma'am. [*Having waved his hand.*] I'll go through with it since I've made a little profit before.

RAISA. Remember I must have the money tomorrow.

VOSMIBRATOV. Just take it easy. I'll bring it. But you should have the note ready, so you won't worry tomorrow about being paid in full for timber cut and sold.

RAISA. That means you'll bring exactly three thousand.

VOSMIBRATOV. What's right and proper, I'll bring, ma'am. You have a note for the money on the first deal. When it comes to this deal, it's up to you. The way I feel about it, I'm ready to forget it. You never take my word, anyway. You pick up notes and receipts on every trifle, so why should you doubt me this time? I can't read or write. Time and again I don't know myself what's put down on the note, exactly. I've worried my boy here up to the point I always drag him with me, so he can add his own name. All right if I say good-by?

RAISA. Good-by. [VOSMIBRATOV *and* PETR *exit.* KARP *enters.*]

KARP. Ma'am, you asked for the young lady. She's waiting to come in.

RAISA. Call her. [KARP *exits.*] Oh, she's a cunning, impudent hussy, all right. She's never grateful, never ready to please me. She gets on my nerves. Oh, does she! [AKSYUSHA *enters.*]

AKSYUSHA. [*Lowering her eyes and speaking in a soft voice.*] What do you want?

RAISA. I suppose you know why I invited Aleksey Sergeich here?

AKSYUSHA. Yes, I do.

RAISA. Please don't put on your high and mighty ways around me. Well, I'm not certain about it yet. You know you might get emotional and make a mistake or two. [*With a laugh.*] I'd be sorry for you.

AKSYUSHA. Why should I get emotional?

RAISA. Oh, good Lord! Don't you think he's good enough for you? Silly, silly question. But I plan to keep my eyes open and see if you deserve him. I've told everyone that he is your suitor, and I hope they will spread the news. But I'm going to think about it, do you hear? I'm going to think about it. [ULITA *enters.*]

ASKSYUSHA. You must ask me, too, you know.

RAISA. I know when to ask you. Don't you try to tell me. At the moment I want everyone to think that he is your suitor. That's the way I want it. But God help you if you flirt with him, or start taking any liberties!

AKSYUSHA. What liberties? You're not serious!

RAISA. Don't tell me you've been insulted? Oh, that's sweet, isn't it? She's been insulted. You know, don't you, my dear, that I can say whatever I think about you? You're a girl right off the streets. In fact, you spent most of your time sledding with brats.

AKSYUSHA. I wasn't sledding all the time. By the time I was six years old, I was helping my mother, working day and night. On holidays, it's true, I did go sledding with the gang. Well, I grew up without a single doll or toy. And you know very well that by the time I was ten I was living in your home, and I was told to follow your example.

RAISA. Bad inclinations are rooted in childhood. That's the reason you shouldn't get angry, my dear, if we keep you under rather strict supervision. [*With a laugh.*] Although he's your suitor, the grapes are still green.

AKSYUSHA. A suitor! Who wants a suitor like that?

RAISA. Well, I see it's beyond your understanding.

AKSYUSHA.   He doesn't amount to a thing. Besides, he's not very bright.

RAISA.   Nonsense! You are stupid, while he is clever, handsome, well-educated. Go ahead and tell me. Yes, tell me. You said it on purpose, didn't you? You're not blind. You're only trying to irritate me, aren't you?

AKSYUSHA.   What difference should it make to you?

RAISA.   What difference? He's my choice, that's what. And you're questioning my taste. Obviously, he's no match for you. Fashionable ladies, women who know, have simply been enchanted by him.

AKSYUSHA.   That scarcely brings honor to them.

RAISA.   Oh, oh, she's arguing with me. And how can you, of all people, tell the difference between honor and dishonor?

AKSYUSHA.   I'm a girl right off the streets, scarcely a fashionable lady. So I'm not tempted with treasures like that.

RAISA.   But I tell you to marry him.

AKSYUSHA.   You know I'm not going to marry him. So why continue this comedy?

RAISA.   Comedy? Don't you dare say . . . All right, let's say it is a comedy.[13] I feed you and clothe you, and I shall force you to play this comedy. You haven't the right to ask about my intentions. I'll do what I like, and that's all there is to it. He is the bridegroom, and you are the bride. Only you will sit in your room under lock and key. That's what I want, and that's what you'll do.

AKSYUSHA.   [*Having looked into her eyes.*]   Nothing more?

RAISA.   Nothing. Now get out of here. [AKSYUSHA *exits.*]   No, just wait and see. Better people than you have danced to my tune. [*To* ULITA.]   Come here.

ULITA.   Oh, ma'am, what can I do for you, dear ma'am?

RAISA.   Come closer, sit down where you are, and listen.

ULITA.   [*Crosses and sits on the floor.*]   Yes, dear ma'am, I'm listening.

RAISA.   You understand me, don't you? You know how strictly I keep watch over everyone in the house?

ULITA.   Yes, I know. How can I help knowing?

RAISA.   I don't trust Aksyusha. She's a cunning witch. She sees Aleksey Sergeich a lot. I don't like to see her around him that much. When I'm around, of course, she doesn't dare try anything. But you know I'm not with them all the time. They can meet in the garden and in rooms when I'm somewhere else. So I ask you . . . In fact, I'm going to order you . . .

ULITA.   I understand, dear ma'am, I understand. Your little hand, please. [*Kisses* RAISA's *hand.*] It's miraculous how well I understand you. Been sticking to them for a long time, like I was a shadow. I hang round and when they leave, I'm a step behind. Where they are, so am I.

RAISA.   [*Having thought a bit.*]   I'm very fond of you because you're sensible and sharp.

ULITA.   That I am, dear ma'am, sensible and sharp. Why, only yesterday I ripped my little old dress to shreds, crawling in the bushes. Yes, and pricked and stung all over, creeping through the nettles. Just so I could hear everything they were saying to each other.

RAISA.   Ripped your dress? No great loss there. In the future don't go thinking about your dress. I have plenty. I'll give you a better dress than the one you tore.

ULITA.   [*Furtively.*] Well, only a little while ago, they were together, right here.

RAISA.   What do you mean, only a little while ago?

ULITA.   Oh, that fool Karp kept getting in the way. But all the same I was able to see a thing or two.

RAISA.   What was it you saw?

ULITA.   Well, you might say she was acting pretty sweet on him. And as for him, well, it looked as if he . . . [*makes gesture with hand*]   turned her down, like he couldn't care less.

RAISA.   No? You're certain about that, aren't you? [*Looks directly into her eyes.*]

ULITA.   Well, it looked as if he . . .   [*Makes gesture with hand.*]

RAISA.   Well!

ULITA.   It looked as if . . . as far as I could see, that he wasn't exactly altogether . . . that he was now very . . .

RAISA.   I think you're lying to me.

ULITA.   Oh, no, dear ma'am. I've got eyes that're real good for seeing something like that. It looked as if he had something different on his mind.

RAISA.   Now, just tell me how on earth you can know what he has on his mind? Seems to me, you've gone too far.

ULITA.   But with my passion for duty . . .

RAISA.   No matter how great your passion for duty may be, you just can't climb into somebody else's mind. Which means, there's no use chattering about trifles. [*Silence.*]   Ulita, we're both the same age. . . .

ULITA.   Dear ma'am, I just know I'm older than you.

RAISA.   I don't want to hear that. It's useless. And I know, and you know, we're both the same age.

ULITA.   Really, dear ma'am, I've always thought . . . But why should we even count? We are both orphans, widows, sick at heart.

RAISA.   Come now, you're not very sick at heart. You remember, don't you, what you've done since you've lived with me? No matter how kind I was, or how stern, nothing much seemed to help you.

ULITA.   Yes, that's the way it was, dear ma'am, exactly the way. But it all happened so long ago. The last six years since you've been here, in such a quiet . . .

RAISA.   But I haven't even looked . . .

ULITA.   Damn me if I have, either!

RAISA.   Listen, Ulita. Tell me, only speak frankly. When you happen to see a handsome young man, don't you get the feeling, or doesn't it suddenly strike you, how wonderful it would be to fall in love?

ULITA.   Go on with you! An old woman like me? I've forgotten, dear ma'am, I've forgotten everything.

RAISA.   Come now. You, an old woman! No, go on, tell me.

ULITA.   Well, only if you order me.

RAISA.   All right, I order you.

ULITA.   Perhaps when I'm dreaming. [*Softly.*]   Then sometimes it comes over me like a sort of cloud.

RAISA.   [*Deep in thought.*]   Go away, you disgust me!   [ULITA *rises, crosses to one side, and looks askance at* RAISA. RAISA *rises and crosses to the window.*]   You know he's not a bad boy.[14] The first time I saw him he made a good impression on me. Oh, I'm still young, in my heart. I think I'll know how to fall in love when I'm seventy. If only common sense didn't . . . He doesn't see me . . .   [*Makes gesture with hand.*]   Oh, you beautiful boy, you! Yes, strict rules in life mean a lot. [*Turns and sees* ULITA.]   Well, let's go. Instead of one dress, I'll give you two.   [*They exit.*]

ACT TWO

The forest. Two narrow roads, leading from opposite sides up-stage, meet near the proscenium at one corner. In this corner is a painted post on which are attached two signs. The sign on the right says, "To the city of Kalinov." The sign on the left, "To Penky estate, Landowner Madame Gurmyzhskaya." Next to the post is a wide, low stump. Behind the post, in the triangle between the roads, along the cleared space is small shrubbery—no taller than a man's height. Sunset. AKSYUSHA *enters from the forest, the left side, and sits on the stump.* PETR *enters from the forest, the right side.*

PETR. [*In a loud voice.*] Terenka! [A BOY *enters from the forest, the right side.*] Climb up that tree over there, the one by the edge of the forest. Be sure you keep looking on both sides of the road. Better not go to sleep, or somebody'll shoot you down for a grouse. Hear me?

TERENKA [*Shyly.*] Yes, I do.

PETR. If it turns out it's daddy, then you'd better somersault out of that tree like a baby bird learning to fly and get straight to me. [*Turns* THE BOY *around and gives him a light slap.*] Now get going. [THE BOY *starts off.*] Come on, fellow, you haven't got all day. [THE BOY *exits into the forest.*]

AKSYUSHA. [*Crossing to* PETR.] Hello, Petya!

PETR. [*Kissing her.*] Hello. How's everything?

AKSYUSHA. About the same, maybe a little worse.

PETR. Seems I've heard everything's a lot better.

AKSYUSHA. Oh, that's a good story. Why do you say that?

PETR. But you're marrying a nobleman? It's better, ma'am. Maybe he knows various languages. And it sure beats everything that he wears short overcoats, not the kind I wear.

AKSYUSHA. [*Putting her hand over his mouth.*] Now that's enough. Stop it. You know, don't you, that it won't happen. So why go on and on?

PETR. What do you mean, it won't? When your aunt herself a little while ago . . .

AKSYUSHA. Don't be afraid, don't.

PETR. Then better say right out, whose you are? Your own, or somebody else's?

AKSYUSHA. My own, my darling, my own. And I know for sure she won't force me, either. Something different's going on.

PETR. You mean, she's bluffing?

AKSYUSHA. Something like it.

PETR. If you only knew what I was going through a little while ago. Daddy was starting to put in a good word for you, but she tells him right off, "The girl's spoken for." Believe you me, while they went on talking it was just as if they scalded me in boiling water. And then daddy swore for two hours on end. He rested a little, and then started all over again. "You," he says, "made me a fool in front of the lady."

AKSYUSHA. She'd be happy to get me off her hands, but she'd hate to part with the money. What about your father, still looking for a dowry?

PETR. He won't be happy with less than three thousand. "If we can't get three thousand for you," he says, "then it wasn't worth even feeding you." "Why," he says, "I'd marry you off to a nanny-goat, if she came with money."

AKSYUSHA. There's nothing to do, then. I can't get three thousand anywhere. You asked me whose I was? Well, whose are you? Your own, or not?

PETR. I belong to someone else. But why talk about me? I'm condemned to hard labor, bound hand and foot forever, and I can't break out.

AKSYUSHA. Why are you so sad, distant?

PETR. And what do I have to be happy about? You know, when I go through the forest, I find myself looking at the trees, trying to see which bough is the stronger. I suppose you're no happier than I am.

AKSYUSHA. I'm neither bored nor happy. I died a long time ago. But forget your unhappiness, at least when we're together.

PETR.   All right, let's. But there's damn little to be happy about.

AKSYUSHA.   Oh, you silly boy, you. How can you be unhappy, when you have a girl who loves you?

PETR.   Well, why shouldn't you love me? I'm not one of your Mordovian heathens. And what better thing do you have, except to love? That happens to be your only responsibility.

AKSYUSHA.   [*Angrily.*]   You can leave right now, if that's what you think.

PETR.   Now, don't get upset over nothing at all. I'm all mixed up now. I've been thinking for three days, and my brain won't come up with anything. My thoughts have been going this way and that.

AKSYUSHA.   What is it you're thinking about? You ought to think about me. You know you should.

PETR.   I am thinking about you. I've got two things I can do. One is to keep after daddy. Today, of course, he'll swear at me a little, but I'll go after him tomorrow, for sure. Well, tomorrow we'll go over it again, even if he lays me out. And day after tomorrow I'll go after him again, and so on until he gets sick of swearing. I'll keep it up day after day, and I won't let up. Either he'll club me to death, or he'll do it my way. Either way we'll find a solution.

AKSYUSHA.   [*Having thought a little.*]   What's the other thing you can do?

PETR.   The other's a little out of the ordinary. I have three hundred rubles of my own. But if, for luck, I slip a fistful out of daddy's money-drawer, then you can be sure we'll be rolling in cash.

AKSYUSHA.   And then what'll we do?

PETR.   And then it's "Good-by to misfortune!" Grab the money, then together we'll jump on a little troika, and shout, "On with you, my darlings!" We'll drive to the Volga. Zzip-whoa! On to a steamer. It travels so fast downstream that no one on shore can catch up to us. In one day we'll reach Kazan; in another, Samara; in a third, Saratov. We'll live to our heart's content. Nothing'll cost too much for us.

AKSYUSHA.   And if you meet someone you know?

PETR.   Before you know it, I've closed one eye. There you are, blind in one eye, and no one can recognize me. That's the way

I'll go about for three days. I'll tell you about a situation that really happened to me once. You see, daddy sent me to Nizhny on business, and warned me not to dally. But wouldn't you know I met some friends in Nizhny, and they trapped me into going with them to Lyskovo. What could I do? If they found out about it at home, there'd be trouble, for sure. Then and there I slipped on a kaftan,[15] bound up my face, and left. Sure enough, one of daddy's acquaintances was on the steamer. I don't hide from him, you see. I walk around pretty boldly, and he looks me up and down. Then I see him coming up to me. "You," he says, "where are you from?" I answer, "From Myshkino." I've never been there in my life. "Somehow," he says, "your face is familiar." So I answer, "No wonder," and then, you see, I go right past him. He comes up to me a second time, like he did before. He comes up a third time, and tries the same thing. He's starting to get to me by now. So I say, "Your face is familiar to me, too. Weren't we in jail together in Kazan?" That's what I said in front of everybody. He acted like he couldn't jump back fast enough. Just like I'd shot him out of a rifle. What a meeting that was!

AKSYUSHA. When we've run through the money, what happens then?

PETR. I haven't thought that one out yet. Either we go and confess, or pick out a pretty steep bank. A deep place where the water swirls around like a funnel, and then like an axe, we'll go swimming the way axes do. Better think a little more about that.

AKSYUSHA. No, Petya, we'd better try the first thing you thought of.

PETR. You mean, worry him to death?

AKSYUSHA. Yes. Well, but maybe then, if . . . then we'll see. Tomorrow late at night be sure to sneak over to our garden. They go to bed early at our place.

PETR. Sure enough. [THE BOY *runs in.*] What is it?

THE BOY. Daddy. [*Exits, running.*]

PETR. [*Quickly.*] Well, that's it, my girl. Dig in and start running as fast as you can. Good-by. [*The kiss and exit in opposite directions. From the right side upstage appears* NESCHASTLIVTSEV. *He is about thirty-five, but appears much older. Dark hair, with a large mustache. His features are sharp, deeply marked, and quite mobile—traces of an unquiet and intemperate life. He is dressed in a long and wide coat, made of sail-cloth. He wears a gray shabby hat with a wide brim, and large Russian boots. He carries a thick, knotted stick. Strapped on his back is a small traveling case, like a knapsack. Apparently he is worn out; he often stops, sighs, and casts gloomy and sullen glances. At the same time* SCHASTLIVTSEV *appears from the opposite side. He is about forty. His face looks as if it were rouged; the hair on his head, like threadbare fur; his mustache and imperial are thin and fine, the color of red ashes. His eyes are quick, expressive; both shy and mocking at one and the same time. He wears a light blue necktie, short jacket, short close-fitting trousers, colored half-boots, and a boy's cap on his head— all quite threadbare. On a stick, over his shoulders, are hanging an overcoat of light shiny material and a bundle in a colored handkerchief. He is worn out, breathes heavily, and looks around with a smile that is neither sad nor happy. They meet.]*

NESCHASTLIVTSEV.   [*Gloomily.*]   Arkashka!

SCHASTLIVTSEV.   It's I, Gennady Demyanych.[16] Seems I'm all here.

NESCHASTLIVTSEV.   Where are you going, and where are you from?

SCHASTLIVTSEV.   From Vologda to Kerch, sir, Gennady Demyanych. How about you, sir?

NESCHASTLIVTSEV.   From Kerch to Vologda. You traveling on foot?

SCHASTLIVTSEV.   On my own legs, sir, Gennady Demyanych. [*In a half-fawning, half-joking manner.*]   How about you, sir, Gennady Demyanych?

NESCHASTLIVTSEV.   [*In a deep bass.*]   In a four-wheeled coach. [*Heatedly.*]   Can't you see for yourself? What are you asking for? Jackass!

SCHASTLIVTSEV.   [*Shyly.*]   No, I just, sir . . .

NESCHASTLIVTSEV.   Let's sit down, Arkady!

SCHASTLIVTSEV.   On what exactly, sir?

NESCHASTLIVTSEV.   [*Pointing to the stump.*]   I'll sit here, and you—wherever you like. [*Sits, takes off traveling case, and puts it next to himself.*]

SCHASTLIVTSEV.   What kind of a knapsack do you have, sir?

NESCHASTLIVTSEV.   An excellent piece. Made it myself, brother, for the road. Light and roomy.

SCHASTLIVTSEV.   [*Sits on the ground next to the stump.*]   Good enough for the person who has something to pack. What exactly do you have in it, sir?

NESCHASTLIVTSEV.   A suit of clothes, brother, good ones made by a Jew in Poltava. Later on, when I was playing during the Ilinskaya, following a benefit performance, I received a lot of clothing. A collapsible hat, brother, two wigs; I have a good pistol here, which I won at cards from a Circassian in Pyatigorsk. The lock is broken; somehow or other, when I'm in Tula, I'll get it repaired. Too bad I don't have a frock coat. Had one all right, but in Kishinev I traded it off for a Hamlet costume.

SCHASTLIVTSEV.   Why on earth do you need a frock coat, sir?

NESCHASTLIVTSEV.   I can see you're still stupid, Arkashka, now that I take a good look at you. Well, I'm on my way now to Kostroma, Yaroslavl, Vologda, Tver. Say I join a troupe; then I must appear before the governor, the chief of police, make visits to the city, won't I? Comedians don't make visits, because they're jokers; but tragedians—why, they're up in society, brother. And what do you have in your bundle?

SCHASTLIVTSEV.   A library, sir.

NESCHASTLIVTSEV.   A big one?

SCHASTLIVTSEV.   Thirty plays with music, besides.

NESCHASTLIVTSEV.   [*In a bass voice.*]   Do you have dramas?

SCHASTLIVTSEV.   Only two, sir, both of them vaudevilles.

NESCHASTLIVTSEV.   Why carry trash like that?

SCHASTLIVTSEV.   Worth money, sir. I also have some small stage properties, such as decorations, ribbons . . .

NESCHASTLIVTSEV.   What'd you do, grab all that?

SCHASTLIVTSEV.   I don't think of it as a sin. They withhold my salary.

NESCHASTLIVTSEV.   And where are your clothes, hmm?

SCHASTLIVTSEV.   Here, what you see on me, sir. And I haven't had any others for a long time, sir.

NESCHASTLIVTSEV.   Well, what on earth do you do in the winter?

SCHASTLIVTSEV.   I, Gennady Demyanych, am accustomed to it, sir. On a long trip it's especially hard, sir. You know it yourself: everybody is good at something; and the beggar, at inventions. They carried me all the way to Arkhangelsk, rolled up in a large carpet. When they arrived at a station, then they unrolled it; but whenever we started off in the carriage, then they rolled me up again.

NESCHASTLIVTSEV.   Warm?

SCHASTLIVTSEV.   Not bad. I got there, sir. And it was a lot lower than thirty below. The winter trip was by the Dvina; a draught between the banks, the wind from the north, and we rode right into it. So you're on your way to Vologda, sir? There're no troupes there now.

NESCHASTLIVTSEV.   And you're bound for Kerch? And there are no troupes in Kerch either, brother.

SCHASTLIVTSEV.   What's to be done, sir? Gennady Demyanych, I'll set off for Stavropol or Tiflis. Not too far away from here, sir.

NESCHASTLIVTSEV.   The last time you and I met was in Kremenchug, wasn't it?

SCHASTLIVTSEV.   In Kremenchug, sir.

NESCHASTLIVTSEV.   At that time you were playing the lover. What was it, brother, you did afterward?

SCHASTLIVTSEV.   Afterward, I changed to playing comedians, sir. But nowadays everybody and his brother are trying to take over. The educated have conquered us: bureaucrats, army officers, university graduates—all are climbing on stage. You can't make a living nowadays. One day I was a comedian, the next day, sir—a prompter. How's that for a fellow with inspired talent, Gennady Demyanych? A prompter!

NESCHASTLIVTSEV.   [With a sigh.]   Everyone ends up there someday, Arkady, my boy.

SCHASTLIVTSEV.   We had one little path open, Gennady Demyanych, and they've closed that now.

NESCHASTLIVTSEV.   Simple to see why. Doesn't take much cleverness at all to play the clown. You ought to try playing the tragedian! No one tries to take over the tragedian's line.

SCHASTLIVTSEV.   You know yourself that there are no good players among the educated, Gennady Demyanych.

NESCHASTLIVTSEV.   No. What performances they give! Riffraff!

SCHASTLIVTSEV.   They go on and on. Never know when to stop.

NESCHASTLIVTSEV.   That's it, brother. They go on and on and on. Even in the two capitals. Oh, my, how they put plays on the stage. I saw it myself: a tenor lover, a tenor *raisonneur,* a tenor comedian. [*In a bass voice.*] There's no foundation in the play. I didn't stay to see the end. I left. Why on earth did you start that goatee?

SCHASTLIVTSEV.   What's wrong with it, sir?

NESCHASTLIVTSEV.   Nasty. Are you Russian or not? It's repulsive, that's what. I won't put up with it. Shave it off or let a beard grow, at least.

SCHASTLIVTSEV.   I tried a beard, sir, but nothing came out.

NESCHASTLIVTSEV.   Oh, come now. Why lie about it?

SCHASTLIVTSEV.   But instead of a beard, feathers grew, Gennady Demyanych.

NESCHASTLIVTSEV.   Hmm! Feathers! Go on, tell me another one. Shave it off, I tell you. Otherwise, if you fall into my hands when I'm angry . . . with your goatee . . . Just look out!

SCHASTLIVTSEV.   [*Shyly.*]   I'll shave, sir.

NESCHASTLIVTSEV.   And do you know, Arkashka, my boy? I fell all to pieces there in the south.

SCHASTLIVTSEV.   How did that happen, sir, Gennady Demyanych?

NESCHASTLIVTSEV.   Disposition, brother. You know me. You know I am a lion. I dislike small-mindedness. That's my undoing. I started quarreling with all my managers. They're insignificant, brother, filled with intrigue. They don't value art, and they're pinching kopeks all the time. I want to try my luck here, up north.

SCHASTLIVTSEV.   Well, you know it's the same with us up here, and you won't get along any better up here, Gennady Demyanych. I couldn't get along here, either.

NESCHASTLIVTSEV.   You . . . either! You compared yourself with me.

SCHASTLIVTSEV.   [*Insulted.*]   My disposition is even better than yours. I'm more humble.

NESCHASTLIVTSEV.   [*Menacingly.*]   Wha-a-t?

SCHASTLIVTSEV.   [*Moving away.*]   Well, that's how I am, Gennady Demyanych, sir. I'm humble, humble, sir. I've never hit anyone.

NESCHASTLIVTSEV.   Whoever wasn't so lazy beat you, then. Ha, ha, ha! It always turns out that way: there are people who beat, and there are people who get beaten. Which is better—I don't know. Everyone to his own taste. And you dare . . .

SCHASTLIVTSEV. [*Moving away.*] I don't dare anything, but you said yourself you couldn't get along.

NESCHASTLIVTSEV. Couldn't get along? And what city was it the governor chased you out of? Well, out with it!

SCHASTLIVTSEV. Out with what, exactly? Don't believe everything people jabber about. He chased me out. But why did he chase me out, and how did he?

NESCHASTLIVTSEV. How did he chase you out? Even I heard about that. It's all over the country, brother. They kicked you out of the city three times. They drove you out one gate, and you came right back in another. Finally, even the governor lost patience. "Shoot him," he says, "I don't care, if he never comes back."

SCHASTLIVTSEV. Shoot! Go on with you. Don't tell me they can get away with shooting?

NESCHASTLIVTSEV. They didn't shoot to kill. But Cossacks chased you four versts with whips.

SCHASTLIVTSEV. Not quite four.

NESCHASTLIVTSEV. That's enough, Arkady! Don't upset me, brother. [*Authoritatively.*] Start moving a little. [*Rises.*]

SCHASTLIVTSEV. I'm moving a little, Gennady Demyanych. [*Rises.*]

NESCHASTLIVTSEV. Well, Arkady, my boy, I've broken off from the theatre. And I'm sorry about it already. How I used to act! Good Lord, how I used to act!

SCHASTLIVTSEV. [*Shyly.*] Were you very good, sir?

NESCHASTLIVTSEV. Listen, I was so good that . . . But why talk to you. How can you understand? The last time in Lebedyan I acted Belisarius,[17] and Nikolai Khrisanfych Rybakov[18] himself saw me. I finished the last scene, walked behind the wings, and there was Nikolai Rybakov. He put his hand on my shoulder thus . . . [*Drops his hand forcibly on* SCHASTLIVTSEV'S *shoulder.*]

SCHASTLIVTSEV. [*Cowering from the blow.*] Oi! Gennady Demyanych, dear fellow, have mercy. Don't kill me. Really and truly, I'm scared to death.

NESCHASTLIVTSEV. It's nothing, brother, nothing at all. I'm doing it gently, as an example. [*Again drops his hand on* SCHASTLIVTSEV'S *shoulder.*]

SCHASTLIVTSEV. Really and truly, I'm scared to death. Let me go. You know they killed me once before like this. I almost died.

NESCHASTLIVTSEV. [*Takes him by the collar and holds him.*] Who? How?

SCHASTLIVTSEV. [*Shriveling up.*] Bichevkin. He was acting Lyapunov, and I was acting Fidler,[19] sir. During rehearsal he kept on fattening his role. "Arkashka," he says, "this is the way I'm going to toss you through the window: I'll grab you by the collar with this hand, pick you up with that hand, and then, sma-a-sh." "That's the way," he says, "Karatygin[20] handled it." Oh, I begged him, I did. Begged and got down on my knees. "Oh, dear, sweet man," I says, "don't kill me." "No need to worry, Arkashka," he says, "no need to worry at all." Well, came the night of performance, and we get to our scene. The audience claps when they see him. I sneak a fast peek at him. Oh, good Lord. His lips are trembling, his cheeks are trembling, and his eyes—his eyes are spitting blood. "Put some kind of bed or other," he says, "right under the window for this fool, so I don't really kill him." Well, I see that my end is coming up fast. How I mumbled through the scene, I don't remember now. He comes up to me, his face—inhuman. Oh, the wildest of wild animals. He grabbed me by the collar with his left hand, picked me up into the air, and swinging his right hand, whacked me on the back of my head with his fist. Everything went dark before me, Gennady Demyanych. I flew eighteen feet through the window and broke through the door of the women's dressing room. Oh, tragedians get the best of everything. The audience called him back thirty times for that scene. In fact, they almost pulled down the theatre. Why, I could've ended up a cripple the rest of my life, if God hadn't been a little bit merciful. Let me go, Gennady Demyanych!

NESCHASTLIVTSEV. [*Holds him by the collar.*] Very effective. I'm going to remember this. [*Having thought a little.*] Hold on, there. What do you say? Shall I try it?

SCHASTLIVTSEV. [*Falling on his knees.*] Oh, dear, dear Gennady Demyanych!

NESCHASTLIVTSEV. [*Drops him.*] Well, it's not necessary. Off you go, now. Some other time . . . Oh, that's what he did. He put his hand on my shoulder. "You," he says, "and I," he says, "are going to die," he says. [*Covers his face and weeps. Wipes his tears.*] It was flattering. [*With complete indifference.*] Do you have tobacco?

SCHASTLIVTSEV.   What do you mean, tobacco? For pity's sake. Not a snitch.

NESCHASTLIVTSEV.   How can you go on a trip, and not lay in a supply of tobacco? Silly fool.

SCHASTLIVTSEV.   How come you haven't got any?

NESCHASTLIVTSEV.   "How come you haven't . . ." How dare you say that to me? Listen, I had some, I did. Like you've never seen before, from Odessa—the finest brand from Krion. But it's all gone now.

SCHASTLIVTSEV.   And mine's gone, too, sir.

NESCHASTLIVTSEV.   Do you have much money with you?

SCHASTLIVTSEV.   Never had much money in my whole life, and now I don't have a kopek to pay for my soul.

NESCHASTLIVTSEV.   What on earth are you doing on a trip without money? No tobacco and no money! Silly fool.

SCHASTLIVTSEV.   Better off. Nobody will rob me, sir. Doesn't seem to make much difference, does it? I mean, sitting around without money, or going on a trip without money?

NESCHASTLIVTSEV.   Well, I imagine you could make it to Voronezh, if you went with pilgrims and ate and drank in Christ's name. But farther than that? Across the land of the Don Cossacks? You wouldn't make it across there. Even if you had money, they'd never feed a person who smokes tobacco. You don't even look like a Christian, but you want to go through Cossack country. Why, you know the Cossacks would think you the Evil Spirit. And they'd scare the kids to death with you.

SCHASTLIVTSEV.   Think you'd like to give me something on loan, Gennady Demyanych? To tell the truth, tragedians have the only souls left nowadays. There was the late Kornely. Why, you know he never turned away a friend, but shared his last kopek with him. All tragedians should follow his good example.

NESCHASTLIVTSEV.   Now, don't you dare talk to me like that. I've got a big heart, too. But I'm not about to give you money, simply because I'm short of it myself, for pity's sake. I'm sorry for you, Arkashka, my boy, I really am. Don't you have any close relatives or acquaintances around here?

SCHASTLIVTSEV.   Not one. But, you know, even if I had, they wouldn't give me money. That's for sure.

NESCHASTLIVTSEV.   We're not talking about money. But wouldn't you like to get away from traveling, take a rest, try some home-made pirog and a little nip of brandy? Why is it, brother, you don't have relatives or acquaintances? What kind of a man are you, anyway?

SCHASTLIVTSEV.   Well, you know you don't have any, either.

NESCHASTLIVTSEV.   Yes, I do. But I wanted to go right by them. I'm a very proud man. Well, it looks as though we'll have to turn in.

SCHASTLIVTSEV.   You know, living with relatives doesn't add up to much enjoyment for us, Gennady Demyanych. We're pretty free and easy. We like to move around a lot, see the country. Best of all, we like life at the inns. I've lived with relatives, so I know what I'm talking about. There's this uncle of mine. A shopkeeper in a god-forsaken town about five hundred versts from here. I stayed as a guest with him, and if I hadn't run away, well . . .

NESCHASTLIVTSEV.   Well, what?

SCHASTLIVTSEV.   Not so good, sir. Not good at all. All right, I'll tell you about it, sir. I'd been fooling around on the road about three months, and I was sick and tired of it. Suppose, I thought, I visit dear uncle. Then and there I did, sir. They wouldn't let me in the house for a long time. Instead I saw all kinds of faces peeking out at me on the porch. At last the old man himself came out. He says, "How come you're here?" "Dear uncle," I say, "I've come to visit you." "Do you mean," he says, "you've given up art?" "Yes, I have," I say. "Well, do tell," says he, "here's a bit of a room for you; you can stay with us; only first, better get down to the bathhouse." So I began living with them. They get up at four in the morning, eat dinner at ten, and go to bed around seven or eight at night. At both dinner and supper, you drink as much vodka as you like; and right after dinner you sleep. And everybody in the house is so quiet, Gennady Demyanych, you think you're in a graveyard. Uncle takes off for the shop in the morning, and you're left with auntie, who spends the whole day drinking tea and heaving sighs. Auntie takes a quick look at me, breathes heavily, and says, "Oh, you unlucky man, you; you've ripped your soul to shreds, haven't you?" That's the only thing we talk about. For example, she says, "Isn't it time . . . you've ripped your soul to shreds, haven't you . . . Isn't it time you had supper and went to bed?"

NESCHASTLIVTSEV.   Did you expect anything better?

SCHASTLIVTSEV.   Well, sir, seems as if I was getting well and even started to put on some fat. Then, all of a sudden at dinner one day, a thought crossed my mind: maybe I'd better hang myself ? Well, don't think I didn't shake my head to get rid of that idea. A little while later in the evening the same thought struck me again. I can see the whole thing's pretty bad, so at night I jumped out the window and ran away. Just see what fellows like us have to go through with our relatives.

NESCHASTLIVTSEV.   I wouldn't go, either, brother. Only, I must confess, I'm worn out. And it's still a full week's traveling by foot to get to Rybinsk. Once you're there, you can't be certain you'd find work. You know, if we could find a dramatic actress, young, good-looking . . .

SCHASTLIVTSEV.   Then there'd be nothing to worry about, sir. You and I'd simply . . . Oh, it's easy to pick up the others, and with a troupe like that . . . I'd handle the money.

NESCHASTLIVTSEV.   There's a bit of a problem. We don't have the actress.

SCHASTLIVTSEV.   And nowadays there's nowhere to find them, sir.

NESCHASTLIVTSEV.   You understand, don't you, what a dramatic actress is, exactly? You know, don't you, the kind of actress I need? I need soul, brother; life, fire.[21]

SCHASTLIVTSEV.   No matter how fired up you get, Gennady Demyanych, I doubt if you can smoke one out these days.

NESCHASTLIVTSEV.   Don't crack jokes around me when I'm talking seriously. You vaudeville actors have only jokes on your mind. As for feeling, you don't have even a half-kopek's worth. If a woman throws herself headfirst into a whirlpool, just for love, then there's our actress. If I saw it myself, I'd never believe it. But if I pulled her out, then I'd believe it. Well, I can see we ought to go.

SCHASTLIVTSEV.   Where, sir?

NESCHASTLIVTSEV.   It's none of your business. It's been fifteen years since I've been here, brother, but you know I was almost born here. Childhood years, harmless games, pigeon roosts, don't you know I remember every bit of it. [*Drops his head.*] Why on earth shouldn't she welcome me? She must be an old lady by now. The way women count their ages, she must be way past fifty years old. I've not forgotten her, brother, and I've sent presents to her many times. I sent her Tartar slippers from Karasubazar, a frozen white salmon from Irkutsk, turquoise from Tiflis, brick-tea, old fellow, from Irbit, balyk [22] from Novocherkassk, malachite rosary from Ekaterinburg. Oh, I can't remember everything. Of course, it'd be better for us to drive up to the porch in a four-wheeled coach. The servants would meet us. But now, on foot, in rags. [*Wipes tears.*] I am proud, Arkady. Yes, I am. [*Straps on traveling case.*] Let's go. And I'll find a corner for you.

SCHASTLIVTSEV.   Which way is it, Gennady Demyanych?

NESCHASTLIVTSEV.   Which way? [*Points to the post.*]   Read.

SCHASTLIVTSEV.   [*Reads.*]   "To Penky estate, Landowner Madame Gurmyzhskaya."

NESCHASTLIVTSEV.   That's the way my poor lot sends me. Your hand, comrade. [*They slowly exit.*] [23]

ACT THREE

An old, densely planted garden. To the left of the audience, a low terrace of the manor house, where flowers are planted. Three or four steps from the terrace to the ground. RAISA *is on the terrace;* BULANOV, *in the garden. Having seen* RAISA, BULANOV *helps her down from the terrace and kisses her hand.*

BULANOV. Good morning, Raisa Pavlovna!

RAISA. Hello, my friend.

BULANOV. [*With concern.*] How are you feeling, ma'am?

RAISA. Thank you, my dear. I'm fine, and somehow today I feel especially fresh and well-rested, despite the fact I slept poorly last night. I tossed and turned and had all kinds of disturbing dreams. Do you believe in dreams?

BULANOV. How can I keep from believing in them, ma'am? Perhaps if I'd studied a little more, I wouldn't believe in them, ma'am. [*Smiles wickedly.*] But you know I didn't complete my education, ma'am, and I don't go around with my hair uncombed. I wash myself every day, and I believe in dreams, ma'am.

RAISA. I've some dreams I can't get out of my head all day.

BULANOV. What was it, Raisa Pavlovna, you saw?

RAISA. Well, let's say that I won't tell you everything.

BULANOV. I beg your pardon.

RAISA. No need to apologize. I'll tell you the next dream I have, but not this one.

BULANOV. Why is that, ma'am?

RAISA. Because telling your dreams is a little like telling your own secret thoughts and desires. And that isn't always suitable. For example, I am a woman, and you are a man.

BULANOV. What's wrong with that—I mean, my being a man, ma'am?

RAISA. Why, that's the most innocent thing I've heard yet. Very well, I saw you in my dream.

BULANOV. Me? Oh, I like that a lot, ma'am.

RAISA. Really?

BULANOV. Yes. You were thinking of me, ma'am, when you lay down to sleep.

RAISA. Oh, that's what you say! Then you're really pleased?

BULANOV. How can I help being pleased, ma'am? I'm always afraid that you'll get mad at me over something or other and ship me home to mama.

RAISA. Oh, now that's funny! Why on earth should I get angry with you? Are you that afraid of me, poor thing?

BULANOV. Why shouldn't I be? Everyone says how very strict you are.

RAISA. I'm glad they say that. But with you, my dear, I shan't be strict. Why, it'd be just terrible for you, if you were afraid of me.

BULANOV. Very well, ma'am. But if I only knew . . .

RAISA. What?

BULANOV. How to please you.

RAISA. Go on and guess.

BULANOV. Do you think it's easy to guess, ma'am? Oh, I don't have brains enough to do that.

RAISA. Then what are your brains for?

BULANOV. For anything you tell me to do. For managing the estate and peasants, ma'am. If we had serfs, you'd never find a better manager than I. No, you wouldn't, young as I am.

RAISA. Oh, that dream! I can't get it out of my mind. That's all there is to it.

BULANOV. What is it that bothers you?

RAISA. It's pretty hard to explain. But I can talk frankly to you. I see that you're loyal to me. Well, you see, I have a nephew.

BULANOV. I know, ma'am. You love him a lot, and you often talk of him.

RAISA. My friend, people sometimes say one thing, but mean something quite different. Why should I tell everyone how I feel? As a relative I must love him. And so I say that I love him.

BULANOV. But you really don't, do you?

RAISA. I don't mean that I don't love him, but . . . Oh, how can I say it . . . He doesn't need me now. I feel comfortable enough. In fact, I've made up my mind how to settle my estate. But say that he shows up all of a sudden. I can't turn him away, I know. So I must then give him some part or other from the estate. And to do that, I must then take from the person whom I love.

BULANOV. Then don't divide it up, ma'am.

RAISA. No, it's impossible. I can't turn him away, if he is respectful and knows how to behave himself. Oh, I've put myself into a situation here that I can't refuse a relative. And what if he shows up without means at all? I'll have to take care of him. Very likely he'll want to live here. You know I can't drive him off, exactly.

BULANOV. Only tell me, and I'll drive him off.

RAISA. [*With fear.*] Oh, God help you! Take care of yourself. Take care. That's what I saw in my dream. It seems he came and shot you to death with a pistol right before my eyes.

BULANOV. Me? Well, we'll see about that, ma'am, we will. But, Raisa Pavlovna, you'd better not think about him, or you'll dream about him all the time.

RAISA. He's been very wise up till now. He hasn't dropped in once in fifteen years. I only hope . . . Indeed, I hope with all my heart that another fifteen years will go by in the same way.

BULANOV. Then, Raisa Pavlovna, you'd better forget about him completely. And don't even talk about him. Otherwise, for all I know, you're just begging for trouble, very likely.

RAISA. Really? Well, I won't go begging for trouble, then. [KARP *enters.*]

KARP. If you please, mistress, tea is served. The samovar is ready, ma'am.

RAISA. Let's go, Aleksis!

KARP. Mistress, the master arrived last night.

RAISA. The master? What master?

KARP. Gennady Demyanych, ma'am.

RAISA. [*With fear.*] Oh, no, it can't be. Do you hear, Aleksis? [*To* KARP.] And where is he?

KARP. I took him to the summerhouse and prepared a bed for him there, ma'am. He said he was staying at the tavern in the city. He left all his luggage there. He happened to go out walking our way and just stopped by.

RAISA.   Didn't he say anything else?

KARP.   Nothing, ma'am. He was in a bit of a mood, ma'am.

RAISA.   What do you mean, a bit of a mood?

KARP.   As if he'd lost his memory, ma'am. I imagine it's from traveling, ma'am. He asked for paper and ink. He walked back and forth in the summerhouse for a long time, just thinking. Finally he sat down at the table, wrote a note and told me to give it to you. [*Hands over the note.*]

RAISA.   What is it? Some sort of verses. [*Reads.*]
> Oh, cruel, cruel, my lot,
> My fate, so cruel, I blot.
> What's left but now to rot . . .

What is it, Aleksis? I don't understand.

BULANOV.   If you don't understand it, then how can I, ma'am?

RAISA.   [*To* KARP.] Is he sleeping?

KARP.   No, ma'am. He got up early and left. Probably to take a bath. I haven't seen him this morning, ma'am.

RAISA.   Well, when he shows up, ask him to have tea in the dining room.

KARP.   Yes, ma'am. [*Exits.*]

RAISA.   [*Shrugging her shoulders.*] Oh, so I shouldn't believe in dreams? Let's go, Aleksis. [*They exit. Enter* NESCHASTLIVTSEV, *rather well dressed; he wears a black collapsible hat. With him comes* SCHASTLIVTSEV, *dressed as he was before.*]

NESCHASTLIVTSEV.   Now then, Arkady, my auntie is a respectable, strict woman; and I don't want her to know, brother, that I am an actor. What's more, a provincial actor. [*Threatens* SCHASTLIVTSEV *with his finger.*] Just see that you don't let it out. I am Gennady Demyanych Gurmyzhsky, a retired captain or major—take your own choice. In short, I am the master, and you are my flunky.

SCHASTLIVTSEV.   What do you mean, flunky?

NESCHASTLIVTSEV.   Simply what I said, flunky. That's all there is. I'm not about to take you into the drawing room, I can't. You don't expect me to present you to my aunt, do you? She is a devout woman, and in her home, brother, it's peaceful. Yes, and everything in its place. And then all of a sudden you show up. Just imagine it yourself, the way you look in a place like that. With a mug like yours, brother, better be a flunky. That's all there is to it.

SCHASTLIVTSEV.   Beg your pardon, but hold on. Don't be too sure yet.

NESCHASTLIVTSEV.   Too sure about what?

SCHASTLIVTSEV.   About my mug, I mean.

NESCHASTLIVTSEV.   No, that's you, Arkady, my boy. No doubt about it.

SCHASTLIVTSEV.   No, you've no right. No right at all . . .

NESCHASTLIVTSEV.   [*Threateningly.*] That's the way it's going to be, I'm telling you. What more do you want? You'll get fed pretty good here, and the only one you'll serve is me.

SCHASTLIVTSEV.   But you know I am proud, Gennady Demyanych.

NESCHASTLIVTSEV.   Doesn't mean a damn to me if you are proud. There's no comparison with you, but Martynov[24] himself played flunkies. And here you are, feeling embarrassed about it. Oh, brother, are you a silly fool!

SCHASTLIVTSEV.   But you know that was on the stage.

NESCHASTLIVTSEV.   Well, brother, you just think of yourself as on the stage.

SCHASTLIVTSEV.   No, I won't. Just see what you've trumped up. Good Lord! Better I take off right now. I've got ambition, at least.

NESCHASTLIVTSEV.   I know you've got ambition, but have you got a passport?

SCHASTLIVTSEV.   What business is it of yours?

NESCHASTLIVTSEV.   Just this. Try to take off, and then you'll see. Brother, all I've got to do is blink an eye, and you're on your way back home under guard. The charge? Being a tramp. I know it, and don't think I don't, that you've been waltzing around twelve years without a passport. In place of a passport, there's an article in your pocket, right out of the Kursk District Register, which says that a certain actor arrived in Kursk and gave a stinking show. That's all the identity card you've got. Well, how come you're so quiet, hmm? 'Bout wraps it up, doesn't it? Now, go ahead and do it for me, brother. Just think who's asking you! Well, what do you say? From one buddy to another. Hmm?

SCHASTLIVTSEV.   If it's from one buddy to another, I'm at your service.

NESCHASTLIVTSEV.   Now don't think, brother, that I look down on my calling. It's just a little awkward, brother, that's all. The house is peaceful, quiet. You know that you and I are almost devils—a little better, maybe. You know it yourself: a buffoon is no friend to the priest. Only remember to stay away from quarrels, or fights, and more important, keep your hands off things that belong to someone else, Arkashka. Even though it'll be hard for you; just try, brother, to behave yourself the same way as a regular flunky. All right, brother, first of all, take off your cap, and move over to the side. Someone is coming.   [KARP *enters*.]

KARP.   Hello, dear master. Pray, how did you sleep?

NESCHASTLIVTSEV.   Not badly, brother. Napped pretty well.

KARP.   How'd it happen, sir, that you've grown old?

NESCHASTLIVTSEV.   Life, brother.

KARP.   I understand, sir. Yes, I do. Also, you know life in the military . . .

NESCHASTLIVTSEV.   Yes, brother, life in the military . . .

KARP.   The marches, sir, over and over again . . .

NESCHASTLIVTSEV.   [*With a sigh.*]   Oh, the marches. Yes, indeed.

KARP.   From one place to the next, sir.

NESCHASTLIVTSEV.   Yes, brother. From one place to the next. How are you getting along here?

KARP.   Oh, you call this living, sir? We live in the forest: offering up prayers to stumps of trees; too lazy to plant, idlers we be. Please, sir, please. Your aunt is expecting you for tea.

NESCHASTLIVTSEV.   [*Crossing to the terrace.*]   Listen, Karp, don't forget my Arkashka. Give him tea to drink, brother.

KARP.   Yes, sir. Don't worry.   [NESCHASTLIVTSEV *exits*.]

SCHASTLIVTSEV.   Oh, go to the devil. He's gone, and I'm left with a peasant, no less. Oh, just look. He's crawling over to talk to me.

KARP.   What do they call you?

SCHASTLIVTSEV.   Sganarelle.

KARP.   What are you, exactly? You're a foreigner, aren't you?

SCHASTLIVTSEV.   Yes, a foreigner. What's your name?

KARP.   Karp Savelich.

SCHASTLIVTSEV.   It's not possible.

KARP.   It's the truth.

SCHASTLIVTSEV.   But you know carp. It's a fish.

KARP. That's *Cyprinus carpio.*

SCHASTLIVTSEV. Oh, well. Whether it's *carpio,* or carp, it's one and the same. It'd be better to call you Salmon Savelich.

KARP. Well, have it your own way. Do you want some tea?

SCHASTLIVTSEV. No.

KARP. Why do you say, no?

SCHASTLIVTSEV. That's it. No.

KARP. That means you don't want any. Honestly?

SCHASTLIVTSEV. Honestly I don't.

KARP. Now, why do you say that?

SCHASTLIVTSEV. Simply because.

KARP. I don't understand it.

SCHASTLIVTSEV. Very simple. It'd be better to have tea after something to eat.

KARP. Stands to reason that it'd be better. Only where can I get something?

SCHASTLIVTSEV. You could try a little, Perch Savelich.

KARP. But it's not Perch. It's Karp. Might ask the housekeeper for something.

SCHASTLIVTSEV. Then ask her to bring us something there in the summerhouse.

KARP. Well, I'll try it, just for you.

SCHASTLIVTSEV. You do that, Eelpout Savelich! [*Bows and exits.*]

KARP. Oh, wouldn't you know it, a first-rate clown. What kind of country did they pick him up in? No doubt, one that's pretty far off. There's a gintlemun's gintlemun[25] for you. Only one way to figure it out—because of education. And what's here for us? Nothing but the forest, our own backwoods. [*Enter* VOSMIBRATOV *and* PETR.] What do you want?

VOSMIBRATOV. I'd like to see your mistress, little fellow.

KARP. You can just wait a spell. When they want you, they'll call you.

PETR. Listen here, you silly fool. You know daddy and I have business here.

KARP. A lot I care about your business. It's just impossible, for pity's sake. What gave you the right, I'd like to know, to worm your way in?

PETR. Now you just run along and announce us. Try.

KARP.   How can you talk about being announced, when she's busy with a colonel? Her nephew has arrived.

VOSMIBRATOV.   A colonel?

KARP.   Of course, a colonel. We haven't seen him in fifteen years.

VOSMIBRATOV.   Is he staying long?

KARP.   What do you mean, staying long? He's here, for good and sure.

VOSMIBRATOV.   [*Having thought a little.*]   Is he pretty strict?

KARP.   Strict? Goes without saying. And how! Why talk about it anymore? What a title! Colonel, no less. Just put that in your brains.

VOSMIBRATOV.   [*Having waved his hand.*]   Oh, go to hell! You'll get yours when the time comes.   [*Exits.* PETR *follows him.*]

KARP.   You'll have to show me first.   [NESCHASTLIVTSEV *and* BULANOV *enter from the house.* KARP *exits.*]

NESCHASTLIVTSEV.   Don't you think I have a nice little cousin, brother?

BULANOV.   Yes, sir.

NESCHASTLIVTSEV.   Get married, brother, do.

BULANOV.   Then you approve?

NESCHASTLIVTSEV.   Why is it any of my business? People are born, they marry, they die. I mean, if you must, then go ahead.

BULANOV.   I hope you'll like me, sir.

NESCHASTLIVTSEV.   Why should you want me to like you? What's in it for you, brother?

BULANOV.   Well, after all, sir.

NESCHASTLIVTSEV.   Don't tell me you're waiting for the inheritance? Keep waiting, brother, do. But here's something for you. You should try to get around auntie. She is a rich woman. You're still a young man; and yet, who knows, abilities like that might show up early. Know how?

BULANOV.   [*Bashfully.*]   I know how, sir.

NESCHASTLIVTSEV.   Bravo. But tell me how you learned it so young?

BULANOV.   What, sir?

NESCHASTLIVTSEV.   To get around somebody, brother. To play up to people, learn to crawl?

BULANOV.   Necessity teaches us, sir.

NESCHASTLIVTSEV.   Necessity? And how come you know about necessity?

BULANOV.   How can I help knowing, sir? All my life I've been very unlucky, sir.

NESCHASTLIVTSEV.   Nonsense. I don't believe you. You're lucky. The unlucky ones are those who don't know how to play up to people, or how to lick the dust. Tell me what you've been unlucky in.

BULANOV.   First of all, papa didn't leave me much of an inheritance.

NESCHASTLIVTSEV.   And how much do you need?

BULANOV.   Maybe about two or three thousand desyatin[26] of land, sir, or around forty thousand in cash, sir.

NESCHASTLIVTSEV.   You'd be happy, then? You only need a little, don't you, brother?

BULANOV.   That's it exactly, just a little. But it's possible to live right and proper on it, sir.

NESCHASTLIVTSEV.   Now, just hold on, brother. I'll leave you more.

BULANOV.   Are you joking, sir?

NESCHASTLIVTSEV.   No, go on with you. I don't have relatives, and I like you a lot. What else have you been unlucky in?

BULANOV.   Unlucky in my studies, sir. I never even finished the gymnasium, sir.

NESCHASTLIVTSEV.   [Takes off his hat and bows.] Oh, brother, I hope you'll excuse me. Do me the favor, please.

BULANOV.   Excuse you for what, exactly, sir?

NESCHASTLIVTSEV.   That I can't help you to finish your schooling. I'd like to, but I can't.

BULANOV.   Oh, that's nothing, for pity's sake, sir. I don't want that, sir. Getting the money will be good enough. Mama says I don't have the brains for studying, sir.

NESCHASTLIVTSEV.   What kind do you have?

BULANOV.   Practical, sir.

NESCHASTLIVTSEV.   Well, thank the Lord you have some kind of brains. So much of the time, people don't have any at all.

BULANOV.   But it's nothing to get by without, sir. If I only had a little more land, and received the interest myself, as the owner, then it'd be possible to live without brains at all, sir.

NESCHASTLIVTSEV.   Wouldn't that be better? At least, your head would be lighter. So you don't have brains? How about cigarettes, then? Have any of those?   [RAISA *appears on the terrace.*]

BULANOV.   [*Laughs.*]   I don't have those either, sir.

NESCHASTLIVTSEV.   Why are you laughing, brother? Do you smoke, or don't you?

BULANOV.   [*In a low voice.*]   I smoke, sir, and I have cigarettes. Only here comes Raisa Pavlovna, and I don't take chances in front of her.   [RAISA *crosses down to the garden.*]

RAISA.   I'd never have recognized you, since you've changed. I'm thankful that you didn't forget me completely. You were in my thoughts almost every day.

NESCHASTLIVTSEV.   I couldn't forget you. You don't know my heart. I've remembered you, I remember you, and I shall remember you.

RAISA.   I know, my dear, and I thank you for remembering me. Nothing could have made me happier than the rosary you sent.

NESCHASTLIVTSEV.   When I sent the rosary, I thought: "Dear, kind lady, receive thou this rosary in hand and begin to pray. Oh, remember me in thy holy prayers."

RAISA.   I remember you, my dear, I do. However, up to now I've not asked a single question of you. Judging by your wardrobe, you no longer serve in the military.

NESCHASTLIVTSEV.   No. No longer. Bad health, little strength, the enemy no longer storms outside the gate. But, if . . . alas! My heart cries out for the bloody sport. But, you know, to serve in time of peace for the sake of rank, for the sake of military honors! I am not the ambitious type.

RAISA.   But I don't think you can live without doing something. I expect you've shifted to another line of work.

NESCHASTLIVTSEV.   Yes, I've shifted.

RAISA.   And you are satisfied with your position?

NESCHASTLIVTSEV.   My work, auntie, is right for me. I am satisfied, and they're satisfied with me.

RAISA.   Then, you've taken a leave.

NESCHASTLIVTSEV.   No, I'm passing through, and decided to take a rest.

RAISA.   I'm so pleased you've decided to visit me. Are you comfortable in the summerhouse?

NESCHASTLIVTSEV. Oh, don't trouble yourself. The garden, nature, verdure, seclusion. Oh, that is simply paradise for my soul. [KARP *enters.*]

KARP. Mistress, Vosmibratov has been waiting a long time, ma'am.

RAISA. Oh, yes. I completely forgot I told him to come early. Call him in here! [KARP *exits.*] Wouldn't you like to take a stroll in the neighborhood? Aleksis here will go with you.

NESCHASTLIVTSEV. No, I take walks only in the evening. [*To* BULANOV.] Let's go, brother, to the summerhouse.

BULANOV. Let's go, sir. [NESCHASTLIVTSEV *and* BULANOV *exit. Enter* VOSMIBRATOV *and* PETR.]

RAISA. Excuse me, please. I simply forgot about you.

VOSMIBRATOV. It's nothing, ma'am. Your little nephew showed up?

RAISA. Yes, my nephew.

VOSMIBRATOV. Pretty good deal, ma'am. Only, mistress, don't hold back.

RAISA. No, I shan't detain you long, now.

VOSMIBRATOV. Just what I said. Don't hold back.

RAISA. No, of course. We'll do it at once.

VOSMIBRATOV. Pretty good, ma'am. [*Silence.*]

RAISA. Did you bring it?

VOSMIBRATOV. Why not? I remember my part, ma'am.

RAISA. Well, then let's do it now.

VOSMIBRATOV. All right, ma'am, let's. [*Silence.*]

RAISA. Very well, then, how much do you have there?

VOSMIBRATOV. Please, ma'am.

RAISA. What?

VOSMIBRATOV. The note, ma'am; our agreement, exactly.

RAISA. Oh, come now, really. I don't know what I did with it.

VOSMIBRATOV. Look around for it, ma'am.

RAISA. Where exactly should I look? Really, I don't know. I probably lost it.

VOSMIBRATOV. Now, how's that, ma'am? You know, you just might try to swindle me.

RAISA. What nonsense. Why should I swindle you?

VOSMIBRATOV. Why, the way you'd like, that's how you'll swindle me. You lost the note. I was too stupid to take it when

I could have. Now, you'll say you sold it to me for ten thousand. But, you know I've already cut trees and carted 'em off. So, don't try none of your trading with me.

RAISA.   Well, I've never! Surely you know me better than that.

VOSMIBRATOV.   Well, I've hopes you'll do right by me, ma'am. Because everything I got's in your hands, ma'am.

RAISA.   But, then again, why should you doubt me, Ivan Petrovich? I've had a new note prepared for you.

VOSMIBRATOV.   Prepared, ma'am?

RAISA.   Yes. That I have received the money in full.

VOSMIBRATOV.   Yes, ma'am. That's something else, ma'am. I thank you a lot. If you don't mind, I'd just like to run my eye over this little note.

RAISA.   Here it is. [*Hands over the note.*]   Look it over.

VOSMIBRATOV.   [*Taking it.*]   Without glasses, exactly, I don't see too good, ma'am. But with glasses, it's even worse. But my son here can read through it. Petr, read it. [*Gives note to* PETR.]

PETR.   [*Reads.*]   "For sale by me to the merchant of Kalinov, Ivan Petrov Vosmibratov . . ."

VOSMIBRATOV.   Yes, ma'am. That's it exactly, ma'am.

PETR.   [*Reads.*]   "for cutting trees in the waste plot, Gorelaya and Palenaya . . ."

VOSMIBRATOV.   They are the ones, ma'am.

PETR.   [*Reads.*]   "and two desyatin in Pylaeva, I have received the money paid in full. Landowner of Kalinov, Raisa Gurmyzhskaya."

VOSMIBRATOV.   [*Takes note.*]   Very good, ma'am. [*Takes out pocketbook and carefully folds the note in it.*]   If you please, ma'am, the money.   [*Takes out the money and counts it.*]   One thousand, one thousand three hundred, five hundred. [*Deep in thought; then, as if he remembers.*]   Eight hundred. There you are, ma'am.   [*Hands the money over to* RAISA.]

RAISA.   What do you mean, a thousand eight hundred? But you know I need . . .

VOSMIBRATOV.   It's my fault, ma'am. Forgive me with all your heart. That's my memory, for sure. [*Takes out money and hands it over.*]   Here's two hundred rubles more. Now it's just right. Seems it is, isn't it? Petrushka,[27] that right? Why don't you say something? [*Threateningly.*] Speak up, you silly blockhead, you!

PETR.   Right, ma'am.

RAISA.   Ivan Petrovich, you're teasing me, aren't you? Three, not two.

VOSMIBRATOV.   [*Insulted.*] What's this, three? What do you mean, for pity's sake?

RAISA.   Don't tell me you've forgotten? Fifteen hundred for one piece of land, and fifteen hundred for the second.

VOSMIBRATOV.   That was impossible, ma'am. Don't come out that way, according to calculations, ma'am.

RAISA.   According to what calculations?

VOSMIBRATOV.   Don't tell me you think I've gone blind? Now, who'd ever buy that forest for three thousand? You know I couldn't do it without a loss.

RAISA.   I put my faith in you. And I praised you to everyone, saying you're a good family man.

VOSMIBRATOV.   That's not part of the bargain.

RAISA.   If you're going to act like that, then I don't agree with you.

VOSMIBRATOV.   It's up to you, ma'am. I'll just say good-by. Let's go, Petr.

RAISA.   No, I just can't agree to sell Palenaya and Gorelaya at that price. Well, think it over yourself. Surely, you have common sense enough, don't you?

VOSMIBRATOV.   Why shouldn't I have common sense? Why, if I didn't, I just couldn't get along, ma'am. Your Worship's the one who don't need common sense, exactly, 'cause you're all set to get by on cash. If you don't agree to sell, give me back the money, please. I've got to finish this up, somehow.

RAISA.   I'll keep fifteen hundred for Gorelaya, then you take the five hundred.

VOSMIBRATOV.   No, I see we're going to be trading for a long time, ma'am. I won't take Palenaya and Pylaeva for less than two thousand, and that only from you.

RAISA.   What do you mean, won't take less?

VOSMIBRATOV.   Well, that's it, exactly, ma'am. I bought them from you. And whatever I want, it means that's what I'm selling them for.

RAISA. If I give you two thousand, then there's nothing left to me for Gorelaya.

VOSMIBRATOV. That's your business, exactly, ma'am.

RAISA. No, no. I won't do it, I won't.

VOSMIBRATOV. If you'd do something for us, why we'd do something for you. But, no. You look down on my birth and my calling, if you please . . .

PETR. Daddy!

VOSMIBRATOV. [*To* PETR.] I'm going to kill you.

RAISA. No, no. You take this five hundred rubles.

VOSMIBRATOV. No use going on like this, so there's no use talking. Let's go, Petr.

RAISA. Now, what's going on?

VOSMIBRATOV. Why, a little child could understand it. I bought the forest from you, gave you money for it, and you gave me a receipt. Very simple: the forest is mine, the money is yours. So I'll bow low, and off I go. I'll say good-by. [*Exits.* PETR *follows him.*]

RAISA. Well, what do you know? A robbery—in broad daylight, too. The remarkable thing is that I've never been successful, either in buying or in selling. I've been cheated every time. Apparently, it was preordained at my birth. [*Crosses to the terrace. Enter* NESCHASTLIVTSEV *and* BULANOV.]

BULANOV. It's terrific the way you do card tricks, sir. How is it exactly that your nine . . .

NESCHASTLIVTSEV. It's the *volte*,[28] brother.

BULANOV. Teach me how to do the *volte.*

NESCHASTLIVTSEV. Why?

BULANOV. Well, you see, don't you, the landowners here are rich, and sometimes they play cards, sir. Why should I lose money on that account? I am a poor man, sir.

NESCHASTLIVTSEV. No, brother, you're some boy. Yes, indeed.

RAISA. [*Crossing down from the terrace.*] Just imagine, Aleksis. I sold the lumber to Ivan Petrov for three thousand, but I received only two.

BULANOV. How did it happen, ma'am?

RAISA. Oh, I'm to blame. I gave him a receipt beforehand, saying that I'd received full payment. Well, he then gave me only two thousand.

NESCHASTLIVTSEV.   [*Threateningly.*]   Oh, the damned villain.

BULANOV.   How on earth could you do it, ma'am? Oh, what a pity! It would've been better . . .

RAISA.   Well, there's nothing to do now, my dear. It's good he gave me at least two thousand.

NESCHASTLIVTSEV.   [*Heatedly.*]   What do you mean, nothing? Bring him back here.   [*Raises his eyes to the sky.*]   What I'll do with him! Good Lord, what I'll do.

BULANOV.   But you know he has the receipt.

NESCHASTLIVTSEV.   Oh, keep on prattling about that, will you. I don't give a damn about receipts. Where is he? Just hand him to me. What I'll do to him.   [*Enter* KARP *and* SCHASTLIVTSEV.]

RAISA.   [*To* BULANOV.]   Oh, he's absolutely frightening! Let's go, please.

BULANOV.   Permit me to stay. I'm curious, ma'am.   [RAISA *exits.*] Has Ivan Petrov gone?

KARP.   Not yet. He's here, in the courtyard, sir.

NESCHASTLIVTSEV.   Bring that swindler back here. When I see him! Drag him in by the collar.   [KARP *exits.*]   Arkashka, hand over my decorations.   [SCHASTLIVTSEV *exits.*]

BULANOV.   What is it you're going to say to him?

NESCHASTLIVTSEV.   How do I know, brother, what I'm going to say?

BULANOV.   But surely you don't expect to go in the face of documents, sir?

NESCHASTLIVTSEV.   In a minute I'll show you what's possible. What are documents worth to me? I'm no paper-dropping, pen-pushing bureaucrat. Just get away from me. Right now, brother, I've nothing to do with you.   [SCHASTLIVTSEV *brings theatrical decorations.* NESCHASTLIVTSEV *pins them on.*]

BULANOV.   What kind of decorations do you have, sir? Are they foreign?   [*Enter* KARP, VOSMIBRATOV, *and* PETR.]

VOSMIBRATOV.   What's this all about? What more do you want? I've got my own affairs to attend to, and I'm sick and tired of all this talk.

KARP.   If you'll come along. I do what they tell me to.

BULANOV.   Are those foreign decorations, sir?

NESCHASTLIVTSEV.   Yes, foreign. Now, let me alone, brother. [*To* VOSMIBRATOV.]   Come here.

VOSMIBRATOV. I wish you the best, your Excellency. I don't know your name, sir.

NESCHASTLIVTSEV. Come here, I tell you.

VOSMIBRATOV. [*To his son.*] Petrushka, step aside. Another step or two. There, that's it. [*To* NESCHASTLIVTSEV.] What is it I can do for you, sir?

NESCHASTLIVTSEV. I can't talk with you standing a verst off from me.

VOSMIBRATOV. Maybe, you're hard of hearing, sir, so we'll go up to you. Don't matter in the least.

NESCHASTLIVTSEV. How is it you even dare think . . .

VOSMIBRATOV. Permit me, sir!

NESCHASTLIVTSEV. Shut up. With a woman like that. And you . . .

VOSMIBRATOV. What woman? Permit me, sir . . .

NESCHASTLIVTSEV. What woman? So, he even asks me! Shut up, and I'll tell you. A woman, before whom everybody, yes, everybody, even I, venerate. And you, you filthy kopek-pinching . . .

VOSMIBRATOV. What's this all about, sir?

NESCHASTLIVTSEV. Don't interrupt me. Better thank the good Lord that I've got a dribble or two of patience left. God help you if I didn't. [*Shakes his finger.*]

VOSMIBRATOV. Petrushka! Why are you standing there with your mouth hanging open? Just stand up and look the way you should.

NESCHASTLIVTSEV. Oh, better watch out, you poor boy, you. Don't get between the lion and his . . .

VOSMIBRATOV. Why is it you're shouting? If you start shouting, then I'll start shouting, and before you know it, it will turn out like the marketplace. Won't make any sense. No sense at all.

NESCHASTLIVTSEV. You! Oh, what are you . . . What do you mean, you'll start shouting?

VOSMIBRATOV. And why shouldn't I shout, if that's the way you do things around here? Where I live we talk quietly to one another, 'cause we don't have deaf people around.

NESCHASTLIVTSEV. [*To* BULANOV.] What's he saying? Did you hear what he said? Don't tell me he has the audacity to . . .

BULANOV. Yes, sir.

NESCHASTLIVTSEV. Good God Almighty. And he is still alive? Don't tell me I haven't killed him yet?

VOSMIBRATOV.   Why are you going on like that, sir? Permit me to ask what can I do for you? 'Cause there's nothing much in it for me standing around visiting.

NESCHASTLIVTSEV.   What can you do for me? Listen to him, will you? Asking me what can he do for me? Oh! Ha, ha, ha! I'd just like to tell you that you are a swindler.

VOSMIBRATOV.   No, better you leave off that tune. Keeping that up won't get us anywhere. It's just uncalled-for right now.

PETR.   Listen to those compliments, will you.

VOSMIBRATOV.   Petrushka, come here.

PETR.   I am here, daddy.

VOSMIBRATOV.   [*To* NESCHASTLIVTSEV.] If you've got business, then speak up. If not, then permit me to leave. Now, see here, you'd better come to my place, please. I can talk a little easier at home. Let's go, Petr.

NESCHASTLIVTSEV.   [*Threateningly.*] Hold on! Stay right there!

PETR.   If you stay over night, then you've got to pay for it.

NESCHASTLIVTSEV.   How is it you could cheat an honest woman?

VOSMIBRATOV.   Cheat? Oh, that's a good one, it is. Why is it you believe your aunt, and you don't believe me?

NESCHASTLIVTSEV.   You heard him ask it, didn't you? She is gentle, like an angel, and he . . . [*Throws up his hands.*] And he has the audacity to talk. Just look at him, will you. With a snout like his, god-forsaken as it is. Just tell me what it's worth.

VOSMIBRATOV.   Petrushka, stand over here.

PETR.   But, daddy, don't you think we've heard plenty of silly songs already?

NESCHASTLIVTSEV.   Gentleness! The living picture of gentleness.

VOSMIBRATOV.   Nobody would ever deny that. But as for common sense? She's a bit shy on that score.

NESCHASTLIVTSEV.   To hell with your common sense. What's that got to do with it, I'd like to know? Common sense is worth an inch or two, four or five grains, a smidgen, no more. But honor? You can't measure it. And you don't have a single, solitary snitch.

VOSMIBRATOV.   Don't go on like that, master. Say what you want, but don't rub away my honor. I'll take you to court for that. How can you say I don't have honor? I'll prove it to you with my own documents. There is my honor. Go ahead, and ask anyone within a hundred versts, and they'll all say the same thing. Maybe it's not enough for you. Then I'll speak for myself. I am an honorable man. You won't hear me boast about anything else. As for my honor, I'll just say this. I'm not a man. I'm a walking yardstick.

NESCHASTLIVTSEV. [*Sits at the table and drops his head.*] Go on. Leave!

VOSMIBRATOV. What do you mean, leave?

NESCHASTLIVTSEV. That's all. Just get out of here. Oh, people, people!

VOSMIBRATOV. What do you mean, that's all? No, just a minute. If you like, master, shall I slay you with one word?

NESCHASTLIVTSEV. Me?

VOSMIBRATOV. Yes, you. [*Crosses, takes out pocketbook, and throws it on the table.*] Do you see that?

NESCHASTLIVTSEV. What is it?

VOSMIBRATOV. Maybe your aunt forgot about it herself. Well, the devil with her. So, you believe her. All right, then take what you think is fair. Take as much as you want. I'm not going to stop you. Go ahead, take it.

BULANOV. Better take it as fast as you can.

NESCHASTLIVTSEV. [*To* BULANOV.] Get out of here. [*To* VOSMIBRATOV, *handing over the pocketbook.*] Give it to me yourself.

VOSMIBRATOV. All right, I'll do it myself. [*Counts the money.*] Now you can see the kind of person I am. Just write it down on the credit side for prayers in church.

NESCHASTLIVTSEV. Your hand!

VOSMIBRATOV. What do you want my hand for? [*Holds out his hand.*] I'd have done it long before. Don't you know the kind of person I am? Master, you probably know my nature, don't you? If somebody rubs me the wrong way, I get all hot and bothered, and then give everything away. No doubt your aunt and I traded for three thousand. It strikes me we did, but I won't say for sure. I've got no documents to prove it, only my say-so. Oh, well then, give her a thousand rubles. But all the same, I'll say that it's not right. [*Raisa enters.*]

NESCHASTLIVTSEV. [*Handing the money to* RAISA.] There you are, take your money. [*Crosses to one side of the stage and stands, folding his arms and hanging his head.*]

RAISA.   I thank you with all my heart, my dear.

VOSMIBRATOV.   Did you get it, ma'am? Only thing is, if the master hadn't come along, you'd never have seen this money. And I'd have blamed myself for it. I've got a conscience, too, you know.

RAISA.   Don't be angry at me, Ivan Petrovich. I am a woman; you can't demand too much of me. Do me the honor of having dinner here tomorrow.

VOSMIBRATOV.   You can't turn down either bread or salt. And there's still the matter about the stumps.

RAISA.   Well, about the stumps, then.

VOSMIBRATOV.   It's all right if I go, isn't it? Good-by, angry master. Petr, let's go. [*Exits.* PETR *and* KARP *follow him out.*]

RAISA.   [*To* NESCHASTLIVTSEV.] Oh, I don't know how to thank you. You know, don't you, that it's the exact same amount I owe you? [*As though suddenly remembering something, she quickly hides the money.*]

NESCHASTLIVTSEV.   I don't believe it.

RAISA.   [*Locking the box.*] I treasure your money, my dear, I do.

NESCHASTLIVTSEV.   Oh, auntie, don't try your cleverness on me. Aren't you ashamed of yourself? Oh, the heart of a woman. You want to offer me money, but you don't know how to do it tactfully. You are in my debt. Well, that's excellent. Some time or other, we will settle accounts. Don't refuse me should I ever be in need. But for the moment I don't want money. I'm a rich man.

RAISA.   Well, if that's your desire, my dear.

SCHASTLIVTSEV.   [*To himself.*] Just look at him putting on airs, when he hasn't a kopek to his name.

RAISA.   [*Glancing at* BULANOV.] I hope that you'll stay on here with us.

NESCHASTLIVTSEV.   Two or three days, no longer. If it's all right with you.

RAISA.   Why such a short time?

NESCHASTLIVTSEV.   It'd be long enough for me. To visit my native woodland, to recall the days of silly childhood, of light-hearted youth. Who knows, if I'll have the chance again before the gates of eternity . . .

RAISA.   You're not thinking, are you, that a longer visit would inconvenience me? On the contrary, I'd be very happy to see you . . .

NESCHASTLIVTSEV.   Noble, noble woman. Waste not in vain the treasure of thy heart on me. My path is thorny, but I shall never leave it.

RAISA.   [*With glances at* BULANOV, *she shows that she is very pleased.*]   If that's your desire, my dear. I thought you'd find it more peaceful here.

NESCHASTLIVTSEV.   I'll find peace when I'm dead. But here it is paradise. And I'm not worth it. Oh, thank you. Thank you. My heart is filled with gratitude, filled with love for you. My soul is full of warm tears.   [*Wipes away tears.*]   Oh, your mercy, your tenderness, I've enough and to spare. I shall become an idolater. I shall pray for you.   [*Covers his face with his hand and exits.* SCHASTLIVTSEV *follows him, but stops and watches from behind a bush.*]

RAISA.   He's gone. Well, I feel a little better now, more calm. His being here doesn't upset me. But he must be some sort of fanatic. It seems to me, pure and simple, that he is a stupid man. But I was scared to death just now. How frightening he was.

BULANOV.   No, it was nothing, ma'am. It's the best way to handle common people, ma'am.

RAISA.   All the same, you be careful. Just protect yourself, my dear. I still can't get that dream out of my head. You can see for yourself, the fellow has a violent streak in him.

BULANOV.   Oh, don't worry. I've made friends with him.

RAISA.   I'd never have expected it. He refuses to take the money. Isn't that sweet of him? And it was useless to remind him of the debt. Oh, why did I take it so much to heart? You go on playing a role too long, and then all of a sudden you forget you're playing. You're caught up in the reality of the moment. You don't know, my dear, how much I love to hold on to money.

BULANOV.   I wouldn't know. I'm still young, ma'am. But smart people say, Raisa Pavlovna, that tightfistedness is scarcely thick-wittedness.

RAISA.   Well, I am scarcely tightfisted. I'll give everything to the one I grow to love.

BULANOV.   Do you have a lot of money, ma'am?

RAISA.   Yes, I do. Just take a look.   [*Opens the box.* BULANOV *looks and sighs.*]   And I'll give all this money to the one I grow to love.

BULANOV.   [*With a deep sigh.*]   Oh, ma'am.

RAISA.   There's something I wanted to tell you, Aleksis. You are much too obsequious, and you still act like a boy. I don't like it at all. Of course, it's impossible to judge you too harshly. I expect it's because of your background. Poverty, and all that. Well, somehow or other we'll overcome that misfortune. We'll give you something a little more solid to build on. I'd like you to be more reputable, distinguished. In a day or two you must go to the city in our province; order a lot of good clothes, loose-fitting; buy an expensive gold watch and chain; and, so on and so on. Besides that, you ought to have money in your pocket, all the time. It will give you aplomb.   [*Out of her box she takes the money which* NESCHASTLIVTSEV *gave her.*]   This is mad money. I received it by accident. I give it to you.

BULANOV.   [*Flustered.*]   Me, ma'am?   [*Takes the money.*]   I thank you, ma'am.   [*Kisses her hand.*]   So you want me reputable, distinguished? That I'll become, ma'am.

RAISA.   Let's go. I'll prepare a list of what you must buy in the city.   [RAISA *and* BULANOV *exit.*]

SCHASTLIVTSEV.   Farewell, oh money to burn. Oh, damn these tragedians! A world of noble actions, but never a smidgen of common sense.

ACT FOUR

Another part of the garden. To the right, a summerhouse; to the left, a garden bench. In the distance, through the trees, a view of a lake. A moonlit night.

NESCHASTLIVTSEV.   Arkady, have you eaten supper?

SCHASTLIVTSEV.   Yes, I've eaten.

NESCHASTLIVTSEV.   Did they feed you pretty good, brother?

SCHASTLIVTSEV.   Excellently. A smart fellow, Gennady Demyanych, never gets lost at the table.

NESCHASTLIVTSEV.   Smart? Now, who is it you're talking about?

SCHASTLIVTSEV.   About myself, sir.

NESCHASTLIVTSEV.   And who was it said you were smart? Don't believe it, brother. Somebody was putting you on.

SCHASTLIVTSEV.   I'll just show you how smart I am, sir. Well, first of all, I eat from the master's table; I said that you expected me to do that. And, second, I've taken up with the housekeeper. To top it off, Gennady Demyanych, I've even borrowed money from her. What's more, I have a bottle of brandy in the corner next to my bed. The bottle looks like it has shoe blackening.

NESCHASTLIVTSEV.   Not bad, Arkashka, for your first debut. Now, brother, try and play your role the best you can.

SCHASTLIVTSEV.   That I am. But how about you?

NESCHASTLIVTSEV.   I'm happy now, Arkady. I did a good thing.

SCHASTLIVTSEV.   Yes, sir, a good thing. But it'd been better if the money'd . . .

NESCHASTLIVTSEV.   What?

SCHASTLIVTSEV.   *Amposhé.*[29]   [*Pantomimes action of putting the money in his pocket.*]

NESCHASTLIVTSEV.   I'll give you your *amposhé.*

SCHASTLIVTSEV.   Oh, the money, the money right there in your hands. Oh, Gennady Demyanych!

NESCHASTLIVTSEV.   Yes, and it trickled right through my fingers.

SCHASTLIVTSEV.   Why on earth did you give it up?

NESCHASTLIVTSEV.   Have you gone mad, Arkashka? Why, exactly? It wasn't mine.

SCHASTLIVTSEV.   As if that mattered! God help me, we could've taken to our heels at once. To town, where we'd have picked up a troika. Then, off we'd go on a dead run. Then on a steamer to Yaroslavl, hither and thither. From there to Nizhny for the fair.

NESCHASTLIVTSEV.   I think I'll strangle you, Arkashka. It'd be better for you, and a little more peaceful for me.

SCHASTLIVTSEV.   Strangle? Here you've been saying you're pretty smart. The way I see it, the schoolboy's smarter. He's playing his role here a little better than you.

NESCHASTLIVTSEV.   What role, brother? Well, what is he, exactly? Nothing more than a brat.

SCHASTLIVTSEV.   What role? Why, first lover, sir.

NESCHASTLIVTSEV.   Lover? [*Threateningly.*] Whose?

SCHASTLIVTSEV.   [*With comic obsequiousness.*] Your auntie's.

NESCHASTLIVTSEV.   Ha, ha, ha! Well, Arkashka, you not only have the figure but also the soul of a flunky. Only better be more careful, and don't blab so much. Fellows like you get beaten for that.

SCHASTLIVTSEV.   Well, yes, beaten . . .

NESCHASTLIVTSEV.   And a good beating, at that.

SCHASTLIVTSEV.   Well, why not? [*Crosses to the bushes.*] He plays the lover, but you [*from behind a bush*] the simpleton.

NESCHASTLIVTSEV.   [*Crossing toward* SCHASTLIVTSEV.] Me, the simpleton? Me?

SCHASTLIVTSEV.   [*Running to the opposite side.*] The one everybody laughs at.

NESCHASTLIVTSEV.   Is it me they're laughing at? Who is it, who? Speak up, you unlucky man, you.

SCHASTLIVTSEV.   [*Retreating.*] Now, that's enough of your scaring me to death. I'll run away. Don't blame me. Just because I heard it with my own ears.

NESCHASTLIVTSEV.   Well, who? Damn it.

SCHASTLIVTSEV.   Auntie and Bulanov.

NESCHASTLIVTSEV.   [*Clutching his head.*]   Oh!

SCHASTLIVTSEV.   They called you a silly fool.   [*Hides behind a bush.*]

NESCHASTLIVTSEV.   Arkashka. You're sick to death of your vile life, aren't you? Then go on and strangle yourself. Don't force me to dirty my hands with you.

SCHASTLIVTSEV.   We had the money, but you didn't dare take it. It dribbled through your mustache, but it wouldn't drop into your mouth. And you called me your buddy. If we're buddies, then we go half-and-half. And my half went down the drain with your half.

NESCHASTLIVTSEV.   But you know I didn't call you my buddy, just for the sake of robbing people.

SCHASTLIVTSEV.   Hand over my half. Hand it over.

NESCHASTLIVTSEV.   Arkashka. You're drunk, aren't you?

SCHASTLIVTSEV.   And, so what if I am drunk? I'm proud of it.

NESCHASTLIVTSEV.   No, I'm going to kill you. Yes, that's it. Then I'll hear the last of it. And there's nothing more to say, either.

SCHASTLIVTSEV.   [*Retreating.*]   Well, why don't you go ahead and kill me?   [*From behind a bush.*]   Your arms are too short. [*Runs off.*]

NESCHASTLIVTSEV.   He was lying. Yes, stood there barefaced and lied. Oh, man is vile. Yes, vile. What if . . . Oh, let him lie, rather than speak the truth. I'll just flatten him. What if my devout auntie, that image of gentleness and humility . . . Oh, then I'd tell her a thing or two. To laugh at the feelings, at the warm tears of an actor. No, an insult like that Neschastlivtsev would never forgive.   [*Exits to the summerhouse.* KARP *enters.*]

KARP.   Everyone's had supper. The mistress has gone to her bedroom. Perhaps, I can relax now.   [*Sits on the bench.* ULITA *enters and looks around.*]   Come out for a stroll?

ULITA.   Yes, Karp Savelich. The night is already very . . .

KARP.   Indeed, we might say, quite disposed. Well now, have a good stroll. You might even say that people are lively, and lively people think about lively things.

ULITA.   What's all that about, exactly?

KARP.   Maybe even about you.

ULITA.   In what sense?

KARP.   You might even understand it yourself.

ULITA.   No, you don't say so?

KARP.   Oh, what's it to me? Think what you like. I am not your husband.

ULITA.   Whatever you're saying sounds pretty stupid to me.

KARP.   Go on, think whatever you want.

ULITA.   I don't understand why people forever and always see only the bad in everything.

KARP.   I don't see anything bad or good. But it's certainly surprising . . .

ULITA.   What do you mean, surprising?

KARP.   That when you get to your age . . .

ULITA.   My age? You weren't at my christening. I can see there's no use talking to you.

KARP.   You won't lose anything listening to me.

ULITA.   You sit there, like a horned owl, and sound off on whatever pops into your head.

KARP.   Turns out I'm bothering you here?

ULITA.   And what do you mean by that? You can just stop turning that around in your head, because you are wrong. [SCHASTLIVTSEV *enters.*]

SCHASTLIVTSEV.   Honorable company.

ULITA.   Welcome.

KARP.   Your master asleep?

SCHASTLIVTSEV.   [*Sitting.*]   Who knows what he's doing?

ULITA.   Are you staying with us a long time?

SCHASTLIVTSEV.   What on earth can we do here?

KARP.   But you ought to stay. Everything's different now. Why, just now Ivan Petrov had to return the money.

ULITA.   Of course, he is a man.

KARP.   But the mistress really can't handle things. Good people keep on buying, but we keep on selling. I can't guess how much timber we've sold, or how much of everything else, either. The mistress stuffs her box full of money, closes it, and then just try and get even half a kopek out of it. Then, all of a sudden, out fly thousands, and they keep flying.

SCHASTLIVTSEV.   Don't tell me they fly?

KARP.   They fly.

ULITA.   Right straight into the hands of poor people and relatives.

SCHASTLIVTSEV.   [*Not listening.*]   Not a bad idea to hook a few.

KARP.   Well, they get hooked, all right.

ULITA.   Every one by the poor people and relatives.

KARP.   I wouldn't say by the relatives.

ULITA.   And by whom then, do you think?

KARP.   I know, don't think I don't, by whom.

ULITA.   You ought to be ashamed to talk in front of outsiders like that.

KARP.   Why be ashamed? He's just like us. So, what's it matter . . .

ULITA.   Seems to me, the whole district knows only too well what good lives we lead around here.

KARP.   I'm not talking about the village. Don't think they won't be saying something else later on. What about in Petersburg, or in Moscow?

ULITA.   All the same, you shouldn't go around talking down the mistress.

KARP.   Well, don't think I'm talking her down. The mistress is kind, and a good one to serve. But why shouldn't you tell the truth? I carry the money to the post office, so I know for sure who it is she sends it to, relatives or not.

SCHASTLIVTSEV.   Sure is a curious conversation.

ULITA.   There's nothing curious about it. Go on with you. He's making it all up.

KARP.   Did she send it to a French doctor? To an Italian? To a topographer, who measures the earth?

ULITA.   Oh, oh! Why is it you're not ashamed?

KARP.   Well, what do you have in mind? What would you like to hear? I love the truth. So, it's time to go to bed. Go on with you. Good luck!

SCHASTLIVTSEV.   Good-by, Sturgeon Savelich.

KARP.   Oh, to hell with you. You joker, you.   [KARP *exits.*]

ULITA.   Did you taste the brandy? I don't know if it's good or not. I wanted to treat you to something, but I really don't know.

SCHASTLIVTSEV.   Very good, excellent. You probably made it yourself.

ULITA.   Come on now, you're joking me, aren't you? If you like, I'll bring some cream for your tea tomorrow.

SCHASTLIVTSEV.   Do me the favor, but only from a mad cow.

ULITA.   Oh, 1 don't understand you.

SCHASTLIVTSEV.   That is, rum. That's what we always call it.

ULITA.   I'll look for some.

SCHASTLIVTSEV.   Do that, if you love me.

ULITA.   Listen to you, will you? "If you love me." Do you know what I'll say to that?

SCHASTLIVTSEV.   No, what?

ULITA.   You said that just to scoff at me. You shouldn't go around convicting all us women.

SCHASTLIVTSEV.   Convicting you of what, for pity's sake? Don't think I haven't been pretty well satisfied.

ULITA.   Well, men are forever and always satisfied, 'cause they don't have to answer to anyone for it. I'd like to see you live the way women have to. It used to be . . . and I die every time I remember it . . . that our life wasn't worth much. We just existed. They wouldn't let you get married. They wouldn't let you fall in love, either. They even put a ban on love. Well, there was only one way out: to get on the good side of the mistress. So, you crawled. Yes, you crawled before the mistress. Worse, it seems to me, than the lowest creature on earth. Well, by crawling, you picked up a little privilege and got a little courage in your heart. Your heart, you see, is alive, and expects something to keep it alive. You should see how servitude cripples people. I'll tell you about myself. But it'd bore you to listen. Stands to reason, my life was wretched and worthless. But I don't want to upset either you or me, 'cause you're very dear to me. [*Glances around.*]   That's your master, isn't it?

SCHASTLIVTSEV.   He's coming to beat me.

ULITA.   Oh, that's terrible.

SCHASTLIVTSEV.   I'll squat down, and you fence me in. Maybe he won't notice. [*Squats down.*]   What do you say, is he coming? Getting closer?

ULITA.   No, he went back. He looked just like a wild man. Oh, can he stare you down! Simply terrible. I shudder every time I see it.

SCHASTLIVTSEV.   [*Rises.*]   Barbarian!

ULITA.   How is it, my dear, you can live with a master like that?

SCHASTLIVTSEV.   Master? Oh, that's a good one. I'm the same as he is. Just see the way he prances around, thanks to his big mouth.

ULITA.   What did you say? He has a real gentlemanly manner about him. He was born with it, and it's impossible to take it away from him.

SCHASTLIVTSEV.   Who's taking it away? I just said that we're equals. We're both actors. He is Neschastlivtsev, and I am Schastlivtsev, and both of us are drunkards.

ULITA.   Actors? Oh, you're not serious, you can't be!

SCHASTLIVTSEV.   Listen, for more than ten years we've been wandering around Russia, from theatre to theatre, like gypsies. The reason he's never been at his aunt's before is that he's ashamed to look her in the eye.

ULITA.   Oh, it's terrible, terrible.

SCHASTLIVTSEV.   Right now he's walking to Vologda, with a little bag. It was impossible for him to show up without a flunky. He's a nobleman, so he got down on his knees and begged me to take on the job. Then, he'd better start treating me a little kinder. I've got a better name than he has in the provinces. Nowadays, stiff-handled plows have gone out of fashion.

ULITA.   Why, I can't believe my ears.

SCHASTLIVTSEV.   He thinks he'll get something useful out of auntie here. He ought to ask her straight out. He's poor enough, God knows. But, you see, he's ashamed to. A little while ago, he made a mistake. He failed to snatch up the money. So, right now, he's mad as hell at me because of it. Why, he's the orneriest man I know. A little while ago he was playing cards with the schoolboy, and trying his best to trap the kid. Well, I just walked off. I bet he'll win from him, snap up the money, and give the kid a good beating besides. That's what'll happen, all right. And don't think it's the first time, either. He'll kill somebody or other, and I'll land up in prison with him. Why, he looks and acts like a robber. A Pugachev, [30] come alive.

ULITA.   I'm glad you told me. Good-by.

SCHASTLIVTSEV.   *Adue, mon plezir.*[31]

ULITA.   [*Frightened.*]   I'm on my way. Oh, it's terrible, terrible.

SCHASTLIVTSEV.   Oh, you were frightened! You know, I used to play devils all the time. This is the way I jumped around on stage. [*Jumps and screams.*]   Ai! Ai!

ULITA.   Saints in heaven! Excuse me. I can't stand it, I can't.

SCHASTLIVTSEV.   Oh, what's it to me? Go on with your excuses.

Damn you and damn your estate, too. I'm going to run away from you. Go to hell! [ULITA *runs off.*]   I'd leave right now, but I'm afraid. There's a world of dogs in the village. Damn these people, anyway. They have nothing to eat for themselves, but they raise dogs. And it's terrifying to walk through the woods alone. I must spend the night in the summerhouse. I have to go there, since my library and brandy are there. But how can I slip in? He's not asleep yet. He's still reciting monologues. No doubt, I'll fly through the window, just like Fidler did. I'll go tramp through the garden, even if I snap off all the dahlias. All the same, it's easier than facing him. [*Exits.* PETR *timidly steals along in the shadow of the bushes and looks around.*]

PETR.   Well, seems like everybody in the house has gone to sleep. The only unhappy fool tramping around is me. All right, then offer the fool half a ruble in silver, and he'll sell his own father. It's very bright tonight. Maybe Aksyusha won't even show up. She'll be scared to death somebody will see her. But she must show up, she must. It may be the very last time we can be together. And then it's over, finished, done for. I hate the life I lead, forced to do everything somebody else wants. My heart shakes like a lamb's tail, that's for sure. You can't do a thing with yourself; both your hands and feet are shaking so much. It'd be easier to rob somebody. If you come to somebody's house to be with your girl, why they make an example out of it and deal with you worse than a thief. And you call this love? Daddy calls it nothing but fooling around. He says it grabs hold of you for a year or two, no longer. After that you start working to make money. I must wait until she comes, and in the meantime just put up with the torments of the damned. Wait a bit, is she coming? Sure enough, she's here. [AKSYUSHA *enters. Having seen* PETR, *she runs to him.*]

AKSYUSHA.   Oh, here you are.

PETR.   I've been tramping around here a long time. Hello! It's really you, isn't it? [*Kisses her.*]

AKSYUSHA.   You see, it's really me. Well, hurry up and say what you have to say. You know we haven't much time before they miss me.

PETR.   I had another talk with daddy again.

AKSYUSHA.   Well, what did he say? Hurry up and tell me. I'll die if you don't tell me.

PETR.   He's backing down. As usual he swore at me for an hour. Finally, "For a silly fool like you," he says, "I see we won't find a bride with a dowry; if they'd give two thousand, then I'd go along with it." Hear that?

AKSYUSHA.   But you know there's no place to get it.

PETR.   You must get it.

AKSYUSHA.   You can't pry it out of Raisa Pavlovna, and there's not much use in groveling for it, either.

PETR.   Why not ask your cousin? Ask Gennady Demyanych.

AKSYUSHA.   Ai, you're not serious! I'd be scared to death. Besides, I'd be ashamed to.

PETR.   But, when it's all said and done, he is your cousin. Up to now there's nothing else you can do.

AKSYUSHA.   You know I'll have to tell him everything.

PETR.   Well, so what? Tell him. He's one of the family. He's our very last chance.

AKSYUSHA.   Yes, our very last.

PETR.   After all, who knows him, really? You can't tell what might happen. With a mug like his, you'd guess him to be a fine gentleman. Then hurry up. Tell him before tomorrow morning. Then, at noon when daddy and I come, you can tell me.

AKSYUSHA.   All right, I'll do it.

PETR.   Only don't drag out the whole conversation. Keep it short. Like this, I'd say, I need the money desperately. Then, that's it. Whole hog, or nothing.

AKSYUSHA.   Yes, yes. Of course. Why be ashamed even, when . . .

PETR.   What do you mean, when?

AKSYUSHA.   When death will come.

PETR.   Now, enough of that. You're not serious, are you?

AKSYUSHA.   Listen to me, Petya! Everything seems so futile to me now.

PETR.   Why do you say that?

AKSYUSHA.   I just can't tell you why. Nobody's taught me the answers. Futile, that's all. Futile. My own guess is, I've known nothing but grief and weariness my whole life long. I imagine that's what's eaten me up inside. And so, I feel everything's futile. Besides, I am alone all the time. Other people have a mother, a grandmother, or a nurse or friend, at least. Somebody with whom they can talk about life, and what it means. But I don't have a single person to turn to. So everything has just built up inside, to the point it's getting me down. I can't even cry. I want to, but no tears come. I don't feel overcome by grief. But I tell you, I'm empty inside. I feel it's all so futile. Everything's spinning around inside my head. I think, and I think, but I'm all mixed up.

PETR. Well, just stop all this thinking. When you start thinking, you're only asking for trouble.

AKSYUSHA. I just can't stop. I've no strength left at all. If someone would only tell me what to do, then I know I'd listen. If only someone would hold me, hold me tightly. But I imagine I see water all the time.

PETR. What do you mean, water?

AKSYUSHA. Oh, don't you know, my darling? Don't you know everything's pressing me closer and closer to the water's edge?

PETR. Oh, you can't be serious. Stop it.

AKSYUSHA. I go walking through the garden, and I keep looking at the lake. I walk far away from it, on purpose. Then something presses me closer to it, and I must look at it. And in the distance, through the trees, I'll see the lake, sparkling. Then all of a sudden, something very powerful seizes me, presses me toward it. Then I feel as if I must run, run, and throw myself into it.

PETR. Oh, good Lord, why? You know it's a sin. Why?

AKSYUSHA. I don't know myself. Remember what you said yesterday? Well, I can't get it out of my mind. When I sit at home, then I imagine constantly that I'm going straight to the bottom, and everything around me seems green. It isn't that I despair and want to destroy my own soul. No, that isn't it, at all. I know I can go on living. I could hide for a while and somehow deceive them. You know they won't kill me when I show up. And they'll probably feed and clothe me as they do now. Bad as it is.

PETR. Well, it's a hell of a life.

AKSYUSHA. At least we're alive, aren't we? And I can go on living just as before.

PETR. That's the way for animals, the way dogs and cats live. Seems to me, a person ought to have something better.

AKSYUSHA. Oh, my darling! Why do I even talk about it? Always the same thing. You know it's possible to live that way, but it just isn't worth it. And I don't understand why it's all happened. You know I'm barely fifteen years old. I used to have pretty good sense, and here all of a sudden . . . Living as I do and doing for others all the time have dried up my soul. I'd like to have a little fun before I die. I need a little holiday. There you have it, my silly darling. Just see what I go through because of you. [*Embraces him.*]

PETR.   Oh, my poor darling, you. And where did you learn to love like that? And why is it your caress tears me up inside and means more than anything else in the world? Oh, my darling, what can I do? I must be with you, always. I can't escape it. Never.

AKSYUSHA.   But you must try, my dearest, you must. Right now I'm not sure if you will pity me or laugh at me when I'm gone. I can't stay away from what I must do. But you, my dearest, you must try to keep away from me, from what I must do. It will be easier for me, my darling, if you leave me.

PETR.   No, please stay a little longer. If only for a little while, we must still try to live in our own way. Let's don't even think of tomorrow! And we don't know yet what your cousin will say.

AKSYUSHA.   Yes, let's wait. If there's a chance, we must call on him.

PETR.   Maybe he'll come to our rescue.

AKSYUSHA.   Maybe. You didn't see anyone in the garden, did you?

PETR.   Gennady Demyanych's servant was tramping around.

AKSYUSHA.   Then you'd better leave. It's time.

PETR.   And you, Aksyusha, go home, so that . . . May the Good Lord protect you, my darling.

AKSYUSHA.   I'm going home, my dearest, I am. Don't worry. It doesn't bother me now. Because, because I have something to look forward to.

PETR.   Well, even so, watch out. [*They kiss.*]   I believe in you. [PETR *exits.* AKSYUSHA *starts to go home, she turns around and sees* NESCHASTLIVTSEV, *who is coming out of the summerhouse.*]

NESCHASTLIVTSEV.   [*To himself.*]   Woman, oh beautiful woman. [*Crosses to* AKSYUSHA.]   Tell me. Are you a woman or a shadow?

AKSYUSHA.   Cousin.

NESCHASTLIVTSEV.   Ah, I see now that you are a woman. Right now I wanted to speak, on this beautiful evening, with those who live beyond the grave.

AKSYUSHA.   Cousin.

NESCHASTLIVTSEV.   Oh, they carried to the grave so many secrets, so much suffering. My soul is dark and gloomy. What care I for the living! There is nothing on earth for me to tell the living. I must speak with those from that other world. Off, away with you!

AKSYUSHA.   Cousin, I too have gone through so much pain, and I suffer even now.

NESCHASTLIVTSEV.   You?

AKSYUSHA.   Yes, me. I am terribly unhappy.

NESCHASTLIVTSEV.   If you are terribly unhappy, then come to me, put your head on my chest. [AKSYUSHA *crosses and puts her head on his chest.*]   I am your cousin twice over. Cousin by blood, and cousin by misfortune.

AKSYUSHA.   [*Falling to her knees.*]   Oh, dear cousin, I'm to blame.

NESCHASTLIVTSEV.   [*Raises her.*]   No, no, not before me. How is it possible that you are to blame? You, who are so young, so very beautiful? And you fall on your knees before whom? What am I? One of the rabble, rags thrown off from mankind.

AKSYUSHA.   I'm to blame, and I'll say it before everyone. Even before myself. I love . . .

NESCHASTLIVTSEV.   Oh, my child. Love whomever you choose. God gave you a heart so you might love.

AKSYUSHA.   Oh, what are you saying? To love. I love, beyond all human bounds. You know I must marry him. I must. Yes, I must.

NESCHASTLIVTSEV.   And who's trying to stop you?

AKSYUSHA.   People are stopping me. People who have the power.

NESCHASTLIVTSEV.   Oh, don't even listen to them. Go to the man whom you love. And upon your head I shall give my own blessing.

AKSYUSHA.   But he can't marry me without a dowry. His father just won't agree to it. I need a dowry, but I just don't have one.

NESCHASTLIVTSEV.   What nonsense! Happiness is worth far more than money.

AKSYUSHA.   But I'm not going to get happiness without money.

NESCHASTLIVTSEV.   But do you need much money?

AKSYUSHA.   Two thousand rubles.

NESCHASTLIVTSEV.   It's only a trifle. Don't tell me Raisa Pavlovna refuses to give you a little thing like that?

AKSYUSHA.   Yes, she refuses. She keeps me out of charity, feeds me out of charity. How can I even dare ask her for a dowry? She'll give me a crust of bread, but not a single kopek.

NESCHASTLIVTSEV.   And a girl's happiness depends on an insignificant amount of money, the happiness of a young soul . . .

AKSYUSHA.   No, not happiness, but life itself.

NESCHASTLIVTSEV.   Life itself? Heavenly powers, was it you who spoke?

AKSYUSHA.   It was me, cousin.

NESCHASTLIVTSEV.   At last, thank God. Don't tell me I see a woman? And your love, then, is not a passing fancy? Are you ready for every kind of sacrifice?

AKSYUSHA.   I have already sacrificed almost everything for this love. But my life is so bitter, so bitter that any sorrow would be worthless.

NESCHASTLIVTSEV.   Are you without fear?

AKSYUSHA.   Without fear, even if right now . . .

NESCHASTLIVTSEV.   [Raises his hand above her head.]   Oh, angels of the Lord, give her shelter with your wings.   [AKSYUSHA drops her head in silence and folds her arms. A short pause.]

AKSYUSHA.   Cousin, don't be angry with me. Don't think badly of me. It's really hard for me to say . . .

NESCHASTLIVTSEV.   Tell me, my child, do.

AKSYUSHA.   Cousin, don't think me a cheat, a poor begging relative. Dear cousin, mother and I lived in severe poverty. I was a child, but not once did I bow and scrape, not once did I stretch out my hands to beg from rich relatives. Instead, I worked. This is the first time, cousin, that I have ever asked anyone for anything. And I'm doing it at night, so you can't see the shame in my cheeks. Cousin, you are a rich man, and you are single. Oh, give me happiness, give me life itself.   [Falls to her knees.]

NESCHASTLIVTSEV.   [Raises her; he is deeply moved and speaks with a tremble in his voice.]   My child. My child.

AKSYUSHA.   If it were not for fear of shame because of my sinful love, I should never, never . . . Oh, be a father to me. I am a good girl and honest. I'll teach my little children to bless you and pray for you.

NESCHASTLIVTSEV.   Oh, be quiet, please do. I'll tear out my hair. Oh, my child. I am the criminal. I might have had money, might have helped you, might have made your life happy. But I squandered my money, spent it all in debauchery. I trampled it down in the mud together with my youth, my life. And now when the money's needed, I have none to give. If I had known . . . Oh, dear God, if I had known, I'd have existed on bread alone. I'd have gone around in rags; and every ruble I had, I would've sewed up in those rags. We drink, raise hell, embody vulgar, false passions, praise to heaven our tavern heroism. And here my poor cousin stands between life and death. Weep, you drunkard, weep.

AKSYUSHA.   Cousin. Oh, cousin.

NESCHASTLIVTSEV.   Forgive me. Please, forgive me. I'm poorer than you. I've walked hundred of versts to see my relatives. I never cared for myself, but I cared for these clothes, so that I could dress a little nicer—so they wouldn't chuck me out. You think me a man. Well, I thank you for that. You have asked thousands of me, and I have nothing to give. Oh, cousin, cousin. Don't ask money of me. It's you who shouldn't refuse me a copper five-kopek piece, when I knock at your window and cry for money to cure my drunk the night before. A five-kopek coin for me, a five-kopek coin! Now you can see what I really am.

AKSYUSHA.   [Clutches her heart.]   Oh, oh! Will grief never, never end? Another deception for my heart. Why did I cheat myself, why? I was stupid to think, to hope. How can I dare hope? Why should I think there was hope for me! Good-by!   [Goes off, swaying to and fro; then faster and faster until finally she runs off stage.]

NESCHASTLIVTSEV.   [Looks at her as she exits.]   Where is she off to? She is running. Now she's thrown away her kerchief. She's by the shore. No, no, cousin! It's too soon for you to die.   [Exits, running. SCHASTLIVTSEV enters.]

SCHASTLIVTSEV.   Well, he's gone, running off somewhere or other. To drown himself, maybe? Wouldn't that be wonderful! That's one way out for him. I'll drop into the summerhouse, pick up my library, and then off I'll go. I'll sit in the bushes until daylight, and then—off, down the road. I have money. Thank God, I finally borrowed some at the last moment. It's a good trick to get money, but up till now I never had any luck at all. People have always been a bit nervous letting me have some. Well, right now I've got to get to some theatre or other.   [Exits into the summerhouse. NESCHASTLIVTSEV enters, supporting AKSYUSHA, who can scarcely walk.]

NESCHASTLIVTSEV.   No, my child, no! I don't care how great your misfortune is, I shan't let you die. You must live. You are so very young. Is it possible you've been eaten up by sorrow? Are you sick to death of life so soon? Forget your sorrow, put your way of life aside. We shall begin a new life, cousin, for the sake of glory, for the sake of art.

AKSYUSHA.   I know nothing, I feel nothing at all, I must be dead. Let me rest a moment.

NESCHASTLIVTSEV.   [*Putting her on the bench.*] You think you know nothing, do you? No, my child, you know more than others. You know storms, my dear; you know passions. And that, my child, is quite enough!

AKSYUSHA.   Do what you want. I see nothing ahead for me. Wherever or why you call me, or what lies ahead, I don't know. It shan't be worse than it is now.

NESCHASTLIVTSEV.   There is sorrow there, my child. But there is also joy—a joy which other people never know. Why use up your soul in vain! Is there anyone here who can possibly react to your wealth of feeling? Who will value these pearls, these diamond brilliant tears? Who, except me? But there, up ahead . . . Oh, if you throw even half these treasures to the public, why the theatre itself would tumble down from the clapping, stamping, shouting audience. They will smother you with flowers, with presents. Here you will find no reaction to your sobbing, to your groaning. But there, just for one of your tears, a thousand eyes will weep. What do you say, little cousin? Look at me. I am a beggar, a pitiful tramp. But on the stage I am a prince. I live his life. I am tortured by his thoughts. I weep his tears over poor Ophelia, and I love her with a passion that forty thousand brothers could not match. But you, my child. Oh, you are young, beautiful. There is fire in your eyes, music in your speech, beauty in your movement. You will enter on the stage as a queen, and you will leave the stage as a queen. And you will remain a queen the rest of your life.

AKSYUSHA.   I am dead, cousin. I am dead.

NESCHASTLIVTSEV.   You will return to life, dear cousin. The first sounds of the orchestra will resurrect you.

AKSYUSHA.   But what about Petya?

NESCHASTLIVTSEV.   Cousin, you are a woman, and women forget pretty fast. You will forget him, in the same way all women forget their first love. There are many handsome young men, as well as many rich men, who will hang on every word you utter and try to catch every glance you make.

AKSYUSHA. [*Shaking her head.*] No, I don't like it. It's wrong.

NESCHASTLIVTSEV. Even better, my child. The more honor to you. Yes, throw aside, push away scornfully the rich man's gold and fall in love with a poor actor. Make your decision, my child.

AKSYUSHA. If that's what you want. Then I'm ready for whatever comes.

NESCHASTLIVTSEV. You shall be my pride, my glory. And I shall be a father to you, my child. I shall be your nurse, your maid. Let's go to my place. It's a sin to sleep on a night like this. I have several parts I shall read to you. I shall give this night over to you. This night I shall confer on you the title of actress.

AKSYUSHA. Let's go. [*They cross toward the summerhouse, and* SCHASTLIVTSEV *with bundle meets them halfway.*]

NESCHASTLIVTSEV. Stop, right there. You fugitive, you. I shall be generous. Therefore, I forgive you. Let's celebrate, Arkashka! We have an actress. We three shall play all the theatres and astound all Russia. [*The three exit into the summerhouse. Enter* RAISA *and* ULITA.]

RAISA. Have you talked to him?

ULITA. You can say that again, dear mistress, I sure did. And I talked to him pretty keen, if I do say so myself. "The mistress," I said, "couldn't go to sleep, 'cause the weather's unusual; she's walking around in the garden, and even, just maybe, she's bored to death, being alone like she is, with no one there to pass away the time. And look at you, will you, coddling yourself, lying around; what kind of cavalier do you think you are, after all this?" Well, he hops right up and starts to dress.

RAISA. Hmm. Good.

ULITA. Well, there's more, dear mistress. But really I don't know how to put it to you.

RAISA. Speak up. What is it?

ULITA. The young lady's hiding out somewhere.

RAISA. Has she gone?

ULITA. She's not in her room, and her bed's not mussed up.

RAISA. Oh, that's excellent.

ULITA. How's that, dear mistress?

THE FOREST   435

RAISA. Well, only this. I am very pleased. I've been sick and tired of her for some time now. But I haven't known just how to drive her out of the house. And right now I have reason enough. Why should I feel sorry for her, when she doesn't care that much for herself? I told you she wasn't worthy of him.

ULITA. No, she isn't. Not by a long shot. You know, I could never figure out why you could hand away a beautiful, handsome, sweet man to a . . .

RAISA. Now, just a moment. That's none of your affair.

ULITA. Yes, ma'am. There's a little something else or other I found out, only to spit it out would be horrible, just horrible. The moment I heard it, why the whole thing just struck me with terror. So much so that every single one of my limbs started shaking and trembling.

RAISA. How many times have I told you to stop talking like a stupid ninny? You know how nervous I am. Then you always come along and frighten me to the point of hysterics. And when I've stopped screaming, then you drop a tidbit that means nothing. Just stuff and nonsense.

ULITA. Oh, that's what it is, dear mistress. Stuff and nonsense. Pray, don't work yourself up. Stuff and nonsense. It's about Gennady Demyanych.

RAISA. What about him?

ULITA. Well, you know he's cheated you. He's not a gentleman, but an actor. And he's gone back on his family name and now calls himself Neschastlivtsev. And he's not only in the theatre, that's bad enough; but more than that, it turns out he's a drunkard. And the only clothes he's got is what's on him. Now I can swear to that for certain. And he came here on foot with a little knapsack.

RAISA. Then he is Neschastlivtsev. I've heard of him. Yes, I have. Well, that's even better.

ULITA. And the man with him is also an actor. Only, dear mistress, out of all the actors around, he is the very worst criminal. You should see how he acts out the devils. All by himself.

RAISA. So much the better. Yes, indeed. How cleverly all this has turned out for me.

ULITA. But in what way, dear mistress, is it so good?

RAISA. In that by tomorrow morning they shall no longer be here. I don't run a hotel or tavern for gentlemen like that.

ULITA. That's for sure, dear mistress. Your hand, please. [*In a low voice.*] Aleksey Sergeich is coming. [*On her way out.*] Looking at him right now, you could say he's more than a gentleman . . . just as pretty as a picture. Hmm. [*Exits.* BULANOV *enters.*]

BULANOV. [*Hurriedly puts himself in order.*] Why is it, Raisa Pavlovna, you didn't tell me ahead of time? You should have told me, ma'am.

RAISA. What?

BULANOV. That you love to stroll in the evenings, ma'am.

RAISA. And what business is it of yours? I love nature, but maybe you don't?

BULANOV. But you know I do as you say, ma'am. If you are bored being alone . . .

RAISA. But aren't you bored on a night like this? Aren't you affected by the moon, or this air, or the fresh breeze? Look how the lake gleams reflecting the shadows from the trees. Are you cold to everything here?

BULANOV. No, ma'am, how could I be cold? I just don't know what pleases you, ma'am, or what it is gives you the most pleasure.

RAISA. But, my dear, undoubtedly you like to enjoy yourself, don't you? What is it you like to do?

BULANOV. As for me, God knows what I'd give, if only I knew what you love. Then I'd do my best to . . .

RAISA. Well, what do you think I love? I'm curious to know what you'll say.

BULANOV. The moon, ma'am.

RAISA. How simple-minded he is. Oh, my dear, I loved the moon. But all that was a long time ago. I'm no longer sixteen.

BULANOV. [*Having thought a little.*] Your relatives, ma'am?

RAISA. Ha, ha, ha! I beg your pardon. He's going to make me die laughing. Oh, simplicity! [*Laughs.*] How very sweet that is, "Your relatives, ma'am."

BULANOV. It's my fault, ma'am.

RAISA. Tell me. Right now, tell me. I order you to.

BULANOV. Don't know, ma'am.

RAISA. Oh, you fool, you! It's you!

BULANOV. Yes, ma'am. I thought it myself, but I didn't dare come out with it, ma'am. If you'd only a long time ago, ma'am

. . . You see, I've been around quite a while . . . Oh, but this is so much better, Raisa, sweetie! If only you'd a long time ago . . . [*Embraces* RAISA *and starts to kiss her.*]

RAISA. [*Pushes him away.*]   What's wrong with you, have you gone mad? Get out of here, right now! You ignorant scoundrel, you. You brat, you! [*Exits.*]

BULANOV.   Why did I mess it all up? Silly, silly, silly! Tomorrow for sure . . . I'll be out and away. [*Calls after* RAISA.]   It's all my fault, ma'am. Tomorrow they'll drive me out, and there goes my neck—in three parts, too. She didn't hear me. [*Calls louder.*] It's all my fault, ma'am. She doesn't want to hear me. [*Falls on the bench.*]   It's all over! All over! All over!

ACT FIVE

The setting is the same as in Act One.

KARP. [*Clears cups from the table and sees* RAISA's *workbox.*] Look at that, will you? She forgot her money-box, and then she'll start to look for it. Better not to touch it. Just let it lie there. [BULANOV *enters.*] Aren't you going to wait tea for Gennady Demyanych?

BULANOV. Well, I like that! I doubt it very much.

KARP. Whatever you like, sir.

BULANOV. But let me know when he comes, and don't bother Raisa Pavlovna.

KARP. Yes, sir.

BULANOV. I ask you, Karp, to carry out my instructions exactly right. I won't stand for disorder in this house. I am not like Raisa Pavlovna. When I'm around, all the right chords must be struck, or it's out the door with you. Every mistake you make I chalk up against you.

KARP. What's to be done, sir, we will carry out. Believe me, we've gone through worse things. Live long enough in this world, and you'll see everything and as much as you want to see. More wonders than these you're speaking about certainly exist.

BULANOV. That's enough of your chattering. I don't like it.

KARP. If I can't chatter anymore, then that's even better. Why talk around here? About what? Whole thing's pretty obvious.

BULANOV. Well, you can go now. [KARP *exits.* NESCHASTLIVTSEV *enters.*] Hello, Mr. Neschastlivtsev!

NESCHASTLIVTSEV. Neschastlivtsev? You know that I'm Neschastlivtsev?

BULANOV. I know.

NESCHASTLIVTSEV.   I am very glad, brother. Because you know with whom you are dealing, and therefore you'll handle yourself with care and with proper humility.

BULANOV.   Come now, what's this all about? You, a provincial actor, and you think you're that important?

NESCHASTLIVTSEV.   Well, I see that you don't know who Neschastlivtsev is, or how to talk to him. What a shame! I must teach you some sense, which, it stands to reason, will be unpleasant for you, and even more unpleasant for me.

BULANOV.   Well, that remains to be seen. In the old days, you know, physical strength amounted to a lot.

NESCHASTLIVTSEV.   Wha-a-t? Don't tell me that you and I must resort to firearms, hmm? No, brother, I am a simple man, and I'm very fond of simple, natural methods.

BULANOV.   Let's get off this subject, right now. Would you mind telling me what is it you want?

NESCHASTLIVTSEV.   Well, you can be damn sure it's not you.

BULANOV.   Who, then?

NESCHASTLIVTSEV.   What-a-t? Were you born a silly fool, or did you just become one today? Who, you ask? Who? I've finally figured out what you're like in this house. You're just like the person they call "the unknown" in operas. Look, brother, I'm here right in the middle of my own family. So, I've come to drink tea with my aunt. That too hard for you to understand?

BULANOV.   Beg your pardon.

NESCHASTLIVTSEV.   Pardon you for what? You know what you should do, brother? Slip a bag over your shoulder, tie a slate to your button, then take off and finish your schooling.

BULANOV.   Beg your pardon.

NESCHASTLIVTSEV.   Well, I beg your pardon.

BULANOV.   Not mine, but Raisa Pavlovna's pardon. She doesn't want to see you. Her health's not too good, and she feels that visits and various guests, even if they are relatives, are very much an imposition right now.

NESCHASTLIVTSEV.   Is she driving me away? But for what reason, exactly?

BULANOV.   That's not my concern. As a matter of fact, she begs you to free her of your presence, which upsets her.

NESCHASTLIVTSEV.   But what can I do? I loved her. I looked upon her like a mother. [*Wipes away a tear.*]   What does it matter if I am an actor? The duty of everyone is to do what he knows how to do. You know I'm no robber. I get my bread by honest, hard labor. I didn't come to beg favors of her, but a word of tender feeling. Of all the nerve! Oh, women! If she had to insult me, couldn't she find anybody worse than you?

BULANOV.   [*Heatedly.*]   Listen here, my good sir.

NESCHASTLIVTSEV.   Oh, God in heaven! He's going to chat about it. Listen, you. You gymnasium punk, you schoolboy, you parochial school kid, you! Out of respect for this house, I'll show mercy to you; but, so help me, if you ever show up some place else . . .

BULANOV.   We'll just see about that.

NESCHASTLIVTSEV.   Shut up, you multiplication table, you! Cornelius Nepos[32]! Pythagorean trousers,[33] you! Better grab the image of my saint and start praying morning and night that we'll never meet. But if you so much as catch sight of me, then you'd better run without looking back once, and don't forget your prayers, either.

BULANOV.   Now, who do you think you are, really! Not so loud, you! You're going to upset Raisa Pavlovna.

NESCHASTLIVTSEV.   It's all her fault, anyway. Why on earth didn't she send a man, instead of a kitten? You can't be thick-skinned when it come to kittens, let alone talking to them.

BULANOV.   Seems to me, there's nothing to talk about.

NESCHASTLIVTSEV.   Whether I've got anything to say or not, you don't have brains enough to understand it. You haven't even come to that stage yet.

BULANOV.   If you want to say something or other to Raisa Pavlovna, tell me and I'll let her know.

NESCHASTLIVTSEV.   Who do you think you are? The sword-bearer, or the page perhaps, of Raisa Pavlovna? Her minstrel? Well, to finish it up, her message-runner? Or her jester? Speak up and tell me.

BULANOV.   Whatever I am, you'll find out later on.

NESCHASTLIVTSEV.   I don't want to. Well, whoever you may be, tell Raisa Pavlovna that I'm not angry with her. That I want to say good-by like a relative should. And if she doesn't want to, then to hell with her.

BULANOV.   All right, I'll tell her, sir.

NESCHASTLIVTSEV.   [*Having caught sight of the workbox, speaks to himself.*]   The box is here. I'd better take that into consideration. Just wait a bit.

BULANOV.   Nothing more, sir?

NESCHASTLIVTSEV.   Nothing. Good-by, slate pencil!   [*Exits.* RAISA *enters.*]

RAISA.   Well, you can be sure he won't look in here again.   [*Sits by the window.*]   But you have style, and you have character. I must confess I didn't expect it.

BULANOV.   [*Walks, with his hands clasped behind him.*]   Everything depends, Raisa, on the surroundings.[34] What was I around here before? A boarder, a parasite—the most spurious situation possible. You must admit yourself that it's very difficult for a boarder to conduct himself with dignity.

RAISA.   Nevertheless, I am angry with you about yesterday evening.

BULANOV.   Raisa dear, put yourself in my place. I was simply overwhelmed.

RAISA.   Everything has a form, my dear. Just imagine how you insulted me with your behavior. Indeed, what must you think of me! How could you even consider acting that way? You know my reputation. The whole district respects me, and you . . .

BULANOV.   [*Kisses her hand, in a free-and-easy manner.*]   Forgive me.

RAISA.   I forgive you, my dear, I do. I am usually very lenient. It's my shortcoming. But you must always respect a woman's delicacy, her chaste feeling.

BULANOV.   Of course, I am still a kid. No need to go on about it. Your love, however, and your experience will help me ever so much. Once I get on a little more solid ground, you'll see how I'll conduct myself. Why, I'll have the whole district right in the palm of my hand. And what concerns your interests, Raisa dear, then just trust . . .

RAISA.   I trust you, my dear, I do. Go along now, and tell them to send Aksyusha to me.

BULANOV.   Yes, we must think a little about that girl.

RAISA.   Think about her? Really. Especially you, my dear. Why, she is no longer any concern of yours. So you might as well forget about her right now. During the night she ran off and stayed out till all hours. I must get rid of her.

BULANOV.   She was with her cousin, Gennady Demyanych. He spent the whole night declaiming monologues to her.

RAISA.   How on earth did you find out? Look in my eyes. Yes, look at me.

BULANOV.   I saw them, as I walked past the summerhouse.

RAISA.   I believe you. All the same, she can't stay here any longer.

BULANOV.   [With a smile.] You're beginning to take precautions.

RAISA.   Not too many, my dear. You are still so young that you can't answer for yourself, and even I can't trust you completely.

BULANOV.   But you know you just can't drive her out into the street. She has no one. No one at all. She ought to be married.

RAISA.   But if I am responsible for her marriage, and if I do it decently, then she must be given a dowry. Why should I start living high, just for her? Why should I suddenly begin spending money now?

BULANOV.   It goes without saying! No, Raisa dear, you're right. Let's have no unnecessary expenses. If only someone would marry her without a dowry.

RAISA.   Oh, that'd be something else again. What could be better? Then all the proprieties would be preserved, and the expenses would be inconsequential. I could be the bride's mother, and you—her father. I'd arrange the customary bride's party here, the night before the wedding; give the young couple the usual blessings; and then, they're on their own. All this would be philanthropic and cheap.   [AKSYUSHA enters.]   Here she is herself. Run along, my dear, do.   [BULANOV exits.]

AKSYUSHA.   What do you want?

RAISA.   [Rises.] Listen, Aksyusha, I don't want you to get the wrong impression. You are staying with me, and I suppose you imagine you'll go on like this forever. I'm to blame for you delusion. At one time I had thought of marrying you to Aleksey Sergeich. Now, you must not even think about him.

AKSYUSHA.   But I don't think about him.

RAISA.   I don't believe you. But it makes no difference. I realized rather soon that you two just don't go together. I'll tell you straight off that you are not worthy of that man. You'd be silly even to dream of him. Why is it you're quiet?

AKSYUSHA.   I'm listening.

RAISA.   Fiancés like him are not for you, my dear. I'm not certain, but maybe he even made love to you . . .

AKSYUSHA. Maybe.

RAISA. But you understand that it means nothing. Nothing at all. Simply a whimsy, a little joke. Maybe you even flirted with him?

AKSYUSHA. No. Out of the question.

RAISA. Let's say you're right. But I must tell you . . . Whether you like it or not, and it's no affair of mine . . . He doesn't like you, one little bit. [*To herself.*] That should take care of you, dear.

AKSYUSHA. I am very pleased.

RAISA. Pleased? Think you're pretty slick, don't you? But you'll find it difficult to outwit me. [*To herself.*] Just wait a bit, I'll find a more sensitive spot to prick. [*To* AKSYUSHA.] I should also say that he likes someone else. Well? Aren't you pleased?

AKSYUSHA. What's it to me?

RAISA. Don't worry. You know I'm not going to be taken in. Not by anyone. Right now he is no longer your fiancé. As far as I'm concerned you are strangers to each other. Therefore, it's impossible for you both to live in the same house.

AKSYUSHA. Whatever you like.

RAISA. You must leave my house.

AKSYUSHA. When must I leave?

RAISA. But whatever will become of you?

AKSYUSHA. I am very grateful for your charity. But when I leave your house, then I ask you not to bother yourself any more about me.

RAISA. But, maybe you're thinking of settling some place or other nearby.

AKSYUSHA. [*To herself.*] The old woman is jealous.

RAISA. What are you whispering? Maybe, you'll move into town?

AKSYUSHA. Maybe.

RAISA. But you can't do that.

AKSYUSHA. And why not? You don't own the whole town, Raisa Pavlovna.

RAISA. But that's terrible. It's too close.

AKSYUSHA. Yes, it isn't far.

RAISA. Listen, Aksyusha, dear. Don't you have relatives some place or other a little farther away? Go to them. I'll even send you at my own expense. I'm really afraid for you, my darling. Aleksis is such a flighty boy. A bit scatterbrained.

AKSYUSHA.   Yes, he is, isn't he? Quite.

RAISA.   So, you've noticed it?

AKSYUSHA.   How could I help noticing it? And if I'd only wanted . . .

RAISA.   Oh, now you've gone and said it. Listen, dear. Well, come a little closer. [*Embraces her.*] Now, do it for me.

AKSYUSHA.   For you? That's something else again, as you'd say. And why on earth should you want to protect me and look after me? To put it simply, you are jealous. You are a distinguished lady, and I am a girl off the street. But here you are, so jealous that I'll snap up your lover.

RAISA.   You can't mean what you're saying.

AKSYUSHA.   Oh, I can't, can't I? I'm telling you the truth. Admit it at least once in your life. You are constantly setting yourself up with your holier-than-thou pose, while the rest of us are sinners.

RAISA.   My darling, I, too, am a woman.

AKSYUSHA.   Admit it! Just admit it, and I'll run a thousand versts away from you.

RAISA.   You want me to tell you my weakness? [*Embraces her.*] Yes, I am jealous.

AKSYUSHA.   That's all I wanted to hear. I'll go away from you. Far, far away. [*Starts to kiss her hand.*]

RAISA.   For what, my dear, for what?

AKSYUSHA.   For having looked after me.

RAISA.   Oh, you mustn't. No, don't. [*Kisses her.*]   God grant you every happiness.

AKSYUSHA.   I'll go and get ready. [*Exits.*]

RAISA.   [*Sits by the window.*]   Well, thank the Lord, everything is settled now, and I can enjoy my happiness fully and completely. How much unpleasantness I've gone through in this silly comedy with my relatives. And I got what I had coming. But in return I feel completely at peace. Aleksis will manage the estate, and I can spend all my time with good works. I'll set aside a certain amount for this. Not a large amount, of course. And I'll do what I know best, right in my own realm, so to speak. [KARP *enters.*]

KARP.   Gennady Demyanych wishes to see you.

RAISA.   Tell him, that I . . .

KARP. But he is here, ma'am. He won't listen to excuses at all.

RAISA. Oh, dear God, again. [NESCHASTLIVTSEV *enters in traveling dress, takes off his knapsack, and puts it and his cane in the corner.*]

NESCHASTLIVTSEV. Run along, Karp, and don't let anyone in. Say that we're busy.

KARP. Yes, sir. [*Exits.*]

RAISA. What kind of costume is that?

NESCHASTLIVTSEV. Traveling. We are travelers on foot. This coat is my old friend and comrade. In bad weather I have tramped around in this coat, like old Lear, through the steppes of New Russia. On many a stormy night I have sought asylum, and I've been accepted in this coat, accepted by strangers more graciously than by my own relatives. Farewell.

RAISA. Farewell, my dear.

NESCHASTLIVTSEV. Only two words, and I shall never bother you again.

RAISA. I'm listening. [*Picks up a handbell.*]

NESCHASTLIVTSEV. What's this? Are you going to ring it? It's too soon. Give me the bell. [*Takes handbell.*] I'll ring it myself, when it's necessary. We don't need witnesses. On the contrary, auntie, better make sure that nobody comes in. Especially Bulanov, if you value his meager life.

RAISA. All right, I'll make sure no one comes in. [*To herself.*] Oh, that dream of mine!

NESCHASTLIVTSEV. Splendid. [*Places the handbell on the table and sits on a chair next to the table.*]

RAISA. [*Seeing her workbox on the table.*] My workbox. I forgot it. [*In the most affectionate tone possible.*] Listen, my dear Gennady, be so good as to trouble yourself and hand me that workbox.

NESCHASTLIVTSEV. Don't worry. It's all right where it is.

RAISA. Well, if you don't want to, I can get it myself.

NESCHASTLIVTSEV. [*Takes out a pistol and puts it on the table.*] Don't trouble yourself.

RAISA. What are you doing? It's terrible. I may die from fright.

NESCHASTLIVTSEV. Don't worry. We're going to talk quite peacefully, even politely. [*Examining the workbox.*] What do you say? Give it to me to remember you by.

RAISA.   [*With fear.*]   Oh, it's impossible, my dear! It contains important papers, documents concerning the estate.

NESCHASTLIVTSEV.   Plans, deeds of purchase, surveyor's books? How on earth did you expect to protect them in this little box? Beg your pardon, but I'd like to satisfy my curiosity.   [*Opens the workbox.*]

RAISA.   It's terrible. I can't stand it.

NESCHASTLIVTSEV.   You're wrong. There's money in here. Oh, gold. Oh, yellow gilt. How much evil-begotten by you? Or should we say, guilt-begotten? Well, we'll close it for the time being. [*Closes workbox.*]   Once there was a provincial actor. A woman, the wife of a theatrical manager, insulted him. He didn't reply to her, but he never forgot the insult. He suffered all through the winter season. At last, on the last Sunday in Shrovetide there was a farewell party at the manager's. Listen to me, auntie.

RAISA.   I am listening.

NESCHASTLIVTSEV.   At the close of the party, when everyone began to leave, the actor walked up to his hostess and said, "Permit me to kiss your hand." She gave him her hand; and he, auntie, went and bit off her finger.

RAISA.   Why on earth did you tell me this story?

NESCHASTLIVTSEV.   Stands to reason, he acted pretty silly. I know him, and he's a fool, all right. He might have been a bit more clever about it.

RAISA.   And what has it to do with me?

NESCHASTLIVTSEV.   It doesn't harm you, at any rate, does it? Another actor I know was much smarter. It seems a certain rich landowner—a woman, that is—had a nephew. He was a man with noble feelings, but he was poor. He took it into his head to pay a visit to his aunt, who hadn't seen him for fifteen years. Her place was far off, so he traveled a long time on foot. Finally, he arrived at his aunt's and was received as a relative should be received. All of a sudden his aunt found out he was an actor. She drove him out of her house, without saying good-by, and shamed him in front of everyone, even the servants.

RAISA.   Oh, no, Gennady . . .

NESCHASTLIVTSEV.   That is, she made up her mind to treat him like that, but it turned out differently. The tragedian Neschastlivtsev, you see, didn't care to play that role.   [*Opens the work-*

box.] First of all, you know, the tragedian Neschastlivtsev must have money for traveling, and it would be improper for him to walk out on his rich aunt. Walk, no. Ride, yes. In the second place, you have a poor girl living here. Well, not much good would come of it, if she—living here and enjoying your support—decided to drown herself. You agree, don't you?

RAISA. What stories are you making up now?

NESCHASTLIVTSEV. I shall take her with me, and you must give her something or other as her share. Then, since we shall refuse to accept any future inheritance—that's easy to do since you're leaving us nothing and giving it all to the school kid—I ought to take a little something or other right now. [*Counts out the money.*]

RAISA. Stop tormenting me and tell me how much you want.

NESCHASTLIVTSEV. I shall be generous. [*Rises, takes the pistol in one hand and, in the other, the workbox with the money. He gives the workbox to* RAISA.] Here, you give it to me yourself.

RAISA. [*Glancing at the pistol.*] It's useless to continue this comedy. I owe you a thousand rubles. Here it is, but if you need . . .

NESCHASTLIVTSEV. [*Takes the money.*] It's quite enough. I don't want any favors. I thank you. [*Pockets the money.*]

RAISA. Oh, put away that pistol, please. I'm a nervous wreck.

NESCHASTLIVTSEV. What on earth are you afraid of? You know I am not Stenka Razin.[35] If you insulted me too much, then as a last resort, I'd kill the schoolboy. You can be sure I'd never kill you. [*Puts the pistol in his pocket.*] Well, ma'am, now, of course, you'll see me off in a proper fashion. We shall lunch together and kiss each other good-by, exactly the way relatives should.

RAISA. Yes, of course.

NESCHASTLIVTSEV. I showed up here as a gentleman, and I'll go away as a gentleman, with honor and respect. [*Rings the handbell.* KARP *enters.*] Send somebody as soon as possible into town to rent the very best troika for the first steamer landing. And look here, old fellow, I'm leaving, so the mistress wants a good lunch put together as fast as possible. Bring wine that's a little better than champagne.

KARP. Yes, sir. Lunch is ready.

RAISA. Send it to the dining room.

NESCHASTLIVTSEV. Call Arkady. [*To* RAISA.] When we say good-by, I'll introduce him to you. You've not missed very much by not meeting him before now.

KARP. My lady, Ivan Petrov and his son are waiting, ma'am.

RAISA. Tell him he can wait in the dining room. [KARP *exits.*] Excuse me, my dear, I must leave you for a short time.

NESCHASTLIVTSEV. For pity's sake. Among your . . .

RAISA. I must dress. I'm expecting guests. Go along to the dining room, have a bite to eat for the trip, and I'll come in time to say good-by.

NESCHASTLIVTSEV. So, we'll part peacefully, then. You're not angry with me, are you?

RAISA. No, I'm not angry. But it seems to me, you might have behaved a little more delicately. After all, I am a lady.

NESCHASTLIVTSEV. Oh, dear Lord. Have I insulted you? Tell me if I've insulted you? I'll never forgive myself. I'll shoot myself, right in front of you. [*Takes out the pistol.*]

RAISA. Oh, no! No!

NESCHASTLIVTSEV. No, just tell me if I've insulted you? Oh, I . . .

RAISA. Oh, no, not one single bit. On the contrary. [*Exits.*]

NESCHASTLIVTSEV. Oh, that's much, much better. Right now I can't figure out whether I am Neschastlivtsev or Rothschild. [SCHASTLIVTSEV *enters.*] Well, Arkady, now it's possible for us to take a little rest. I have a lot of money, brother. [*Shows a bundle of paper money.*] We're riding off to the Volga in a beautiful carriage, and then it's first class on a steamer.

SCHASTLIVTSEV. Oh, Gennady Demyanych, that's splendid. Oh, that's splendid. If you only knew how I love comfort.

NESCHASTLIVTSEV. If we get a profitable engagement, then we'll take it and start acting right away. If we don't, then it makes no difference. We'll ride to the fair in Nizhny for a benefit performance. But the benefit had better take place in August. If it's in September, nothing much will come of it. So, I won't take it then. Oh, brother, we'll raise Cain. That's for sure.

SCHASTLIVTSEV. And you can be sure you'll never find a comrade better than me. I, don't you know, Gennady Demyanych . . . I was born for a life like this. To hell with poverty! Anyone knows how to live in poverty. That's easy. But to know how to spend money effectively? Oh, Gennady Demyanych, that takes a lot of brains.

NESCHASTLIVTSEV.   And now, brother, let's go drink some good wine and have a little something before our trip. What would you say to a glass or two of champagne?

SCHASTLIVTSEV.   This is really living it up, Gennady Demyanych! It's something I can understand. But to go on foot anywhere, that's when you despise yourself. I don't know if you go along with this, but I despise that old way of life. I'm all for living it up the way rich people do. Now, the one who drinks champagne and smokes good cigars, why he's something to look up to—a man. And everybody else is a nothing, a nobody, a zero. You'll buy that, won't you, Gennady Demyanych?   [*They exit into the dining room.* AKSYUSHA *enters.*]

AKSYUSHA.   Where on earth is my cousin?   [*Peeks through the door.*]   There he is, in the dining room. And Petya's there, too. How can I get him out here? I'd like to say a word or two before we leave. And it won't be easy in front of everyone.   [*In a low voice.*]   Petya! Petya! He heard me and he's coming. [PETR *quietly slips through the door, sideways.*]

PETR.   Oh, so it's you?

AKSYUSHA.   Please, for God's sake, a little quieter. The whole thing's over. My cousin has no money, so I'm going away with him; far, far away, and I'll never come back.   [*Takes his head, presses it to her, and kisses him.*]   Good-by, my darling. And now, go. Quickly.

PETR.   You are going away? Where, for God's sake? Why?

AKSYUSHA.   I'm going into the theatre. I'm going to become an actress.

PETR.   Come on now, snap out of it. Have you gone out of your mind?

AKSYUSHA.   It's settled, I tell you, settled. And now, go. Oh, please go.

PETR.   You're not serious. My heart just sank, as if you'd hit me in the chest with a stone. You know I had another talk with daddy.

AKSYUSHA.   [*Looking around, shyly.*]   Well, what happened?

PETR.   At first, as usual, he swore at me for a couple of hours without taking a breath. Finally, he said, "They ought to give at least a thousand for you, you silly fool, you."

AKSYUSHA. I'll put in a word to auntie before I leave; not that I think there's much hope. Now, off with you. [*Kisses him.*] Good-by. Don't say good-by later on. I'd be embarrassed. Just look at me, and I'll keep looking at you. For as long as I can see you.

PETR. Oh, this is a helluva life! Right now I ought to jump in the lake. I could do it with the greatest pleasure. [NESCHAST-LIVTSEV *enters.*]

NESCHASTLIVTSEV. Aha! Caught you!

AKSYUSHA. Oh, cousin, a little quieter, please. [PETR *exits.*] Just a word, dear cousin, just one word. Even drowning men grab for straws. Please beg auntie, and maybe she'll feel sorry for me. Right now I need only a thousand rubles, only a thousand.

NESCHASTLIVTSEV. And what about your career as an actress, my child? With your depth of feeling . . .

AKSYUSHA. [*Snuggling into his arms, tenderly.*] Cousin . . . my depth of feeling . . . I need it here, at home.

NESCHASTLIVTSEV. [*In a bass voice.*] You hesitate. What on earth can I count on now? Let's go, the company's waiting for me. Better have something pretty good to drink, I need inspiration. Then I'll say a word or two. [*Exits into the dining room. Enter* MILONOV, BODOEV, *and* KARP.]

KARP. If you please, gentlemen. She will be here shortly.

MILONOV. What's new around here, Karp, old boy? Today, everything seems pretty showy, somehow.

KARP. I couldn't say. [RAISA *enters, quite smartly and youthfully dressed. She walks hand-in-hand with* BULANOV.]

RAISA. Forgive me, gentlemen, I kept you waiting.

BODAEV. Well, we haven't been waiting at all.

MILONOV. [*Kissing her hand.*] You look marvelous. [*Walks away from her, turns, and looks at her from a distance.*] Marvelous. You're getting younger every day.

RAISA. And I must keep on looking younger. Gentlemen, I called you here for the signing of my will, but circumstances have changed everything somewhat. I am getting married. I should like to present my future husband.

MILONOV. Marvelous! Marvelous!

BODAEV. I expected as much.

RAISA. [*Sitting.*] Won't you all please sit down? [MILONOV *and* BODAEV *sit.*] Aleksis, sit down.

BULANOV. [*Kissing her hand.*]   Oh, Raisa, permit me. I should like to stand next to you.

RAISA.   Don't you agree that he's sweet? Gentlemen, I see that you have already convicted me in your hearts. Hear me out first, then judge me. Gentlemen, I have ample justification. I was alone and defenseless, and my estate was in ruins. I thought of charging my nephew with its management, but he caught me by surprise. Yes, surprise. Do you know what career he's chosen? He is a provincial actor.

MILONOV.   Terrible, terrible, terrible.

BODAEV.   What did she say?

BULANOV.   About her nephew . . .

BODAEV.   Aha? Well, it's not my business.

RAISA.   And the life he leads—at best, untidy. He is here, in my house. You can see him.

MILONOV.   And your niece?

RAISA.   Her behavior displeases me. What was left for me to do? I ask you. In spite of all my wishes to remain a widow forever   [*languorously*]   and even to relinquish my share in society, I decided to sacrifice myself. I am getting married, gentlemen, simply to put my estate in order and to make sure it doesn't fall into bad hands.

MILONOV.   That's an heroic deed! You are a heroine.

BODAEV.   Come now, what kind of heroine? She's simply perverse.

MILONOV.   A long time ago, you should have . . . Yes, a long time ago . . .

RAISA.   Oh, Evgeny Apollonych, I had to find the man. And nowadays, it's quite difficult. Yes, quite difficult. But, this one, here now. Oho, if you only knew! He's quite a man. [*Tenderly looks around at* BULANOV.]   Oh, my dear.

BULANOV.   [*Kissing her hand.*]   Raisa, dear, not in front of others. You rattle me, when you do.

MILONOV.   [*Threateningly, with his finger.*]   Only watch out, Raisa Pavlovna. Better keep an eye on him for sure. He is still a youngster.

RAISA.   Oh, no. He swore an oath to me, a dreadful oath.

BULANOV.   Believe me, gentlemen, I shall try to be worthy of the honor Raisa Pavlovna gave me when she chose me as her husband. When it comes to Raisa Pavlovna's interests, well, gentlemen, in the shortest possible time, the business itself will speak for me. You shall see our estate the very flower of prosperity.

MILONOV.   What? What's that you say? Marvelous, young man, marvelous.

RAISA.   I told you . . .

BODAEV.   He's lying through his teeth. He's going to squander it all.

BULANOV.   Gentlemen, I may be a youngster, but I'm taking very close to heart not only my own but also public affairs. In fact, I intend to serve the public. Believe me, gentlemen, you'll find me the most fervent defender of our interests and our privileges.

MILONOV.   And here we've been mourning the lack of men in public office, that new institutions require new men, and none have shown up. We were wrong. Here's our man, now.

BODAEV.   So what, for pity's sake! Let him serve the public. We're not picky. That's for sure.

BULANOV.   [Shrugging his shoulders.] You know, my age is against me. I don't understand the reason for all these checks and controls. If I feel myself capable . . .

MILONOV.   Oh, so what? We'll just wait two years; then, we'll find you there on the board, or in some other honorable post.

RAISA.   Gentlemen, we shall eat later on today, but what about a glass of champagne now? Karp, bring the champagne.

KARP.   Yes, ma'am. I have the honor to congratulate you, my lady.   [To himself.] I'll go and tell the others.   [Exits.]

MILONOV.   But where on earth did the youngster get brains and strength like that?

RAISA.   Oh, he has suffered a lot, poor boy. His mother was a rich woman, and as a child he was trained to expect comfort, as well as servility from servants and from all those around him. All of a sudden the family was impoverished, and he came to know dreadful need. It was terrible. He was born to command, and he was forced to study something or other at the gymnasium. [KARP enters with a bottle of champagne and glasses. All rise.]

MILONOV.   [Taking a glass.] Everything noble and everything marvelous is based on variety, on contrasts. Take the most graceful combinations in nature, and what is it we see? Rugged granite and melancholy ivy. Indestructible oak and delicate morning-glory. And now, here, before our eyes: unflinching virtue, worldly wisdom fortified by experience, united with a delicate, young sprout of a noble nursery. Raisa Pavlovna, Aleksey Sergeich! I wish you a long, tranquil life, for your own joy, for the comfort of your friends, and for the benefit of the whole surrounding population living in the farthest boundaries. [*In the dining room, "Hurrah!"* [36]]

RAISA.   What on earth is that?

KARP.   Gennady Demyanych, pray . . . is drinking to your health.

MILONOV.   Gentlemen, I can't say another word. Everything marvelous and everything noble has filled my heart, shut my lips, and called forth abundant, burning tears to my eyelashes. [*He drinks.*]

RAISA.   [*Squeezes his hand.*]   Thank you. Thank you so very much.   [*In the dining room, "Hurrah!"*]

BODAEV.   [*With a glass.*]   Congratulations! Try to live happily, and I'll be the first to celebrate.   [*He drinks.*]

RAISA.   I thank you, humbly.   [*To* BULANOV.]   Oh, he is rude, rude!   [*Everyone sits. In the dining room, "Hurrah!" The doors from the dining room open.* NESCHASTLIVTSEV *enters.* SCHAST-LIVTSEV, VOSMIBRATOV, PETR *and* AKSYUSHA *remain standing in the doorway.*]

NESCHASTLIVTSEV.   Auntie, I congratulate you. You're going to marry? It's time, auntie, time. And it's good for you, and pleasant for your relatives. It does you honor, and for us the greatest enjoyment. As far as I'm concerned, I'm very glad and I approve of your union.   [*Turns to the doors.*]   Gentlemen, why are you standing there?   [SCHASTLIVTSEV *and* VOSMIBRATOV *approach.*]   Auntie, I'd like to present my friend, Arkady Schastlivtsev.

RAISA.   Very pleased to meet you.

MILONOV.   Is he your nephew?

NESCHASTLIVTSEV.   [*To* MILONOV.]   I have the honor to present myself, Gennady Gurmyzhsky.   [*To* BODAEV.]   Gurmyzhsky, Gennady!   [MILONOV *and* BODAEV *rise, shake hands with him, and sit.*]

VOSMIBRATOV.   [*To* RAISA.]   A good deal, ma'am. That is, by law, as is right and proper. What could be better, ma'am? Very pleased, ma'am.

RAISA. Well, Ivan Petrovich, how do you like my fiancé?

VOSMIBRATOV. Not bad, ma'am. A fiancé's a matter of taste, anyway, ma'am. If it turns out he don't have much brains, then it's because he's chicken-hearted. But in time he'll grow out of it, ma'am.

NESCHASTLIVTSEV. [To SCHASTLIVTSEV and VOSMIBRATOV.] Gentlemen, I most humbly beg you to sit down. Auntie, permit me to be in charge as if it were my own house. Karp, brother, go and bring us some wine, and more than enough. Now don't scrimp and save. Events like this are rare, indeed. You know auntie isn't going to get married every year. [He sits on the right side of the stage, the same place where SCHASTLIVTSEV and VOSMIBRATOV sit. KARP exits.] Go on, gentlemen, with your conversation. We won't disturb you.

MILONOV. We're eager to listen to you.

NESCHASTLIVTSEV. With the greatest pleasure, gentlemen. I'm very pleased to talk in such an aristocratic group. Auntie, you're happy, aren't you? Happy, beyond all bounds?

RAISA. Yes, my dear, I am happy.

NESCHASTLIVTSEV. In happiness a person becomes kinder, more noble. That's right what I said, isn't it? The truth, gentlemen, hmm?

MILONOV. Absolutely true. Marvelous, marvelous.

NESCHASTLIVTSEV. Auntie, you have a niece; a dear, gentle creature. She has a fiancé, too. He is not as good-looking or courageous as yours, but she loves him. And here is his daddy.

RAISA. I know, my dear.

NESCHASTLIVTSEV. He, that is the daddy, is a Russian; devout, gentlemen, but his soul is a fried egg smothered with galloping cockroaches. He is a family man; he loves his children a lot; and he wants to marry off his sons. But he wants to get a dowry without fail, because he is greedy and ignorant himself.

VOSMIBRATOV. That's right, mister, it's because of my ignorance. Why, if I didn't have my ignorance, I wouldn't get a single thing; because everything I do depends on it.

NESCHASTLIVTSEV. There you are, auntie. It's an excellent time for you to do a good deed.

RAISA. Oh, no, no. Why did you come up with an idea like that? Forget it please. It's not your concern. So far I've already spent too much money. Then, I have many, many expenses coming up.

BULANOV. Right now Raisa and I can't afford anything extra. I want to buy a stud farm; the ponds must be cleaned; and the ditches should be dug out again.

NESCHASTLIVTSEV. So, you aren't going to give the money?

RAISA. It isn't a lot of money. But you agree, gentlemen, don't you, that circumstances existing as they . . .

NESCHASTLIVTSEV. But why money? I imagine that your noble word in the presence of these gentlemen is quite enough.

VOSMIBRATOV. The way I see it, your word is better than a note.

RAISA. No, no! It's indelicate even, when all of a sudden, in front of outsiders . . . A demand like that . . . It's coercion. You, of all people, plotting against me.

BULANOV. Now, Raisa dear, just flatly refuse. That's all.

RAISA. You agree, gentlemen, don't you, I can do nothing when all of a sudden, you see . . . I flatly refuse.

NESCHASTLIVTSEV. So, you aren't going to give the money?

RAISA. Forgive me, my friend, but I can't.

NESCHASTLIVTSEV. [*To* VOSMIBRATOV.] How about it, my good man, scrape a little something or other off the top? Come on! Take off a bit.

VOSMIBRATOV. Not good figuring, mister. I only said a thousand, since she's from a good house. If she weren't, I never would've paid any attention.

NESCHASTLIVTSEV. [*Rises.*] Dear   auntie,   Raisa   Pavlovna! Benefactress of the human race. Don't malign yourself in front of this honorable group. Don't embarrass the name of Gurmyzhsky. I'm getting red in the face for you. The girl and I, you know, are your only relatives. She won't ask you one more time, and I have no use for a dowry. Surely Raisa Gurmyzhsky won't refuse a sum like this. You are a rich woman, so this is just a mere trifle for you. I am a poor worker, but if I had . . . [*Hits himself on the chest.*] Oh, what am I saying? I have it. [*Takes money out of his pocket.*] Here it is. I confess it would scarcely be a sin if the poor peasant Neschastlivtsev lived it up a little on this money. It wouldn't hurt a bit if the old dog put it aside for a rainy day.

SCHASTLIVTSEV. [*Tugging him by the arm.*]   What are you doing?

NESCHASTLIVTSEV.   Shut up, Arkashka! So you aren't going to give the money?

RAISA.   I already said so.

NESCHASTLIVTSEV.   Well, if a rich landowner refuses a dowry to a poor girl, then a poor actor cannot refuse it. [*To* AKSYUSHA.] Come here, my child.

SCHASTLIVTSEV.   But you said we'd ride in a troika. Well, there goes the troika. And the steamer.

NESCHASTLIVTSEV.   Shut up, Arkashka! [AKSYUSHA *crosses to* NESCHASTLIVTSEV.]   Here you are, my child. Take it.

AKSYUSHA.   You're not serious, you can't be! Oh, cousin, you shouldn't.

NESCHASTLIVTSEV.   Take it, I tell you. When I've made up my mind, I don't change it. When I've done something, I don't try to alter it.

AKSYUSHA.   [*Embracing him.*]   Oh, cousin. Darling cousin! [KARP *enters with a bottle of wine and glasses and places them on the table.*]

NESCHASTLIVTSEV.   Well, enough said. I feel like crying, and that's not good. Not good at all. Shameful.

AKSYUSHA.   How can I thank you?

NESCHASTLIVTSEV.   How? Why, just say "thanks," and that's all there is to it. Here now, let's drink. [*Crosses to the table and pours two glasses.* AKSYUSHA *hands over the money to* PETR.]

PETR.   [*Giving the money to his father.*]   Please accept, sir. [VOSMIBRATOV *crosses to one side and counts it.*]

RAISA.   [*To* NESCHASTLIVTSEV.]   That's very generous on your part.

NESCHASTLIVTSEV.   I hope so. Come on, Arkady, drink up. [SCHASTLIVTSEV *approaches and drinks.*]

RAISA.   [*To* AKSYUSHA.]   I am very glad, my dear, that everything's been arranged so well. And I'm ready to further your happiness in whatever way I can. In fact, I'd be happy to take your mother's place at the wedding. [AKSYUSHA *bows.*]

VOSMIBRATOV.   We thank you a lot, ma'am. The way we see it, ma'am, we couldn't manage the thing without you. If you're at the wedding, ma'am, that's like adding 50 per cent to the dowry. That's how much we think of you. I'll fix you up a banquet, your Ladyship, that'll be the talk of the town for two months afterward. At least, we'll let them know about it.

MILONOV.   [*Crossing to the table.*]   Marvelous! Marvelous! Your deed must be printed in the newspapers.

NESCHASTLIVTSEV.   To the devil with newspapers! Come now, let's drink to *Brüdershaft!*

MILONOV.   But, my dear boy, it's impossible. Really.

NESCHASTLIVTSEV.   If you don't want to, then don't. Then beat it. Get moving, you! Let's drink, Arkady.   [MILONOV *moves away.*]

BODAEV.   [*To* BULANOV.]   Who does he think he is? Hmm?

BULANOV.   An actor.

BODAEV.   An actor? Oh, the hell you say! Bravo! Bravo!   [*Crosses to* NESCHASTLIVTSEV.]   Your hand. Aha! I've been listening to how well you talk, nobly, I'd call it. It happens so rarely around here.   [*Points to* SCHASTLIVTSEV.]   And is he an actor, too?

NESCHASTLIVTSEV.   Yes, an actor.

BODAEV.   But can't he talk?

NESCHASTLIVTSEV.   Oh, yes, he talks.

BODAEV.   What is it he says?

SCHASTLIVTSEV.   I whistle like a starling. I jump like a magpie.

BODAEV.   Oh, bravo, bravo!   [*Moves away and immediately returns to* NESCHASTLIVTSEV.]   I'll make him a present of a meerschaum pipe. Come to my house. You'll be more than welcome.

NESCHASTLIVTSEV.   To entertain you? Get jesters or fools for that. Let's drink to *Brüdershaft!*

BODAEV.   What? Ha, ha, ha! He's a funny man.   [*Moves away.*]

RAISA.   [*To* BULANOV.]   We must find some way or other to get him out of here. God knows what he might do.

BULANOV.   [*To* NESCHASTLIVTSEV.]   Seems to me you were getting ready to leave?

NESCHASTLIVTSEV.   Brother, I've been getting ready a long time now.

BULANOV.   Don't you think it's about time you went?

NESCHASTLIVTSEV.   Arkady, they're driving us out. Yes, indeed, Arkady, old fellow, why did we drop by? How was it we found ourselves in this forest, in this damp, thick pine forest? Why is it, brother, we scared these owls and eagle-owls? Why should we even bother them? Let them live as they like. Here, everyone has his place, just as is right and proper in the forest. Old women marry schoolboys. Young girls drown themselves because of the bitter life they lead with relatives. Yes, indeed, brother. We've stumbled right into the forest. Yes, right into the backwoods.

RAISA. [*Shrugging her shoulders.*] Comedians.

NESCHASTLIVTSEV. Comedians? Oh, no. We are artists, noble artists, and you are the comedians. If we love, then we really love. If we don't love, then we quarrel or pound each other. If we help, then we give our last, hard-earned half-kopek. But what about you? Your whole life long you chatter about public welfare, about love of humanity. And what have you really done about it? How many have you fed? How many have you given comfort to? You give comfort only to yourselves, and you entertain only yourselves. You are the comedians, the jesters. Not we. When I have money, then I feed—at my own expense —two or three swindlers like Arkashka here. But my own aunt stretched herself to the breaking point feeding me for a couple days. The girl here runs off to drown herself. But who pushed her into the water? Her own aunt. Who saved her? The actor Neschastlivtsev. "Mankind, oh, mankind. You race of crocodiles, you. Your tears—nothing but water. Your hearts—made of hard damascus steel. Your kisses—daggers in our bosom. Lions and leopards nourish their young. Predatory ravens care for their fledglings. And she, what does she do? Is this love for love? Oh, if I were only a hyena! Oh, if I could send enraged all the bloodthirsty inhabitants of the woods against this hellish generation!"

MILONOV. If you please, you can be made to answer for those words.

BULANOV. Yes. Right to the district police officer. We are all witnesses.

NESCHASTLIVTSEV. [*To* MILONOV.] Me? You're mistaken. [*Takes out* SCHILLER's *play, "The Robbers"*] "Passed by the Censor." Just look. "Approved for Stage Presentation." Oh, you vicious man, you. Where do you get off talking to me? I feel and speak like Schiller. And you, like a potboiler! Well, I've had enough. To the road, Arkashka. Good-by.   [*Bows to every-one.*]   Auntie, your hand, please!

RAISA.   [*Hides her hand.*]   Oh, dear Lord. No, no!

BULANOV.   Permit him. He will get out of here sooner.

NESCHASTLIVTSEV.   Don't be afraid. I won't bite.

MILONOV.   Of course, he won't bite.

BULANOV.   Of course . . .

RAISA.   Oh, no. You don't know.

NESCHASTLIVTSEV.   Oh, mankind! Mankind!   [*Crosses to the corner and puts on the knapsack.* AKSYUSHA *helps him and kisses him. Takes his cane in hand.*]   Well, Arkady, you and I have feasted and raised a little Cain, brother. Now, back to work again.   [*Crosses to the center of the stage, calls* KARP *and speaks to him in an impressive manner, using measured tones.*]   Listen to me, Karp. If the troika comes, send it back to town, brother. Just say that the gentlemen have gone on foot. Your hand, comrade!   [*Gives his hand to* SCHASTLIVTSEV *and they exit, slowly.*]

TEXTUAL NOTES

IT'S A FAMILY AFFAIR

1. Lipochka mispronounces the Russian equivalent of Eros or Cupid.
2. *Tphew (T'fu)* is the traditional Russian stage business of spitting to show contempt or disapproval. See Ustinya's last line in Act Four.
3. Ustinya mispronounces the Russian equivalent of appetite.
4. Ustinya mispronounces the Russian equivalent of order or "decoration round the neck."
5. The name Psóvich is derived from an adjective which means "having been brought about with the help of a dog."
6. The name Makár is associated with successful endeavor, especially by crafty means.
7. The phrase past taxes has been substituted for the Russian *quitrent*, or fiscal property which has been given over to an individual in return for certain periodical payments.
8. Fedót Selivérstov Pleshkóv. Selivérstych.
9. Antíp Sysóev Enótov. The name Enotov denotes raccoon.
10. The word vegetarian has been substituted for the Russian word which means people who strictly observe the fast and will not use milk, butter, etc.
11. Efrém Lúkin Poluarshínnikov. The last name means half an *arshin* (half of twenty-eight inches), or half a yard.
12. Samopálov means something like old smoothbore dueling pistol, himself.
13. Tíkhon Savostyánych. This is the only moment in the play when Tishka's complete first name and patronymic are given. He is daydreaming of adulthood when he will be addressed by his first

name and patronymic. The two names together connote "quiet and calm like the son of a man with the conscience of a janissary."

14. Alimpiyáda. Podkhalyuzin mispronounces Olimpiada's name. In addition to the various meanings in her name, the Russian word for poison or venom is introduced with this mispronunciation.

15. In the eighteenth century the term townsmen *(meshchane)* officially classified those individuals in the city who owned less than five hundred rubles and hence could not belong to the merchant guilds. Historians estimate that over half of the urban population in 1850 consisted of the *meshchane.*

16. Podkhalyuzin mispronounces the Russian equivalent of document.

17. Ustinya mispronounces the French *mademoiselle.*

18. The phrase was a coarse popular expression at that time which meant "having lost one's mind."

19. Ustinya mispronounces the Russian equivalent of report.

20. The comic sequence between Bolshov and Fominishna is based on Fominishna mishearing Bolshov's questions and comments. Similarity of sounds, *e.g.,* the Russian equivalent of attorney resembles a verb form of to cook, is a technique repeated by Ostrovsky in Grigory's scenes in *The Scoundrel,* Act Three.

21. The Russian phrase, *Vladei, Faddei, nashei Malan'ei,* indicates Bolshov's high spirits. John L. Seymour and George R. Noyes have translated the phrase as "Johnny's the boy for our Jenny!" See *Plays by Alexander Ostrovsky,* edited by George R. Noyes (New York, 1917), p. 267.

22. The word princess might be substituted for *tsarévna,* "daughter of a tsar."

23. In the Table of Ranks, established by Peter the Great in 1722, the rank of general corresponded to ranks (from the lowest to the highest) four to one. Hence, a general's daughter was classed among the highest possible ranks in the army or in the civil service. References to rank occur throughout Ostrovsky's plays and indicate the character's social position, aspiration, envy, or disdain.

24. The phrase is an ironic reference to high social position contrasted with Ustinya's own inflated pride of position. As the wife of a man in the civil service at the fourteenth rank (the lowest rank in the Table of Ranks), Ustinya rarely forgets her own social position. For example, see the scene between Ustinya and Podkhalyuzin in Act Four.

25. The correct pronunciation of Olimpiada by Rispolozhensky occurs for the first and last time in the dialogue. In the first three acts, the parents call her either Lipochka or Lipa. There is one exception, in Act III when Bolshov speaks to Podkhalyuzin about Olimpiada. In the last act, Bolshov says either daughter or Alimpiyada, while Agrafena never once uses her first name. Podkhalyuzin consistently says Alimpiyada throughout the play, whereas the remaining characters, with the exception of Rispolozhensky at this moment, never say her name. In designating the names of characters in the text, Ostrovsky used Lipochka in the first three acts but substituted Olimpiada in the last act. The playwright apparently wanted to show the altered status of Olimpiada from unmarried girl to established wife.

26. This is a proverb, in Russian, *Vot tebe, babushka, i Yur'ev den'!*, dating from the sixteenth century and referring to the abolishment of a certain right on the day celebrating the memory of Georgy-Yury. The proverb means the unexpected stopping of free action, the sudden collapse of hopes and dreams, etc.

27. Podkhalyuzin mispronounces the Russian equivalents of sirens and Eros.

28. Podkhalyuzin mispronounces the Russian equivalent of corsage.

29. When Sadovsky as Podkhalyuzin finished this speech in the 1861 production at the Maly Theatre, one of the reviewers noted that an "involuntary bravo was expressed by the spectators."

30. This sentence, censored in the nineteenth century, was restored in the 1920s.

31. The Russian sentence, *Na kakogo mne zhida treprashel'chatoe-to!*, combines the following words: an abusive term for Jew; the Russian equivalent of babbling which resembles in sound the equivalent of crepe; the Russian equivalent of Rachel which is inserted between the first and second syllables of babbling.

32. Ustinya refers to the contrasting social positions.

33. The Russian phrase, *meshchanskaya-to krov'!*, or blood of the *meshchane*, which was an official class lower than that of the merchants, is not only insulting to Podkhalyuzin but is also an accurate statement of his family background. That is, by serving an apprenticeship with Bolshov and by putting aside money, Podkhalyuzin was able to enter the Merchant Guild of the second class.

34. This sentence, censored in the nineteenth century, was restored in the 1920s.

35. The meeting of creditors was held by an institution, *konkursnoe upravlenie*, which dealt with matters at a lower level than that of the Commercial Court.

36. Olimpiada's remark stresses the social and economic differences between the merchants and the *meshchane* (tradesmen). The intelligentsia of the day readily noted the irony of her statement. That is, to the intelligentsia, the term *meshchane* and its variants had a cultural meaning, summing up a mode of life *(byt)* and typified in the behavior of the characters in *It's a Family Affair*.

37. That is, Agrafena observes the fast on Mondays, Wednesdays, and Fridays.

THE POOR BRIDE

1. See notes 15 and 36 on townsmen *(meshchane)* in *It's a Family Affair*.

2. Másha is a nickname used informally for Marya (Mar'ya).

3. Máshenka (Mashen'ka) is another nickname for Marya and is used affectionately.

4. Márkych is the shortened form of the patronymic Markovich.

5. The name Darya (Dar'ya) suggests "free of charge."

6. The nickname Dásha is used informally.

7. Merich's patronymic Vasilevich (Vasil'evich) incorporates the Russian equivalent of power or strength. The name Merich suggests measure and perhaps speech, while Vladimir, a fairly popular name, connotes to possess, to own.

8. Stepánida incorporates the Russian equivalent of several meanings: degree, dignity, quality.

9. Martýn Martyánych.

10. The suitors nominated by Pankratevna are in the civil service, and although they are in the nobility, they are obviously members of the impoverished nobility and must depend on their salaries for support. In *The Poor Bride* the government official or civil servant *(chinovnik)* is represented chiefly by Milashin, Merich, and Benevolensky. The civil service and the military were organized on the ladder system of rank or *chin*, in which each member moved step by step up the ladder from the fourteenth to the first rank. If he was promoted, he received a salary increase, sometimes a decoration, and often a new title of address.

Technically, all ranks conferred membership in the nobility, although only those ranks above the ninth granted the status of hereditary nobility. Those individuals in the lower ranks received low salaries. Milashin, for example, has not been promoted to higher ranks and must subsist on a low salary. Merich, however, is well-to-do. As Milashin says later in this act, Merich has sufficient money from his rich father and is in the service only to receive first rank. Benevolensky, on the other hand, does not hold particularly high rank in the service; but through the taking of bribes, he has put aside both money and gifts. Dobrotvorsky exemplifies still another means of "getting on in the world," e.g., by knowing the right person at the right time. His meeting with Marya's father insured the beginning of his moderately successful career.

11. Sáva Sávich Belúgin. The last name derives from *beluga,* a white sturgeon.

12. The nickname Mísha is one of the variants used informally for Mikhailo. Another variant, Míshka, has the meaning of bear or teddy bear.

13. Khorkova's reference to rank and social position is repeated in various ways by other characters throughout the play.

14. Andrévna, the shortened form of the patronymic.

15. Iványch, the shortened form of Ivanovich, and its variants Ivan and Ivanov were popular names, similar in frequency to the names of Johnson or Jones in the United States. That Ostrovsky selected the patronymic Ivanovich for Mikhailo suggests the common origin for the son of Ivan. Even though Mikhailo's background is in the *meshchane,* he has received a university education, and he should be viewed as an intellectual of the fifties. In his dissertation on the *raznochintsy,* literally "men of various ranks," in Ostrovsky's plays, Albert Kaspin discussed the character Mikhailo as the first full portrait of a *raznochinets,* or "an intellectual not belonging to the nobility."

16. Ostrovsky selected the names Ivan Ivanovich for Milashin to stress the character's common status as well as his common origin. Perhaps Ostrovsky also implied that Milashin is typical of many low-ranked government officials. Thirty-five years later in his play *Ivanov,* Chekhov chose his leading character's name to represent a personage typical of many individuals. In a recent article, Albert Kaspin compared the character Mikhailo, an example of the superfluous man, with the character Milashin, an early example of "the man from the underground."

17. Vasílich (Vasil'ich) is the shortened form of the patronymic.

18. Official, or *chinovnik*.

19. Sófi Baráshkova. The last name incorporates the Russian equivalent of lambskin.

20. The names used by Merich show the changing attitude of Merich toward Marya, from the usual first name and patronymic to the affectionate Mashenka and eventually to Méri, which is Merich's pronunciation of the French equivalent of Marya, *Marie* (Mary, Maria). In the same speech, Merich switches from the formal *vy* (you) form to the familiar *ty* (you) form of address. In the speech beginning "I hope so," Marya also makes the same change.

21. Although Darya's insulting barb is aimed at Anna offstage, its vivid contrast with Marya's prior speech—her declaration of love and dream of future happiness with Merich—immediately undercuts Marya's dream, prepares for Marya's eventual disillusionment, and balances reality with illusion. In his last plays, Chekhov incorporated and perfected this technique of association.

22. Doroféich is the shortened form of the patronymic.

23. A *drózhky* was a lightweight open carriage.

24. *Peresemkin* suggests meanings such as "getting all worked up" and "starting to go to seed." *Akulína* incorporates the name of a specific day (July 13) when buckwheat should be planted and when cattle were supposedly driven mad by the heat and flies. Several phrases were associated with this day, *e.g.*, "chasing their tails." *Nezamaikina* suggests the phrase, "don't start suffering."

25. Benevolensky's rank as Collegiate Secretary was step number ten in the Table of Ranks.

26. Benevolensky's Latin phrase, "is the mother of learning," reveals the insufficiency of his copper-money training.

27. Andréy Petróvich.

28. Again, Ostrovsky contrasted Marya's last line with Darya's first line, which prepares for Marya's disillusionment. Darya's next line, "She loses everything all the time," ostensibly refers to Anna, but by association the line is an accurate statement of Marya's subsequent condition.

29. *Aksínya* (Aksin'ya) incorporates the name of a specific day (January 24), which was identified as halfway through the winter season. The day may have signified the coming of spring, but in contemporary folklore various phrases stressed the difficulty of the winter months. For example, if there were a snowstorm on this day, the "feed would be bad." The proverb, "Divide winter

in half, and it still is not equal," implied to the *muzhik* that the remaining time until spring meant even greater hardship. Ostrovsky probably chose the *Aksin'ya* to contrast Marya's fortune—the illusion of happiness with Merich—with the forthcoming reality of hardship with Benevolensky. Her fortune, "an admirer enticed," turns out to be Benevolensky, not Merich; immediately following the fortune-telling scene, Benevolensky's letter of proposal arrives. This scene is an example of Ostrovsky's skill in using the technique of association.

30. Darya mispronounces the Russian equivalent of interest.

31. According to the rules of the game, the players turned up one by one the assigned cards, which must then be covered. This scene was particularly effective in production. When E. N. Vasil'eva performed it in the 1853 production at the Maly, critics were impressed with her artistic transition from laughter to hysterical weeping.

32. Anna's accusation embodies ironic comment on her own motivation as well as on the mode of life *(byt)* of all the characters except Marya.

33. The patronymic (pronounced *simyónavna*) means "daughter of Semen (Simon)." In Greek the name *Semen* (Simon) denotes "the state of being heard."

34. *Dunya* connotes the sense of a wind or a draft blowing.

35. *Pasha*, or the Turkish title, is an ironic comment on the character's social position.

36. In this speech Merich continues to play the role of disappointed lover, but his comment is an accurate statement of his behavior.

37. In this speech Merich reveals his own thoughts; but as soon as Milashin enters, he immediately switches to playing a role.

38. In this long speech Milashin prepares the role he will play in Marya's presence by checking his facial expression in the mirror. The illusion of what he would like to see in the mirror is contrasted with the reflected reality of what he does see.

39. Maksímka, a nickname of Maksim, is used affectionately.

40. Dunya mispronounces the phrase, "Adieu, monsieur," and connotes the meaning of foaming or frothy. The mispronunciation implies drunkenness and rage, two qualities which characterized Benevolensky in his relationship with Dunya.

41. This speech by a voice in the crowd describes Marya's forthcoming life of hardship with Benevolensky.

THE STORM

1. "Kuligin, *a tradesman*" and "Shapkin, *a tradesman*," or of the *meshchane*. See the notes on *meshchane* in *It's a Family Affair*.

2. "Feklusha, *a pilgrim*," or literally a "wanderer," typical of those wandering pilgrims who lived by charity.

3. Kalínov. Although no town of this name existed, Kalinov was typical of towns in the upper Volga region.

4. The lines are from a poem by A. F. Merzlyakov (1778–1830).

5. Grigórich *(Grigor'ich)* is the shortened form of the patronymic.

6. Prokófich *(Prokof'ich)* is the shortened form of the patronymic.

7. Early in the play, Ostrovsky linked Dikoy with Marfa. Both are characterized by the qualities of petty tyranny *(samodurstvo)*.

8. Dikoy uses the traditional Russian stage business of spitting to show contempt.

9. Anfísa Mikháilovna.

10. The separation between classes is underscored by Boris' explanation of his family background.

11. The Moscow Practical Academy of Commercial Sciences.

12. *Meshchane.*

13. Lomonósov, M. V. (ca. 1711–1765). Derzhávin, G. R. (1743–1816). Later in the play, Kuligin quotes lines from poems by Derzhavin and Lomonosov.

14. Kuligin mispronounces the Latin for "perpetual motion." Three speeches later Boris gives the correct pronunciation. This is one of the devices Ostrovsky used to link Kuligin with Boris and at the same time to show the difference in their educational backgrounds. In his dissertation on the *raznochintsy* in Ostrovsky's plays, Albert Kaspin classified Boris as a *raznochinets* and Kuligin as a "near *raznochinets*," exempt primarily by his lack of formal education.

15. The line reads literally, "Take a look from behind the corner."

16. Tíshka, a nickname for Tikhon.

17. Várya, a nickname for Varvara.

18. This line and Katerina's following speech have been among the most difficult for Russian actresses playing the role. Their problem has been one of creating belief in Katerina at this moment.

19. At the funeral of Gogol in 1852, the actress L. P. Kositskaya-Nikulina told Ostrovsky the story of her childhood. The playwright incorporated part of the story in this speech.

20. As Pascal observed in his French edition of *The Storm,* cypress wood was often the material on which icons were painted.

21. In his examination of customs in the upper Volga region, Ostrovsky noted the public attitude toward unmarried girls and wives. The unmarried girls were allowed considerable freedom, while the wives were shut away inside their houses.

22. Ostrovsky manipulated the character of the Old Lady both to prefigure and to advance the action of Katerina.

23. According to custom, whenever the husband left for a trip, the wife must show her sorrow in public by wailing.

24. Maknút.

25. "According to popular legends," as Norman Henley observed in his excellent edition of the Russian text, "traitors were changed into creatures with dogs' heads."

26. Kibítka, a covered vehicle.

27. A verst is equal to 3,500 feet.

28. Kátya, a nickname for Katerina.

29. Tísha, a nickname for Tikhon, is used affectionately.

30. The nickname Varenka was added in order to distinguish between Katerina's address to an absent Tisha and her address to Varvara.

31. Just before leaving on a trip, everyone sat silently for a moment or two.

32. A locomotive.

33. Feklusha saw a chimneysweep and thought he was the devil.

34. From an ode, "An Evening Meditation on the Divine Majesty on the Occasion of the Great Northern Lights," by Lomonosov, written in 1748.

35. The line reads literally, "The watchman beat the board (metal plate)." The hours were beaten on a board or metal plate by the watchman.

36. "This is the folk name for the Polish-Swedish intervention," Norman Henley noted, "during the Time of Troubles at the beginning of the seventeenth century."

37. Tártar or Tatár.

38. From Derzhavin's ode to "God," 1784.

39. From Lomonosov's same ode spoken by Kuligin on page 248.

40. From Lomonosov's translation of *Anacreon,* 1748.

41. Tikhon mispronounces Kyákhta.

THE SCOUNDREL

1. By virtue of her social position, *i.e.* her aunt Turusina through marriage holds high rank (step two or one), and by her rich dowry, Mashenka can expect suitors from the aristocracy and the highest levels in the army or civil service. Neither Glumov nor Kurchaev has the necessary qualifications.

2. In his first long speech, Glumov sets forth his line of action and outlines the basic plot of the play. This opening scene between Glumov and Glafira resembles the "happy idea" and agon of Aristophanic comedy. Conceiving the happy idea of using flattery to gain his ends, the protagonist (Glumov) is opposed in debate by the antagonist (Glafira). In keeping with the episodes in Greek old comedy, many of the remaining scenes demonstrate the working out of the happy idea.

3. The line reads literally, "Alone, in the dark of night, I shall keep the chronicle of human vulgarity *(poshlost')*."

4. The line reads literally, "The latest self-instructor."

5. This line, added by the translator, explicates an implied thought in the preceding line of Russian dialogue.

6. Kleopatra Lvovna *(L'vovna)*.

7. Mamaev is at step five in the Table of Ranks.

8. Mamaev refers to the emancipation of the serfs and subsequent reforms in the sixties. Both he and Krutitsky are opposed to the reforms.

9. Combining both verbal and gestural implications, the joke centers on trying to find Mamaev's absent heart.

10. In the 1935 production at the Maly, V. O. Massalitinova played Manefa as a "dreadful, rude, fat *baba* with protruding eyes, covetous hands, loud voice; an insolent fraud, loving to eat, drink, and use the superstition of her surrounding masters."

11. Mátushka is a variant of *mother* used to show respect.

12. This specific length of time, added by the translator, coincides with the number of occasions Glumov has been in the Mamaev home. See the scene between Kleopatra and Glafira in this act.

13. M. V. Lomonósov (ca. 1711–1765) established a system of three literary styles—high, middle and low—as well as a rhetoric and a grammar. A. P. Sumarókov (1718–1777) wrote tragedies and comedies based on the neoclassical unities.

14. The line reads literally, "All the truth, all the truth, Kleopatra Lvovna!"

15. In the 1935 production at the Maly, V. N. Ryzhova played Glafira; and N. A. Smirnova recalled the occasion. "It is hard to forget her grimaces and mimicry, when she narrated to [the Mamaevs] the kind of dream her son had when he was five years old . . . [Ryzhova] in some way pursed her lips and looked at Mamaev with eyes covered with tears."

16. Iványch is the shortened form of the patronymic.

17. In the first Petersburg production. V. V. Samoilov played this scene by pretending "to be Don Juan in conversation with the woman of the world. . . ."

18. Glumov is a member of the impoverished nobility. He had been in the civil service, but left it to write and sell epigrams.

19. M. M. Klimov played Gorodulin in the 1935 Maly production, and S. N. Durylin described his interpretation. "He is slightly aging, a quite heavy Khlestakov [in Gogol's *Revizor*]. He has 'absolutely no time' to think: he is a smart dealer; he is creating an era; he builds railroads (that is, he cuts coupons of railway stock); he is carrying out the reforms of the 1860s (that is, under a couple drinks of champagne he talks all sorts of rubbish at the club); he . . . now is it possible to count what he does?"

20. The French *ma tante*, literally my aunt, which Mashenka uses as a term of endearment, was probably inserted by Ostrovsky to serve a double purpose: to show the educational level of Mashenka and to connect its implied and ironic meaning with Turusina.

21. Turusina's negative attitude toward reform, which is summed up in her term freethinking, links her with the conservatives Mamaev and Krutitsky.

22. *Yuródivy*, God's fools.

23. Sófya *(Sof'ya)* Ignátevna *(Ignat'evna)*.

24. Vasilevich *(Vasil'evich)*.

25. The speech reads literally, "I shall be rich, I shall live gaily. You used to live gaily, *ma tante*, didn't you?"

26. The speech reads literally, "I know, I know, that you lived very gaily."

27. The line reads literally, "I also want to live very gaily."

28. In the Russian, Grigory pronounces *uródlivy* (misshapen) in place of *yuródivy* (God's fools).

29. Ulíta Shmygáeva. The last name derives from a verb meaning to twitch, to shuffle, to run here and there. The rank of her late husband was step fourteen in the Table of Ranks.

30. In the Russian, the word denotes blissful or blessed but connotes simple (in the religious sense) and stupid.

31. Iván Yákovlich.

32. Matresha, Anfisa. The names of the companions to Turusina were added by the translator. Ostrovsky identified the women as the first and second hangers-on or as parasites.

33. *Shabalá* means skimmer or large spoon; it is also an insulting term meaning babbler or empty windbag.

34. "Just you keep silent! What's the color of his hair?" This following version of the ending of Act Three has been made by the translator so that the role may be played by either blond or brunette actor.

    TURUSINA. Just you keep silent! What's the color of his hair?

    MANEFA. Toward some, a devil, bark and all; but to you, a bridegroom, dark and tall.

    MASHENKA. That means, he has dark hair. Kurchaev is dark, you know. Perhaps it's he?

    TURUSINA. Now you just heard—she's had a vision. Is it possible for a hussar to appear in a vision to God-fearing people? How silly you are.

    MATRESHA. Oh, it's happened, it's happened!

    ANFISA. I knew it, I knew it.

    MATRESHA. It's in the cards, it's Egor.

    TURUSINA. How shallow you've become! [*To* MASHENKA.] How could she see a name in the cards?

    MATRESHA. [*To* ANFISA.] Wouldn't you know it! A bit of a slip. I mean the cards turn out "tall and dark."

    TURUSINA. [*To* MANEFA.] To you all is known, while we sinful creatures remain in doubt. There are many Egors and plenty of dark-headed men.

    MANEFA. All alien ones have met their fate, but the intended husband is at the gate.

    TURUSINA AND THE OTHERS. At the gate?

    MANEFA. Let all be garbed, assemble all; guests are coming, down the hall.

    TURUSINA. When?

    MANEFA. This very hour, this very moment. [*All turn to the door.* GRIGORY *enters.*] Here they have come, here they have come, with Sinament and Ginger, Nutmegs and Rum. [*Rises.*]

    GRIGORY. Nil Fedoseich Mamaev.

    TURUSINA. Alone?

GRIGORY.   A young gentleman is with him, and he has dark hair.

MATRESHA.   Ah! Are we really alive?

ANFISA.   Is it possible we're dreaming?

TURUSINA.   Ask them in!   [*Embracing* MASHENKA.]   Now, Mashenka, my prayers have been heard!   [*Sits down, sniffs spirits.*]

MASHENKA.   This is so unusual, *ma tante.* I'm trembling all over.

TURUSINA.   Go, calm yourself, my dear. Come back later.   [MASHENKA *exits.*]

MANEFA.   If in trouble, never drown. Virtue ends with the bridal crown.   [*Goes to door.*]

TURUSINA.   [*To the companions.*]   Let each of you accompany her and she needs some tea . . . tea.

MANEFA.   Whoever drinks tea is desperate.

TURUSINA.   Then give her anything that pleases her.   [*The companions take* MANEFA *by her arms and go to the door. At the door they stop.*]

MATRESHA.   If only we can get a glimpse of him.

ANFISA.   I'll just die if I don't see this miracle.   [MAMAEV *and* GLUMOV *enter.*]

MAMAEV.   Sofya Ignatevna, allow me to present my nephew, Egor Dmitrievich Glumov.

MATRESHA.   [*At the door.*]   Ah, it's Egor!

ANFISA.   [*At the door.*]   Ah, he has dark hair.

MAMAEV.   Be good to him.

TURUSINA.   [*Rises.*]   I thank you! I shall love him like my own son.   [GLUMOV *respectfully kisses her hand.*]

35.   This specific length of time, added by the translator, approximates the length of time suggested in this scene.

36.   The title of address used by Glumov places Krutitsky at either step four or step three in the Table of Ranks.

37.   V. A. Ózerov (1769–1816) based his plays on French neoclassical tragedy, but introduced elements of sentimentalism.

38.   The play *Dmitry Donskóy* written by Ozerov in 1807.

39.   Ostrovsky increased the comic effect in this scene by quoting lines which characterize Kleopatra's growing awareness of Glumov's duplicity. At the same time the quotations prefigure her attitude and forthcoming action.

40.   The scene reads literally as follows.

GLUMOV.   Unhappiness? Don't you really know what a crime that would be? To cause you the slightest distress would take a black soul and a savage heart.

KLEOPATRA.   A black soul and a savage heart! Yes, you are speaking the truth.

GLUMOV.   But I have neither a black soul, nor a savage heart, that means . . .

KLEOPATRA.   What does that mean?

GLUMOV.   That means I could never cause you the slightest distress.

KLEOPATRA.   Come now, am I to believe that?

GLUMOV.   Yes, you should!

KLEOPATRA.   All right, I will believe it.

GLUMOV.   [*To himself.*] She doesn't know. [*Aloud.*] How could I ever cause you distress! I, a passionate, timid youth, have been searching long for affection; I've searched long for a girlish heart. My soul has ached in loneliness. With beating heart, with passionate yearning, I sought the eyes of that woman who would command me to be her slave. I would call her my goddess; I would give her my whole life, all my dreams and hopes. But I was poor, unknown, and they all turned away from me. My supplications, my sighs perished, extinguished in vain. Then you appeared before me; my beating heart grew stronger. But you were no cruel beauty; you did not push me aside. You descended to the unfortunate sufferer. You warmed the poor heart without misgivings, and I'm happy, I'm happy, infinitely happy. [*Kisses her hand.*]

41.   Glumov's speech here reads literally as follows. "He wants me to marry for money. He doesn't want me to be a clerk forever; it's time I should become independent, amount to something. Naturally, he wants to be kind. I'm only sorry he didn't ask how I felt about it."

42.   The line reads literally, "People like that should never gain entrance to your home—under no circumstances."

43.   The speech reads literally as follows: "That means you're comfortable. Ah, poor one! How he upset you! Then you are really going to relinquish your fiancée?"

44.   The scene reads literally as follows:

GLUMOV.   Doesn't it strike you as predestination? I haven't even had time to inquire about my fiancée's thoughts and feelings . . . [*To* MASHENKA.] Forgive me, Mar'ya Ivanovna! I was completely satisfied when she consented.

TURUSINA.   Nothing more is really needed.

GLUMOV.   Perhaps if I don't quite appeal to her now, then I will later on. A marriage like ours ought to prove happy and prosperous.

KURCHAEV.   Undoubtedly.

GLUMOV.   A marriage arranged by fate cannot be marred by human error.

TURUSINA.   Those are principles! Everyone should know them by heart, if he wants to know how to live.   [GRIGORY *enters.*]

GRIGORY.   Ivan Ivanych Gorodulin.

TURUSINA.   I shall go and dress in something warmer. It's getting damp here.   [*Exits.*]

MASHENKA.   [*To* KURCHAEV.] Let's go into the garden.   [*They exit into the garden.* GORODULIN *enters.*]

45. In the Russian text, Kleopatra enters alone; and the scene between Glumov and Kleopatra takes place. Mamaev and Krutitsky enter with Turusina on page 408, and the two men play their short scene and cross upstage. Then Turusina begins her long speech to Kleopatra, "It seems quite fashionable nowadays . . ."

46. This reading of Glumov's diary resembles the reading of Khlestatov's letter in Gogol's *Inspector General.* The situation and the comic effect are about the same in both plays.

47. Glumov's long accusatory scene which continues until his exit resembles Chatsky's monologue in Griboedov's *Woe from Wit (Gore ot uma),* and several critics reproached Ostrovsky for the similarity. The scenes are different both in purpose and ending. In *Gore ot uma* Chatsky accuses and leaves Moscow forever. In *The Scoundrel,* Glumov accuses, suggests the circle needs him, threatens to discredit his own accusers, and then leaves—quite ready to return. After all, Glumov needs the circle as much as the circle needs him.

48. When A. P. Lensky as Glumov played this scene at the Maly and then left the stage, the audience always applauded vigorously.

THE FOREST

1. A verst is equal to 3,500 feet.

2. Karp Savélich *(Savel'ich).*

3. Sergéich is the shortened form of the patronymic.

4. Karp uses the traditional Russian stage business of spitting to show contempt.

5. Father Grigóry.

6. Aleksís, a nickname of Aleksey used by Raisa Gurmyzhskaya.

7. *Zemstvo.*

8. ". . . a soldier's bastard son," or *kantonist*. Tied from the day of his birth to the military lists, the *kantonist* was prepared for performing a soldier's work, especially at the lower levels of the military school.

9. Milonov looks back to life in Russia before the reforms of the sixties. Milonov holds the same conservative position as Mamaev and Krutitsky in *The Scoundrel*.

10. Bodaev's description characterizes the actions of Raisa Gurmyzhskaya.

11. Ványa, a nickname for Ivan.

12. The selling of the forest to the rising peasant-merchant was a theme repeated in Russian literature long before Chekhov's *The Cherry Orchard*.

13. The reference to comedy not only prefigures the arrival of the traveling actors, but also is a direct statement of role-playing in life situations.

14. Raisa's thoughts of Bulanov are a culmination of several hints introduced by Ostrovsky in the first act to prepare for Raisa's subsequent action in the play. That the act ends by raising unanswered questions is an example of Ostrovsky's skill in building interest step by step to the end of Act One.

15. Kaftán is *chuika* in the text. The *chuika*, which resembled the kaftan, was popularly worn by men of the *meshchane* from the middle of the nineteenth century to the beginning of the twentieth.

16. Gennády Demyánych *(Dem'yanych)*. The first name suggests noble.

17. The title role in a play by Eduard Schenk, translated by P. G. Obodovsky. The play opened in 1839 at the Aleksandrinsky with Karatygin in the part.

18. Nikolái Khrisánfych Rybakóv (1811–1876) was a well-known provincial actor. From 1872 to 1876, however, he acted in Moscow. Ostrovsky apparently drew upon Rybakov's characteristics for the creation of Neschastlivtsev, and the role itself was played by Rybakov.

19. Lyapunóv and Fídler, characters in a play written by N. V. Kukol'nik in the thirties.

20. V. A. Karatýgin (1802–1853) was a famous actor at the Aleksandrinsky. He was the first to play the role of Lyapunov.

21. Neschastlivtsev's description of a dramatic actress is similar to the characteristics of Aksyusha.

22. Balýk, salted or dried fish.

23. The two actors enter the backwoods exactly as they leave at the end of the play.

24. A. E. Martýnov (1818–1860) was a noted actor at the Aleksandrinsky. He played in several Ostrovsky works. Among his famous roles was that of Tikhon in *The Storm* (1859).

25. Karp mispronounces the Russian equivalent of valet or gentleman's gentleman.

26. 2.7 acres.

27. Petrúshka, a nickname for Petr.

28. *Volte* is a French term used of horses, in fencing, etc.

29. Schastlivtsev mispronounces the French *empoché*, to pocket.

30. Emilyan Pugachév, leader of the Cossacks of the Ural, headed a peasant uprising against Catherine the Great.

31. Schastlivtsev's phrase for *Adieu, au plaisir (de vous revoir)* underscores the relationship between Ulita and him.

32. Roman historian and writer.

33. Neschastlivtsev uses a humorous term, which is based on the resemblance of a Pythagorean theorem to the cut of men's trousers.

34. In this speech and throughout the remainder of the play, Bulanov uses the familiar you *(ty)* form of address to Raisa Gurmyzhskaya.

35. Sténka Razín, leader of a Cossack revolt in the seventeenth century.

36. Milonov's toast to the couple on the stage is contrasted with the "hurrah" in the dining room. This technique of association creates a satiric and comic effect.

A SELECTED
BIBLIOGRAPHY

I. EDITIONS OF OSTROVSKY'S WORKS

Sobranie sochinenii, 4th ed., 8 vols., St. Petersburg: N. G. Martynov, 1885.

Polnoe sobranie sochinenii, 10 vols., ed. by M. I. Pisarev, St. Petersburg: "Prosveshchenie," 1904–1905.

Novye mater'yaly, pis'ma, trudy i dni, stat'i, ed. by M. D. Belyaev, Leningrad: Gos. Izdat., 1924.

O teatre: zapiski, rechi i pis'ma, ed. by G. I. Vladykin, 2nd ed., Moscow-Leningrad: Gos. Izdat. "Iskusstvo," 1947.

Polnoe sobranie sochinenii, 16 vols., Moscow: Gos. Izdat. Khudozh. Lit., 1949–1953.

Sobranie sochinenii, 10 vols., ed. by G. I. Vladykin, Moscow: Gos. Izdat. Khudozh. Lit., 1959–1960.

Groza, ed. by Norman Henley, Letchworth, Hertfordshire: Bradda Books Ltd., 1963.

II. GENERAL REFERENCES

Dal', V. I., *Tolkovyi slovar' zhivogo velikorusskogo yazyka,* 4 vols., Moscow: Gos. Izdat. Inos. Nat. Slov., 1955. (Reprint of orig. publ., 1880–1882.)

Evreinov, N. N., *Istoriya russkogo teatra,* New York: Chekhov Publ. House, 1955.

Institut Yazykoznaniya Akademiya Nauk SSSR, *Slovar' russkogo yazyka,* 4 vols., Moscow: Gos. Izdat. Inos. Nat. Slov., 1957.

Karpovich, Michael, *Imperial Russia, 1801–1917,* New York: Henry Holt & Co., 1932.

Mirsky, D. S., *A History of Russian Literature*, ed. by Francis J. Whitfield, New York: Knopf, 1964.

——————————, *Russia; A Social History*, London: Cresset Press, 1931.

Seton-Watson, H., *The Decline of Imperial Russia* (1885–1914), London: Methuen & Co., 1952.

Tolkovyi slovar' russkogo yazyka, 4 vols., ed. by D. N. Ushakov, Moscow: Gos. Institut "Sovetskaya Entsiklopediya," 1935.

Varneke, B. V., *Istoriya russkogo teatra XVII–XIX vekov*, 3rd ed., Moscow-Leningrad: Gos. Izdat. "Iskusstvo," 1939.

Vsevolodskii (Gerngross), V., *Istoriya russkogo teatra*, 2 vols., Leningrad-Moscow: Tea-kino Pechat', 1929.

Weiner, Leo, *The Contemporary Drama of Russia*, Boston: Little, Brown & Co., 1924.

III. BIOGRAPHICAL AND CRITICAL STUDIES

Derzhavin, K. N., *Aleksandr Nikolaevich Ostrovskii, 1823–1886*, Leningrad-Moscow: Gos. Izdat. "Iskusstvo," 1950.

Dobrolyubov, N. A., *Izbrannye sochineniya*, Moscow: Gos. Izdat. Khudozh. Lit., 1947.

Durylin, S. N., *Mastera sovetskogo teatra v p'esakh A. N. Ostrovskogo*, Moscow: Vsesoyuznyi Dom Narodnogo Tvorchestva im. N. K. Krupskoi, 1939.

Filippov, V. A., *Dnevniki i pis'ma; teatr Ostrovskogo*, Moscow-Leningrad: Academia, 1937.

——————————, *Velikii russkii dramaturg A. N. Ostrovskii*, Moscow: "Pravda," 1948.

Grigorenko, V. V., ed., *A. N. Ostrovskii v vospominaniyakh sovremennikov*, Moscow: Izdat. "Khudozh. Lit.," 1966.

Kaspin, Albert, "A Superfluous Man and an Underground Man in Ostrovskij's *The Poor Bride*," *Slavic and East European Journal*, VI (Winter, 1962), 312–321.

——————————, "Ostrovsky and the *Raznochinets* in His Plays," unpubl. diss., California, 1957.

Kholodov, E. G., *Masterstvo Ostrovskogo*, Moscow: Izdat. "Iskusstvo," 1963.

Patouillet, Jules, *Ostrovski et son théâtre de moeurs russes*, Paris: Plon-Nourrit et cie., 1912.

Pirogov, G. P., *A. N. Ostrovskii; seminarii*, Leningrad: Uchpedgiz, 1962.

Ralston, William, "Sochineniya A. N. Ostrovskago (The Works of A. N. Ostrovsky) 4 vols., St. Petersburg: 1859–67," in *The Edinburgh Review*, 128 (July, 1868), 80–97.

Revyakin, A. I., *Groza A. N. Ostrovskogo; posobie dlya uchitelei*, Moscow: Uchpedgiz, 1962.

————————, *A. N. Ostrovskii; zhisn' i tvorchestvo*, Moscow: Uchpedgiz, 1949.

Shambinago, S. K., ed., *Tvorchestvo A. N. Ostrovskogo*, Moscow-Petrograd: Gos. Izdat., 1923.

Shtein, A. L., *A. N. Ostrovskii; sbornik, statei i materialov*, Moscow: Vse. Teat. Ob., 1962.

Vladykin, G. I., ed., *A. N. Ostrovskii v russkoi kritike; sbornik, statei*, Moscow: Gos. Izdat. Khudozh. Lit., 1953.